HURON COUNTY

P9-EIF-167

HURON COUNTY LIBRARY

2 008 200773 1

Date Due

Seaforth	MAY 0 6 2000	
OCT 2 8 1996	MAY 2 7 2000	

813
.3
Moodi

CLINTON
PUBLIC LIBRARY

22121

MOODIE, S.

SUSANNA MOODIE:

SUSANNA MOODIE:
LETTERS OF A LIFETIME

Susanna Strickland Moodie

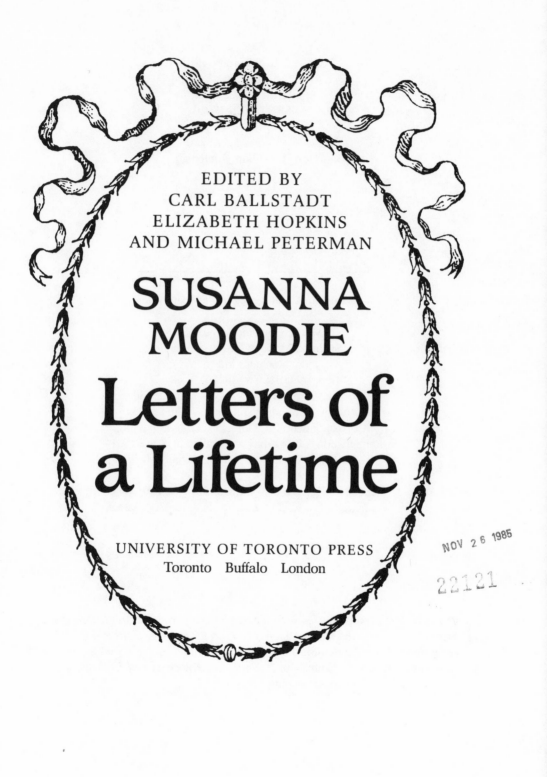

EDITED BY
CARL BALLSTADT
ELIZABETH HOPKINS
AND MICHAEL PETERMAN

SUSANNA MOODIE

Letters of a Lifetime

UNIVERSITY OF TORONTO PRESS
Toronto   Buffalo   London

NOV 2 6 1985

22121

© University of Toronto Press 1985
Toronto   Buffalo   London
Printed in Canada
ISBN 0-8020-2580-3

Design: William Rueter RCA

Canadian Cataloguing in Publication Data

Moodie, Susanna, 1803–1885.
Susanna Moodie: letters of a lifetime
Includes index.
ISBN 0-8020-2580-3
1. Moodie, Susanna, 1803–1885 – Correspondence.
2. Authors, Canadian (English) – 19th century –
Correspondence. 3. Ontario – Emigration and
immigration – Biography.   I. Ballstadt, Carl, 1931–
II. Hopkins, Elizabeth.   III. Peterman, Michael
A., 1942–   IV. Title.
PS8426.062Z54 1985   C813'.3   C85-098749-0

This book has been published with the help of a generous gift to the University of
Toronto Press from the Herbert Laurence Rous Estate, a grant from the Canadian
Federation for the Humanities, using funds provided by the Social Sciences and
Humanities Research Council of Canada, and block grants from the Canada
Council and the Ontario Arts Council.

Contents

Illustrations

Acknowledgments

D URING THE PAST SIX YEARS the search for Susanna Moodie's letters and for information relating to her life and work has involved many persons and agencies that have given generously of their time. We would particularly like to thank the following for their assistance and support: the Social Sciences and Humanities Research Council of Canada for funds to pursue the project; Trent University, Glendon College of York University, and McMaster University for the facilities and services they have provided; Anne Goddard and Judy Roberts-Moore of the Public Archives of Canada; Richard Landon of the Thomas Fisher Rare Book Library at the University of Toronto; Desmond Neill of Massey College, University of Toronto; Bernadine Dodge of the Bata Library, Trent University; William Morley of the Douglas Library, Queen's University; Brooke Whiting, curator of Rare Books and Manuscripts, the University of California at Los Angeles; Stanley Triggs, curator of Photography, McCord Museum of McGill University, Montreal; the staff of the Osborne Collection of Children's Books, Toronto Public Library; and the *Journal of Canadian Studies*.

Descendants and friends of the Moodie and Traill families have been kind and generous in their responses to our phone calls, letters, and visits: Mr T.R. McCloy of Calgary; Miss Kathleen McMurrich of Thornhill, Ontario; Mrs Margaret Hunter and Miss Kaye Richmond of Southwold, England; Mrs Le Gries of Reydon Hall, Suffolk; the Skinners of Stowe House, Bungay, Suffolk; Mrs Robert Moodie of Huntingdon Beach, California; Mrs F.F. McDermid of Saskatoon; Mrs Sheila C. Stewart of Dauphin, Manitoba.

The knowledge and encouragement of our own friends and colleagues has been invaluable to us: Gerry Boyce, Jean Cole, Anne Joyce, Joyce

Lewis, Donna McGillis, Norma Martin, Catherine Milne, Mr and Mrs F. Ridley, Mary Jane Edwards, Grace Jolly, Mary Lu MacDonald, John Robson, Gordon Roper, Eric Rump, Rupert Schieder, Clara Thomas, and the late Brian Heeney.

For their patience, hard work, and good humour, we thank our research assistants, Sherry Lee Powsey and Martin Dowding; our word-processing stenographers, Mary-Lou McKenna and Rita Pignataro-Bruno; and our editor, Gerry Hallowell.

For their love and endurance, our love and gratitude to our children and to Cara, Dorothy, and Tony.

Glendon College
March 1985

Editorial Preface

THE LETTERS of Susanna Moodie reproduced in this volume exist in three different 'original' forms: manuscript letters or fragments written in Susanna Moodie's own hand; transcriptions or copies of letters made by descendants or collectors such as the late nineteenth-century antiquarian John Glyde; and printed letters written to newspapers or published in other letter collections such as the Rev. A.G. L'Estrange's *The Friendships of Mary Russell Mitford* (New York 1882).

In preparing the letters for publication we have generally followed the principle of minimal emendation. Those changes that have been made were dictated by the difficulties of printing such manuscript oddities as inserted phrases or cross-written lines, a common nineteenth-century practice for saving paper and postage. We have also occasionally found it necessary to interpolate a word or phrase rendered unreadable by folds in the paper, seal tears, or the careful cutting out of an autograph by former owners of the manuscript letters. Such interpolations are indicated by square brackets.

Susanna Moodie's handwriting is not difficult to read, her grammar and punctuation are generally complete, and her spelling is remarkably consistent. However, the reader will sometimes run across sentence fragments, irregular spellings, and unusual punctuation patterns. Some of these convey her personal writing habits, such as the tendency to underline phrases she intended to be read ironically or her peculiar and varied spellings of place-names like 'Otonabee' or 'Katchewanook.' Others belong to nineteenth-century conventions of formal writing, such as the insertion of a comma between a subject and a predicate or immediately before a prepositional phrase when the writer wished to measure a prose rhythm in a lengthy sentence.

Instances of errors in Susanna Moodie's own hand are clarified in notes where necessary, while errors in earlier transcriptions or previously published sources are indicated by inserting [*sic*]. Very occasionally the editors have seen fit to correct a minor slip in an original letter when such a change would not in any way detract from its character.

The reader will find variations in the spelling of 'Susanna.' Based on the evidence available to us, she always signed her own name without an 'h,' but members of her family often referred to her or wrote to her as 'Susannah,' and Glyde and L'Estrange use both spellings of her name in their transcriptions.

Because the letter headings and salutations are irregular in the original letters, sometimes appearing at the end rather than at the beginning of a letter, we have adopted the practice of placing all such information at the beginning of a letter's text. Where internal evidence has enabled us to deduce unstated dates and places, this information has been added in square brackets. Each letter is numbered and identified by the name of Susanna Moodie's correspondent. For the sources of letters, see page 365.

While everything possible has been done to ensure the accurate rendering of Susanna Moodie's letters through all the stages of conversion from their original forms to these pages, errors may have crept in, for which, of course, we accept responsibility.

To facilitate informed and comfortable reading of the letters, they have been divided into five sections, uneven in length but representative of the main periods of Susanna Moodie's life. Each section is introduced by an essay offering those facts about her life, work, friends, and correspondents necessary to understand the letters that follow. These essays cannot, nor are they intended to, provide a detailed and complete picture of her life. Because of the limitations of space, the annotations for the lettters have been kept to a minimum and much interesting and useful commentary has had to be reserved for future work. However, we hope the material presented here will contribute to a more comprehensive and accurate assessment of Susanna Moodie than has hitherto been available.

1826~1832

'The wild Suffolk girl'

IN THE LOW AND UNDULATING Suffolk countryside, on the Wangford Road about a mile and a half inland from the North Sea coast town of Southwold, stands Reydon Hall, a large brick country house distinguished by towering, ornate chimneys and several prominent front and rear gables in the seventeenth-century Flemish style. Built in 1682 it still stands today, though much altered, behind a high brick wall set close to the road, almost immediately opposite St Margaret's, the Reydon parish church. It was here that Susanna Moodie spent most of the first thirty years of her life. These years, normally marked by the idealism and extreme emotions of youth, had such an effect on her volatile personality that she would, years later, remember herself as 'the wild Suffolk girl, so full of romance.'[1]

She was born in the village of Bungay, on 6 December 1803, the sixth and final daughter of Thomas and Elizabeth (Homer) Strickland, the first of the Strickland children to be born in Suffolk, whence her father had retired after a successful career as an importer and manager of the Greenland Docks at Rotherhithe near London. Elizabeth (Eliza), Agnes, Sarah, Jane Margaret, and Catharine Parr had all been born in Kent, to Elizabeth, Thomas's second wife (his first wife, Elizabeth Cotterell, who had no children, was a relative of Sir Isaac Newton, a source of family pride to the young Stricklands). Having made a good deal of money but suffering from what was regarded as hereditary gout, Thomas moved his family to the Norwich area in Norfolk, there to watch over business interests and his health, and to look for a rural estate where he might enjoy his later years and undertake the task of educating his daughters. The baptismal records of St Mary's (Anglican) Church in Bungay state that Susanna was christened on 12 December 1803. By then her father had rented Stowe House, a large farm two miles from Bungay on the Flixton Road, overlooking the Waveney River that serves as the border between Suffolk and Norfolk. Though Strickland maintained his Norwich connections and kept a house there, Stowe House was Susanna's home until December 1808, when her father purchased and moved his family to Reydon Hall, some twenty miles distant from Bungay and thirty miles from Norwich.

Reydon Hall was the summit of Thomas Strickland's ambitions, the tangible sign of his business success and the dream of his retirement. For nearly ten years after he bought it, he devoted himself to the improvement of the Hall and its tenant farms, overseeing those operations as well as the education of his daughters and two young sons, Samuel and Thomas, born after Susanna at Stowe House. With his health failing, however, and with his financial situation severely hampered by a defaulted loan, he was increasingly forced to spend time in Norwich. There he died in May 1818,

Reydon Hall

leaving his family in very restricted circumstances. Under his wife's inspiration, they rallied and made what they could of the farm and their limited inheritance. Despite little capital, they struggled to maintain Reydon Hall, though that meant closing off parts of the house and curtailing many activities.

The early disruptions of the Stricklands' life in Suffolk help to account for the paradox of their social position. While they had a wide range of literary and social acquaintances in Norwich, Ipswich, Bungay, Yoxford, and Southwold, they were socially isolated at Reydon Hall, the manor house of the area. James Ewing Ritchie, in his memoir *East Anglia* (London 1883), recalled the curious Strickland clan of the 1820s, living in a half-closed house and eager for a society not to be found either among the tenant farmers and poorer classes of the immediate environs or the established and titled well-to-do like the Earl of Stradbroke and Sir Thomas Gooch of nearby Benacre Hall:

The Stricklands had, I fancy, seen better days, and were none the worse for that ... Mr. Strickland had deceased some years, and the widow and the daughters kept up what little state they could; and I well remember the feeling of surprise with which I first entered their capacious drawing-room ... It must have been, now I come to think of it, a dismal old house, suggestive of rats and dampness and mould, that

Reydon Hall, with its scantily furnished rooms and its unused attics and its empty barns and stables, with a general air of decay all over the place, inside and out ... It must have been a difficulty with the family to keep up the place, and the style of living was altogether plain; yet there I heard a good deal of literary life in London ... (40)

The family's isolation was further emphasized by the expense and difficulty of travel. Regular coach service was costly, and while the Stricklands had their own donkey-chaise for local travel they apparently had to borrow a neighbour's donkey to pull it, a situation Susanna makes fun of in her letters.

The Strickland sisters fell, as it were, into two distinct groups. The older triumvirate – Eliza (born in 1794), Agnes (1796), and Sarah (1798) – had the advantage of their father's severe but well-planned tutelage, learning academic subjects like geography and mathematics under his guidance. Eliza became an accomplished accountant as well as a writer and editor; she was the first to leave the family circle in the 1820s to make a career for herself in London's literary world. As the older and more responsible sisters, Eliza, Agnes, and Sarah often had to oversee the younger group – Jane Margaret (born in 1800), Catharine Parr (1802), and Susanna, as well as young Samuel (1805) and Thomas (1807). Because of their father's recurring illnesses and his business reversals, the younger children had less opportunity to develop under his instruction. The family was, in fact, often split, some staying in Norwich while others remained at Reydon.

In such a situation clashes between the older and younger sisters were inevitable. In an unpublished memoir of her early life,[2] Catharine recalled one occasion in which both she and Susanna secretly began writing their own novels to while away 'the tedium of the dull winter.' The year was likely 1816 and Sarah was in charge. When, however, Eliza returned from Norwich and discovered the enterprise she was severe in her response, calling their labours unproductive 'trash.' An indignant Susanna, her romantic feathers ruffled, 'snatched the despised MS. and threw it in the fire.' The harshness on Eliza's part and the precipitous emotional reaction of Susanna were characteristic of these particular sisters who, because of age and temperament, remained distant from one another despite family solidarity.

Catharine, Susanna, and Jane Margaret grew up in the shadow of these older, talented sisters, spurred on to some extent by their achievements. In *The Backwoods of Canada* (1836), Catharine regretted not having paid closer attention to Eliza's attempts to instruct her in botany and the natural sciences. Both Catharine and Susanna eagerly followed Agnes's advancing reputation as a poet and writer, while they were particularly fond of Sarah, the only Strickland daughter not drawn to writing as a vocation; her gentle temperament made her a friend to all the sisters, for no rivalries of a literary sort concerned her.

The Strickland brothers, who were the only children to receive formal educations – first at Miss Newsome's Academy in Southwold and then at Norwich Grammar School during the tenure of the notorious disciplinarian Dr Edward Valpy – seem to have reacted to the poverty-stricken, female-dominated household they found themselves heirs to in 1818 by preparing for travel and adventure as expeditiously as possible. At fourteen Thomas joined the merchant navy and sailed between India and England throughout the 1820s. Samuel learned what he could of farming at Reydon for a few years, then set out for Upper Canada in 1825.

Life at Reydon Hall in the 1820s was, generally speaking, a brave attempt to dignify genteel poverty and to live up to a social position Thomas Strickland had created for his family. For the young women opportunity for travel was infrequent, depending upon the good graces of sympathetic and interested relatives and to a lesser extent upon the small amounts of money the scribbling sisters could earn by writing for the available literary markets. We know from Catharine's reminiscences of Susanna's early life that Susanna, at the age of sixteen, first went to London. Though the results of the trip were far from satisfactory, at least in terms of the first stop at the home of an aunt (Susanna may well have used this event as the factual basis for her narrative *Rachel Wilde, or, Trifles from the Burthen of a Life*, which appeared in the *Victoria Magazine* in 1848), the visit provides a sort of model for many more the sisters would take individually to London, usually to stay with their 'aunt,' Mrs Rebecca Leverton of 13 Bedford Square, or with their eccentric cousin, the artist Thomas Cheesman of Newman Street. At both places they met a variety of interesting Londoners and had the opportunity to make connections helpful to their own work.

To judge by Letter 3, Susanna was by the autumn of 1827 familiar with the 'fashionables' who attended Mrs Leverton's salon in Bedford Square. A Strickland by birth and Thomas Strickland's second cousin, she was the wealthy widow of Thomas Leverton, an architect who had designed Bedford Square and been one of His Majesty's justices of the peace for several counties. She seems regularly to have invited the Strickland sisters to visit her. It was typical of her thoughtfulness that in 1831, with the breaking-off of Catharine's engagement to Francis Harral, she invited her to accompany her on a trip to Waltham (where she maintained a home),

Bath, and Oxford. When she died in 1834 she provided each of her nieces with a modest inheritance (an inheritance that may have prompted Susanna and her husband to leave their first home in Upper Canada and move to the backwoods north of Peterborough).

Many years later Susanna vividly recalled another London relative in 'My Cousin Tom: A Sketch from Life,' which appeared in the *British American Magazine* in May 1863. Thomas Cheesman occasionally visited Reydon Hall and for several months in 1826 Susanna stayed at his home in Newman Street as a companion to his niece, Eliza. 'Some of the happiest months I ever spent in London were spent in that dirty home in Newman Street,' she observes in describing Cheesman's paintings, musical and linguistic skills, and unusual habits. Though he was over sixty when she first met him, he was quick to encourage both Susanna and Agnes in their writing, helping them both with the Italian he had learned as a student to 'the great Bartolozzy' and schooling them in matters of taste. It was likely Cheesman who produced the miniatures of the Strickland sisters during the 1820s, which Susanna asked a friend to send to Canada in 1869 (see Letters 93 and 99).

Another London address familiar to Susanna was 24 Clarendon Square, the home of Thomas Harral, an old friend of the Stricklands, likely through Ipswich connections, who eventually died in 1853. A fervent Tory and royalist, Harral seems to have been a Suffolk literary man. He started a short-lived literary magazine and miscellany in Ipswich in 1814 called the *East Anglian*; later he edited the *Suffolk Chronicle* (Ipswich) and the *Bury Gazette* before becoming involved in London with *La Belle Assemblée* (c. 1823–31), a court and fashion magazine. It had been taken over by G. and B.W. Whittaker in April 1823, and thereafter items signed by 'T.H.' begin to appear, as do notes implying Harral's editorship.

As a writer himself Harral had published polemical essays in opposition to parliamentary reform and in strong support of George iv at the time of what he called 'the follies of Queen Caroline.' He also wrote a novel, *Scenes of Life* (1805); a masque, 'The Apotheosis of Pitt' (1822); and various celebratory poems including 'A Monody on the Death of Mr. John Palmer, Comedian' (1798) and 'Claremont' (1818). In 1828 he would complete William Gray Fearnside's *The History of London*. For *La Belle Assemblée* he regularly contributed biographical sketches of contemporary literary figures.

Though his output was large and his influence considerable, Harral is a figure about whom very little is known; few memoirs of the period refer to him and much of his life remains a mystery. However, in Susanna

Susanna Strickland
Miniature by Thomas Cheesman, 1820s

Strickland's life he was an important and disturbing figure, as these early letters indicate. Most significantly, he was one of the first established literary men to encourage her writing, regularly publishing her poems, stories, and sketches in *La Belle Assemblée* from 1827 to 1830. His opinion meant a great deal to her and she seems often to have feared the strength of his views and principles, especially since inclination led her in these years from Anglican worship to the 'Enthusiasm' of Congregationalism, a break with tradition Harral would doubtless have scorned.

Catharine Parr Strickland
Miniature by Thomas Cheesman, 1820s

Likely Susanna's original link to Harral was through his daughter, Anna Laura, who, as she later said (Letter 59), was 'one of the friends of my girlhood.' Catharine Parr, who was for years engaged to Harral's son Francis, was also an intimate friend of Laura. Susanna dedicated two poems in *La Belle* to her, 'To ___' (November 1827) and 'To A.L. H___ 1' (December 1827), while an earlier poem by Thomas Harral himself in June 1824 ('To Her Who Deserves the Best') suggests his own belated discovery of the kind of sympathetic individual Laura was. She was also something of a poet and linguist, her translations of French and Spanish stanzas occasionally appearing in *La Belle*. It was perhaps Harral's willingness to publish his daughter's poetry that led Susanna to submit her own work (see Letter 2) to *La Belle Assemblée*.

Life at 24 Clarendon Square must have been unsettling. Increasingly Harral was plagued by financial problems and Laura's health was precarious, though the nature of her illness is not clear; she died in London in 1830, and it is likely her death that Susanna refers to in Letter 24. The Harral family life seems also to have been affected by the curious behaviour of Mrs Harral, whose planting of a false wedding announcement involving Catharine and her son Francis in a London newspaper in 1831 was interpreted as an act of wanton maliciousness by the Stricklands (see Letter 31).

Thomas Harral's Suffolk origins are further suggested by his close friendship with James Bird (1788–1839), whose poetry he occasionally published in *La Belle*; indeed, it was Harral who, after Bird's death, edited and wrote an introductory essay to a memorial volume of his poetry.[3] James and Emma Bird (1792–1872) lived at Yoxford, the 'Garden of Suffolk,' or, to the Stricklands, 'La Belle Village,' about nine miles southwest of Reydon. In his youth James had been apprenticed to a miller and in 1814 he had occupied a mill in Yoxford. In 1816 he married Emma Hardacre, daughter of a bookseller in Hadleigh, thereafter abandoning the mill to become a bookseller and druggist. According to historian and bookseller John Glyde, who included Bird among his 'Suffolk Worthies' in his column for the *Suffolk Chronicle*, Bird's social disposition, geniality, literary interests, and conversational skills made him the centre of a large circle of friends that in the 1820s came to include the Strickland sisters. By this time he had published several volumes of poetry, including *The Vale of Slaughden* (1819), *Machin, or the Discovery of Madiera* (1821), *Cosmo, Duke of Tuscany* (1822), and *Poetical Memoirs: The Exile, a Tale* (1823), and was beginning to pay more attention to the poetical possibilities in Suffolk places and legends. As an established writer keenly interested in East Anglian history and antiquity, he had a considerable influence on the Stricklands at a time when their own careers were beginning to take new directions. Not incidentally, he also provided them with a means to acquire and distribute books and magazines. And as the father of a large family, he welcomed the young women into his domestic circle.

Of the thirty-four letters in this section of the book, twenty-five are addressed to James and/or Emma Bird, providing vivid glimpses of family life at Reydon Hall and of Susanna's temperament and aspirations during

James Bird of Yoxford

her twenties. She was twenty-two when, likely in the autumn of 1826, she
and Agnes first met the Birds, a happy occasion for all parties because of
their shared passion for writing poetry, for literature in general, and for
local history. The Bird letters are among those collected by John Glyde and
currently housed in the Suffolk County Public Records Office in Ipswich; of
the twenty-five, only six have been preserved in original form, the rest
having been copied by hand, likely by Glyde himself, with material
regrettably excised in the process. The Glyde papers include many letters
as well from Catharine and Agnes, and a few from Jane Margaret and
Sarah, revealing the close and convivial relationship between the Bird and
Strickland families. In fact, when Susanna and her husband emigrated to
Canada in 1832, they took away with them the Birds' fourteen-year-old son
James, who was to seek his fortune in the New World initially as an

agricultural apprentice to Susanna's brother Samuel, by then comfortably settled on his farm near Herriot's Falls (Lakefield).

Of all Susanna Strickland's literary friends, the most influential and important to her was Thomas Pringle (1789–1834). A Scottish poet and literary man, Pringle befriended her and took a strong paternal interest in her writing and prospects. How and where they met is not clear, though they were both friends of Thomas Harral. From the summer of 1830 Susanna often stayed with Pringle and his wife in their Pentonville residence on the northeastern outskirts of London or at Hampstead where they occasionally holidayed. Indeed, she came to refer to him fondly as 'Papa,' a term he used in signing letters to her.[4]

Pringle's career was an interesting one. Born of an agricultural family and lamed for life by a childhood accident, he attended the University of Edinburgh and later undertook editorial positions with the *Edinburgh Monthly Magazine*, *Constable's Edinburgh Magazine*, and various Edinburgh newspapers. With James Cleghorn he helped to found *Blackwood's Magazine* in 1817, though he severed that connection shortly thereafter. Following his marriage to Margaret Brown, and feeling increasing financial pressure, he enlisted his family in a government program encouraging emigration to South Africa. There he lived until 1826, leaving only after his attempts to establish a magazine and newspaper in Capetown had been curtailed by a repressive administration inordinately sensitive to any criticism of its policies regarding slavery. The literary fruit of these years, *Narrative of a Residence in South Africa* (1834), along with sketches and poems such as 'Afar in the Desert,' have made him a figure of continuing interest in South Africa to the present day.

Back in England at the very time Susanna was testing the London literary market, Pringle, a congenial and much-liked man, resumed his literary interests and connections, particularly his kinship with Scottish writers such as Walter Scott, Leitch Ritchie, Thomas Campbell, and Allan Cunningham. Among his endeavours he edited the annual, *Friendship's Offering*, and seems, at least during 1830, to have had an editorial hand in the operations of the *Athenaeum*, which included several of Susanna's poems. In 1826 and 1827 his outspoken views on slavery, published in Campbell's *New Monthly Magazine*, brought him to the attention of leading anti-slavery figures in England. In March 1827 he was invited to become secretary of the Anti-Slavery League, a position he held with distinction until his death in 1834. In his house and under his encouragement Susanna wrote two anti-slavery pamphlets, transcribing the stories and sufferings of Mary Prince and Ashton Warner (Letter 29). *The History of Mary Prince, a West-Indian Slave* (1831) went through at least three editions, the third containing a letter in which Margaret Pringle attested to the evidence of severe flogging upon Mary's body, a statement Susanna Strickland 'certified and corroborated.'

Letter 29 is a glowing testimonial to the social and literary opportunities Susanna had opened to her by the kindly Thomas Pringle. Not only did he introduce her to a variety of well-known literary and artistic figures – notably the celebrated painter John Martin, the caricaturist George Cruickshank, who was a near neighbour of the Pringles in Pentonville, and the writer-editor Thomas Roscoe – he also expanded her sense of the literary and social possibilities of London. Most importantly, it was Pringle who introduced Susanna to another Scotsman recently returned from South Africa. John Wedderburn Dunbar Moodie (1797–1869) had left his South African farm to enjoy a taste of London and to negotiate a book about his colonial adventures with Richard Bentley (1794–1871), an enterprising young publisher. Likely he also came in search of a wife who would accompany him back to the colony where his brother Donald had similarly established himself.

These letters provide a telling picture of the early stages of Susanna's writing career, the ways in which she sought out publishers, the kinds of publishing opportunities available to her, and, most interestingly, her continuing uncertainty about the merits of pursuing literary recognition and fame. Regrettably, only a portion of what must have been a much larger correspondence has survived. The loss of Pringle's papers, as reported by Jane Meiring in *Thomas Pringle: His Life and Times* (Capetown 1968), is but one example of a vanished source. Nevertheless, the letters here collected do give substantial evidence of her literary efforts on various fronts. We see her as a regular contributor to Harral's *La Belle Assemblée* and as a young writer eager to ingratiate herself with established figures like Mary Russell Mitford and prominent editors like Frederic Shoberl.

Mary Russell Mitford (1787–1855) is best known as the author of poetic tragedies such as *Foscari* (1826) and the rural sketches she published in a series of five volumes under the title *Our Village: Sketches of Rural Character and Scenery* (1824–32). In *Memories of a Literary Life* (1852), she claimed that she began writing because of financial losses incurred by her father; having to support herself, she became, in W.J. Keith's phrase, 'a decidedly professional writer,' her sketches characterized by an 'intimacy of tone' and 'colloquial directness.'[5]

It was Thomas Pringle who initiated the correspondence between the two women by passing on Susanna's poem (Letter 15). Unfortunately, the

Mitford papers cannot be located and only the four letters reprinted in *The Friendships of Mary Russell Mitford* (New York 1882), edited somewhat casually by the Rev. A.G. L'Estrange (Letters 15, 19, 21, and 24), are available as evidence of Susanna's admiration for her work.[6]

Frederick Shoberl (1775–1853) was Susanna Strickland's connection with the first of the English annuals, *Ackermann's Forget-Me-Not*, which made its initial appearance in 1823. Determined to emulate in England the decorative and elegant books of literary and artistic matter published in France and his native Germany, Rudolph Ackermann employed Shoberl to design the format and seek out a seasonal market, as the subtitle, 'A Christmas and New Year's Annual,' suggests. The new *Forget-Me-Not* combined poems, stories, and sketches with impressive illustrations by well-known artists, the whole packaged in well-tooled, attractively bound, boxed volumes. An indication of the publishing success of the annuals during the 1820s and early 1830s is Shoberl's announcement in his preface to the 1827 volume that the previous year's sales had topped ten thousand. By 1829, the year in which Susanna began to enjoy a certain recognition among annual editors and readers, there were at least seventeen annuals competing for the fashionable seasonal trade. Andrew Boyle's *An Index to the Annuals* (Worcester 1967) offers meticulous documentation of this literary fare and helps to disclose the relative prominence Agnes, Susanna, Jane Margaret, and Catharine (despite her affectation of anonymity) attained during this period.

Shoberl himself, to whom Susanna and her sisters first wrote unsolicited, had attained early literary prominence as an editor, publisher's reader, and writer. With Henry Colburn he founded the *New Monthly Magazine* and later served as a reader for Richard Bentley. For Ackermann he edited not only the *Forget-Me-Not* and the *Ackermann's Juvenile Forget-Me-Not* but also *Ackermann's Repository for the Arts*. As a writer he produced poems for the annuals and was a prominent translator of French and German literature into English, notably travel literature by Chateaubriand and Hugo's *The Hunchback of Notre Dame*. He also compiled a *Biographical Dictionary of Living Authors of Great Britain and Ireland* (London 1816). Susanna's letters to Shoberl (11, 13, 16, 28, and 30) provide useful additional knowledge of a man Boyle praises as 'an admirable editor,' whose 'workmanship was excellent,' but who, according to the editors of the *Wellesley Index of Victorian Periodicals* (Toronto 1966), is 'now almost forgotten.'

At the height of her early English popularity, Susanna's work found its way not into five annuals in 1830, as she proudly reports to James Bird

(Letter 20), but seven, *The Amulet, Friendship's Offering, Ackermann's Juvenile Forget-Me-Not, The Iris, The New Year's Gift, The Juvenile Keepsake*, and *Emmanuel*. Experimenting with pseudonyms like 'Z.Z.' and 'Sophia Sandys' (she used the latter signature at least twice in the *Athenaeum*), she continued to struggle with her uneasy feelings about her own literary worth, the goal of literary fame, and the disagreeable aspects of familial rivalry. While she quickly dropped the affectation of not using her own name, she remained vigilant in placing her material in the annuals right up to the year of her emigration.

Whatever her reservations about fame, Susanna did her best always to have an available outlet for her work. When Harral lost control of *La Belle Assemblée* she was already beginning to publish in the *Athenaeum* and thereafter in the *Lady's Magazine*, over which her sister Eliza, by 1831, exercised some literary control. At the same time, though these letters provide scant reference, she wrote with some regularity for A.K. Newman, the publisher who after a brief partnership took over the Minerva Press of William Lane. It was Newman who published her first known work, the romantic historical novel *Spartacus* (1822), which Susanna later recalled had been taken to London by a family friend. Through Newman, who had an agreement to co-publish children's or juvenile works with the firm of Dean and Munday, Susanna's stories – *The Little Quaker or, Josiah Shirley* (likely based to some extent on her friendship with the Ipswich Quaker Allen Ransome); *Hugh Latimer; or, the Soldier's Orphan*; *Roland Massingham; or, I Will Be My Own Master*; *The Little Prisoner*; and *Practice and Principle; or, the Vicar's Tales* – were printed in the 1820s. They remain, however, very difficult to date because of Newman's and Dean and Munday's publishing practices and because the latter's successors, Dean and Son, reissued certain of these works in later years, occasionally attributing works like *Little Downy; or, the History of a Field Mouse*, written by Catharine, to Susanna. It is not clear what book, written jointly by Susanna and Jane Margaret, is referred to in Letter 12.

But while Susanna flirted on many fronts with literary recognition, perhaps the major publishing event of her English years – the appearance of *Enthusiasm, and Other Poems* (London 1831) – had its roots in her brief but emotional conversion to Congregationalism. Two important families in her early life had much to do with it, the Ritchies of Wrentham and the Childses of Bungay.

The latter connection likely went back to the years the Stricklands had spent at Stowe House. The Childses were prominent Methodists who ran a flourishing printing business in Bungay. Led by John (1783–1853) and his brother Robert, they specialized in cheap editions of the Bible and inexpensive series of 'Standard Authors' (Burke, Gibbon, Bacon, etc.) as a way of increasing public literacy and raising intellectual standards. Politically they were radicals. John Childs gained local fame in 1831 as a vocal opponent of printers' patents granted by the King, especially in the area of the Bible printing monopoly. Four years later he went to jail in a much-discussed dispute over his public refusal to pay the church rates imposed upon all Nonconformists by the Church of England, becoming the first Englishman not a member of the Society of Friends to be imprisoned on such grounds. Robert Peel was to label him 'the Bungay martyr.'

While it is not easy to imagine that Agnes Strickland, a redoubtable royalist and Anglican, would have been comfortable in the radical atmosphere of the Childs home, it is clear that the Childses were, above all, affable and generous hosts, who kept a friendly lookout for publishing possibilities for the Strickland sisters. Certainly they were genial conversationalists much interested in 'cultivated politics and phrenology,' both of which had a strong appeal for Agnes. Catharine's story, 'Cousin Kate; or, the Professor Outwitted' (*Anglo-American Magazine*, May 1853), and Susanna's tale, 'Washing the Black-a-moor White' (*Canadian Literary Magazine*, 1871), provide amusing glimpses of Robert Childs and his 'skull' museum. It was the eccentric Robert who married Sarah Strickland, but who in the late 1830s committed suicide.

John Childs must have been the family's major attraction. The famous and the intellectually adventurous gathered 'round his hospitable board,' among them Daniel O'Connell and leading Suffolk Nonconformist ministers like Andrew Ritchie and John Notcutt of Ipswich. James Ewing Ritchie remembered him as 'A self-made man, almost Napoleonic in appearance, with a habit of blurting out sharp cynicisms and original epigrams, rather than conversing. He was a great phrenologist, and I well remember how I, a raw lad, rather trembled in his presence as I saw his dark, keen eyes directed towards that part of my person where my brains are supposed to be. I imagine the result was favourable, as at a later time I spent many a pleasant hour in his dining-room, gathering wisdom from his after-dinner talk and inspiration from his port – as good as that immortalized by Tennyson.'[7]

The Childs family, on Robert's initiative, had a hand in the publication of *Enthusiasm, and Other Poems* and the small collaborative venture by Agnes and Susanna, *Patriotic Songs*, which, though supported by Robert, was published by John Green of Soho.

According to Susanna's letters, it was really Pastor Andrew Ritchie

(1780–1848) of Wrentham, a village about three miles north of Reydon, who effectively brought her to join his Congregational church on 2 April 1830. As many accounts point out, Suffolk was a notorious Nonconformist region during the early 1800s. Disturbed by the excesses of a lax Anglican clergy, exemplified by characters such as the Rev. Henry Rouse-Birch of St Margaret's Church at Reydon (later of St Edmund's in Southwold), who seems to have enjoyed the hunt more than the pulpit, many local inhabitants, particularly those of the lower classes, turned to the simpler ritual and more austere conduct of such Nonconformist denominations as the Methodists and Congregationalists. According to Ritchie's son, 'The churches round were mostly filled by the baronet's relatives, who came into possession of the family livings as a matter of course, and took little thought for the souls of their parishioners. In fact, very few people did go to church. In our chapel, of which my father was the minister for nearly forty years, we had a good congregation, especially of an afternoon, when the farmers with their families, in carts or gigs, put in an appearance.'[8]

Andrew Ritchie had come to Wrentham in 1808 and by the time Susanna met him was a much respected and well-loved member of his community. A cultured man, he published *The Christian Preacher's Assistant* (Southwold 1826), and he and his talented wife conducted reading classes for local children and encouraged charitable activities. Mrs Ritchie apparently gave Susanna lessons in watercolour painting, while Susanna certainly contributed to the Ritchies' little school.

Conversion from the Church of England and all that it implied in terms of respectability and gentility was not easy for a Strickland, particularly one who valued her friendships and guarded her reputation as highly as Susanna did. But her exposure to the reform cause in London, her ingrained habit of self-examination, and her emotional nature gradually subdued her misgivings. The Wrentham Congregational Chapel's record book for 1830 lists her as one of those 'admitted' to the assembly during April of that year.

Intense though this experience clearly was for her at the time, Susanna does not appear to have remained a 'Dissenter' for long. In the early autumn of 1830, at the age of twenty-six, she became engaged to J.W.D. Moodie and, despite a brief estrangement during the winter, they were married at St Pancras (Anglican) Church in London on 4 April 1831, exactly one year after the date of her 'conversion.' That summer they left London and rented a cottage in Southwold, presumably so that Susanna could be near her family while she awaited the birth of her first child, Catherine Mary Josephine Moodie, born on 14 February 1832 and baptized at St Margaret's, Reydon.

Sometime during the previous autumn Dunbar Moodie had decided to emigrate as soon as the baby was born. Certainly, as Susanna reports in *Roughing It in the Bush* (1852), 'a Canada mania pervaded England' at that time. William Cattermole, formerly of Bungay and an agent of the Canada Company, delivered recruiting lectures in Suffolk late in 1831, and Robert Reid, Samuel Strickland's father-in-law, also paid an influential visit that winter. By the spring of 1832, when the last of these early letters was written, the Moodies' departure for Canada was imminent.

1 See Letter 93.
2 'Reminiscences of the Life of Mrs. C.P. Traill Written by Herself,' Public Archives of Canada, Traill Family Collection, MG29 D81
3 *Selections from the Poems of the Late James Bird with a Brief Memoir of His Life by Thomas Harral* (London 1840)
4 See Thomas Pringle to Susanna Strickland, 26 May 1829, Public Archives of Canada, Susanna Moodie Collection, MG29 D100.
5 Keith, *The Rural Tradition: A Study of the Non-fiction Prose Writers of the English Countryside* (Toronto 1974), 83–103
6 Carl Ballstadt, 'Susanna Moodie and the English Sketch,' *Canadian Literature* (Winter 1972), 32–8
7 Ritchie, *Christopher Crayon's Recollections: the Life and Times of the Late James Ewing Ritchie. As Told by Himself* (London 1898), 23
8 *Ibid.*, 37

---

1 To Emma Bird

Reydon
Sunday Night
[autumn 1826][1]

Dear Mrs. Bird

I take the opportunity of my dear Brother passing through Yoxford on his way to London to beg your acceptance of a basket of apples for the children. Whom I doubt not, like the feathered race whose names they bear, are exceedingly fond of fruit. Mamma would have sent some before but we could not find a conveyance without occasioning a greater expense than such a trifling tribute of our esteem and friendship was worth.

My brother received a hasty summons last night to join his ship bound for India immediately so that you may imagine the bustle and confusion his sudden departure has occasioned but we are scarcely allowed time to think of the long and painful separation that is about to take place and shall feel his absence more tomorrow than we do tonight. I love him so tenderly that I feel my heart none of the lightest which will excuse this

scrawl. My Sister Agnes, Mamma and all the unknown sisterhood join
with me in best regards to Mr. Bird and the dear children and believe
me to remain with the most lively feelings of interest in the welfare of
yourself and family.

Yours Very Sincerely
Susanna Strickland

1 The formality of address and tone in this letter as well as Emma Bird's limited acquaintance with the Strickland family suggest an early date; the gift of apples hints at late
summer or early autumn.

---

2   To James and Emma Bird   [spring 1827][1]

My Dear Friends

For I must address you both, but pray do not fight for your respective
portions of this elegant epistle. The fact is *this here* half sheet contains
the summum bonum of my stationery therefore you can have no more nor
less than all ... You must if you can save me 6 quires of the best 6(d)
paper your shop, can furnish. You had some nice thick outsides and they
answer quite well for copy and scribbling ... I have written a little
sketch for *La Belle* which I despatch today. I rather think of becoming a
regular contributor to the Mag, but must do so, on the usual terms of
author and editor ... Our damsel the pert Marjoram proved a bitter weed
and no herb of grace and left us in the glories of a six weeks wash ... [2]
Any book you may feel disposed to lend for Mamma will be greatly received.

1 This seems a likely date because of the reference to *La Belle Assemblée*, which had
printed poems by Susanna in April and May and her first prose sketch, 'Sketches from
the Country No. 1 – The Witch of East Cliff,' in July 1827.
2 Because of its sweetness, marjoram symbolized honour and happiness, characteristics
obviously wanting in the personality of the servant referred to. 'Six weeks wash' is a
folk saying for a troublesome predicament.

3 To James Bird
Reydon House
Nov 9th [1827]

My sister Agnes wishes to consult you on some matters relative to her
New Poems[1] of which she received the first bound copies today and if
fine we promise ourselves the pleasure of seeing you tomorrow and if
perfectly convenient to Mrs. Bird will avail ourselves of her kind offer and
stay all night. We have borrowed a donkey for the expedition and mean to
start early to arrive late for tis a sorry beast whose paces will not
exceed two miles an hour and you might compassionate the character of
this long eared Pegasus but poor Poets must put up with all shifts, such
trifles do not ruffle them. I think a little inconvenience often enhances the
pleasures we afterwards feel in meeting our friends. If the day should
be unfavorable we will postpone our Journey till Monday. I am fearful that
like children I shall pray for wet that out of contradiction it may be fine.
Mamma has just started a new plan and John is to drive us as far as
Thorington[2] and we can then walk on to the prettiest village in Suffolk
and I must descend from my dignity my poetic dignity and condescend to
carry a basket. What would the fashionables I know in Bedford Square
say could they see me. I almost wish they could I pride myself on my
independence

    And dare be poor for a' that

as dear Burns says. Had I been a man that should have been my song.
How perfectly I agree with one clause in it

    An honest independent Man
  Is chief of men for a' that[3]

I am quite impatient for my last communication from London. No Lover
of romance ever wished so ardently for a peep at his mistress as I do for
the sight of my packet. Now don't be saucy. It contains no love letters, but
the reminiscences of friends are as dear to my heart as the light is to my
eyes. Their correspondence constitutes almost the whole sum of my happiness ... When I begin to write I never know when to lay down my pen.
Closing a letter, to me is as hard as saying adieu to a friend. I liked your
sermon as you were pleased to call the reflective part of your letter
amazingly. I should like to hear you preach just such another. Do sensible

women prate? I thought wisdom wore a grave aspect in the weaker sex,
that it might be the better distinguished from such merry madcap vendors
of nonsense as myself! Was it not Dr. Clarke that once said to his
scholars who were at play when a grave bigwig entered the ground Boys!
Boys! be wise. Here comes a fool![4]

My wisdom must reside in an organ of my brain as yet undiscovered by
the lynx eyes of philosophy for I never could find it out though I have
made many useless voyages of discovery through my pericranium to that
effect but was as much disappointed as Capt. Parry in his North West
Passage.[5]

Susannah Strickland

1 The year is likely 1827, a year in which Agnes published her second book of poems, *The
Seven Ages of Woman, and Other Poems* (London 1827). Earlier she had published
Worcester Field; or the Cavalier. A Poem in Four Cantos, With Historical Notes (London
[1826]) and several books for children. One subject of consultation with Bird would be
the sale of this new book in his shop.
2 John was a hired man on the Strickland estate, Thorington a village situated half way
between Reydon and Yoxford.
3 Here Susanna misquotes from Robert Burns's 'For A' That and A' That.' These lines were
probably committed to memory in this way since Catharine, in one of her sketches,
makes the same mistake.
4 Likely John Clarke (1687–1734), schoolmaster and classical scholar
5 Sir William Edward Parry made three voyages between 1819 and 1824 in a futile search
for the North-West Passage.

---

4 To James Bird

Reydon
Nov 17th [1827][1]

The wetness of the day by hindering me from saying my prayers like a
good girl at church inclines me to be very ungodly and to dissipate my
own ennui by writing a saucy epistle to you and give some account of our
voyage home. It was well for you that I did not insist on a wager! Half
past ten! To arrive home with our mouse coloured Pegasus at such an
unpoetical hour. No! No! The fates had decreed that our journey
should terminate at a more romantic period. For my own part I think the
beauty of the night must have inclined Mistress Dushfoot to Astronomi-
cal observations at our expense and she walked so slowly out of Yoxford
for the better convenience of viewing the stars in the puddles that I

thought we should never have left the lights of that dear friendly beautiful village behind us. Even the driver of the Halesworth coach took com-passion on our speed and for fear that our steed should run away and endanger a rude meeting between our poetical brains and the stones offered us a lift as far as Halesworth[2] whither he supposed us distressed damsels were crawling. The offer was as politely declined as it was kindly given and off drove the coach and on walked Pegasus. For my own part I was not at all displeased with the violence of her motions my mind being so completely occupied with pleasing reminiscences of the two last happy days that while the voices of our dear friends still sang in my ears and your cheerful fireside and the dear childrens smiling faces floated before me I could have wrapped myself in my cloak and have been contented to sit behind her till day break. At half past ten we reached the toll gate and the heavens which had been so bright with their starry hosts were almost obscured by heavy clouds and the air turned exceeding-ly cold. Coming at foot fall under the darkest parts of the Earls planta-tions[3] Agnes was somewhat alarmed by a man over the hedge exercising his lungs by making a most diabolical scream and, oh! horrible, fancied some one pulled her behind by her veil an incident which would just have been adapted for the pages of *La Belle*. I was angry with the provoking fellow for recalling my thoughts from absent friends all of whom I had separately visited long before I hailed the chimnies of our old fashioned mansion peeping from among the trees. I had perambulated the busy streets of London and strayed by the banks of the wild and rapid Otan-abbe in Upper Canada, had shaken hands with our friend Mr. Harral and Laura and I had taken sweet counsel together. Oh do you believe in Sympathies? Did you never feel a secret intelligence which unites the thoughts of one friend with another? This belief is to me the greatest happiness I enjoy and reconciles me to the absence of those who are dearer to me than life. I have often been laughed at for the faith I have in this fanciful theory; at length I was determined to prove the truth of what I felt myself. I entered into a compact with a young female friend to whom I was devotedly attached and whose affection for me I knew by that secret intelligence of mind existing between us was equally at-tached to me, to put down on a piece of paper the day and the hour whenever she felt as it were irresistibly compelled to think of me and I would do the same. If you never experienced you would hardly believe that our dates when compared were true to an hour and a minute in a long list and a hundred miles apart so that cheating was impossible. I can now laugh at philosophy! Philosophy would doubtless laugh at me. I

once wrote a little poem on this subject and sent it to an absent friend but
can only remember the first lines

> 'Say didst thou never feel within thy soul
> That strange mysterious link which doth unite
> The thoughts and sympathies of absent friends
> Bringing them back though distant to the view
> All fresh with the realities of life?
> Oceans may flow between us but the soul
> Bound in this viewless chain can traverse space
> And hold communion with a kindred spirit
> E'en in the cold dark chambers of the tomb.'

… What do I not owe you for the pleasure that the perusal of your sweet
poems has given me. *Machin* is *my favourite*. I think it is a beautiful
thing the closing lines are delightful. I admire the *Vale of Slaughden* the
next, but you must forgive me for being candid when I say I do not like
the *Exile* near so well as the others and yet there are passages in it rich
with poetic beauties. You are most happy in your descriptive scenes and
I care not for Story in a Poem. I know most of Scotts descriptive scenes by
heart while I scarcely remember his stories. It is the same with Lord
Byron whose four Cantos of 'Childe Harold' I prize beyond all his stories.[4] Descriptive poetry often goes so home to my heart that I cannot
read a beautiful drawn scene of this kind without weeping. While I am
hurried on by a story and cannot pause to examine or fully appreciate
its excellence. *Cosmo* is an elegant and beautiful dramatic poem …

Before I close this letter I must tell you of an odd misfortune that happened to me last Monday. I was so impatient to read my letters from
London that in spite of not arriving home till past 12 and being rather
fatigued with my journey – in spite of the rain which fell pretty smartly I
put on my pattens and marched off to Southwold to fetch my despatches.
The parcel contained a very kind note from Mr. Harral enclosing one
for Agnes and letters from Laura. Mr. H. in his note requested me to write
him a Tale for the commencement of the year in the German style –
allowing me 12 pages for the extent of it. It was to be a story with a plot
characters, etc. wild wonderful and horrible even diabolical and could
not possess too much of the *deeply pathetic*! and he must have it by the
latter end of this month. I read his directions over coming along and put
Agnes's note in the Envelope of mine for better security and alas dropped
both by the way! On my arrival at home I found what I had done and

sent the boy step by step back to look for it but in vain. I passed Mr.
Kighlaff twice on the road, but no other person but I fear my note was
not picked up by a good Samaritan for I can hear no tidings of it and what
is worse if any person belonging to Southwold picked it up I might as
well have employed the Town Crier and it is doubtless all over the place
that Miss Suky Strickland is commissioned by some wicked wretch to
write a tale on the Devil and as the good folks are mostly Methodists I
should not wonder if the Parson, today, made it the theme of his discourse. Agnes quizzes me enough about the *deeply pathetic*. Alas! I am
the creature of extremes, the child of impulse and the slave of feeling ...
I know your lines on Mr. Pander seeing the Dead Man at Dunwich by
heart.[5] Is it a portion of that wicked passion Envy when I say I wish I
had written them and would exchange all that I have ever penned to have
been the Author. I have not much number ten[6] with regard to my poetical talents. Nature gave me the mind and the imagination but withheld the
power of language to express correctly what I feel.

Susanna Strickland

1 From Letter 3 we know that Susanna and Agnes planned to visit Yoxford over the night of
   Saturday, 10 November, returning on Sunday evening; the news here of the arrival of a
   parcel from London on a Monday, following the sisters' return from Yoxford, suggests the
   sequence. The appearance of Susanna's 'Count Ravenstein' in two parts in *La Belle
   Assemblée* (January, February 1828) confirms the date.
2 A village seven miles northwest of Reydon on the Blythe River; a coach service ran regularly from London through Yoxford to Halesworth at this time.
3 The estate of John Edward Cornwallis Rous, the second Earl of Stradbroke, lay in the
   vicinity of Henham, a village about two miles from Reydon.
4 Scott and Byron were particular favourites of Susanna; her book of poems, *Enthusiasm*,
   reflects their influence. She copied passages of their poetry into a small black-covered
   notebook that is now held in the Norwich Public Records and Local History Reference
   Library.
5 Likely a reference to Bird's poem, 'The Drowned Man,' in which the narrator discovers a
   dead man, 'His face with blood clotted o'er,' on Dunwich shore. Pander may be the
   name of an individual upon whose actual experience the poem is based.
6 In the phrenological system the number ten indicates the organ of self-esteem or vanity.

---

5 To James Bird

Reydon
April 27 [1828][1]

I felt dissatisfied at this extemporaneous production,[2] for such it literally
was and was composed in the garden without slate, pen or pencil a few

minutes after I received that welcome letter which informed me of the joyful event of the birth of your son and his dear Mothers safety.

The information you ask is as follows – Miss Agnes Strickland, Mrs. Levertons 13 Bedford Square, a very pretty part of the Town, though not quite so fashionable as my ambitious sister poet would wish. Do send your 'Dead Man' to Pringle. I would give all I have ever written to have been the author of that piece.

1 Likely 1828, since Emma Bird gave birth to a son, Walter, in the spring of that year, and Agnes visited London about the same time.
2 This may be the poem published in *La Belle Assemblée* (June 1828), 257: 'To the Son of a Bard (By a Lady who had been requested to answer for him at the Font).'

---

6 To James Bird   May 18th [1828]

Agnes has introduced herself to Sir Walter Scott at a public exhibition. He shook hands with her and complimented her on her Poems, she is delighted.

Mr. Pringle accepted 'O Come to the Meadows' and has requested me to send him up some more to choose out of.[1]

1 The year 1828 seems probable since both Agnes Strickland and Scott were then in London in the early summer. 'O Come to the Meadows' cannot be found in print before the 1830 *Juvenile Keepsake* (93); Pringle likely passed the poem on to his friend, Thomas Roscoe, editor of the annual; it was reprinted in *Enthusiasm*.

---

7 To James Bird   Reydon
                                     August 16th [1828][1]
                                     given from my bedroom

Agnes and Catharine had walked to Southwold and about six in the evening Sarah and I went to meet them. My Kitty ever the bearer of glad tidings gave me the packet. Oh how my heart fluttered and danced for joy at the sight of the well known hand ... Kitty and I are only waiting for a fine day to pay you a flying visit of a few brief hours but they will be hours of pleasure. Green spots in the desert of life. We propose getting up early and coming with the donkey to be with you in the forenoon and start for home at seven ... All here are pretty well, Jane excepted ... I must lay down my pen. It is very late. My Bible is unread before me. It is already Sabbath Morning.

1 The date is either Saturday, 16 August 1828, or Sunday, 16 August 1829, depending on whether Susanna dated the letter according to her last sentence or on the evening before.

---

8 To James Bird

Reydon
Sept 5 1828

I have about 3 chapters to write of the Tale I am upon.[1] I hope it may do some good among the young folks of the rising generation. I think of offering the MS. to Westley and Davis. Could you ascertain whether there is any notice for me in this months *Spirit and Manners of the Age?*[2] I have no means of gaining the desired information here ... Today I had a letter from Asker.[3] He is now in Norwich, but he gives me no hope of seeing him again this year. I am vexed with him on many accounts. If he was not Asker I should positively hate him. I query now whether I shall ever be his wife certainly not if he goes on in his present extravagant career. You will smile and say lovers quarrels. Perhaps I shall smile myself tomorrow at my present indignation. But I abhor selfishness and this trait in a husband of mine would drive me mad. I would rather marry a plain matter of fact man who was liberal than one who only thought of himself. Surely extravagant people are the most mean and selfish people on the face of the earth.

I am at last reading Cowper.[4] Of his merits as a Poet I will say but little. I think his works have little poetic merit. But his sentiments are noble, excellent, sublime! I venerate the independent spirit which pervades his works. He possesses a mind so clear and comprehensive, so divested of prejudice that I consider him as a Reformer of the Vices of mankind to stand unrivalled. His satires particularly his 'Progress of Error' must strike home to every heart. I am pleased with the 'Task,' particularly the second and last books, the close of the fifth and part of the first, but much as this Poem has been admired I think it far inferior to his Satires. His smaller pieces ('To Mr. Gilpin' excepted) are trash beneath the dignity of his pen ... I now read at night in my own chamber an hour before I go to bed. A *stolen treat*, but I think the stillness and solemnity of the hour impresses more forcibly on my mind what I read.

1 Perhaps 'The Curate's Daughters,' mentioned in Letter 10 and possibly in Letter 9. However, the Edinburgh publishing firm of Westley and Davis did not publish a juvenile-didactic work by Susanna in the period 1828– 30.
2 F. Westley was publisher of *The Spirit and Manners of the Age: A Christian and Literary Miscellany*, which printed Susanna's poem, 'The Spirit of Spring,' under the initials 'Z.Z.' in December 1829 (901). No notice of her appears in the September 1828 issue.
3 Asker is mentioned by name in this letter only. Nothing is known about him apart from the information provided here and in Letter 10.
4 William Cowper (1731–1800), a poet and chief exponent of the moral and humanitarian values of the Evangelical revival in England.

---

9 To Emma Bird

Reydon
Oct. 2nd [1828][1]

Mamma has just presented me with a few apples for the dear Children and I send a few Reydon Nuts for Sir James and your Ladyship to crack … I have been busy writing for the last month and hope in a few days to terminate my hateful job. I liked it very much at first it amused me but now I am near the conclusion I almost abhor the sight of pen, ink, and paper … I have increased my cold at the Church this afternoon in teaching eight dunces their A.B.C.[2] Little Frank Childs is still with us, he helps me not a little with my class in the school and hears the elder Children their Catechism while I teach the little ones to read. I am serving an apprenticeship at tuition. Surely all children are not so stupid as my class. I never knew I possessed a grain of patience till today. I do assure you my dear friend it was tried to the utmost … My sisters were much amused today by a visit from a deaf and dumb doctress, a sort of quack fortune teller who pointed out in a book the diseases of every body who consulted her. Agnes declares that she guessed her complaint in a moment. I think I could have done that, without being a deaf and dumb doctress. I wish I had seen her, she must have been a clever woman of shrewd abilities to act a part so well as she appears to have done, very unlike the dumb man whom my father asked how long he had been dumb and he answered in the most natural tone imaginable 'just five years.' Prince Hohenloe[3] never performed a better miracle yet no one ever considered my father a Saint!

1 This letter was written before Susanna's break with the Established Church, and seems to follow on the preceding letter dated 5 September 1828.
2 In a letter to Susanna, part of which is published in the *Albion* (17 May 1851), 237–8,

Agnes recalls the founding of a Sunday School at St Margaret's Church, near Reydon Hall, 'on the first Sunday of 1828.' The Strickland sisters helped to found the school and taught in it; indeed, Agnes was still associated with it in the 1850s, hoping to 'be able to build a school-house' in the community with profits from the sale of her royal biographies.
3 Prince Franz Josef of Hohenloe Schillingsfurst (1787–1841), Bavarian soldier and legislator, claimed to have a prophetic soul and predicted many current events.

---

10 To James Bird

Reydon
Nov 3, 1828

This has been a day of severe trial, of shuddering agony. I have written him his final dismissal. My eyes were tearless but my brain seemed to burn and my heart to wither but it must be. The blow has fallen. I must now strive to forget him. I could not write to him in scorn or anger and when I signed the warrant that gave the death blow to the hopes of years my heart was overflowing with tenderness to the author of my Sufferings. But I will never be his wife – No Never! ... I have read your two pieces in the *Forget-me-Not* with much pleasure particularly 'The Altar' which is in every way worthy of your pen ... I have not yet received the *Friendship's Offering.*[1] 'My Rover' is but a trifle and why they took it, in preference to the other little piece surprises me ... My MS. is now in Mr. Pringles hands but I dare not form a hope ...[2] I am sending to friend Harral 'The Pope.'[3] From various hints in poor Laura's letter, I fear they are struggling with unusual pecuniary difficulties. I have absolved our kind friend from his debt to me which would amount to £15 a great sum for him, but I trust I shall never want it and have promised to write only for a Copy of the magazine. I would gladly exert my abilities to the utmost if by so doing I could serve him. If my means and my heart could keep the same pace none of my dear friends should want ... Should Mr. Pringle be able to sell 'The Curates Daughters' for me, after I had settled my own pecuniary affairs dear Laura should come. It is only that bitter worm poverty which prevents her now.

1 Bird's poems, 'To the Altar' and 'Constancy,' appeared in *Ackermann's Forget-Me-Not* for 1829. *Friendship's Offering or Annual Remembrancer* was first published by a German bookseller, Lupton Relfe, late in 1823. T.K. Hervey, who was identified as the editor in the volume for 1825, remained with the annual until 1827, when ownership passed into the hands of Messrs Smith, Elder and Co. In 1829 the editorship fell to Thomas Pringle, a position he held until his death in 1834. Susanna's poem, 'There's Joy,' appeared in the annual for 1829 (148); Pringle sent her, along with £1 1s., a copy of the volume for 1829. Poems by Susanna also appeared in this annual for 1830, 1831, and 1834.

2 'The Rover's Farewell to his Mistress' appeared in the *Forget-Me-Not* for 1829 (369). The manuscript mentioned is likely 'The Curate's Daughters,' named later in this letter (see also Letters 8 and 9). This story both Harral and Pringle judged to be too didactic.

3 'The Pope's Promise: A Historical Sketch' was printed the next month in Harral's *La Belle Assemblée* (December 1828), 245–50; the same sketch was reprinted in the *Victoria Magazine* (October 1847), 27–31.

---

11 To Frederic Shoberl   Reydon Hall
Nov. 14th 1828

Miss Susanna Strickland, presents her compliments, to the Editor of the *Forget-me-not*, and feels highly gratified by the insertion of her little piece, and the Editor's polite attention, in forwarding the volume, the perusal of which, has afforded Miss S. Strickland, and her young friends great pleasure. The contributions from the pen of the Editor are not among the least of its attractions; and the little piece entitled the '*Wish*' has been read many times with increasing interest and pleasure.[1] Emboldened by the success of her first venture, Miss S.S. transmits for the Editor's inspection; a prose tale: entitled, 'The Royal Election,' and a poetical sketch, 'Winter Calling Up His Legions' both of which, she hopes may suit the pages of the Annual, being original matter. Miss S.S. also encloses a sweet little poem, from the pen of Mr. Bird, which was written, and presented to her during the summer, by her kind friend.[2] Miss S.S. is anxious that it should not sink into oblivion, in her portfolio; and would feel highly gratified by the Editor giving it a place in his ensuing volume of the *Forget-me-not*. It is the property of Miss S.S. and she has permission to dispose of it, in any way she pleases.

Miss S.S. is a contributor this year, to the *Friendship's Offering*, and is happy to find, that her piece entitled, 'There's Joy,' has been given by her friend Mr. Harral, as an extract from that Annual, a favour, unexpected, and unasked. Miss S.S. will likewise be a contributor, to that Annual for the ensuing year.[3]

Should the enclosed pieces *not* suit the pages of the *Forget-me-not*; Miss S.S. would feel obliged by the Editor forwarding them to 24 Clarendon Square – as soon as convenient –

1 Shoberl's 'The Wish' appeared in the *Forget-Me-Not* for 1829 (330).

2 Shoberl did not include any of Susanna's material in the *Forget-Me-Not* for 1830; 'Winter Calling Up His Legions' did appear in 1831 (321–4), along with a shorter poem, 'Love

and Ambition' (144). He did, however, include 'The Son of Arminius: A Tale of Ancient Rome' in the 1830 *Ackermann's Juvenile Forget-Me-Not* (241–61), and two of James Bird's poems, 'Frank and his Kite' (41–5) and 'To My Child at Play' (150–1). 'The Royal Election: A Historical Sketch from Polish History' first appeared in print in the *Lady's Magazine* (February 1831), 62–6.

3 Under her pen-name 'Z.Z.', Susanna contributed 'The Child's First Grief' to *Friendship's Offering: A Literary Album, and Christmas and New Year's Present for 1830* (217).

---

12 To James Bird   Jan. 14th 1829

My cough is so very troublesome that it allows me but very little respite either by night or day. It keeps my head constantly aching, my chest as sore as if it had been flayed and completely wears down both my health and spirits. I do think it has quite a churchyard twang with it and every mess I take for it only seems to increase its violence ... We are getting on with our Newman MS.[1] Jane has only to finish her tale and copy it out and my part of the job is already completed. I have been so busy copying that I too have nearly discarded the Muses and excepting a couple of sacred pieces have left my lyre tuneless and stringless till a fresh fit of inspiration should incline me to –

'Ride upon the horse with wings.'

I have never been able to leave the house not even to take a stroll in the garden but twice since I quitted Yoxford.

I forgot to tell you in my last that R. Childs asked me seriously to write a small volume of Psalms and Hymns as an accompaniment to the Hora Religiones (I forget how that word is spelt so I must say it like an old clerk, no matter for that) and he is sure he could get a publisher for me if we could obtain the sanction of the Bishop of London. This we can do through Dr. Tyler, a friend of the Bishop's and likewise a friend of Mrs. Leverton's.[2] I did not like to undertake this important engagement by myself and Agnes and I are to enter into partnership together and I felt both flattered and pleased by it for her opinion of my capacity must have increased greatly of late for her to wish our names to appear together. We have got some few of the Hymns ready but I feel a great diffidence in my own powers; the subject itself requires so much serious consideration that I tremble lest I should throw a discredit on it.[3] As these Hymns are to be written with a view to be set to music they require to be composed to regular Church Tunes. I have only written five. I will give you one as a specimen

Hark! Hark! the cry is heard without
The Bridegroom comes – arise and meet Him
Dost hear the trump – The Angels shout?
With songs of triumph rise and greet Him.

The Hills are mov'd, the mountains smoke
The earth to her foundations reel
Death bows beneath the Victor's yoke
A captive at his chariot wheels!

He comes! the grave's dark Portals yield!
He calls! The trembling earth replies
And spirits by the Godhead seated
To meet their mighty King arise.

All space returns the thrilling cry
Hosanna! to the prince of peace!
His arm hath won the victory!
He reigns! and sin and sorrow cease.

Hosannah the King of Heaven
Resounds from all the mighty host
To Him! be praise and glory given
To Father! Son and Holy Ghost!

I am fain to consult you on literary matters. Do give me your candid opinion whether you think such hymns are likely to succeed. You need not fear of offending me by saying no. True friendship is above such little-ness. If you read me a passage in your Framlingham[4] which I did not like, I should think myself a base hypocrite to praise it.

1 There is no firm bibliographical record of a Newman or Dean and Munday book with tales written by Susanna and Jane Margaret. *The Little Prisoner; or Passion and Patience and Amendment; or Charles Grant and his Sister* was a joint effort published (according to the *English Catalogue of Books*) by Newman in 1829: its authors, while not specifically identified, were described as 'the authors of *Hugh Latimer, Little Quaker, Rowland Massingham, Tell Tale, Reformation, Disobedience*, etc.'; but Susanna wrote the first three of these, while Catharine wrote the others. Another possible candidate is a small book

entitled *Happy Because Good* (containing two stories, 'The Tame Pheasant' and 'The Blind Brother and Kind Sister') in Dean and Son's series 'Tales of Goodness, Truth and Kindness.' Here the author is listed as Miss S. Strickland, but clearly this is a reprint of an earlier edition. Both on the title page and in an appended list of other works in the series, Miss S. Strickland is given credit for the authorship of Catharine's *Little Downy*.

2 In suggesting a religious project to Susanna, Robert Childs may well have been thinking not only of her interest in writing 'sacred pieces' but of such recent publications as *Horae Religiosae; or Daily approaches to God; in a series of Prayers, Meditations, and Hymns, Selected from the Most Eminent Writers* (London: C. Tilt 1828). The bishop of London at this time was Charles James Blomfield (1796–1857), one of the contributors to *Horae Religiosae*. As in other areas of printing related to the Church of England, it would seem that publishers had to receive official sanction in order to undertake such a work; apparently, the bishop had discretionary power in this area. Dr James Endell Tyler (1789–1851), a divine and tutor at Oriel, who became residentiary canon of St Paul's Cathedral in 1845, was at this time in charge of St Giles-in-the-Fields Church, London, and a Bedford Square neighbour of the Stricklands' relative Mrs Leverton.

3 It is not clear if this project reached fruition, though Agnes and Susanna did collaborate on a small book of *Patriotic Songs*, published by John Green of Soho Square in 1830. There is no known copy of the book, but it was reviewed in the *Lady's Magazine* in August 1831 (155), and by Thomas Harral in *La Belle Assemblée* (82) the same month.

4 *Framlingham: a Narrative of the Castle* (London: Craddock 1831), the sixth of Bird's long poetic works to appear in print

---

13 To Frederic Shoberl

Reydon Hall
April 22, 1829

Sir,

My sincere thanks are due to you, for the very genteel manner, in which you have pointed out the errors in my little tale of the Miner – I had been informed that such was the custom in the tin mines some years ago, that there were even houses and chapels constructed underground and that many of the Miners had never been above ground. Miss Edgeworth must have written her tale of Lame Jervis, under the same mistake[1] – Such I believe is the practice to this day in the Mines abroad, if the information I have received from travellers be correct – You must however be right, and again, I repeat, that I feel obliged to you, for the useful information that you have conveyed so well in a few words – The tale I now transmit to you,[2] I hope will be more fortunate. I wish I could say that it was strictly historical. This you will perceive it is not – as the son of Arminius could scarcely have been twelve years of age at the period of his father's death, and I have represented him as a youth – Tacitus has given us the promise in his history of these singular adventures he says that afterwards made him the sport of fortune. The record is lost. All we know of this youth is that he was born at Rome – that he was educated at Ravenna and that he walked some years afterwards in the triumph decreed by Germanicus on his return from Germany, and was called by the Romans Thumelicus – I have presumed to fill up the blank thinking that the story might interest the ardent minds of youth, as I well remember when a child, being most deeply interested in those tales that were founded on ancient history – I leave my work in your hands – I feel assured that I am at the bar of not only a kind, but a candid judge, and it will be my own fault if I do not succeed –

I likewise transmit a few stanzas which were written for a great Annual which I lament to find, has suddenly departed this life.[3] Let us hope that your projected juvenile, will live to witness many generations –

If you think the small poem you retained for the F.M.N. – entitled 'Winter calling up his Legions,' would be more suitable for this, you have my free leave to transfer it –

I should be glad to illustrate a plate, should my present venture prove unsuccessful –

My sister Catharine, the author of *The Young Emigrants*, and many other popular works for children, and who is a contributor to all the Juvenile Annuals has requested me to enclose the little prose tale of Francesca Martelli.[4] She will expect the usual remuneration.

The stanzas entitled the Woodlane[5] were not returned in the packet – Am I to infer from this circumstance that you have retained them? – With grateful acknowledgements for your kindness, believe me Sir, yours very sincerely,

Susanna Strickland

I should feel obliged by an early answer directed to the care of my friend, Mr. Harral –

1 'The Miner. A Tale' did not appear in the annuals but in the *Literary Garland* (January 1844), 28–32. In spite of Shoberl's observation of the erroneous conception of mining, Susanna could not change it, for the whole tale depended on the idea of miners living constantly below ground. Maria Edgeworth's 'Lame Jervis' was published in *Popular Tales* (1804).

2 'The Son of Arminius: a Tale of Ancient Rome'

3 *The Anniversary*, edited by Allan Cunningham, lasted only one year, 1829.

4 There is no entry for Catharine Parr Strickland titled 'Francesca Martelli' in Andrew Boyle's *An Index to the Annuals*.

5 *Juvenile Forget-Me-Not* (1831), 145

14 To James Bird

Reydon
May 24 1829

I was much alarmed at not hearing from Mr. Harral and paced the road in
front of our garden on Friday till 10 o'clock when the carrier came in.
When I asked for a parcel and he said 'no' I was so completely bewildered
that I still stood where he left me. My communications to Mr. Harral
were of that nature which made me dread his displeasure and his silence
had wound up my feeling to a pitch somewhat beyond anxiety and I fear
even now to open his letter when it shall arrive.[1]

Dear Agnes left us yesterday on a short visit to Bungay where I hope
the change of air will prove beneficial. She is indeed in a very poor way
I fear not very long for this world and no inducement will prevail upon her
to resign her pen. What use will fame be to her when she is mouldering
in the dust. She is killing herself by inches.

1 It is not clear why Susanna should have felt so uneasy about Thomas Harral's delays and
   reactions to her submissions. He had printed 'The Harper's Song' in *La Belle Assemblée* in April 1829, placed a notice in the May issue that 'The Promised Favour' by 'S.S.'
   had been received, and printed the latter as 'The Lover's Promise' in June. As a conservative Anglican, Harral may have disapproved of Susanna's increasing interest in Congregationalism as it emerged in her poetry and letters.

15 To Mary Russell Mitford

Reydon Hall,
near Wangfield[1]
Suffolk
June 2, 1829

To Miss Mary Russell Mitford

> Thy 'sister poetess,' thou gifted one!
> Never for me will lyre like thine be strung:
> Never to me will Nature teach the art
> To sketch the living portrait on the heart;
> With her own magic pencil to portray
> The storms and sunshine of life's varied day,
> The fond anticipations, hopes, and fears
> That gladden youth, or shade our riper years;

With Nature's untaught eloquence to trace
The joys and sorrows of a fallen race,
Till the heart's fountains at thy page run o'er;
We know the author, and the scene adore
From infancy my steps have wandered far
Through flowery fields, beneath Eve's dewy star,
And I have flung me on the earth's green breast,
Till my heart heaved against the sod I press'd,
And tears of rapture blinded fast the sight
Of eyes that ached with fulness of delight.
In this our souls are kindred, for I love
The flowing corn-field and the shady grove,
The balmy meadow and the blossom'd thorn,
The cool fresh breezes of the early morn,
The crimson banner of the glowing west
Flung o'er the day-god, as he sinks to rest;
The witching beauty of the twilight hour
In hazel copse, green dell, or woodland bower;
The plaintive music of the wind-stirr'd trees,
The song of birds, the melody of bees;
The kine deep lowing on the marshy mere,
The sheep-bell tinkling on the common near;
The reaper's shout, the sound of busy flail,
The milkmaid singing o'er her flowing pail;
The voice of ocean heaving in my view,
Reveal'd through waving boughs in robe of blue.
Or when the moon has risen high and bright,
Girdling the east with belt of living light.
'Mid Nature's solitude my days have pass'd;
Here would I live – here breathe in peace my last!
Fame is a dream! the praise of man as brief
As morning dew upon the folded leaf;
The summer sun exhales the sparkling tear,
And leaves no trace of its existence here –
That world I once admired I now would flee,
And to win heaven would court obscurity.

                                        Susanna Strickland

1 L'Estrange, in *The Friendship of Mary Russell Mitford*, has misread Wangford.

16 To Frederic Shoberl

Dear Sir,

Reydon Hall
n[ear] Wangford
Suffolk
June 3 [1829]

I never received your very obliging communication of the 6th of May until
this morning, and I now hasten to give you what I hope will prove a
satisfactory answer. I was much surprised that any remuneration had
been demanded in my name for the trifling little poem which I gratu-
itously offered for insertion in the *F.M.N.* of last year and which I considered myself handsomely paid for by the vol. and I think I expressed
myself to that purpose in a note written to you shortly after I received it.
You must labour under a great mistake if you suppose me guilty of such
meanness, not to say falsehood, in presenting you with poems for which I
afterwards demanded payment. My sister and I seldom communicate
our literary business to each other, as our friends in the world of letters
are often of different parties and totally unknown to each other, but I
am sure Agnes is too honourable ever to have demanded payment for me,
without apprizing me of her intention. She stated I believe that she
expected the usual remuneration for her articles when she sent them. I
expected nothing, and you I fear have confounded one with the other,
but I hope Mr. Shoberl you will do me the justice to believe that I should
scorn to forfeit my word for a thousand pounds, much less for five
shillings. I was much pleased with the kindness and liberality with which
you have ever treated me, and was grateful for it, and however some
authors may complain of the illiberality of Editors, I have received from all
to whom I have applied the kindest attention and even friendship. It
was my elder sister Miss Strickland who wrote the little article in Mrs.
Watt's *Juvenile Annual* entitled the 'Little Gardeners.'[1] Her address is
13 Bedford Square.

Let me assure you that I shall be perfectly satisfied with the terms you
propose, half a guinea per page for verse and 10 or 12 guineas per sheet
for prose, in which both my sisters agree. My friend Mr. Harral took out
of the packet the stanzas you mention[2] as I believe Mr. A Cunningham
retains them for *The Three Chapters*.[3] Do not regret keeping my 'Ruins'
so long.[4] I know that it is out of an Editor's power to retain all the
pieces that please him. It was a long affair. I transmit on the blank page of
this a little poem which would not occupy a couple of pages which
perhaps you may take as a substitute. My sister Catharine presents her

Compliments and will transmit shortly a juvenile sketch.[5] With renewed and sincere thanks for your kindness, believe me to remain yours in all sincerity

Susanna Strickland

1 The year 1829 is suggested by several details in the letter, most directly by the reference to Agnes's 'Hints to Juvenile Gardeners,' which appeared that year in *The New Year's Gift and Juvenile Souvenir* (London: Longman, Lees), edited by Mrs Alaric Watts. Andrew Boyle rates this as one of the best of the juvenile annuals then flourishing. Shoberl's confusion lay in the fact that the writer was identified only as 'the Author of *The Rival Crusoes*' (167). In his bibliography of the annuals, Boyle suffers the same confusion, believing that Susanna wrote *The Rival Crusoes*; in fact, Agnes and Eliza had written it together and had it published in 1826, without their names, by J. Harris in London.
2 The two sisters were Catharine and Jane Margaret. It is not clear what stanzas are in question here, but Thomas Harral did often redirect material sent to him by Susanna to other editors in London.
3 Allan Cunningham (1784–1842) founded his own annual, *The Anniversary*, in 1828, published by John Sharpe. While *The Anniversary* for 1829 was well received, both for its literary and its artistic matter, and seemed to have a promising future, it was changed in format the following year to a monthly magazine called 'The Three Chapters,' to be edited by Cunningham. When the magazine finally appeared in July 1830, however, it was called *Sharpe's Magazine*, and nothing of Susanna's was in it.
4 Susanna wrote several poems in the 1820s celebrating local Suffolk ruins, including 'On the Ruins of Walberswick Church in Suffolk' (*La Belle Assemblée* [March 1828], 119, later reprinted in *Enthusiasm*, the *North American Quarterly Magazine*, and the *Literary Garland*); 'Written in the Ruins of Covehythe on the Coast of Suffolk'; and 'The Ruin.' The latter two, dated 1820 and 1822 and considerably longer than the first, apparently were never published. They are to be found in a notebook of poems dedicated to her daughter, Agnes Dunbar Fitzgibbon, dated 1866, located in the Thomas Fisher Rare Book Library, University of Toronto.
5 The poem, not included with the letter, is unidentifiable. Catharine's submission may well have been 'Uncle Philip's Last Voyage,' which did appear in the 1831 *Juvenile Forget-Me-Not* (123–43).

---

17 To James Bird

Reydon
June 1829

I should think myself unworthy of life if I could regard any sect of Christians with indifference because they did not agree with me on *doctrinal points* ... I have friends of all persuasions and they have now become dearer to me in a tenfold degree.[1] I never knew what real interest was before. I never felt that their lives was [*sic*] of more value than the mere

gratification of the selfish affections ... Should you withdraw your friendship and confidence it would only make me pray more earnestly for you
and yours ... I shall apply to some friends to procure me a place in a
mission abroad I care not where and then poor Susy will be alike unregret-
ted and forgotten and those who once knew me and loved me will know
me no more. Yet wherever may be my destination I shall bear with me
across the foaming waters a heart too true to its human feelings too
faithful to the objects of its earthly idolatry. Oh! when will these mental
struggles be over. When holy Father will you call hence your erring
child. I sometimes glance on the spot I once chose in our quiet churchyard
for my grave. How peacefully the sunbeams sleep upon it and I sigh and
think how calmly and sweetly I could lie down in the dust beneath that
dear old tree – but this is wrong.

1 This letter is implicitly a justification of Susanna's growing commitment to Congregationalism. She did have friends of various religious persuasions, including Allen Ransome,
who was a Quaker. In a Newman tale, *The Little Quaker* (also published as *Josiah
Shirley*), she had spiritedly defended the nobility, charity, and selflessness of Quaker
principles. James Bird and his family were formally members of the Church of England,
but his religious sympathies were broad and he was, according to John Glyde in his
'Suffolk Worthies' (Public Record Office, Ipswich), 'a disciple of the Unitarian school.'

18 To James Bird   June 22 1829

When I told you I expected to lose some of my friends in consequence of
the step I had taken, I argued it from no superior merit of my own but
drew the inference from human nature. Have I not already been termed a
mad woman and a fanatic by one whom I believed had loved me as her
own child at whose sick bed for the last 10 days I have been a daily visitor.
Yet as death drew near did she not turn to the despised faith I had
forfeited the good opinion of the world to claim, for consolation in her
dying hour.

19 To Mary Russell Mitford   Reydon Hall
                                   July 31, 1829
My Dear Miss Mitford,

Your kind and generous letter, while it afforded me the deepest pleasure,
affected me almost to tears, so totally undeserving do I feel myself to be

of so great and distinguished a favour. I can scarcely believe that it is to one so little known and who has such slight claims to literary merit that Miss Mitford had addressed herself in such friendly and liberal terms. I fancy you mistake me for my second sister, Agnes Strickland, the authoress of *Worcester Field*, and the *Seven Ages of Woman*, and many other minor poems that have appeared in the *New Monthly Magazine* and the annuals, and who is a very talented and accomplished woman, quite the reverse of the plain, matter-of-fact country girl, her youngest sister, who is now writing to you.

My name is almost unknown to the world. A solitary piece of poetry in the *Pledge of Friendship* for 1828,[1] a few stanzas in *Friendship's Offering* for this year, entitled 'There's Joy,' and some sketches from the country both in prose and verse that have from time to time been inserted by my friend, Mr. Harral, in *La Belle*,[2] are all the articles of mine that ever came before the public with my name or initials appended to them. I candidly confess that I consider none of these worthy of notice, and they were written more with the view of serving several dear friends to whom I was tenderly attached, than with any idea of establishing my reputation as an authoress. I cannot, therefore, appropriate to myself your flattering opinion of my merit, though I am not less gratified with the kindness and benevolence which induced you to give such encouragement to a young and nameless authoress to pursue her literary career.

You have written to me as a friend, and I shall reply to your kind queries with the same frankness with which I should answer an old and valued correspondent. I have been one of Fancy's spoiled and wayward children, and from the age of twelve years have roamed through the beautiful but delusive regions of Romance, entirely to gratify my restless imagination, to cull all that was bright and lovely, and to strew with flowers the desert path of life. I have studied no other volume than Nature, have followed no other dictates but those of my own heart, and at the age of womanhood I find myself totally unfitted to mingle with the world. I perceive with regret that I must hereafter render an account to my Creator for those precious hours and talents that were wasted in forming those vain theories, those fanciful dreams of happiness that have faded in my grasp. Experience has traced upon the tablets of my soul with many tears, that

'There's nothing true but heaven.'

A desire for fame appears to me almost inseparable from an author, especially if that author is a poet. I was painfully convinced that this was one of my besetting sins. You would have pitied my weakness could you have read my heart at the moment of receiving your sweet verses, directed in your own hand to me. I had always ranked Miss Mitford as one of the first of our female writers, and though my knowledge of your writing was entirely confined to the sketches in the annuals, and to some extracts from the *Foscari*,[3] these were sufficient to make me feel the deepest interest in your name, and even rejoice in the success that ever attended the publication of your works. But when you condescended to place me in the rank with yourself, all my ambitious feelings rose up in arms against me, till, ashamed of my vanity and presumption, I stood abashed in my own eyes, and felt truly ashamed of being so deeply enamoured with a title I did not deserve, and I felt that that insatiable thirst for fame was not only a weak but a criminal passion, which, if indulged, might waken in my breast those feelings of envy and emulation which I abhor, and which never fail to debase a generous mind; conscious, too, that I had employed those abilities with which heaven had endowed me, doubtless for a wise and useful purpose, entirely for my own amusement, without any wish to benefit or improve my fellow creatures, I resolved to give up my pursuit of fame, withdraw entirely from the scene of action, and, under another name, devote my talents to the service of my God.

It was this determination which induced me to conclude the few lines I ventured to address to you in the manner I did, and could you read my mind, and enter fully into my motives for seeking to withdraw from all notoriety, I feel confident that I should gain from you, my dear Miss Mitford, an approving smile.

Mrs. Hemans is indeed a child of song – a complete mistress of the lyre. She possesses at all times the key of my heart. It will require another age to give birth to another Felicia Hemans![4]

Should I ever again visit London, I should indeed consider it a privilege to be allowed a friendly interchange of hands with Miss Mitford, an honour which a few months ago I should not have imagined it possible for me to expect, and which I do not deserve from any individual merit of my own, but owe entirely to your generosity.

I have pictured to myself your little cottage, and your poor lame maid Olive – 'is it not Olive Hathaway'[5] – who is a great favourite of mine. And now, I almost fancy I see your surprise, but I cannot tell you now how I came to know your maid Olive. Should you ever visit the eastern coast of Suffolk, my mother, my sister, and myself would feel ourselves highly honoured by Miss Mitford becoming an inmate of our old-fashioned mansion. The country is well wooded, but flat, and is not remarkable for its picturesque scenery, though it abounds with such sweet woodland lanes as you so intimately describe. Sometimes I think that you have rambled down all my dear old lanes, about which I could preach for an hour. Our coast is interesting, from the many beautiful and venerable relics of antiquity which form the chief attraction to strangers. The ruins of Dunwich, Covehythe, Walberswick, Blythburgh (which still contains the tomb of Ina, king of East Anglia), and Leiston Abbey, would not fail to excite your attention.[6] But I must not dwell upon my favourite spots – spots endeared to me from infancy – but hasten to conclude this unceremonious epistle, which I hope my dear friend and yours, Mr. Pringle, will obtain a frank for,[7] and with sincere wishes for your mother's health and your own,

> Believe me, dear Miss Mitford,
> With a grateful sense of your
> kindness,
> Your truly obliged friend
> Susanna Strickland

1 'Stanzas on War' (London: John Marshall), 356–9; see also *Enthusiasm*.
2 By 31 July 1829, twenty-seven poems, five 'Sketches from the Country,' and four historical tales by Susanna had appeared in *La Belle Assemblée*.
3 In *La Belle Assemblée* (January and June 1827), under the title 'Contemporary Poets, and Writers of Fiction,' Harral wrote a two-part sketch of Mitford, in which he quoted extensively from *Foscari*, a play that had lasted barely a fortnight in its London début.
4 Felicia Hemans (1793–1835) was one of the most popular women writers of her time, along with Mitford, Mrs S.C. Hall, Mary Howitt, and Laetitia Elizabeth Landon. A prolific contributor to the annuals, who was praised by Matthew Arnold for her moral poetry for children, she made her reputation as a writer of poems of sentiment and affection, collected under such titles as *The Forest Sanctuary* (1825), *Records of Woman* (1828), and *Songs of the Affections* (1830).
5 Mitford's 'Olive Hathaway: a Village Sketch' was published in *The Pledge of Friendship* (1828), 95.
6 References here are to Dunwich, the once-great coastal city, part of which, through erosion, had been lost under water; the ruins of St Andrew's Church at Covehithe; the site of another ruined church of St Andrew at Walberswick near Southwold; Holy Trinity at Blythburgh, a fifteenth-century church, where the signs of Cromwell's rebellion are still evident; and Leiston Abbey, founded in 1182 for Premonstratension Canons, the ruins of which still stand near the sea north of Sizewell, on the coast below Southwold.
7 Franking was a system of superscribing a letter with a signature to ensure free delivery.

20 To James Bird   Reydon Nov. 11 1829

I am not very well and yesterday or rather last night frightened all the girls
by fainting away as I sat by the fire. Today that frightful strengthening
plaster allows me no peace. I might as well live in the midst of a wasp's
nest ... Would you believe it, I received a copy of *Amulet* yesterday.
Hall has inserted a single stanza of my 'Spirit of the Spring.'[1] All in fact
which Papa Pringle sent him. It is a splendid book and I am glad that I
am one of its contributors even at the expense of the mutilation of one of
my best pieces. Mr. P. is much pleased with my Poems ... Mr. Dale
means to pay me for 'Zebah and Zalmunna'[2] but they do not mean to give
the book to any of their contributors whom they pay. If this is really the
case I shall be obliged to get you to order the 12s copy of the *Iris* for me and
pay you out of the proceeds for I would like to have the book ... It was
with joy that I saw a most favourable review of your little Poem of 'My
Child at Play' in the *Juvenile Forget-Me-Not* in the *London University
Mag.*[3] It was given as the best Poem in the book though without mentioning the name of the Author ... My 'Arminius' has been highly spoken of
Laura tells me in the *Literary Gazette* and this is more flattering as I am
perfectly unknown to the Editor[4] ... Mr. Harral is quite in a panic at my
dropping my own name but I do not think I was wrong to change my
initials. Last year I got into two Annuals under the signature of S.
Strickland. This year I have got into five under the signature of Z.Z. and
was rejected by all under my own name, save by Ackermann, and if I
remain S.S. to Mr. Harral I do not think it will at all matter.[5] I find from
Laura that there is a prejudice against the name of Strickland, that the
prejudice against A[gnes] extends to me. I shall [not] stand in her way and
a feeling of Xtianity prompts me to relinquish the odious task of compe-
tition. My dear friends will recognize their dear Susy under Z.Z. and
what is all the rest of the world to me ... Mary and William Howitt[6]
have sent me their Autographs requesting mine in return while to Mr. P.
they make most flattering mention of my work. These things would
make me vain if I did not know my own insignificance ... I have not
forgotten the Unitarian Tracts or your letter on the subject but it will
require a serious and less hurried hour to answer them.

1 *The Amulet* was edited in London by Samuel Carter Hall (1800–89), whose wife was
   herself a well-known poet and editor. Andrew Boyle characterizes it as 'a semi-religious
   annual.' A single stanza of 'The Spirit of Spring' did appear in 1830 (367).

2 Rev. Thomas Dale, editor of *The Iris: A Literary and Religious Offering*, for 1830 included 'The Overthrow of Zebah and Zalmunna' (153–7); see also *Enthusiasm*.

3 James Bird's poem 'To My Child at Play' was in *Ackermann's Juvenile Forget-Me-Not* for 1830 (150–1).

4 The editor of the *Literary Gazette* was William Jerdan (1782–1869), a London man of letters who exerted a significant influence over the reputations and successes of writers and their books, gaining a reputation of his own as a 'puffer.'

5 In 1829, Susanna's work actually appeared in four annuals: *The Juvenile Keepsake*, *Friendship's Offering*, *Ackermann's Juvenile Forget-Me-Not*, and the *Forget-Me-Not*. In 1830, using the initials 'Z.Z.,' her work was included in *Emmanuel*, *Friendship's Offering*, *The Amulet*, *The Iris*, and *The Juvenile Keepsake*; under her own name, however, she also had work in *The Iris*, *The New Year's Gift*, and *The Juvenile Keepsake*.

6 Mary Howitt (1799–1888) and William Howitt (1792–1879) were popular miscellaneous writers of the time. Married in 1821, they wrote together a poetical volume entitled *The Forest Minstrel*. This initiated a lifelong career of shared authorship that included *The Desolation of Eyam and Other Poems* (1827), *The Literature and Romances of Northern Europe* (1852), *Stories of English and Foreign Life* (1853), *Howitt's Journal of Literature and Popular Progress* (1847–9), *The People's and Howitt's Journal* (1849), and *Ruined Abbeys and Castles of Great Britain* (1862). William wrote many such works independently, and Mary is known singly for her productions for children, some translating, and various editing ventures. Both wrote poetry and prose pieces for the annuals and other periodicals, and William, in particular, is known for his contributions to the *Spiritualist Magazine* in the 1860s.

---

21 To Mary Russell Mitford   [n.d.]

... There is another very interesting gipsy family of the name of Chilcot – ditto Barwell; perhaps you may have met them in their peregrinations. In your delightful sketch of Grace Nugent[1] I was much amused by the donkey messengers. Such mercuries are common in Suffolk, and I greeted your boys as old acquaintances. My eldest brother, who is settled in Upper Canada, was a famous cricket-player, and I used often by his earnest solicitations to walk across Southwold Common, to witness his dexterity, and I felt no small degree of interest in his éclat. He was a fine handsome fellow, and promises to do something for himself in the country to which he has emigrated, and to which I often feel strongly induced to follow him, having many dear friends in that land 'of the mountain and the flood.' He gives me such superb descriptions of Canadian scenery that I often long to accept his invitation to join him, and to traverse the country with him in his journeys for Government.[2] But I fear my heart would fail me when the moment of separation came, and my native land would appear more beautiful than any other spot in the world, when I was called upon to leave it. Yes, I do agree with you that a

woman would miss the smile of affection more than all the applause of
the world. I know I would rather give up the pen than lose the affection of
my beloved sister Catharine, who is dearer to me than all the world –
my monitress, my dear and faithful friend. She is the author of several
popular works for children: *The Step-brothers*, *Young Emigrants*, *Juvenile Forget-me-not* (the first series),[3] and many other works of the same
nature. But it is not for her talents that I love my Kate; it is for herself.
She is absent now for a few days, and I feel lost and lonely without her;
she is the youngest of the six girls, next to me. We are all authoresses
but Sarah, the third; but then she is a beauty, and such a sweet girl withal,
that everybody loves her, and I often think she is the best off, for she
has elegant tastes and pursuits, and no clashing interests to interfere with
the love her sisters bear to her. I am writing a sad, egotistical letter; my
tongue and my pen never know when to lie still, and I quite forget your
dignity as a celebrated writer when I am scribbling to you as a friend.
Mr. Pringle will, I know, kindly enclose this in the next packet he transmits to you, In the meantime, believe me, dear Miss Mitford, to remain,

Your grateful sincere friend
S.S.

1 This should read 'Grace Neville.' The sketch appeared in the *Forget-Me-Not* (1827), 57.
2 Samuel did not travel for the government; he was hired by John Galt to work for the
   Canada Company, which he served from February 1828 to February 1831, chiefly as a
   superintendent of projects at Guelph and Goderich.
3 *The Stepbrothers* (London: Harvey and Darton 1828); *The Young Emigrants; or, Pictures
   of Canada. Calculated to amuse and instruct the minds of youth* (London: Harvey and
   Darton 1826); *The Juvenile Forget-Me-Not; or, Cabinet of Entertainment and Instruction*
   (London: N. Hailes 1827), the latter jointly written by Catharine and Agnes

---

22 To James Bird

Reydon
April 15, 1830

It is with a spirit of rejoicing my dear friend I enclose the amount of your
little bill, and wish that I had been able to do it last night by Mr.
Potter,[1] but you were a naughty Bard and would not send me anything so
unpoetical. Your letter of yesterday was a treat which I did not expect. I
walked down to Wangford with dear Agnes and received them from the
hand of Mr. Read the postmaster, and was so pettish at your not

sending my bill that I paid a visit to my dear Aunt instead of writing to my kind friend the Bard. I must say that I feel vexed that Mr. Roberts should be hurt at my not calling. I was so greatly fatigued with a walk of seven miles and I had not seen you and dear Emma for seven months, that I found the short space of four hours hardly sufficient for a friendly renewal of old times. I have a great respect for Mr. R., and feel much affection for Mary Anne[2] whom I shall ever be glad to see either at home or abroad so that I hope you will assure both from me that my not calling was a matter of necessity not choice. Had I staid all night I should certainly have seen them before I quitted La Belle Village. I agree with you that Mr. R. is a clever, gentlemanly and kind-hearted young man and with cultivation of mind might become an ornament to society. I cannot but own at the same time that I feel ever in his presence, particularly in his house, that I am personally disagreeable to him, and an intruder, and this conviction has made me rather diffident of calling, and at one time I had determined never to recross his threshold, but that old grudge has been forgotten and I shall always be happy to own him as a friend. Pray make for me the kindest apologies. I will pay this debt when I see Yoxford again. And did you really think of me on the 4 of April, that memorable never to be forgotten day when I first received the cup of salvation from the hand of my beloved pastor and felt that I was indeed bound to the Church in which I had been admitted by the indissoluble bonds of Christian union. I was admitted on the Friday previous. It was a dreadful day – Rain, hail, blow and snow; I was obliged to brave all. I was two hours getting to Wrentham, and almost drenched to my skin. The kind fatherly welcome I received at the dear parsonage, the tenderness and care of sweet Amy and the joy of all my pets soon restored my spirits, and I did not feel all that I had to go through with till Mr. Ritchie gave me his arm to accompany them to chapel. It was a starless, moonless, pouring night, and the dreariness of the evening seemed to give an additional gloom to my mind. There was no joy in my heart; like the heavens above me not one gleam of light on my mind. The unusual tenderness of my dear Pastor only made me more sad. The only cheering conviction was that I was obeying the dictates of conscience and that I was right. The service was beautiful, the sermon most touching, and so deeply was I interested that I never thought of my admission till Mr. R. came to the pew door, and led me to the vestry. He left me alone for about a quarter of an hour whilst he read to the congregation my reasons for dissent from the establishment and proposed me for a member. During this interval my mind underwent all the deep excitement so peculiar to my nature. The first five minutes I could not help feeling bitterly that this step would ultimately make me an alien to all my old friends, that I should never kneel down in the same place of worship with any of them again. These worldly thoughts were soon banished. Better hopes and feelings succeeded. I prayed long, deeply, and fervently, and my whole soul seemed broken and dissolved in tears. But the storm passed away and a sweet calm was beginning to steal over me when Mr. R came for me. This renewed all my violent agitation. I was placed in a pew opposite the pulpit and stood up. All the rest of the congregation were seated. I trembled from head to foot. Every eye was upon me. I buried my face in my hands and the tears streamed fast through my fingers during Mr. R.'s most pathetic address. He was much agitated and though I did not see him, his faltering voice assured me how deeply he felt for me. But when he gave me the right hand of fellowship in the name of the whole congregation, my spirit revived, and during his last beautiful prayer I rejoiced that the ordeal was past, that I was the member of a free church and blessed with such a friend and spiritual adviser. I dare not indulge myself dear friend by entering more fully into this subject lest you should think me a mere visionary enthusiast. I am happy now – so happy when I attend our holy little sanctuary. 'Tis a sweet looking place – One of the first independent chapels ever built. 'Tis some little way from the main street up a beautiful lane-full of fine old trees. The meeting yard is full of old pines and lilac and liburnam trees, covered with velvet sod and spangled over with flowers. I have chosen my grave under two pine trees in which the wind sighs lulaby through the long day. And then there is such a beautiful ash by the gate, that Shakespeare might have eulogized. No person has ever been buried there. I mean to plant roses and honeysuckles and make the place as pretty as I can. Guyer[3] has said

> I dearly love the ancient pile
> The venerable place
> Where many a holy man of God
> Has preached the word of grace

And I dearly love it. I shall carry the cards to Mrs. R. on Saturday. Many many thanks for the kind present for the dear children. May will be out of her wits with joy. Thank dear Emma for me. I would write today but am preparing a packet for London which will tire me out of my five wits. I felt grieved for poor young Potter. I thought him a very interesting man. But he is happy now. Weep not for him but for the living dead. He has found glory and life and immortality.

You have written out 'La Belle Village' beautifully; it has added ten guineas to the value of the book, and wherever this book travels your sweet verses will be one of its chief attractions.[4]

I mean to keep my word and see you within a month, but cannot pitch my tent with you on the sabbath for I have a class of children to teach at Wrentham and should miss my dear Pastor's prayers and preaching. You disputed with me dear friend the truth of the atonement and defied me to produce the text mentioned. I now give you it, just to show you that our glorious hope in remission of sins through the blood of the blessed Redeemer has its foundation in holy writ:

1 John 1:7 The blood of Christ cleanseth us from all sin.
Eph. 1:7 In whom we have redemption through his blood, the forgiveness of sins according to the riches of his grace.
Gal. 1:4 Who gave himself for our sins.
Matt. 26:23 This is my blood which is shed for many, for the remission of sins.
John 1:29 The lamb of God which taketh away the sin of the world.
Heb. 10:14 By one offering he hath perfected for ever them that are sanctified.
Heb. 1:3 When he had by himself purged our sins.
1 Cor. 15:3 Christ died for our sins.
1 Tim. 1:15 This is a faithful saying and worthy of all acceptation that Christ Jesus came into the world to save sinners.
Acts 13:38 Through this man is preached unto you forgiveness of sins.
Matt. 1:21 He shall save his people from their sins.
Zech. 13:1 In that day there shall be a fountain opened to the house of David and to the inhabitants of Jerusalem for sin and uncleanness.
Isa. 53:5 He was wounded for our transgressions, he was bruised for our iniquities: The chastisement of our peace was upon him and with his stripes we are healed. All we like sheep have gone astray, we have turned every one to his own way and the Lord hath laid on him the iniquity of us all.
2 Cor. 5:21 He hath made him to be sin for us, who knew no sin, that we might be made the righteousness of God in him.
Isa. 53:11 By his knowledge shall my righteous servant justify many, for he shall bear their iniquities.
Romans 3:24 Being justified freely by his grace, through the redemption that is in Christ Jesus.
Romans 5:1 Being justified by faith we have peace with God, through our Lord Jesus Christ; (9) Being justified by his blood, we shall be saved from wrath through him.
1 John 2:1 If any man sin we have an advocate with the father Jesus Christ the

righteous. He is the propitiation for our sins: and not for ours only, but for the sins of the whole world.

1 John 3:5 He was manifested to take away our sins.

1 Peter 2:24 Who his own self bore our sins in his own body on the tree, that we being dead to sin should live unto righteousness: by whose stripes ye are healed.

Rev. 1:5 That loved us and washed us from our sins in his own blood.

Romans 5:10 God was in Christ reconciling the world to himself not imputing to them their trespasses.

Eph. 2:13 Now in Christ Jesus ye who sometimes were afar off are made nigh by the blood of Christ for he is our peace.

1 Peter 1:18 Ye know that ye were not redeemed with corruptible things as silver and gold, but with the precious blood of Christ.

Gal. 3:13 Christ hath redeemed us from the curse of the law, being made a curse for us.

Heb. 9:14 How much more shall the blood of Christ who through the eternal spirit, offered himself without spot to God, purge your conscience from dead works to serve the living God.

1 Cor. 5:7 Christ our passover is sacrificed for us.

Rev. 5:9 Thou wert slain, and hast redeemed us to God by thy blood.

I might multiply texts to show you that I believe not in a cunningly devised fable [but] that through the blood of Christ pardon and remission of sins is freely offered to the Jew first, and also to the Gentile. So read these texts without prejudice and you will see that the atonement is fully revealed both in the Old and New Testament. I did not mean to end my long letter with a controversial discussion. I have given you some of the plainest texts from which I have received the noble hope of life eternal through the blood of my redeemer.

I send you the *Iris* as I promised. Tell me what you think of the beautiful *Magdalen* and the Madonna and Child. 'Tis an elegant book; Dale's pieces are beautiful.[5] This paper puts me out of all temper. Y[ou] will never be able to decipher this scr[awl]. Agnes and Katy desire their love. A. [sent] the *Emmanuel* – 'Tis a loathsome affair. Maunder has not sent the books. I am sure he ought to pay me for figuring away in his odious book.[6]

My poem was announced last week in the *Athenaeum*. Papa P. put in a famous puff.[7] Edward Taylor has brought out my song which has been received with great applause.[8] I mean to write to him for a few copies. I cannot write longer today. Will let you know the result of my Wrentham visit next week. Adieu my dearest friend with kindest love to our sweet Emma and bairns.

> believe me ever
> your affectionately
> attached friend
> Susie

1 T. Potter ran a coach line from Ipswich to Coddenham in 1816; presumably by 1830 he had a larger business, which also included Yoxford and Southwold.
2 Robert Roberts of Yoxford was a currier, Mary Anne his sister.
3 Mr Guyer of Ryde, Suffolk, was another Congregationalist pastor and Ritchie's brother-in-law; they married sisters by the name of Brett from Wrentham.
4 Bird's poem, 'My Village,' was in *The Pledge of Friendship* (1828), 316; likely he had inscribed one of his volumes with the poem and presented it to Susanna.
5 The reference here is to *The Iris* for 1830. The Rev. Thomas Dale, the editor, had contributed nine poetical descriptions of engravings depicting biblical events: 'The Madonna and Child' is the title of the frontispiece, 'The Magdalen' the title of another engraving of a painting by Samuel Sangster, which is accompanied by a sonnet written by the Rev. Baptist W. Noel. Susanna and Agnes had contributed to the issue and Susanna's poem, 'The Deluge,' appeared in the 1831 volume.
6 *Emmanuel: A Christian Tribute of Affection and Duty* (1830), edited by the Rev. William Shepherd, a Unitarian minister, and published by Samuel Maunder, was much criticized for its 'almost blasphemous' title. The criticism was effective, for there were no subsequent issues. The volume included two poems by Susanna, three poems and a prose tale by Agnes, and a tale by Jane Margaret.
7 The *Athenaeum* (3 April 1830), 202, included the following 'puff:' 'Shortly will appear, 'Enthusiasm, and other Poems,' by Susanna Strickland, a young lady already favourably known to the public by several compositions of much merit and more promise, in the Annuals, etc.'
8 Edward Taylor, Gresham professor of music, had property in Wrentham. The song he published is not known, but it may have been either an earlier version of 'God Preserve the King,' later published by Green of Soho, or 'England's Glory,' published in the *Lady's Magazine* (15 January 1831), 46.

---

23 To James Bird   August 3d 1830

I should have turned scribbler long ere this and given you some account of my journey home but at Sotherton the fever fiend met me in the shape of a heavy sea fog and chilled me to the heart.[1] This is one of the *refreshing dews* of this very healthy place. After having been so warm all day this wet blanket of a fog, enfolding me in a close embrace set all my teeth chattering and gave me such a headache that when at ten o'clock the coach stopped at our gate after stopping at every petty public house by the wayside to accommodate Mr. Plant's thirst, I was so fatigued and so ill that I could neither stand nor speak. The next day I was attacked with sore throat and fog fever and have been reduced to an anatomy and kept my bed ever since rising for the first time to dine last Sunday.

I send you the Anti Slavery Pamphlets Mr. Pringle was anxious you should have ... Do try and get up a petition for the poor fellows in Yoxford; it will be no expense but a good sheet of paper and will do much to rive asunder the burning fetters of the Negro. Will you dear friend forward the enclosed papers to Allen;[2] it contains some Anti Slavery papers and I think he is a very likely person to further our cause. I call it ours because it ought to be the cause of every free man who enjoys the privilege of freedom ... I send you some prospectuses of my book.[3] I know you will distribute and do the best you can with them for me. I must depend upon my wits to buy my wedding clothes, rather a hard alternative for a smart damsel like me, but I hope Apollo and the Muse will befriend me and if they will not, why then Cupid must.

What think you of this French Revolution.[4] It has put me into an ecstasy of fear lest my Dunbar's Regiment should be called into action.[5] I must hope for the best, but my worst fears are too often realized. I received a most delightful letter from my soldier just before he sailed from Caithness. Moodie's Uncle is delighted with his nephew's intended marriage and wishes to see me. This is a good omen. I wish the old North Briton would invite us to spend the winter with him ... Will you send my bill by Potter. I should like to have it that it may be the first on my list to pay. I should not like to marry till all such little accounts are discharged. Thank God my doctor and a few pounds to Mr. Ritchie is all I owe besides. I would not willingly bring one pennyworth of debts to my husband.

1 Susanna is describing her trip home from London in July 1830. Sotherton is a village three miles northwest of Reydon, likely on the coach route providing roundabout access to Southwold and Reydon.
2 Allen Ransome (1806–75), a Quaker from Ipswich whom J.E. Ritchie recalled as 'one of the best known men in East Anglia ... who was on very friendly terms with the Strickland family and who cultivated literature and business with equal zests.' See *East Anglia* (London 1883), 24. He would in the 1860s re-establish contact with Susanna (see Letter 89).
3 *Enthusiasm, and Other Poems* was in the hands of John Childs of Bungay, whose Bungay Printing Press was preparing the text for the London publishers, Smith and Elder. This project seems to have been initiated and encouraged by Andrew Ritchie.

4 The revolution in France in 1830 was sparked by the publication of royal ordinances, issued on 26 July by the rightist ministry of the aged Charles x, imposing rigorous censorship on the press, dissolving the newly elected Chamber of Deputies, and changing the election laws to favour conservatives. Charles x and his minister, Polignac, fell, arousing considerable social and political unrest in England during the autumn of 1830.
5 As a half-pay officer attached to the 21st Royal Scottish Fusiliers, Lieutenant J.W.D. Moodie could be called back into full service, should conditions require it.

---

24 To Mary Russell Mitford   Reydon Hall
August 12, 1830

It was with regret, my dear Miss Mitford, that I quitted London without seeing you. It was not so much on account of the literary fame you have so justly earned that I was anxious for a personal interview, but for the sake of those kindly and benevolent feelings towards all of woman born which are so naturally and touchingly scattered through those pages we admire and read with such pleasure. All probability of a personal acquaintance, I fear, is at an end, as it is very likely I shall bid adieu to my native land in the course of a few months forever. I am yet selfish enough to be unwilling to resign the privilege of addressing you, and I am perhaps too proud of the kindness you have shown to me. I have at length seen and been domesticated with my dear adopted father, Mr. Pringle, who more than realized my most sanguine expectations by his worth and genius. To me he has ever shown himself a kind and disinterested friend, and I think the faculty of memory must be extinguished in my breast when I cease to recall with gratitude the obligations he has conferred upon me. I came to town in very poor health for change of air, and joined Mr. and Mrs. P. at Hampstead. The few weeks I spent in this delightful village restored me to my former strength, and I greatly enjoyed our long morning and evening rambles upon the heath. We wanted Miss Mitford's pen to describe the picturesque groups of Irish haymakers bivouacking upon the heath. Every little declivity had its human tenants, and presented a scene of mirth or misery, of pastoral simplicity, or extreme distress and wretchedness; some of these poor people were laughing care in the face, while their haggard and wasted features told of sorrows which belied their affected gaiety. Poor Ireland! How my heart aches when I think of her degraded state, of the sufferings of her rash but warm-hearted children![1]

My stay in London was greatly saddened by the loss of a very dear

young friend[2] ... I saw but few of the literary lions. Most of them had
retreated into the country to enjoy air and liberty. Mrs. Lee (the Mrs.
Bowdich[3] of the annuals) was the most charming specimen of the female literati to whom I had the honour to be introduced. She is so perfectly the lady that we forget that she is a blue-stocking. Will you excuse
the liberty I am taking, dear Miss Mitford, in enclosing the prospectus of a
small volume of poems which a friend of mine has undertaken to publish for me by private subscription? I should feel greatly obliged to you if
you would circulate them among any of your wealthy friends who are
unfashionable enough to be lovers of poetry. The high opinion which my
friend has of their merit makes him anxious to bring them before the
public. But the method he has taken to give them publicity is most repug-
nant to my feelings. With every kind wish for your health and happiness,
believe me, my dear Miss Mitford,

> Yours most sincerely,
> Susanna Strickland

1 During these years, many Irish emigrants fleeing famine at home had come to England
   seeking agricultural work; without homes or money, they often camped in groups in the
   then unsettled area of Hampstead Heath.
2 Likely Laura Harral, though L'Estrange's editing prevents certainty.
3 Sarah Bowdich Lee (1791–1856) contributed stories and sketches of her African adventures to the annuals, particularly to *Ackermann's Forget-Me-Not* and *Friendship's
   Offering.* She was also noted for books of natural history and for such works as *The
   African Wanderers: or, The Adventures of Carlos and Antonio. Embracing Interesting
   Descriptions of the Manners and Customs of the Western Tribes, and the Natural Pro-
   ductions of the Country* (London: Grant and Griffith 1850). (Susanna mentions her in
   Roughing It in the Bush.)

---

25 To James Bird

Reydon
Oct. 9 1830

I send you a few fresh Prospectuses which have a more respectable appearance than the last. If you could send a couple of them to Mr. Jesup
who is among the rich of the earth I should be obliged.[1] We have got
about 50 orders at present, but then our chief applications have not
been answered. Glasgow, Norwich, Ryde, Sheffield and Framlingham are
still in statuo quo. Several friends have offered their assistance in London and one has already procured 16, another 10 names. We hope some-

thing from Ipswich, not through Allen who has not answered my letter and seems to have deserted us but through Mr. Notcutt the Independent Minister of that place. Mr. Ritchie will begin to print when we have got 150 names ...

I had the Hooping Cough when I was 16 years of age and for 8 months it hung upon me like a tormenting fiend. I became a perfect skeleton in consequence and made my first visit to London for change of air which had the desired effect and gave me my first mortifying knowledge of the world.[2] The curse of authorship like the garment of Hercules cleaves to me and nothing but death will release me from its adherence.

I pine for my dearie's return which I fear I must not anticipate before the spring ... Agnes is looking better than I have seen her for years. Mamma is busy gardening and more interested in housing her potatoes for the winter than the blue stocking fraternity in composing sublime odes or entering into the joys and sorrows of some imaginary heroine ... I have declined several very pressing invitations and do not mean to leave home for more than a few days to Wrentham during the winter. It is the last I may ever spend at Reydon and my heart cleaves to it more closely when I contemplate the probability of quitting it so soon.

1 William Jessup, a Quaker, was a prominent resident of the Leiston Abbey area, and friend to James Bird.
2 She refers to an unhappy youthful love affair, described in Catharine Parr Traill's manuscript, 'A Slight Sketch of the Early Life of Mrs. Moodie,' Public Archives of Canada, Traill Family Collection.

---

26 To James Bird   Reydon
                             Oct 19th 1830

I did not refuse to visit Yoxford through any displeasure but really if the truth may be spoken because I could neither afford the time or the trifling expense of such a visit. I could not make it convenient. I even fear that did my darling come earlier than the spring to claim me that I should realize the words of the old ditty which Pringle used to sing to me ... But truly the gallant fellow whom I love with all my heart and soul would tempt a girl less enthusiastic to contemplate this dreary picture with calmness. His uncle is now Sir Alex Dunbar and he talks of our living near the good old man in Orkney. His long letter is full of hope and pleasing anticipation. It is like the writer well worth the perusal and almost set me beside myself with joy. In spite of the cold I am sure I should be happy with Dunbar anywhere if beneath the burning suns of Africa or building a nest among the eagles of the storm encircled Orkneys. This is my hero's native isle and he possesses all the noble chivalrous and poetic feelings which cling round the hearts of those who have been reared amid scenes of barren grandeur. The prospect of settling in that remote region instead of frightening me called forth a burst of song commencing with

O yes I will go to thy own rocky isle.

I shall hear no 'Annual' news until Mr. Pringle's return. Our girls are dying with impatience. Cannot you tell them if their names appear in any of them and which they are … I send a Song for four voices which has been set to music by Mr. Cruse.[1] The *Sunday Times* and the *Dramatic Gazette* speak of it in such terms and of its writer that it would almost make me write songs for the time to come.

1 'God Preserve the King,' in four voices, with an accompaniment for the pianoforte composed by Edward Cruse, was published by J. Green of Soho Square and announced in the *Athenaeum* on 11 December 1830 (780). The notice observes that the song is imitative of 'God Save the King' and that the words had appeared in the *Athenaeum* on 4 September.

---

27 To James Bird   [November 1830][1]

I feel much indebted to dear Allen for his exertions on my behalf but I heartily wish the book was not to be published at all. You will say why? But I have my own reasons for this strange wish. I believe that we have already got 150 books ordered and I daresay shall get enough to cover the expense of publication. I should like much to be in London during this eventful period. I feel deeply interested in the King's Movements and wish much that he would take a bold step and go to the feast yet[2] … Katie has perhaps told you of my lameness. I have not left the house for the last 6 weeks and Mr. Lay's[3] bill which I received tonight will entirely empty my purse of all Annual Profits. Two Bottles of Medicine, Two Boxes of Pills and two visits regularly come to a pound. This my dear friend is making a fortune.

I think I have lost much of the regard which you and especially which

Emma once felt for me. You will say nay. But I am a shrewd reader of the human heart, a perfect witch in these matters and cannot be deceived.

1 On 9 November 1830, Agnes wrote Bird saying Susanna had been confined to a couch for six weeks. Since letters were often sent in bundles, it seems likely this one was written in November. The lord mayor's civic celebration was scheduled for 9 November in 1830.
2 Opposition to the ministry of the Duke of Wellington and the pressure for reform legislation resulted in riots, both in the country and in London, during the autumn of 1830. Agitation in London caused the cancellation of the Lord Mayor's Day procession and banquet for fear of rioting; William IV and his queen, as well as the Duke of Wellington, were to have attended these functions.
3 Susanna's Southwold doctor

---

28 To Frederic Shoberl

7 Solly Terrace
Claremont Square
Pentonville

Dear Sir

[December 1830 / January 1831]

Being on a visit with my dear friends at Pentonville,[1] I take an early opportunity of forwarding to you the little poem I mentioned for the J.F.M.N.[2] which I think, and my literary friends think, superior to my Squirrel. I am happy to say that that little piece has been most flatteringly spoken of in most of the provincial papers.[3]

I likewise send for your inspection two short poems for the F.M.N.[4] The best I think which I have ever sent you. I hope they will please you, and two prose tales. If the latter should not suit the F.M.N. I will give you a sight of several others of a different cast. A friend of mine has much soiled 'The Miser,' but I have not time to re-copy it.[5] The story is dreadful but partly founded upon facts. I should be greatly obliged by your opinion as to its merits. I believe it is at least original.

Could Mr. Shoberl favour me with a personal interview and give me a line as to the day I would certainly be at home. I should like to return my personal thanks for the very great kindness I have ever received at his hands. In great haste I remain

Dear Sir
Yours truly
Susanna Strickland

1 The date of the letter is based on internal evidence regarding Susanna's publication and writing. The Pringles lived at Pentonville.

2 Likely 'The Boudoir,' a sonnet that appeared in *Ackermann's Juvenile Forget-Me-Not* (1832), 31

3 'The Captive Squirrel's Petition,' which had appeared in the *Lady's Magazine* (October 1830), 238–40, and in *Ackermann's Juvenile Forget-Me-Not* (1831), 59–65. A favourable comment in a magazine like the *Literary Gazette* was likely to be picked up and repeated in 'provincial papers' like the *Ipswich Journal* and the *Suffolk Chronicle*. This was the process of 'puffing' in effective operation. In the *Gazette's* review of the annuals of 9 October 1830 (655), Susanna, Jane, and Agnes were noted as contributors to *Ackermann's Juvenile Forget-Me-Not* for 1831.

4 The poems do not accompany the letter, and no poems by Susanna were in this annual in 1832.

5 One of the enclosed tales may have been 'The Vanquished Lion,' which was included in *Ackermann's Juvenile Forget-Me-Not* for 1832 (97–115). 'The Miser,' which Shoberl passed over, came out in the *Lady's Magazine* (November 1833), 247–57, after Susanna had emigrated; it is, in fact, the basis for the tale she later expanded into 'The Miser and His Son.'

---

29 To James and Emma Bird

21 Chandos Street
Middleton Square
Pentonville
[late January 1831][1]

I really deserve your everlasting anger if your anger, which at all times must be like the dew upon Summer Grass, could last so long ... Circumstances have induced me to break off my engagement with Mr. Moodie and my mind has been so intently occupied with this unhappy business that I could think of nothing else. How is this I hear you say. Ah! friend Bird our engagement was too hasty. I have changed my mind. You may call me a jilt a flirt or what you please, I care not. I will neither marry a soldier nor leave my country for ever and feel happy that I am once more my own mistress. My visit with the dear never to be forgotten Pringles terminated last night. I parted with them with deep regret which was only softened by the pleasing conviction that from this time till the 21st of April I shall live within five minutes walk of them. I have become intimately acquainted with Miss Lawrence the author of London in the Olden Time,[2] with Mr. and Mrs. Leitch Ritchie both of whom I love much,[3] with Mr. and Mrs. Lee, and Derwent Conway and his wife.[4] They all live quite near to me and Leitch has promised to help me on in the literary world. I admire him, he is a noble generous creature and his wife a sweet amiable young woman. By the strong recommendation of my friends I have been induced to board with a family (Harral's old friends the Jones's) for the next three months and to try my fortune in the world of letters. I am to pay £12 s10 per quarter. I have a nice back drawing room to write in and share Miss Jane Jones's bed. I hope to get on and prosper. All my friends promise to call upon me in my new home. Am I not a venturesome girl! Ah! I have seen a great many strangers and have been shown up at Martin the Engravers[5] for a Lioness. I am almost tired with compliments and sick of flattering encomiums on my genius. How these men in London do talk. I learn daily to laugh at their fine love speeches. I was disappointed in Martin. Instead of the grand looking man I imagined from his pictures I saw an elegant dandefied little fellow who looked the favored favorite of the drawing room. He and his wife treated me with distinction and I have an invite for every Monday night to their grand converzationes but I have not since availed myself of it. I saw Allen Cunningham, Hobart Caunter, Mr. Ogle, Daniell the Painter, Whiston the musician, Mr. Picken, the author of *The Church and the Meeting House*, and a host of Mr __'s whose names I could not catch.[6] The Evening passed better than I expected and would have been very pleasant only I left a charming party of friends behind. It was provoking to be forced to go to a Lion rant on such an Evening! ... I have been reviewing books for Mr. Pringle and I said just what I thought of Kennedy's *Only Son* ... Leitch Ritchie's *Romance of History*. Both are excellent in their way. I like reviewing very much indeed but I fear Mr. Swain will not like what I say of his. But 'tis the truth and then to make up for a few critical scratches I extracted the two very best passages in the vol[7] ... The thoughts of Revolution here have died away. We are as quiet as possible and all fear seems now confined to country places. I saw by accident Hunt's procession into Islington. I think my dear friend Bird you would have laughed yourself into pleurisy. It was indeed

> March my boys in your radical rags
> Handle your sticks and flourish your flags.

Mr. Hunt upon a milk white steed most like a Farmer bold, rode foremost of the company in hopes to win some gold. Then came the incomparable blacking mass filled with trumpeters who had expended all their breath before they arrived at Islington and dirty blacking boys who with red Cockades upon their hats shouted 'Hunt for ever' and 'Radical Reform' till our ears would gladly have shut themselves against their teeth jarring jargon. The procession stayed so long at the toll gate that I verily believe they had no money to pay. The farmers carried long poles with red streamers and wound about with whisps of Hay. Whilst gazing upon this motley band of rag tag notoriety I discovered that M.P. after Henry Hunt's name signified 'mischievous person.' Do not you think I am right?[8]

I have been writing Mr. Pringle's black Mary's life from her own dictation and for her benefit adhering to her own simple story and language without deviating to the paths of flourish or romance. It is a pathetic little history and is now printing in the form of a pamphlet to be laid before the Houses of Parliament. Of course my name does not appear. Mr. Pringle has added a very interesting appendix and I hope the work will do much good ... I have given away most of your Prospectuses[9] but I am sorry to say with no success.

You will be surprised when I tell you I met Mr. Burmeister[10] in Paternoster Row. The new Rector seemed delighted to recognize me, his old antagonist, and greeted me with 'How now my little Neophyte, what makes you prowling about Paternoster Row?' ... Among other rarities I have heard the celebrated Edward Irving preach. It was worth enduring a state of suffocation to see and hear him make his defence from the Pulpit. I never took my eyes from off this strange apparition. Methought some man has escaped from St. Luke's or that Legion [and] before he was restored of his right mind had taken possession of the Pulpit. If you never saw him imagine a tall man with high aquiline features and a complexion darkly brilliant with long raven love locks hanging down to his waist, his sleeves so short as to show part of his naked arms and his person arrayed in the costume of the old reformers and you see Edward Irving. Then his attitudes. No posture master ever studied the grotesque more successfully than this extraordinary man. He is like the extravaganzas of the early romance writers and seems to belong to a bygone age.[11]

You know doubtless from Katie that Tom before he went to sea married Miss Thompson. She is a lovely creature and the idol of all who see her. I feel quite proud of my gazetted sister.

1 This date seems likely – shortly after she completed her agreement to stay with the Jones's, an agreement that was to terminate on 21 April.
2 A regular contributor to London magazines and the annuals, H. Lawrance was an historical writer and novelist; her regular contributions to *Friendship's Offering* suggest friendship with Thomas Pringle.

3 Leitch Ritchie (1800–65), a Scot who became a well-known literary figure in London, enjoying particularly warm relations with Pringle and Allan Cunningham, was perhaps best known for his numerous books descriptive of continental tours and picturesque scenery and for readable history such as *The Romance of French History* (1831), which Susanna reviewed for the *Athenaeum*.

4 Derwent Conway (1795–1835) was the pseudonym of Henry D. Inglis, another Scot and a specialist in charming books of travel and romance; he also contributed regularly to various magazines and annuals, and as a close friend of Pringle's took over the editing of *Friendship's Offering* upon the latter's death in 1834.

5 John Martin (1789–1854), one of the most inventive and popular artists in London, was noted for his large-scale, apocalyptic canvasses, rivalling J.M.W. Turner and Sir Thomas Lawrence in reputation. His engravings for the various annuals were much sought-after; certainly, his illustrations were almost universally praised as the outstanding feature of the giftbook trade. From 1825 to 1835 he made his home at Allsep Terrace, New Road, the venue of his weekly 'Evenings at Home' or Conversaziones, where the talented and arrivistes of English art, science, and literature might regularly be met.

6 The Rev. Hobart Caunter (1794–1851) contributed to several annuals in this period; Thomas Daniell (1749–1840) was a landscape painter and member of the Royal Academy; Mr Ogle may have been Nathaniel Ogle, an early writer on Australia who contributed a poem to the *Forget-Me-Not* in 1830.

7 While it is not clear what editorial capacity Pringle held with the *Athenaeum* or whether Susanna wrote other reviews than these, she did review William Kennedy's *Only Son* on 1 January 1831 (7), Charles Swain's *Beauties of the Mind, a Poetical Sketch with Lays Historical and Romantic* on 22 January 1831 (57), and Leitch Ritchie's *Romance of History* on 11 December 1830 (770). Swain (1801–74) was a prolific contributor to the annuals.

8 Henry Hunt, born in 1773 in Wiltshire, was a farmer and a politician. His experience of the sufferings of the poor and the rural administration of his own district inclined him to radical views, and his egotistical and belligerent spirit found expression in much political activity. The parade witnessed by Susanna was a public entry into London arranged by Hunt to mark the occasion of his assuming a seat in Parliament on 3 February 1831. Her perception matched that of a contemporary, Sir Samuel Romiks, who described Hunt as 'a most unprincipled demagogue.' Hunt was to lose his seat in 1833, but before that time took full advantage of the parliamentary platform to attack the ministerial plan of reform, to demand the ballot and universal suffrage, to assail royal grants, and to move for the repeal of the Corn Laws. He died two years later in 1835.

9 For Bird's *Framlingham*

10 George Burmeister, for a brief period during 1829 and 1830 official Anglican minister of Southwold

11 Edward Irving (1792–1834), a Scottish minister and strong advocate of a Scottish national church, was a prominent public figure in London. His extraordinary abilities in the pulpit combined with unusual features of personal appearance (he was apparently tall, gaunt, and had a curious squint) to draw Londoners of all classes and persuasions to his services at the chapel of the Caledonian church in Hatton Garden. St Luke's Asylum or Hospital for Lunatics, a huge institution on Old Street in London, dates from 1751.

30 To Frederic Shoberl

My dear Friend

21 Chadwell Street
Middleton Square
[January / February 1831][1]

I send you a few poems for your Editorial inspection, hoping that a national feeling will ensure your approbation for Arminius which if I may judge by the pleasure I felt whilst writing it, is not deficient in spirit and poetic merit. I should much like to see it in the F.M.N. but I know I must reconcile myself to disappointment in case of a refusal. I know it is long – but for all that, I do not think it would discredit the book. Should it not meet with your approbation, I will try it with the *Gem*, *Friendship's Offering* or the *Winters Wreath*.[2]

I enclose two songs, and a small piece for the young Annual. I have commenced my lion story, but am obliged to write it at my leisure. You shall have it when completed. I hope it will be a pretty tale.

> With great respect
> I remain
> Dear Sir
> Yours sincerely
> Susanna Strickland

1 Susanna has met Shoberl, which accounts for the salutation 'My dear Friend'; she finished her 'lion story, 'The Vanquished Lion,' and submitted it to him for publication in *Ackermann's Juvenile Forget-Me-Not* in 1832 (97–115). 'Arminius' is a poem of 220 lines that eventually appeared in the *North American Quarterly Magazine* (April 1835) and the *Literary Garland* (February 1844).
2 *The Gem* (1829–32) was edited by Thomas Hood and published by W. Marshall; Susanna's 'The Disappointed Politician' was included in 1832. *Winter's Wreath* (1829–32) was edited by William B. Charley.

---

31 To James Bird

My Dear Friend,

Middleton Villa
Near The New River Head
April 9, 1831

I received your poem, and the most kind communication that accompanied it, with equal pleasure. I have read *Framlingham*, with the conviction, that it will rather add to, than diminish your reputation, particularly in your native place. The story is the most interesting you have ever penned, but, upon the whole, I prefer the versification of *Dunwich*. *Framlingham* will be read with greater interest by most people, but there is something in the lonely grandeur of that fallen city which operates more powerfully upon my poetical feelings. There is nothing in *Framlingham* I think so good as the opening of the I and II Cantos of *Dunwich*, and its concluding lines. They were written in one of your happiest moments. I must scold you, (as you know I have turned critic) for dealing so much in extravagant metaphor with which you often spoil a fine passage by giving it a ludicrous cast. I refer you my dear Bard, to the four several descriptions of the speed of our hero and heroine's horses. The Earl of Stradbrooke would give half his estate for such a brace of racers. Your thoughts my friend often outspeed the wind, the lightening, the shooting stars and meteors, but I do not see why your horses' legs should perform miracles to keep pace with the vivid imagination of their Master. 'You are a pretty Damsel, Susy,' I hear you say, 'to find fault with me, when you leave such great windows of your own,' but, my friend, you are welcome to cast at me, that ugliest of all pebbles, a critical stone. That illnatured weapon of offensive, and defensive notoriety, has broken more hearts than you or I ever cracked nuts, for the life of me, I wish they were all pounded up in a mortar and appropriated by the turnpike surveyors to Macadamize the roads. I do not fear your censure, you and I friend Bird, have been too long acquainted to quarrel about trifles. I am heartily glad, that you altered your first plan, and instead of making Helen an only girl, bestowed upon her such a very charming brother. The picture of the old castle makes me long to visit the place, and now I repent me, that I so often refused to accompany you thither when at Yoxford. I feel little doubt as to the success, of the work, which I heartily wish may exceed your utmost expectations. As to my Enthusiasm, it begins to cool, and if the printers and editors, who have dawdled so long over it, do not quicken their movements, it will soon be extinguished altogether.[1] Like a glass of evaporated soda water.

Tell dearest Emma, a piece of now old news, that I was on the 4th instant at St. Pancras Church made the happiest girl on earth, in being united to the beloved being in whom I had long centred all my affections.[2] Mr. Pringle 'gave me' away, and Black Mary, who had treated herself with a complete new suit upon the occasion, went on the coach box, to see her dear Missie and Biographer wed. I assure you, that instead of feeling the least regret at the step I was taking, if a tear trembled in my eyes, it was one of joy, and I pronounced the fatal obey, with a firm determination to keep it. My blue stockings, since I became a wife, have turned so pale that I think they will soon be quite white, or at least only tinged with a hue of London smoke. We are settled in very pleasant lodgings, only a few minutes walk from Mr. Pringle's. I have a large, airy, well furnished sitting room, and a very pretty comfortable chamber. The house is entitled Middleton Villa. A pretty name you will say, and vastly romantic. I am perfectly satisfied with my quarters, and am indeed very happy, in the society of my dear and talented partner. By the by dear friend, I have hardly learned my new name, and it is often twice repeated before I recollect that it is my fortune to be a Miss no longer (a miss of fortune I might have said). My dear Katy was with me today, she looks, but so so. Mrs. Harral has been annoying her in the most unwomanly way, and to shew her spite put the announcement of Katy and Frank's marriage into the *Globe* in which she called him Thomas Harral Apothecary, and Mr. Moodie – John Moodie. K— will I doubt not inform you on her return of all her wickedness.[3] I agree with you, that authors are not the most impartial creatures in the world. That they are gossips in their way, and often attack the works and character of a successful rival with a degree of asperity which would shame an old maid of 50 while discussing the features of a pretty girl of eighteen.

Yet, there is to me a charm in literary society which none other can give, were it only for the sake of studying more closely the imperfections of temper and the curious manner in which vanity displays itself in persons of superior mind and intellect. With the latter I consider the heart has little to do. Mr. Martin improves upon acquaintance. I begin to think him a very fascinating man. Have you seen the first number of the *Englishman's Mag.*[4] and what do you think of it? I am much pleased with its contents, and heartily wish that it may succeed. I send you twenty copies of Mary's *History*, and 2 of *Ashton Warner*. If you can in the way of trade dispose of them, I should feel obliged. I have begun the pudding and dumpling discussions, and now find, that the noble art of housewifery is more to be desired than all the accomplishments, which are to be retailed by the literary and fashionable damsels who frequent these envied circles. I am glad that I am not forgotten. Give my love to dear Emma, to my boy[5] and all the bairns. Not forgetting the rest of my old friends in La Belle Village, and believe me, 'tho' with a new name,

Your old friend
Susanna Moodie

1 *Enthusiasm* finally appeared in April or early May as it was reviewed in the *Literary Gazette* on 21 May 1831.
2 Catharine wrote to James Bird on 6 April 1831: 'our dear Susanna was married last Monday April the 4th to J. Wedderburn Dunbar Moodie of his Majesty's 21st regiment of fusileers. What do you now think of the vagaries of woman kind? ... The dear girl kept up her spirits pretty well though at times a shade of care came over her brow but she rallied as much as possible ... I feel assured that they stand as good a chance for domestic happiness as any two persons I know of.' (Glyde, Public Records Office, Ipswich)
3 Catharine's engagement to Harral's son, Francis, was thwarted by their lack of income and by his mother's interference. In her letter of 12 May 1831, Agnes writes: 'Some malignant person, Mrs. Harral I suspect, put a hoaxing announcement of the event into the "Globe," and not contented with that, announced poor Kitty's marriage as well; but I understand it has been formally contradicted by the editor since.' (Glyde)
4 The *Englishman's Magazine*, published by E. Moxon, first appeared in April 1831 and lasted for only six numbers; edited by Leitch Ritchie, it had a deliberate anti-slavery policy, 'tak[ing] Liberty as handmaid and oppos[ing] slavery.'
5 Walter Bird, her godchild (see Letter 5)

---

32 To James Bird

Southwold
August 31, 1831

I know not what apology to offer to you for my very long silence. I may with justice plead the cares of this life, but certainly not the deceitfulness of riches, however without any excuse at all for I do not think I can stitch together a rag of one. Moodie and I have been coming over day after day and week after week to introduce ourselves to the Bard of Yoxford, his lady and his ladybirds but I have not been well enough to undertake the journey ... Agnes has told you I presume that we are settled for the next nine months in this unquiet little town, but with its politics and its inhabitants we have little to do, finding our own world and society within ourselves. The place agrees with my dear husband's health and we are a pleasant walk from Reydon. Seldom many days intervening without a visit from some of the Girls. Even Mamma forgets her resolution of never leaving home and honors our little mansion with her presence ... I am very happy and comfortable and can truly say that the cares of a married life though numerous are more than counterbalanced by its quiet and rational enjoyments ... A few days ago we walked over to Dunwich but I found the ruins entirely shut out from the inspection of the public and could only gratify M— with a peep into the forbidden fold. He was however much delighted with his visit to the City of the Past.

All the Grandees have called upon us and their visits have been returned with all due solemnity, but it is not among these that I anticipate that friendly intercourse which sweetens the ills of life. We are much pleased with your friend Gooding and his amiable sister ...[1] I received tonight the numbers of the *Athenaeum* for which accept my thanks. The Editor has promised to transmit them monthly to you[2] and you will perhaps send them all in a lump by your good friend Potter ... I have actually let slip the opportunity of sending this by Mr. Potter but am determined to seek up some Messenger. The Mercuries in this country do not wear wings, but generally travel on donkeys which may not unappropriately be termed the Suffolk Pegasus ... I feel rather annoyed by an advertisement of Haynes Bayley's in the *Athenaeum*. Is it allowable for one person to publish a song with exactly the same title as another. Mr. Bayley must have seen advertisements and reviews of my 'God Preserve the King' because it has been reviewed or noticed in most of the public Journals and I think it very mean and dishonorable in him to rob a Lady of her title verbatim. Can I not bring him to book for this? I should much like to see the words of his song to see if he has been equally honorable with them[3] ... We have been greatly pleased with the kind attention of General Darling and his lady during their short stay with Lady Margaret Cameron at Southwold and I spent one of the most delightful evenings at her Ladyship's that I ever remembered to have passed. I recommended your *Dunwich* and *Framlingham* ... We entertain serious thoughts of going next spring to join my brother in Canada. Mr. Read, his father-in-law, was over last week. He promises us independence and comfort on the other side of the water and even wealth after a few years toil. This at present he enjoys after a struggle of 12 years and he has now the satisfaction of seeing a family of ten children all in a fair way of becoming wealthy landowners. You must not be surprised at our flight in the spring ... What a contemptible review was Harral's of my book. A good sound manly hiss would have done more for me than such invidious praise. I cannot thank him for it. It is on a piece with the shabby manner in which he has treated me and is a liberal mode of paying old debts ... Your review was excellent and I am indebted to you for it.[4]

1 Although no direct link to Gooding's sister has been found, Susanna later dedicated *Flora Lyndsay* – 'To Miss Gooding of Cromer in the County of Norfolk. These volumes are affectionately inscribed to her attached friend' – appropriately, since much of that narrative concerns the time of their friendship. It is possible that she is the basis for Mary Binell in that autobiographical novel, and she also became a godmother to Susanna's first child, born a few months before the Moodies emigrated.

2 Likely these were complimentary copies by which Susanna could keep up with the London news.
3 Susanna's 'God Preserve the King' appeared in the *Athenaeum* on 4 September 1830 (555–6). H.T. Bayley's 'God Preserve the King: a Loyal Anthem' was announced in the *Athenaeum* on 13 August 1831 (525) under 'New Publications.' Bayley (1797–1839) was perhaps the best known and most prolific song writer of the day, and many of his songs and poems appeared in the annuals.
4 A review of *Enthusiasm* in *La Belle Assemblée* (July 1831), 36.

33 To Emma Bird   Southwold
                                      Nov. 6, 1831

A letter from you, my dear friend, was quite an unexpected pleasure, but, not the less welcome on that account. I was sincerely grieved to learn from Mr. Moodie that the Bard was ill, and have been watching for an opportunity to write to Yoxford ever since. Your letter put a happy termination to all my fears. I rejoice in my dear friend's restoration to health. My dear husband returned a whole three weeks before I expected,[1] and you may be sure that I was out of my wits for joy. Never did time appear to linger so upon my hands, as during his absence, and though constantly employed in preparing for one, whom my saucy love calls his *juvenile Annual*, I missed the dear one, whose presence is the joy and sunshine of my little home, more than words can express, but you, who have a kind husband, not unlike mine in many points of his character, can well feel. Dunbar was much pleased with his visit to Yoxford, still more, with his short acquaintance with your James. I regret, not a little, that distance and circumstances hinder a more friendly intercourse between them, convinced as I am that they could so well appreciate each other. Before we bid adieu to England, I shall try and spend a last friendly day, at the dear old place, and bid goodbye to all my old friends.
Moodie looked but sadly on his return from town, and since then he has been so far from well that he kept his bed for several days, and I nursed him with an anxiety that I dared not wholly shew to the dear object that occasioned it. Thank God! he is much recovered, but he still looks thin, and occasionally complains of his headaches from which he often suffers severely. The weather too is growing cold upon the coast and he feels it much more than we do, after such a long residence in a burning climate.
    Yes, every thing is settled for our emigration. And if war, in the mean time, does not break out,[2] and our lives should be spared, we shall

embark somewhere in the spring. Directly I am recovered from my confinement which I expect some time the latter end of February. I cannot help looking forward to that period with a secret dread. I am so happy, so very happy now, that I fear such cannot long exist on earth. I will however rely firmly upon that gracious Being, to whose mercy I am indebted for all my present joy. Should baby live, it will be a great pet. I often look at its wee bits o' things whilst making them up, and wonder what sort of a being is to fill them, or whether I shall ever see it. I hope it may be like its beloved father and then I shall be more than satisfied. Ah, he is so kind, so good, so indulgent to all my wayward fits, that I look up to him as to my guardian Angel. I seem to lose my own identity in him, and become indifferent to every thing else in the world. 'Ah,' you will say, this is preaching like a young wife, wait a few years, and then tell me what you think of matrimony. I do not much fear the trial, my heart will never grow old or cold to him.

I am glad your new baby is a boy.[3] What have you called him? Some pretty name I hope. My prophecy only wants one more for its fulfilment. You have been the mother of two since Walter. Another girl will make up the three graces, and the tuneful nine. As to mine, they are to be sturdy tillers of the soil and I will whip every literary propensity out of them by times. I have quarreled with rhymes ever since I found out how much happier we can be without them. Domestic comfort is worth all the literary fame that ever pu[lled] a youthful Bard onto the pinnacle of pub[lic] notice. I congratulate Mrs. Crisp, on her young treasure, and I hope he may prove a blessing and comfort to her future years. Pray give my love to her and kind remembrances to all friends.

Allen Ransom I have not seen since my marriage. I suppose he is as happy as ever, with his Kate, but I do think she is not so sweet tempered as her spouse, if you may form any judgment from looks. I was much obliged to you for sending Mr. Shoberl's parcel. It was a very welcome one. I am quite delighted with that kindest of Editors and my personal acquaintance enhanced the value of his character. Eliza has been staying a few days with me. She and Moodie are gone to dine at Reydon this fine day. I am far from well, and thought it wisest to stay quietly at home. The walk is too far for me now. They are all but Agnes quite well. She is nervous, and ailing, and looks pale and writes more than is good for her health. Dear Katy is still at Bath. I long for her return, but must wait patiently. She is well and happy.

Tell the Bard that I laughed heartily over the disfranchise of Dunwich. It was in his very best vein of humour. Tell him to write on Eye. The member having lost his Eye will make no bad joke.[4] Adieu for the present, with kindest love to you and yours, in which Moodie joins, and with best wishes for your health and happiness, believe me ever,

Your affectionate friend
Susanna Moodie

1 Dunbar Moodie was probably away arranging his affairs for emigration, or perhaps seeing to business relating to the publication of his 'Narratives of the Campaign in Holland in 1814,' in John Henry Cooke, ed., *Memoirs of the Late War* (London 1831), or his *Ten Years in South Africa, Including a Particular Description of the Wild Sports*, which Richard Bentley would bring out in 1835.
2 Traditional British fears of France were aggravated in 1831 by the issue of Belgian independence. Under the Treaty of Vienna Belgium and Holland had been united, but in August 1830 the Dutch were driven out. While independence was acceptable to the British, they would not tolerate French domination, and thus they opposed the selection of Louis Philippe as king of Belgium in 1831, supporting instead Prince Leopold of Saxe-Coburg. The threat of war in the fall of 1831 was the result of a Dutch invasion of Belgium.
3 The Birds' eleventh child, Aleyn, was born in 1831.
4 This apparently refers to a private satire Bird has penned about the disfranchisement of rotten boroughs. In 1831–2 Parliament was busy redistributing the voting areas and reducing representation from communities where the population had diminished, such as Dunwich and Eye.

---

34 To Emma Bird

Southwold,
March 9, 1832

I am indeed the happy Mother of a very fine and healthy little girl whose resemblance to her dear father at this early age is truly astonishing. I had a long and severe labor being taken on the Sunday Evening ... and not abed until half past one on the Wednesday morning. The last seven hours beating all that I ever imagined of mortal suffering ... As a wife I have been the happiest creature in the world and I trust my fair, blue eyed Kate will weave the knot of love still tighter around the heart of that truest and tenderest of all friends, my beloved husband ... My dear Sister Sarah was with me during my anxious moments and has taken the management of the house ever since. Moodie is in London, he was forced to leave me ten days after my confinement to meet his uncle, Mr. Dunbar, who after coming upwards of six hundred miles on his journey to see us, fell ill in Town and found himself incapable of journeying further. Moodie was loath to leave me but I persuaded him to go up and see his uncle at the Hotel ... What time we shall leave for Canada, the return of Mr. Reid, my brother's father-in-law, will determine. He has been a successful settler in Upper Canada for twelve years and from him we received information with regard to the country and the advantages of Emigration which formed the chief inducement for our own ... Moodie promises to bring dear Katie home with him ... Catherine has, I suppose, told you that my brother Thomas is now a Captain of the East Indiaman in which he made his former voyages. She is a ship of 800 tons and he a young man of 23. Too young, I almost fear, for such an important trust and perhaps the youngest Captain of an East Indiaman that ever sailed out of the Thames[1] ... We shall settle near Peterborough within a mile of my brother and two of Mr. Reid. My brother has already secured for my Dunbar 146 acres of excellent land fronting a small lake which he says, when cleared, will command an enchanting view[2] ... If Mr. Bird could get my song of London inserted in either of the Suffolk papers I should feel greatly obliged to him.[3]

1 This reference to Thomas Strickland suggests he was born in 1808 or 1809, though *Lloyd's Captains' Register* (1869) and parish records list 1807 as his birth date.
2 According to Upper Canada Land Petitions 'M,' Bundle 19, 1828–35, File RG1 L3, vol. 360, Public Archives of Canada, Samuel Strickland had purchased several lots in the Newcastle District, County of Northumberland, at a public sale on 1 August 1831. One of these, the west half of Lot 21, Concession 6, Douro Township, became the Moodies' backwoods home from early 1834 to late 1839. However, these records also reveal that J.W.D. Moodie actually owned several parcels of land in Northumberland (later Peterborough County), some obtained as Crown grants, some apparently purchased from previous owners.
3 'London: A National Song' was published in *Fraser's Town and Country* (February-March 1832), 154.

1833~1851

'Muse on Canadian shores'

ALTHOUGH THE LETTERS Susanna wrote about her emigration have not survived, she has left a vivid fictional recreation of her preparations for and voyage to the Canadas in *Flora Lyndsay; or, Passages in an Eventful Life* (1854). The Moodies boarded an Edinburgh-bound steamer off Southwold beach in late May, parting from friends and loved ones. They spent a month in the Scottish capital visiting Dunbar's old friends and looking for suitable passage to North America, finally choosing the brig *Anne* which sailed for Quebec on 1 July 1832. The voyage took a tedious two months because their ship was becalmed for three weeks off Newfoundland, and it was not until 30 August that they anchored near Grosse Isle, the cholera inspection station in the St Lawrence River. Thereafter, as *Roughing It in the Bush* (1852) reveals, the Moodies proceeded upriver to Quebec and Montreal on the *Anne*, travelled by stage coach to Prescott, and there boarded the new steamboat *William IV*, which took them to Cobourg, the port of access to the backwoods country in which they had acquired land and intended to settle.

When the Moodies left Southwold they did not part from all members of the Strickland family. Samuel was, of course, already established in Douro Township north of Peterborough, and Catharine was also in the process of emigrating. On 13 May 1832 she had married Thomas Traill (1793–1859), an Orkney friend and fellow officer of Dunbar Moodie. The Traills chose to sail from the port of Greenock on the western side of Scotland and were fortunate in the selection of a faster brig, the *Laurel*; although they left Scotland in mid-July, they arrived at Montreal in mid-August, and by the time Susanna and Dunbar anchored in the St Lawrence Catharine and Thomas had started inland from Cobourg to take possession of their land adjacent to Samuel's.

Susanna and Catharine were never to see their mother or their elder sisters again, although they kept regular contact with them through the years and often fondly recalled Reydon Hall and depicted it and its surroundings in their writings. Mrs Strickland lived on at the old hall until her death in the autumn of 1864 at the age of ninety-two, watched over chiefly by Jane Margaret, who managed to combine her domestic role with a continued involvement in the world of children's literature. Eliza, the eldest daughter, had moved to London and lived for many years in a rented cottage in Bayswater, collaborating with Agnes on the historical biographies of the queens of England and Scotland which made the Strickland name famous in the nineteenth century, though Eliza, a very private person, would never allow her name to appear on the works. In 1857 she bought her own home, Abbot's Lodge, in Tilford, Surrey, and lived there until her death in 1875. It was Agnes who courted the literary fame that *Lives of the Queens of England* (12 volumes, 1840–8) brought. She returned annually to Reydon, but spent most of her time doing research for the biographies either in London or in the stately homes of aristocratic families into which she was welcomed throughout England and Scotland. Not until after the death of Mrs Strickland and the sale of Reydon Hall in 1865 did Agnes acquire a home of her own. She leased Park Lane Cottage in Southwold from her sister Jane, the latter living in an adjacent cottage, and the two spent the rest of their lives there, sometimes on rather uneasy terms. Following Agnes's death in 1874, Jane Margaret produced the first biography of her famous sister, *The Life of Agnes Strickland* (1887).

The severance of the Moodie and Traill families from those Stricklands remaining in England was not to be absolute. The fourth sister, Sarah, had married Robert Childs in the late 1820s and lived in Bungay until his death in 1839. She married Canon Richard Gwillym five years later at St George's Church of Hanover Parish in London and enjoyed a gentle, comfortable life until his death in 1868. When she inherited Abbot's Lodge from Eliza in 1875 she subsequently welcomed to her home several of the grandchildren of Susanna and Catharine. 'Young' Thomas Strickland, who remained in the merchant navy until his retirement in the mid-1860s, also married twice, and one of his children, Adela, eventually joined her Traill relatives in Lakefield.

By emigrating, Susanna and Dunbar embarked on a very different life. When they arrived in Upper Canada, instead of taking up the unbroken Douro land Dunbar had acquired, they decided to buy a cleared farm in Hamilton Township, Newcastle District. The trials of their life there, the abuses to which they were subjected by antagonistic neighbours, and their own unfortunate financial ventures[1] are vividly recounted in the early chapters of *Roughing It in the Bush* and in Dunbar's informative sketches 'The Village Hotel' and 'The Land Jobber,' which appeared only in early editions of the book. So uncongenial to their tastes were their Hamilton Township experiences that by the autumn of 1833 they were making plans to take possession of their Douro lands and carve out a home in the backwoods near the Traills and Samuel's family. The move was facilitated by a legacy of £700 Susanna had received from the estate of Rebecca Leverton and by the sale of the farm to Charles Clark, the Cobourg merchant and 'land jobber' from whom they had bought it initially. Nevertheless it was with mixed feelings that Susanna left the birthplace of her second daughter, Agnes (born 9 June 1833), and set off for Douro in February 1834; her uncertainty proved to be well founded for the Moodies did not prosper in the bush. Their land was rough and nearly unarable; the cost of supplies and of hired help for clearing and planting soon depleted their financial resources; physical illness and back-breaking labour took their toll on both Susanna and Dunbar and brought them to the realization that they simply were not suited to pioneer life. Their concern about the future was intensified as their family became larger. Three sons were born to them in Douro: Dunbar in 1834, Donald in 1836, and John in 1838. Ironically it was the outbreak of rebellion in Upper Canada in late 1837 that somewhat alleviated their poverty. Dunbar served for some months as a captain in the militia, but his absence placed the burden of the farm entirely on Susanna and left her anxious and depressed.

Determined to find a way out of their circumstances, she wrote to the lieutenant-governor of Upper Canada, Sir George Arthur, in the summer of 1838, describing the conditions of her life and asking him to continue Dunbar in the militia service so that they might pay their debts. The story of this letter and its effects is told in the late chapters of *Roughing It in the Bush*, but, unfortunately, the letter is designated as missing from the Public Archives of Canada holdings of petitions to the lieutenant-governor. Susanna received no direct reply, but the letter brought results. In October 1838 Dunbar was appointed paymaster to the militia in the Victoria District, and, when, in a burst of eleventh-hour appointments, before leaving his post as the last lieutenant-governor of Upper Canada, Arthur granted to Dunbar the much coveted, newly created office of sheriff of Hastings County, Susanna's letter was still in his mind. He wrote to Dunbar in 1840: 'With respect to your office, I hope it is agreeable to you; and as to your loyalty and attachments to British Institutions, it was unnecessary for you to say one word – I took it for granted that you must possess both, or you would not have been the husband of Mrs. Moodie, for whose situation I felt so deeply interested that I was quite mortified it was not earlier in my power to confirm some appointment upon you.'[2]

So began a new phase of the Moodies' life in Canada. Susanna and the children left the woods on New Year's day 1840 to join Dunbar who had preceded them to Belleville. The family eagerly anticipated a more comfortable and satisfying life in town and in many respects the anticipation was realized. In Belleville Susanna gave birth to two more sons, George Arthur (19 July 1840), named in honour of their benefactor, and Robert Baldwin (8 July 1843), named after the famous Reform politician with whom they became friends. Their difficulties, however, were not at an end. In December 1840 their first Belleville home burnt down, and later they suffered the loss of two of their sons.

Unfortunately, the nine letters of the period 1832–1851 reveal little about the Moodies' life during these remarkable and difficult years. For more detailed information on the Belleville years one must turn to *Life in the Clearings* (1853), a less personal and overall less colourful and engaging work than *Roughing It in the Bush*, but still an important source of information pertaining to the Moodie family itself and to the social and political life of the town and of the newly formed province of Canada West. For Susanna in particular life in Belleville allowed her literary career to flourish; she became one of the major contributors to the *Literary Garland* (1838–51) and for one year (September 1847–August 1848) she and Dunbar edited, for Joseph Wilson, the *Victoria Magazine*, a periodical intended for the education of farmers and mechanics. Although contributions were sought, the Moodies were compelled to supply most of the material themselves. It was in fact for the pages of the *Victoria Magazine* and the *Literary Garland* that Susanna began to write the autobiographical sketches that were to form the nucleus of her most famous books.

While it is frustrating that so few of Susanna's letters from the early Canadian years have survived, we do know that she wrote home complaining of her loneliness and discomfort – so much so that her sister Sarah, in a letter contained in the Glyde papers, was convinced that the Moodies would not remain in Canada for long. In spite of the loneliness, however, Susanna's approach to writing in her new country was brisk and pragmatic. Indeed, the letter (35) and poems she sent to Dr John Sherren Bartlett (1790–1863), the respected editor of the *Albion* in New York, in February 1833 were not her first effort to place her poems. Perusal of the Cobourg *Star and Newcastle Commercial and General Advertiser* during this period yields both predictable and surprising results. The Moodies stayed at Oren Strong's newly revamped Steam Boat Hotel in Cobourg from 9 to 22 September 1832. In the *Star* of 19 September 1832 there appeared not only Susanna's 'Lines Written Amidst the Ruins of a Church on the Coast of Suffolk,' a poem taken from *Enthusiasm, and Other Poems*, but also James Bird's 'To Catherine Mary Moodie, An Infant, On her Embarking for North America, May, 1832.' The issue of 17 October contained Susanna's 'Autumn' and the first of two parts of a sketch called 'The Elephant Hunt' by Lieutenant J.D. Moodie 'of the 21st fusiliers, who is now residing near Cobourg.' Other poems by Susanna were included on 31 October, 23 November, and 19 December 1832.

More startling, however, is the fact that three of Susanna's poems had appeared in the Cobourg *Star* in September and October of 1831, many months before she left England: 'The Vision of Dry Bones' (20 September),

'Morning Hymn' (4 October), and 'Elijah in the Wilderness – a Fragment' (18 October). In each case the author was not named. The poems were designated as previously unpublished, though by that time *Enthusiasm, and Other Poems*, which includes the second poem and a revised version of the first, had made its appearance in England. Likely these poems came into the editor's hands through Robert Reid, Samuel Strickland's father-in-law, who, having visited the Moodies in Southwold, may have returned with a manuscript version of the book, parts of which either he or Samuel passed on to the *Star*'s Tory editor, R.D. Chatterton.

But it was to Dr Bartlett in New York that Susanna seems to have addressed her first formal request to find a place for her poems. The letter was written in the 'miserable hut' adjacent to the larger house the Moodies in fact owned but could not move into until the shrewd Joe Harris ('Uncle Joe') and his family decided to leave. The property, Lot 32, Concession 4, in Hamilton Township, was located near Gage's Creek some eight miles west of Cobourg and four miles northeast of Port Hope. Here the Moodies found themselves virtually surrounded by rough-hewn Yankees, whose United Empire Loyalist claims were at best questionable; the Harrises and Seatons (she called the latter clan 'the Satans') in particular both perplexed and taunted them.

While Susanna may seem to gild the lily in her letter by praising the *Albion* so highly, it is important to recognize that it was generally perceived by emigrants to be the most literate and reliable weekly newspaper in North America, specializing in the most up-to-date Old Country news, literature, and politics while steering clear for the most part of the hostile politicking and crude name-calling which Susanna, with good reason, found all too characteristic of Canadian papers. To be published in it was to be in good company and to receive wide exposure. Bartlett, a medical doctor from Dorsetshire, who edited both the *Albion* (from 1822 to 1848) and the *Emigrant* (later called the *Emigrant and Old Countryman* in the late 1830s and the 1840s), welcomed her submission, printing both her letter and her first two Canadian poems – 'The Sleigh-Bells: A Canadian Song' and 'Song: The Strains We Hear in Foreign Lands' – in the 2 March 1833 issue. But Bartlett erred somewhat in identifying her for he confused her with Agnes Strickland as the author of *The Seven Ages of Woman*. For this he apologized in a subsequent issue (25 May), publishing at the same time 'There's Rest,' a poem she had composed during her trip up the St Lawrence River. Throughout the 1830s several more poems were included in both of Bartlett's papers. While he was clearly glad to receive her work, there is no evidence that she was remunerated for her efforts. She would later report to Richard Bentley, however, that Dr Bartlett had at one point urged her to come to New York to pursue her literary career.

Susanna's success in New York was quickly registered by the Cobourg *Star*. On 20 March 1833 Chatterton reprinted the two *Albion* poems of 2 March, commenting as follows on Susanna's provocative letter:

In the first page we have presented our readers two chaste and beautiful Songs by Mrs. Moodie, whose poetical effusions have frequently given lustre and beauty to the pages of the Star. These songs are full of feeling and sensibility, and are written in the usual racy, and pure English style of the fair authoress. With us the beauty and chief attraction of Mrs. Moodie's Poetry arises from the delicacy of sentiment and the enthusiastic feelings, that pervade it. We meet not the lofty, gaudy, oriental language, which so illuminates the poetry of Mrs. Hemans, but a simple and energetic language which cannot fail to reach the hearts of every true lover of poetry. The Songs were originally published in the New York *Albion*, a fortnight since, accompanied by some remarks of Mrs. Moodie complaining of the little respect her muse has received in the wilds of Canada. This apathy, on the part of Canadians if it really exists, must arise from other causes than those she somewhat captiously alludes to, for our experience has convinced us that a want of taste can by no means be imputed to the inhabitants of this province.

Thus, very early on, Susanna met her first ambivalent Canadian reaction, not to her poetry, which had been interestingly commented upon, but to her views on her Canadian surroundings. Certainly, Chatterton had some reason to feel that the Cobourg *Star* had ignored neither Susanna Moodie nor the muse in general.

By 1833, Susanna had several other outlets for her work, including the *Canadian Magazine* and the *Canadian Literary Magazine*, both in York (now Toronto), and the Montreal *Herald*, which had reprinted selections from Bartlett's papers. It was her writing in the short-lived *Canadian Literary Magazine* that caught the attention of the American poet Sumner Lincoln Fairfield (1803–44), during what he called 'our journey through the vast and beautiful Canadas' in 1833 or 1834. Fairfield was editor of the *North American Magazine* and in his December 1834 issue he published a review entitled 'Mrs. Moodie's Poems,' to which he appended three samples. He praised her in glowing terms as 'one of those highhearted women in whom England has so great reason to rejoice and triumph' and as a poet whose 'genius and feeling [are] of no ordinary kind,' continuing effusively:

We desire to contribute to diffuse the reputation of this lady; and we embrace the opportunity, which the publication of one of her charming allegorical tales ['Achbor: An Oriental Tale'] presents, to exhibit to our countrymen the poems of one who is an honour to the continent which she has selected for a home. She is one of that beautiful and brilliant constellation which has shed much glory on the British name; she is one of that bright band who have exalted the female character and adorned human nature. Even the celebrated Hemans, Baillie, Norton, Jameson, Howitt and Shelley, of England, may rejoice in such a sister, for her genius is as lofty as her heart is pure.

Fairfield's Anglophilia was such that he was often at odds with writers and critics in his own country. Born in Massachusetts, a sometime actor and teacher (briefly headmaster of Newtown Academy in Philadelphia), he had visited England and France before turning to editing in the hope of raising literary tastes in America and of finding relief from the poverty and debt that were constant threats to his family. At the same time he appears to have been an aggressive, unstable personality, much given to melancholy and literary controversies.[3] His most notable literary contretemps was his attack on Bulwer Lytton as plagiarist when the latter's novel, *The Last Days of Pompeii* (1834), appeared in the wake of Fairfield's own epic poem, *The Last Night of Pompeii* (1832), a copy of which he had sent to the British author whom he greatly admired. The *North American Magazine* (for a time called the *North American Quarterly Magazine*) regularly featured Fairfield's high-minded, Miltonic poems, which in their style and content alienated many of the very audience he hoped to reach, for he seemed not so much American as an imitator of English verse. Books of his poetry were nevertheless published almost yearly during the late 1820s and early 1830s.

Little wonder, then, that Fairfield felt he had found a kindred spirit in Susanna Moodie. In all, he printed eleven of her poems, and one of her husband's, from December 1834 until November 1836 when he lost control of the magazine. The two letters to him included here (36 and 37) are likely but a part of their correspondence over the years. Both were written from the Moodies' home in the bush in Douro on the shores of Lake Katchewanook north of present-day Lakefield.

Another facet of Susanna Moodie's writing during the 1830s is revealed in Letter 38. In the excited aftermath of the 1837 rebellion in Upper Canada she contributed a number of patriotic poems to the Toronto *Palladium of British North America*, the successor to George Gurnett's *Upper Canada Courier* (1829–37). The editor, Charles Fothergill (1782–1840), was an

Englishman who had emigrated to Canada in 1826, establishing connections in the Port Hope—Rice Lake area before moving on to Pickering, the home of his wife. Dunbar Moodie had likely made his acquaintance during his travels, for numerous poems by both himself and Susanna appeared in the *Palladium*. Fothergill had made a distinguished contribution to his adopted land, as editor of the *Upper Canada Gazette*, as King's Printer from 1822 to 1827, and as the Durham representative in the Legislative Assembly from 1827 to 1830. He was also regarded as one of the most knowledgable students of natural history in the province.[4] Politically, though disposed to worthwhile reform, he was resolutely loyal to the Crown. It is not surprising that the Moodies were drawn to this man of wide and cultivated interests and independent English spirit.

No complete run of the *Palladium* exists, but it is certain that Susanna sent Fothergill 'Canadians Will You Join the Band – a Loyal Song,' a poem she had written expressly for his paper. Dated 20 November 1837, the poem appeared on 20 December with the following comment: 'Who will not admire with us that beautiful and heart-stirring song of Mrs. Moodie (formerly Miss Susannah Strickland) which graces the Poet's Corner of this number? Thanks to that sweet poetess who has so often delighted us from her resting place in the dark-brown woods of the Newcastle District on subjects of softer interest, and who now shews forth with what skill she can strike a bolder strain – Yes; all who will see it, must thank thee, sweet Poetess – Daughter of Genius – and, Wife of the Brave.' Shortly thereafter, on 17 January 1838, Susanna's poem, 'On Reading the Proclamation Delivered by William Lyon Mackenzie, on Navy Island,' appeared in the *Palladium*; it was dated Melsetter, Douro, 2 January 1838. Later she used part of this long castigation of Mackenzie as the epigraph for her chapter 'The Outbreak' in *Roughing It in the Bush*, though she did not include it in the book with her other rebellion songs. It is a powerful and rousing poem, if somewhat contradictory in its romantic championing of historical rebel-heroes, Spartacus and George Washington. She is relentlessly dogmatic throughout in her condemnation of presumptuous, gain-seeking anarchists who would undermine the glory of England's 'mild maternal sway.'

Other poems by Susanna and several by Dunbar were included in the *Palladium* through the late winter and early spring of 1838, among them 'The Burning of the Caroline' and the accompanying letter (38). Though we have only their republication in the Montreal *Transcript* of 11 October 1838 to go by, that fact in itself becomes an important piece of evidence linking Susanna Moodie to perhaps the most important figure in her career as a

John Lovell, editor of the *Literary Garland*

writer in Canada. John Lovell (1810–93), Irish-born, had come to Canada at a young age in 1820. Through hard work, supportive partners, and wise employment practices he had established a flourishing printing and publishing house in Montreal by the late 1830s. With Donald McDonald as editor, he set up the tri-weekly penny newspaper, the Montreal *Transcript*, in 1836 before collaborating with his brother-in-law, John Gibson, in a series of ventures that included the Montreal *Daily News*, the *Canadian Agriculturalist*, *La Revue Canadienne*, the Montreal *Medical Gazette*, and, most significantly, the *Literary Garland* (1838–51). The *Transcript*'s interest in Susanna's spirited rebellion poems reflects shared feelings: Lovell was himself strongly attached to Britain, had much faith in the moral and elevating power of literature, and had served loyally during the rebellion in Lower Canada as a member of the Montreal Cavalry. His wife, Sara, whom he married in 1849, noted in her *Reminiscences of Seventy*

Years (1908) that he had bravely undertaken a dangerous assignment, conveying a despatch from Colonel Wetherall to Major Warde with word that additional troops were en route to St Charles, where the rebels were subsequently defeated.

Though Susanna was unaware of Lovell's interest, it is not surprising, given their common sentiments, that in undertaking to launch the *Literary Garland* in 1838 he did not hesitate to establish contact with her in Douro. Lovell deemed himself 'an Amateur in Literary Horticulture' but nevertheless sought to produce a literary magazine of quality, drawing as much as possible on native talent. Since no such magazine had lasted longer than three years in Canada, this was both a venturesome and forward-looking enterprise, so much so that Lovell took the positive step of actually paying his contributors. It was the very opportunity of which Susanna had long despaired. Her first poems for the magazine, 'The Otonabee' and 'The Oath of the Canadian Volunteers,' appeared in May 1839 – the latter was reprinted in the *Transcript* on 11 June – thereby launching a congenial and enduring relationship between author and publisher. Susanna Moodie, in fact, became the *Literary Garland*'s most consistent contributor, offering stories, poems, sketches, and serialized fiction so regularly that it was the rare issue that did not contain her work.[5]

By November 1842, Susanna and John Lovell were on friendly terms, though it is not clear when they first met; regrettably, very little of their correspondence seems to have survived. Sara recalls entertaining the Moodies in the Lovells' home on St Catherine's Street: 'She was a pleasant companion, could paint well, and told me that she often wrote with her infant on her lap.'[6] Both families were enthusiastic about both literature and music. Sara (née Kurczyn), who came from a family in which music was 'the recreation of the household,' sang in the choir of St George's Church and regularly took part in musicales and soirées. Like Susanna, she considered the piano a vital part of social life, and remarks proudly in her memoirs that 'About the year 1845, I became the possessor of a grand piano with six pedals. One of them was a drum attachment.' Knowing of John Lovell's passion for music – he included music as a regular feature in the *Literary Garland* – Susanna trusted to his expertise to choose a piano to be shipped to Belleville (see Letter 40). The piano was clearly a symbol of refinement to the Moodies, as well as an essential part of family life. Dunbar, himself a lover of the flute, notes this importance in the second edition of *Roughing It in the Bush* by mentioning that 'Twelve years ago there were not more than five or six piano-fortes in Belleville. Now there are nearly one hundred of a superior description.'[7]

The editor of the *Literary Garland* at the time was John Gibson, and the letters directed to him provide glimpses of Susanna's amiable relations with the magazine, her interest in promoting young authors, and her concern for her integrity as a writer. The formal letter (39) that appeared in June 1842 as a preface to the first instalment of 'The Miser and his Son: A Tale' (eventually expanded into the two-volume *Mark Hurdlestone, or The Gold Worshipper*) is worth noting specially for, as the letter suggests, Eliza Strickland had indeed placed the much shorter sketch in the *Lady's Magazine* (London) in 1833, well after the Moodies' emigration.

Susanna was always careful to avoid any possible charge of plagiarism and occasionally went out of her way to praise other writers. She was therefore greatly distressed to discover in the pages of the *Literary Garland* for March 1844 one of her own early stories, 'The Disappointed Politician,' published under the title 'Christina Steinfort. A Tale from the French,' allegedly written by Hugh E. Montgomerie, a respected *Garland* contributor, who had used the pen-name 'Edward Hugomont.'[8] The publication of this story was the result of a curious set of circumstances that say a great deal about the absence of effective copyright controls at the time. Gibson did not publish Susanna's letter charging Montgomerie with plagiarism – regrettably for present purposes – but he did give sufficient indication of her anger in his 'The Editor's Table' column and Montgomerie's reply. It seems that Susanna's original story, published in a London annual, *The Gem* for 1832, was borrowed and translated by the French poet Marceline Desbordes-Valmore. Under its new title, 'Un Soufflet,' it appeared first in the *Revue des Théâtres*, then in 1837 in the literary digest *La Tribune Littéraire*. Herein Montgomerie discovered it and, taken by its possibilities, retranslated it for the *Literary Garland* audience.

The brief, somewhat formal letters to Gibson (41) and to Louisa May Murray (42), an aspiring writer, reveal a Susanna Moodie much concerned with other authors and with the promotion of talent in Canada, an aspect of her personality also evident in her 1853 'Introduction' to *Mark Hurdlestone* where she called attention to the poems of a poor Irishman of Hastings County named Michael Ryan.[9] Similarly, in editing the *Victoria Magazine* she gave considerable space to aspiring writers such as Rhoda Ann Page (R.A.P.), Hamilton Aylmer, and Thomas MacQueen. Louisa Murray (1818–94) deserves particular emphasis, for she went on to notable success as a writer of prose romance. She had emigrated to Canada in 1844, settling with her family at Wolfe Island near Kingston. 'Fauna; or, the Flower of Leafy Hollow' was her first publication, appearing in the 1851 *Literary Garland*, which was edited that year – its last – by Eliza Cushing in the wake of John Gibson's death in 1850. Nothing by her appeared in book form, but she did find outlets for her fiction in magazines such as *Once a Week*, the *British American Magazine*, the *Nation*, the *Canadian Monthly*, and the *Week*.

The final letter in this section (43) appeared in the *Albion* on 17 May 1851, and it shows a Susanna Moodie determined to be vigilant about the reputation and integrity of the Strickland family. The case referred to involved Agnes Strickland and Caroline Bowles (1786–1854), a frequent contributor to English periodicals and annuals. She was much admired by the Strickland sisters especially for her stories in *Blackwood's Magazine*; in 1839 she became the second wife of the poet Robert Southey.

Whatever reservations Susanna may have had about Agnes, and however much Agnes actually was aggressive in her pursuit of social and literary status, publicly Susanna was her zealous defender and advocate, a kind of ambassador abroad. Certainly in the *Victoria Magazine* she published many of Agnes's poems and stories, and she also deeply admired the royalist histories Agnes and Eliza had written, especially *Lives of the Queens of England* (1840–8). Moreover, Susanna's letter of 26 November 1842 to John Lovell suggests her awareness of the worth of her sister's name, a value she capitalized on in dedicating *Roughing It in the Bush* as a 'simple Tribute of Affection' to Agnes Strickland.

In its conclusion, *Roughing It in the Bush* might leave the impression that, upon reaching the thriving town of Belleville, the worst was over for the Moodies. A prestigious appointment and removal from the backwoods, however, did not make life easier for them. There were, in the first place, several family tragedies. Their fourth son, George Arthur, with whom Susanna was pregnant before leaving Douro, died on 8 August 1840, less than a month after his birth. Four months later their first Belleville home was destroyed by fire and they lost much of their furniture, clothing, and winter stores. Then, less than a year after the birth of their last child, Robert Baldwin Moodie, on 8 July 1843, they suffered their most grievous loss when, in late June, John Strickland Moodie, age six, drowned while fishing in the Moira River. The cost of this particular loss to Susanna is not easily measured, but one suspects it played a large part in her estimate of her life as 'sad [and] eventful' in *Life in the Clearings* (27), and in the further testing and strengthening of her Christian faith. One has only to notice how often little John is mentioned in *Life in the Clearings* to feel the weight of the tragedy. During the fire, for instance, it was this same child who was lost during the confusion of the conflagration. 'The agony I endured for about half an hour,' she writes, 'I shall never forget. The roaring flames, the impending misfortune that hung over us, was forgotten in the terror that shook my mind lest he had become a victim to the flames.' Her affinity for this 'lovely, laughing, rosy, dimpled, child' is feelingly recorded in the poem 'The Early Lost,' written on the anniversary of John's death and printed in *Life in the Clearings* (27–8).

Coincident with these troubles, the Moodies faced difficulties of a political and social kind in Belleville. As outsiders, thrust into the public spotlight as a result of Dunbar's much-envied appointment, they found themselves precariously placed. The town in 1840 was only a few decades old, but the foundations of a distinct, conservative identity had been laid among its established, mostly British and Loyalist, families. While their politics were Tory, their base of power, which they sought vigilantly to preserve, owed much to fraternal societies as well as to church affiliation. The Orange Order was particularly strong along 'the Front' (the Lake Ontario shore), so much so that George Benjamin, editor of the outspokenly Tory Belleville *Intelligencer*, had in 1846 sufficient renown to be elected grand master of the Orange Order of British North America. Benjamin's election in fact represented a renewed consolidation of conservative and Orange interests, a unity that had been threatened when his predecessor, Ogle Robert Gowan of Brockville, had antagonized Tories by denouncing the ruling oligarchy, the 'Family Compact.'

Around this Tory core, and at odds with it, was an expanding opposition sympathetic to reform. It found its public voice in the Victoria *Chronicle* (after 1850 the Hastings *Chronicle*) and drew its strength from disparate, seldom-unified sources: political idealists, newcomers, those resentful of the established order, Catholics, and rural voters. Belleville, not untypically, was a place where 'no one was allowed to be neutral.'[10] As Susanna noted in *Life in the Clearings*, 'however moderate your views might be, to belong to the one [political faction] was to incur the dislike and ill-will of the other.' The blame, she felt, lay with the Tories:

The Tory party, who arrogated the whole loyalty of the colony to themselves, branded, indiscriminately, the large body of Reformers as traitors and rebels. Every conscientious and thinking man who wished to see a change for the better in the management of public affairs was confounded with those discontented spirits who had raised the standard of revolt against the mother country ... Their attempt, whether instigated by patriotism or selfishness – and probably it contained a mixture of both – had failed, and it was but just that they should feel the punishment due to their crime. But the odious term of rebel, applied to some of the most loyal and honourable men in the province because they could not give up their honest views on the state of the colony, gave rise to bitter and resentful feelings, which were ready, on all public occasions, to burst into a flame.[11]

So strong was the appeal of party feeling that it seems to have had a greater authority than the claims of good sense, fellow feeling, and moral principle. Rival newspapers had little trouble fanning the fire and elections often resulted in violent confrontations. With evident and lingering disappointment, Susanna recalled that 'Even women entered deeply into this party hostility; and those who, from their education and mental advantages, might have been friends and agreeable companions kept aloof, rarely taking notice of each other, when accidently thrown together.' Such may have been the case in her early contacts with Maria Murney (née Breakenridge), a cousin of Robert Baldwin, who had married Edmund Murney, a prominent Belleville resident, wealthy landowner, Tory politician and lawyer. The Murney house, 'Adjidaumo,' on the brow of Murney's hill, was not far from the Moodies' stone cottage, but the keen political polarization of the town dictated that the two women had to maintain a cool distance.

According to Audrey Morris, the Moodies came to Belleville as Reformers. They came armed with their English ideas of independence and an unwavering commitment to the ideal of integrity in personal and public life. They came eager for a richer social experience than the backwoods had allowed them. And they came with their loyalty to Britain and the Queen, a loyalty which had made Dunbar the eager servant of English interests during the Rebellion and had inspired Susanna's anti-Rebellion poems. It was only after the events of 1837 that, with a larger perspective than they had in Douro, they learned more about what Susanna, in *Roughing It in the Bush*, described as 'the abuses that had led to the present position of things.'[12] After 1837 they began to divest themselves of their naive conservatism and came to share increasingly with Robert Baldwin the view that responsible government as it was practised in England was consistent with loyalty to England, the maintenance of traditional values, and improved government in Canada.

In Belleville their social connections were determined by politics. Among their acquaintances were William Ponton, later Belleville's registrar and mayor; Dr William Hope; Dr James Lister; and John Ross (1818–71), a young lawyer recently arrived from Toronto. Ross, who would later distinguish himself as president of the Grand Trunk Railway, receiver-general in the government of Sir John A. Macdonald, and member of the Canadian Senate, persuaded Baldwin to seek election in the contentious

The Moodie cottage on Sinclair at Bridge Street in Belleville

Hastings County in the early 1840s and acted as his adviser for the area. Thus, he brought the Reform leader into friendly contact with the Moodies. Dunbar's letters to Baldwin give evidence of a warm and enduring relationship. Baldwin was just the sort of man the Moodies would admire: a man of integrity who acted from principle rather than for personal gain, a conservative in his personal tastes, a moderate in his reformist goals, and a man of distinguished family connections. That he continued to mourn his wife long after her death (in 1836) and treated the raising of his children as 'not only a family but a religious obligation' but added to his stature in their eyes.[13]

Though the time Baldwin spent in Belleville was limited, a mutual affection sprang up between the politician and the sheriff and their families. Dunbar did not hesitate to offer partisan reports from Hastings and to petition Baldwin with requests and advice. In return, Baldwin offered the sheriff a new post which Moodie rejected after carefully weighing the loss of income involved.[14] At the same time touches of affection and humour sprinkle these letters. In one postscript Dunbar writes, 'Mrs. Moodie is glad your children are pleased with her books and she will be delighted to hear from your dear Maria [Baldwin's eldest daughter]. So she must write without taking courage at all for Mrs. M. as you know is not so formidable a blue as many I have seen.'[15] On 15 February 1845, Dunbar wrote Baldwin, two years after the fact, that they had named a son after him, noting 'I would not tell you while you were in office.' To this he added an amusing family story that says much about the intense political feelings of the day: 'My poor Johnny, whose melancholy fate even our enemies felt, when the Chief Justice called upon us during the Assizes here, overhearing some remarks we were making to the effect *that dreaded name* might produce on his *conservative nerves*, on being asked the name of the baby shyly replied, "We sometimes call him Robert."'

'I am aware of the objection to strangers in this country,' wrote Dunbar Moodie to Baldwin in 1843, three years as sheriff of Hasting County having made that lesson very clear. His position was not easy. No sooner had he arrived to set up office than he was met by a determined campaign to make his life and work miserable. Realizing he was not a man of independent means, the Tories attempted, with much success, to embarrass him financially. Lawyer Benjamin Dougall, who was both district court judge and chairman of commission, set the tone by doing all in his power to delay official recognition of the bond of security the new sheriff was required to post as a condition of office; it took nearly three years for Dunbar to have his securities accepted.[16]

Further problems resulted from the fact that the office of the sheriff carried no yearly salary. Its income was to be earned from fees received for serving writs and subpoenas, for administering sheriff's sales of im-pounded property, and for making court appearances. While this was, in principle, an effective means of reducing government spending, in practice it left the sheriff vulnerable on a number of fronts even as it placed little priority on the maintenance of public order. Lawyers could withhold or delay payments to the sheriff often on contrived or flimsy grounds. Nuisance suits could be launched forcing the sheriff to risk his own money in court costs if the plaintiff turned out to be bankrupt or had cleverly divested himself of his capital before the trial. Tory lawyers and public officials, notably Thomas Parker, who had been the leading Belleville candidate for the sheriff's position, did their utmost to thwart Moodie's efforts; as a result Dunbar constantly recommended to Baldwin and others that the sheriff's office be made a salaried position. The only effective way of coping under the existing circumstances was to employ a Tory and Reform baillif who could serve writs as the occasion required. Whatever his personal politics, the sheriff was vulnerable: indeed, as the 1840s unfolded, Moodie increasingly felt himself as much victimized by the self-interest of Reformers

John Wedderburn Dunbar Moodie, photograph by William Notman

as by Tory hostility. On 6 February 1845, he ruefully reported to Baldwin: 'While I still feel as strongly as I always did towards the great principle of Responsible Government and to those who have so nobly sacrificed office in defense of it: – still I cannot, after the selfish indifference I have experienced on the part of some of the leading Reformers here, and the base treachery of others of them who have been eagerly watching an opportunity to supplant me and step into my office – feel myself called on to ruin myself to please them.'

This sense of betrayal resulted from Moodie's experience as a returning officer, one of his duties as sheriff. In the spring of 1841, Baldwin, running in Hastings as well as the fourth riding of York, was declared to be the winner by a narrow margin over Tory incumbent Edmund Murney. The Tories were quick to accuse Moodie of political favouritism, but the charge was dismissed as 'frivolous and vexatious.'[17] A year and a half later matters heated up again when, under the new administration of Sir Charles Bagot, Baldwin was required to seek re-election. Since he had made his York seat available to Louis LaFontaine, he had to face again the strong challenge of Murney and the Tories in Hastings. From the start Baldwin seems to have realized that a defeat was almost certain. The Tories were eager and well prepared, abetted by an aroused local Orange Order which chose to view the moderate Baldwin not only as a rebel but as a secretive Catholic. Thus while papers like the *Intelligencer* incited Tory and Orange feelings and while Baldwin astutely made alternative plans for election, Moodie, again the returning officer, prepared for the six days of voting well aware that violence, rioting, and bloodshed were likely once the Tory and Reform voters appeared in armed groups at the poll.

So great was the intimidation of voters that Moodie was forced to call in the local militia as well as two companies of government troops. Obstructionist techniques practised for the most part by Murney's men resulted in the casting of less than half the eligible votes for the District. Moodie's request for additional time was turned down. Hence, as required, he closed the poll with Murney ahead by forty-nine votes. On the basis of Moodie's report, however, Murney was not allowed to take his seat and a new election was called. The blame for the débâcle fell on the returning officer, a convenient scapegoat to all parties. In the re-election William Hutton replaced Moodie as returning officer. Murney's victory was readily confirmed because in the meantime Baldwin directed his energies to securing a safe seat – in Rimouski.

The strain of these experiences must have been considerable. Moodie came slowly to realize the danger of expressing political feelings outwardly while seeking to hold an office demanding impartiality. Yet even with the abuses and vexations he had to endure, his position as sheriff was too valuable to his family's security for him to let go, for it earned him about £250 a year – despite the nuisance suits and manœuvres used to deprive him of income he felt was legitimately his. It was a chastened Dunbar Moodie who wrote to Baldwin on 6 February 1845: 'For some time back I have carefully abstained from taking any part whatever in politics and did not even vote in the last election ... I have no doubt my conduct will be misrepresented to you on this head, but at the age of nearly 50 with a large family entirely dependent on this paltry office I hold for bread, and unable to clothe them as well as respectable mechanics can do – I think you can hardly blame me if I endeavour at last to take some care of myself.'

By contrast, Susanna's anger at the treatment received by her husband in their early Belleville years was not so easily placated. In the wake of the infamous Hastings elections she sent John Lovell a four-part story entitled 'Richard Redpath. A Tale'; it appeared in the *Literary Garland* from September through December 1843, was reprinted in the Toronto *Star* the same year, and was later published by Richard Bentley as part of *Matrimonial Speculations* (London 1854).

On the surface, 'Richard Redpath' is a romance set in Kingston, Jamaica, where three young shipwrecked Englishmen find appropriate marital partners. Its serious subject is slavery. What makes the story interesting with regard to Belleville is its elaborate portrait of one Benjamin Levi, the villainous editor of the *Jamaica Observer*, 'a violent party paper, which most strenuously opposed the abolition of the slave trade, and denounced the few benevolent men who set their faces against the abhorred trade ... as traitors to Great Britain and enemies of their country.' Levi is merely a catalyst to various parts of the plot, but his behaviour is made so much the focus of the story that Susanna's intentions are clear beyond doubt. Substituting the slave trade for the issue of reform in Canada, she mercilessly caricatures the editor of the Belleville *Intelligencer* in the spirit of 'our immortal Cruickshanks'; he is described as a bull-like, bespectacled man, 'a living, laughing, impersonation of gratuitous mischief,' 'a sort of moral hyaena.' Like George Benjamin, Levi, who came to his city as a printer's devil, worked himself into a position of ownership and editorial control. His salient characteristics are all negative. He disguises his Jewishness by passing as a Christian. He delights in printing 'spiteful' slanders and crude sketches of 'the best and most respectable of our citizens' and in working up political hostilities by deliberate falsehood and insinuation. All this he does for love of notoriety and from personal arrogance.

Because so little of the *Intelligencer* for the 1840s is extant, it is impossible to know if Susanna's outrage was merited and her charges fully justified. Certainly partisanship in the press was rampant at this time, but in the colonies it was a particular vexation. As one character remarks when asked why no one prosecutes such an editor for libel, ' "That's all very well in the old country, sir, where if a man is ever such a bully, he must behave himself, or be kicked out of society ... Here, men may call one another liars, and thieves, and traitors in print, without the least fear of punishment." '

George Benjamin's reaction to his caricature as devil figure is not known (though Letter 54 reveals that Susanna still felt strongly about the subject and some pride in the accuracy of her 'picture' in 1854). It is worth noting, however, that in the *Intelligencer* of 26 December 1862, Benjamin's successor, Mackenzie Bowell, upon the newspaper's change of location, noted that 'the old office which was immortalized by the novelist in her *Richard Redpath*, will no longer furnish a theme for the somewhat erratic, though fruitful imagination of her whose forte is fiction.' 'A truce to this.' Bowell added. At least in fiction, Susanna could deliver Benjamin of his comeuppance, but she was too much the writer of fiction not to observe at the same time a kind of delight in his mischievousness. As one of the story's female characters, herself a victim of Levi's insinuations, remarks: 'I don't know what we should do without Benjamin Levi – he keeps us all alive.'

If, as the decade of the 1840s drew to a close, the Moodies had chosen to run a safer course and were at last able to settle into a less contentious existence, the transposition from backwoods struggle to political bearpit had not been an easy one for either of them. It ought not to be surprising that a sense of bitterness lingered on in Susanna's writing about her town, for she and her husband shared their trials together with an affection and trust of which her letters as a whole give ample evidence. They had survived together, and the mutual respect that characterized their relationship had much to do with that ability to endure.

1 Dunbar sold his half-pay commission, fearing that he might be recalled to active duty, and invested the capital in the stock of a steamboat company being organized in Cobourg. See *Roughing It in the Bush.*
2 *The Arthur Papers*, ed. Charles A. Sanderson (Toronto 1957), II, 437
3 Jane Fairfield, *The Life of Sumner Lincoln Fairfield* (New York 1847) and *The Autobiography of Jane Fairfield* (Boston 1860)
4 Ken Dewar, 'Charles Fothergill,' *Kawartha Heritage*, ed. A.O.C. Cole and Jean Murray Cole (Peterborough 1981), 73–80
5 Mary Markham Brown, *An Index to the Literary Garland* (Toronto 1962)
6 A further indication of that friendship is a flower painting by Susanna Moodie, now in the possession of Kathleen McMurrich, which is affectionately dedicated to Sara Lovell.
7 'Canadian Sketches,' *Roughing It in the Bush* (London 1852), II, 323
8 Mary Markham Brown, 'The Literary Garland and a case of Literary Larceny,' *Journal of Canadian Fiction* (Summer 1973), 65–8
9 In 1851 nine poems by Ryan appeared in the *Literary Garland*. Mary Lu MacDonald, in a note for *Canadian Notes and Queries* (spring 1983), reports that Ryan, who also wrote under the pseudonym Charley Corncob, was a strong sympathizer with the Reform movement.
10 Audrey Y. Morris, *Gentle Pioneers* (Toronto 1966), 169
11 *Life in the Clearings* (Toronto 1959), 35
12 Coles facsimile edition of the 1913 Bell and Cockburn edition of *Roughing It in the Bush* (Toronto 1980), 472
13 George E. Wilson, *The Life of Robert Baldwin* (Toronto 1933), 28
14 Moodie to Baldwin, 8 October 1848, Baldwin Papers, Toronto Public Library. Dunbar turned down the position, choosing to wait in hopes that 'something better may turn up.'

15 Moodie to Baldwin, 3 February 1842
16 Morris, *Gentle Pioneers*, chapters 9 and 10
17 Wilson, *Life of Robert Baldwin*, 131

---

35 To the editor of the *Albion*, New York

Hamilton,
Upper Canada
February 14th, 1833 –

Sir,

The pleasure I derived from the perusal of several of the last numbers of your clever and interesting paper, has made me ambitious of the honour of contributing to its pages; and if the assistance of a pen, deemed not unworthy of public notice in my native land, when held by Susanna Strickland, can in any way be acceptable to you, and your readers, it will afford me much pleasure to transmit to you, from time to time, a few small original poems.

I now enclose the first flight of my muse on Canadian shores. But this chilly atmosphere, at present, is little favourable to the spirit of Poesy. The minds of the inhabitants being too much engrossed, in providing for their families the necessaries of life, to pay much attention to the cultivation of literature. However mortifying to the vanity of an Author, this indifference may be, it would be unjust to censure my fellow settlers for suffering more urgent and important duties to render them deaf to the voice of the syren, whose wild flights and vagaries have charmed me from my youth upwards. The close confinement of a log cabin, and the cares of a family, though they engross much of my time, have not been able to chill those inspirations, which in my own beautiful and beloved land were a never failing source of amusement and delight. The little sympathy which such feelings can meet with, in a new colony, where every energy of the mind is employed to accumulate wealth, has made me anxious to seek a more liberal channel of communication with the public, and I know no one to whom I can better apply than to the Editor of a Journal, which finds its way into the study of every respectable family on this side the Atlantic, and is not inferior in literary merit, to any publication of the same class in Great Britain.

Should the trifling specimens enclosed meet with your approbation, and be deemed worthy of insertion in the *Albion*, they are at your service.

I remain, Sir, Yours respectfully,
Susanna Moodie

SONG: THE STRAINS WE HEAR IN FOREIGN LANDS

The strains we hear in foreign lands,
No echo from the heart can claim, –
The chords are swept by strangers' hands,
And kindle in the breast no flame,
Sweet though they be –
No fond remembrance wakes to fling
Its hallowed influence o'er the chords, –
As if a spirit touch'd the string,
Breathing in soft harmonious words,
Deep melody.

The music of our native shore,
A thousand lovely scenes endears;
In magic tones it murmurs o'er,
The visions of our early years –
The hopes of youth, –
It wreathes again the flowers we wreathed,
In childhood's bright unclouded day;
It breathes again the vows we breathed,
At Fancy's shrine, when Hope were gay,
And whisper'd truth, –

It calls before our mental sight,
Dear forms, whose tuneful lips are mute;
Sweet sunny eyes, long closed in night,
Warm hearts, now silent as the lute,
That charmed our ears –
It thrills the breast with feelings deep,
Too deep for language to impart, –
And bids the spirit, joy or weep,
In tones which sink into the heart,
And melt in tears.

THE SLEIGH-BELLS.
A Canadian Song.

'Tis merry to hear at evening time,
By the blazing hearth the sleigh-bells chime;
To know each bound of the steed brings near,

The form of him to our bosoms dear;
Lightly we spring the fire to raise,
Till the rafters glow with the ruddy blaze.

'Tis he! and blithely the gay bells sound,
As his steeds skim over the frozen ground:
Hark! he has pass'd the gloomy wood,
He crosses now the icy flood;
And sees the light from the open door,
To hail his toilsome journey o'er.

Our hut is small, and rude our cheer,
But love has spread the banquet here, –
And childhood springs to be caress'd,
By our beloved and welcome guest –
With a smiling brow his tale he tells;
They laughing ring the merry bells.

From the cedar swamp the wolf may howl,
From the blasted oak the felon owl, –
The sudden crash of the falling tree,
Are sounds of terror no more to me.
No longer I list with boding fear,
The sleigh-bells merry peal to hear.

---

36 To Sumner Lincoln Fairfield

Douro
Near Peterboro
Newcastle District U.C.
Jan. 23, 1835

Sir

It is with pleasure, I embrace the opportunity of a friend going to the United States, to transmit to you a copy of the small volume of poems you have noticed in such flattering terms, in the *North American Magazine*.

Though residing in a small log hut, in the backwoods of Upper Canada, and constantly engaged in the everyday cares of domestic life, I am not so wholly indifferent to praise, as not to feel highly gratified, when the spontaneous outpourings of a mind, vividly alive to the beauties of Nature, meets with the approbation of men, of superior worth and genius.

Mr. Moodie, and myself, were much interested in the three numbers of the Magazine, forwarded to Douro, by yourself, or by some unknown friend. Many, of the prose contributions, are excellent, and the poems from your own pen, original and beautiful. Among these, 'Let the Storm Come,' 'To my son in Heaven,' 'The dream of the Sepulchre,' and the 'Reign of Genius,' pleased me most.[1]

There is only one portion of your excellent periodical which offended my taste. The invectives hurled against a host of contemptible adversaries.[2] This is beneath a man of your genius, and superior attainments. They triumph, in the indignation, their malice calls forth. Silent indifference to their calumnies, would place you beyond the reach of them. Forgive my candour. I too am an author, and I deeply feel for you, and had not your works awakened in my bosom a lively interest, I should not have ventured thus far, to offer my advice to a stranger.

Were we residing in the same country, I should feel much pleasure in contributing to the pages of your Magazine, but the expense of transmitting articles to such a great distance is beyond my means, and my time is too valuable to waste in the pursuit of fame, when I have three sweet children demanding all my care,[3] and a Bush Settler has no 'hours of idleness.'

I take this opportunity of enclosing a few original poems,[4] which I hope may prove serviceable to your work, and you have my hearty good wishes for its success, and a complete triumph over all the petty assaults of your enemies.

Mr. Moodie, unites with me, in compliments, and with feelings of respect,

> I remain, Sir,
> Yours sincerely
> Susanna Moodie.

1 'The Reign of Genius' and 'To My Son in Heaven,' *North American Magazine* (October 1834), 375–6 and 367–8 respectively; 'The Dream of the Sepulchre' (November), 9–17; 'Let the Storm Come' (December), 105–6
2 Fairfield's editorial in October 1834 (416–27) commemorates the second anniversary of the magazine by attacking his critics.
3 Catherine Mary (Katie), born 1832; Agnes Dunbar (Addy), 1833; and John Alexander Dunbar (Dunbar), 1834
4 'Oh Canada Thy Gloomy Woods' by Mrs Moodie and 'Oh Let Me Sleep Nor Wake To Sadness' by J.W.D. Moodie, Esqr., appeared in the July 1836 issue (197–8); in all, Fairfield printed eleven of her poems, from December 1834 to November 1836.

37 To Sumner Lincoln Fairfield

Douro
1836

... You have doubtless heard of Thomas Pringle, late editor of 'Friendship's Offering,' and secretary of the Anti-Slavery Society, a man much loved and respected by all who enjoyed the privilege of his friendship.

A most dear friend he was to me, and deeply have I lamented his untimely death. His widow, a very excellent woman, is now in this country to which her family immigrated some years ago. The poor thing is in ill health and struggling to live respectably on a very limited income.[1] She has a very valuable collection of autographs to dispose of, consisting of most celebrated English authors of the last century.

Should you know any person curious in those matters who would wish to become a purchaser, information on the subject would be thankfully transmitted to you by Mrs. Pringle of her friends ...

Mr Moodie unites with me in kind regard to yourself and family, and with best wishes that the magazine may increase your worldly prosperity and literary fame,

> I remain, Dear Sir,
> Yours most truly
> Susanna Moodie

1 Margaret Pringle apparently joined her relatives, the Browns, who had settled in the Gore's Landing area, after her husband's death in 1834, and seems to have remained in Canada until the late 1840s.

38 To the editor of the Toronto *Palladium*

Melsetter,
Douro,
U.C.

Sir –

October 11, 1838[1]

The enclosed poem was partly written at the period when the important event it celebrates occurred. The absence of my dear husband on the frontier, sickness, the management of our bush farm, and many domestic cares, hindered me from preparing it for publication at the time. With-

out wishing to keep alive the public excitement, so widely displayed on the
perpetration of that gallant action, by Captain Drew, and his brave and
loyal band,[2] – with the vanity natural to my sex and profession, I should
like to see my honest feelings on the subject transferred to the pages of
your valuable paper, and I remain, Sir,

Yours with respect,
Susanna Moodie

1 The letter and poem, 'The Burning of the Caroline,' were reprinted in the Montreal *Transcript* on this date; the original date of publication in the *Palladium* is not known. For
the text of the poem see the *Literary Garland* (February 1841), 176.
2 In early 1838 Commander Andrew Drew, RN, led an attack upon the American-owned
steamer the *Caroline*. The destruction of the *Caroline* strained Anglo-American relations
for several years.

---

39 To the editor of the *Literary Garland*, Montreal

Belleville
March 8, 1842

Dear Sir,[1]

You will be surprised at receiving the commencing sheets of a tale,[2] the
title of which so closely resembles that just published by your esteemed
and talented contributor, E.L.C.[3] For some time past I had been preparing this story for your Magazine, and I thought it better, under the
existing circumstances, to send it to you at once, than to delay it until after
the entire publication of that lady's story, which would make me appear in the odious light of a plagiarist. I do this the more readily, as, at
present, there appears little similarity in the communications, beyond
the titles, and so much of the character of my tale depends upon the title,
that I cannot well rebaptize it. An abridgement of this story, bearing
the same title, was published in the *Lady's Magazine*, in the November
number, for 1833 [247–57]. I should not attempt to send you a story
which had been published before, were it not for the following circumstances: My eldest sister was one of the prinicipal conductors of that
Magazine, and under her auspices it grew into much celebrity, for a periodical of that cast.[4] I left with her many of my papers, and by accident,
an imperfect sketch of this story, which I intended filling up at my leisure,
and offering for publication. This I had nearly accomplished, when, to

my great mortification, my sister sent me a copy of the Magazine, with the rough draft of the story, forming one of the contributions; and, to console me, she likewise sent me the copies of many reviews, speaking highly in its praise. A few mornings ago, I read over the large MS. and thought that it might suit your Magazine, and be favourably received by those who had been pleased with 'Geoffrey Moncton.'[5] I had not proceeded far in my task when I received your last number of the *Garland*. The title of your correspondent's very interesting tale, suggested to me the propriety of sending you the sheets already prepared for the press, and making this rather *egotistical* statement of the facts.

I trust E.L.C. will not imagine that I am vain enough to attempt to rival her in the estimation of the public, as I consider that much of the success of the *Garland* may be attributed to her beautiful tales and poems. As fellow-labourers in the same flower-garden, it has ever given me the greatest pleasure to bestow upon this lady the wreath of praise, which her fine taste and talents so richly have won. My sole object is to escape the title of a plagiarist. –

I remain, dear Sir, yours truly,
S. Moodie

1 John Gibson
2 'The Miser and His Son. A Tale'
3 Elizabeth L. Cushing, 'The Miser's Stepdaughter,' *Literary Garland* (March 1842), 145–56, (April), 224–33, (May), 251–64
4 There is a good deal of internal evidence of Strickland involvement in the *Lady's Magazine*; Eliza contributed a series of 'Biographies of Flowers' and sketches on the months of the year; Agnes wrote many historical tales, rural sketches, and poems; and there were more than a dozen items by Susanna. In these pages, too, were early, short biographies of queens and princesses by the Strickland sisters; the writing of these pieces undoubtedly sparked the writing of their *Lives of the Queens of England* (1840–8) and subsequent series.
5 Serialized in the *Literary Garland* from December 1839 to August 1840.

40 To John Lovell

Belleville
Nov. 26th, 1842

My dear Sir,[1]

The piano arrived quite safe two days ago and sustained no injury from the stormy passage up. I am quite satisfied with it in every respect, and

feel extremely grateful to you for the care and trouble you have taken
about it. My girls will I hope profit by it. Poor things they have both
been seriously ill, and I much fear my beautiful Addy will go into a decline.
We have prized too highly the surpassingly fair face which few pictures
could rival, when the dear child was in health, and I have been too proud
of the universal praise bestowed upon her by all, and now I fear, my
Lily of the Lake, as an old friend used to call her, is doomed to an early
grave. She has excellent talents too, and promised so fair. Alas for
human Love – and human hopes. They end in dust. But we will still hope
for the best. I am so happy that Mr. Ross[2] holds out to us the prospect
of a visit from you. Most happy shall we be to see you an inmate beneath
our roof. We are not such rebels, that we cannot appreciate, aye, and
even love, the worth of those who differ from us in opinion, as I hope you
will find from experience.

   Now for pounds, shillings and pence – I find our account for the last
year, amounts to 6 4/2. sheets of prose, and 1 sheet of original poetry,
which at two dollars per page our original agreement, amounts to 8
pounds, the prose to £32.10 – being a total of forty pounds, ten
shillings.   8
                              40.10 –
This I hope you will put to your account against me for the piano, and the
expenses there unto belonging, and I should feel greatly obliged to you,
to send me in an account of the same, that I may have some idea of the
quantity of writing which it will require for me to pay off the old arrears.

   I am the more anxious on this account, as I am likely to have my arms
filled again, and as life on these occasions is very uncertain, especially
with me. I should like to provide material enough before that time arrives,
to ensure you from any loss in case my life should not be spared
through the trial, or sickness should prevent me from the free use of my
pen.

   I have been busy preparing my boys' winter clothing and have not
touched a pen since I last wrote. I think you will like the story now in
progress. I will try and send you a good portion of it during the next
month.[3]

   Now, is not the 'Miser' my best tale? I do not think 'Geoffrey' to compare with it. But authors are no judge of their own performances.

   Harper and Brothers were in treaty for the copy right of these stories.
But I have not heard from them since their great loss by fire. If I had
time, I would try Moodie's publisher, Bentley of London. My sister Agnes's name would be a great help to me now in selling a book of my

own. I am reading the *Queens*, and greatly delighted with the work.[4] Mr.
Moodie unites with me in best compliments, and hoping to welcome
you to Belleville soon.

> I remain
> My dear Sir,
> Yours very truly
> Susanna Moodie.

1 John Lovell
2 Likely John Ross, or his brother James
3 'Richard Redpath' appeared in the *Literary Garland* in four instalments, beginning September 1843.
4 On 1 June 1842, fire broke out in Harper and Brothers' bindery as a result of a burglary (see Eugene Exmun, *The Brothers Harper*, New York 1965). By the end of 1842, five volumes of Agnes's *Lives of the Queens of England* had been published by Blackwood's.

---

41 To the editor of   March, 1847
the *Literary Garland*,
Montreal

Dear Sir,[1]

Turning over the pages of one of our provincial papers, I was greatly
struck by the beauty of the poem which I offer to your notice. It is, in my
humble estimation, worthy of a wider circulation than it could possibly
obtain in a local journal. The author is a resident within the Canadas;
and the mind which could produce such a gem, should be explored for the
public benefit. Oblige me by giving this poem a place in the pages of
your excellent periodical, and I am certain that those of your readers who
have any taste for fine poetry, will feel grateful for having it presented
to their notice.

> Yours truly
> Susanna Moodie

1 This letter to John Gibson prefaces George William Lovell's 'The Close of the Year,' *Literary Garland* (March 1847), 146.

42 To Louisa May Murray   Belleville
Jan. 13, 1851

My dear Miss Murray[1]

Enclosed, you will find a note to me from Mrs. Cushing the present con-
ductress of the Montreal *Literary Garland* expressing a strong desire to
obtain for the pages of that Magazine, your beautiful story of, 'Fauna,'
which you transmitted to me two years ago for the *Victoria Magazine*.
Writing not long ago, to Mrs. Cushing, I mentioned this tale, to her, and
the high opinion I had formed from it, of the talents of the writer, and
this is her reply.

Sincerely do I hope that this trifling circumstance may be the means of
introducing 'Fauna,' to the Canadian public and prove a source of
emolument and fame to its author.

The low esteem in which all literary labor is held in this country renders
it every thing but a profitable employment but Mr Lovell's offer of
remuneration although small, is not to be rejected without due consideration – 'What is worth publishing,' my good friend Tom Roscoe[2] used
to say, 'is worth paying for' – and I have found the five pounds per sheet,
that I have received from Mr. Lovell for articles contributed to the
Garland for the last twelve years, no inconsiderable help in bringing up a
large family. To a young person, even small sums are always serviceable in procuring extra articles of dress etc.

If you can afford to write for him gratis, you are more fortunate than I
am; and I am sure, he would receive with delight such contributions as
the fine one in my possession. If remuneration is any object to you, I have
named the sum I receive, thinking it might afford you a clue to fix your
own terms with Mr. Lovell, whom I have ever found a most liberal and
kind friend.

In disposing of MS by the sheet, I always reserve the right of copy, as at
some future time I may wish to publish such articles in a collective
form.

My dear Miss Murray, this is a mere business letter, and you must
excuse the matter of fact manner in which it is written, but let me
assure you, that such is the interest that I feel in you from the very brief
correspondence that has passed between us, that it would afford me
great pleasure to be able to render you the least assistance in your literary
career. Pray do not fail to write to me on the receipt of this, and state

your wishes with regard to the MS., and to Mr. Lovell, what your expectations [are] respecting it. In the mean while I remain, my dear young lady, Your sincere friend,

                                    Susanna Moodie

        His direction is –
            J. Lovell Esqr.
            Literary Garland Office
            St. Nicholas' Street
            Montreal

1 In a column on Murray in *The Week* (19 April 1888), A.E. Weatherald quotes briefly from this letter.
2 Thomas Roscoe (1791–1871), a contributor to the annuals, particularly the *Juvenile Keepsake*; Susanna contributed to it in 1829 and 1830 and Roscoe was editor from 1828 to 1830.

---

43 To the editor of the *Albion*, New York

Belleville,
C.W.,
May 6, 1851

Sir, –

The following paragraph appeared in the *Toronto Patriot*, for Jan. 29 1851, relative to my sister, Miss Strickland, the well-known authoress of the 'Lives of the Queens of England.'

'This reminds us still more strongly of a correspondence published very recently in the American papers, by Miss Strickland's authority, purporting to be a series of letters which had passed between Miss Strickland and Mrs. Southey, with reports of conversations between the two ladies; in all which Miss Strickland is represented to have been a very dear and intimate friend of the Southey family; but the whole unfortunately for Miss Strickland's character for veracity – about her good taste there was no question – was denied by Mrs. Southey, who showed that Miss Strickland had intruded herself at a moment of great distress for the purpose of manufacturing literary capital, and that she had given a colouring, unjustifiable by the facts, to suit her own purpose.'

Convinced of the utter falseness of this statement made by the *Toronto Patriot*, against the fair fame of my sister, I had taken up my pen to contradict it: when, it appeared to me, that in order to put a stop to such injurious reports for the future, it would be better to send the offensive paragraph to my sister, and let her contradict it herself. This morning I received her reply, together with a letter from Mrs. Southey to Miss Strickland, which must strike everyone as a complete refutation of the slander set forth by the *Toronto Patriot*. You will confer upon Miss Strickland and myself a great favour, by giving insertion to these letters in your admirable journal.[1] I think it necessary to disabuse the public mind of any belief in so cruel a calumny against the honour of a lady, who has ever borne a reputation of unsullied integrity; and who is more highly prized by her family and those to whom she is intimately known, for her high moral qualities, her truth and faithfulness, than even for those great mental attainments, that have made her one of the most remarkable women of her age and country.

> I remain, Sir,
> Yours with great respect,
> Susanna Moodie

1 Following Susanna's letter, the *Albion* published a brief letter from Agnes saying she had written to Caroline Southey and sent a copy of the *Patriot*'s charges, Southey's reply stating she had never met Agnes but was an admirer of her works, and a long excerpt of another letter from Agnes to Susanna. The latter includes reminiscences of the Stricklands' early admiration of Caroline Bowles' writing for *Blackwood's Magazine*, together with a résumé of Agnes's current literary activities and her ideas on her functions as an historical biographer, particularly with reference to the treatment of religious issues. This letter confirms that the Stricklands helped form the Sunday school in Reydon in 1828.

1852~1862

'My pen as
a resource'

I N LITERARY TERMS the early 1850s were the apex of Susanna Moodie's life, for, with the publication of *Roughing It in the Bush* in 1852 and her subsequent books, she achieved widespread national and international acclaim. During the years of her prolific contribution to the *Literary Garland*, from 1839 to 1851, she seems slowly to have settled upon the idea of writing a book on her experiences of emigration and settlement. The intentions are apparent in the series of 'Canadian Sketches' in the *Garland* in 1847 that would ultimately be the nucleus of the book. But, in fact, the plan began to take shape as far back as 1835. At that time Dunbar Moodie, whose *Ten Years in South Africa* had just been published in London by Richard Bentley, proposed a book on Canada; but Bentley, in a letter dated 21 April 1835, discouraged him on the grounds that 'so much has lately been written on that country, as to make it doubtful how far such a book would succeed here.'[1] The plan was temporarily set aside, but the intention persisted, and both Moodies wrote material suitable for such a volume during the 1840s, publishing it in the *Literary Garland* and in their own *Victoria Magazine*. As internal evidence indicates, as early as 1848 and 1849 Susanna was revising her material to create her famous book.

To bring the book into being, the Moodies sought out an old London friend, the Scot John Bruce (1802–69). How they knew him is uncertain. He was an antiquarian scholar, a man skilled in the collection and appraisal of historical documents, which task he performed as an official in the Public Records Office in London; as an organizer and literary editor of the Camden Society, which was devoted to the study of historical documents; and as an executive of the Society of Antiquaries. Bruce apparently approached Richard Bentley, possibly at the request of the Moodies, and negotiated terms for the publication of Susanna's 'Canadian Life.' Bentley first offered fifty pounds for the copyright to the work, but on 27 December 1851 Bruce countered with a request that the author also receive a share of the profits and that on the day of publication she would be advanced twenty pounds 'on account of half profits.'[2] Bentley agreed to these terms and *Roughing It in the Bush* was published on 9 January 1852. It proved so successful that Susanna was sent another fifty pounds the following September, presumably as a further share of profits. However, negotiation was not the only facet of John Bruce's involvement: he also saw the work through the press, reading the proofs and making alterations and corrections.

When Susanna wrote her first letter to Richard Bentley on 16 April 1852, because of Bruce's illness, she set out to advance her own literary career and so began a warm and productive relationship with one of the foremost

British publishers of the day. Bentley (1794–1871) was well-known for his Standard Novels series; for *Bentley's Miscellany*, which was first edited by Charles Dickens and then by Harrison Ainsworth; and for the publication of works of many of the popular novelists of the time including Charles Reade, Mrs Henry Wood, James Fenimore Cooper, and Herman Melville. The history and character of Bentley's publishing house has been well documented by Royal Gettman in his book, *A Victorian Publisher: A Study of the Bentley Papers* (Cambridge and Chicago 1960), although Susanna Moodie's relations with the firm are not mentioned.

The relationship with Bentley quickly developed into a satisfying and important one for Susanna financially and in terms of friendship with someone at the heart of the British literary scene to whom she might express her views on a wider range of topics than she normally did, at least in the extant letters. That Bentley considered her a friend is apparent from the continuing openness of her letters, the references to personal life, and the visit of Horace Bentley, Richard's second son, to the Moodies in 1858, which itself suggests that the friendship was warmly reciprocated.

Nevertheless, the basis of the friendship was literary business. When Susanna first wrote in April 1852 she was well prepared to seize her opportunity and seek further publication. She already knew of the favourable reception in England of *Roughing It in the Bush*. *Blackwood's Magazine* especially gave it prominent treatment in its March issue, which was available in Canada within the month. *Blackwood's* quoted liberally from the text, so much so, in fact, that at least one reviewer, the editor of the *United Empire* in Toronto, used the article as the basis for his own review. The *Blackwood's* piece stressed Susanna's role as heroine and cited her as an example of noble womanhood to her countrywomen:

deftly embroidering in carpeted saloon, gracefully bending over easel or harp, pressing with nimble finger, your piano's ivory, or joyously tripping in Cellarian circles, suspend for a moment, your silken pursuits, and look forth into the desert at a sister's sufferings! May you never, from stern experience, learn fully to appreciate them. But, should fate have decreed otherwise, may you equal her in fortitude and courage. Meanwhile, transport yourselves, in imagination's car, to Canada's backwoods, and behold one, gently nurtured as yourselves, cheerfully condescending to rudest toils, unrepiningly enduring hardships you never dreamed of. Not to such hardships was she born, nor educated for them. The comforts of an English home, the endearments of sisterly affection, the refinement of literary tastes, but ill prepared the emigrant's wife to work, in the rugged and inclement wilderness,

Richard Bentley, publisher of *Roughing It in the Bush*

harder than the meanest of the domestics, whom, in her own country, she was used to command.[3]

Reviews in the *Literary Gazette* (21 February 1852), the *Spectator* (7 February), and the *Athenaeum* (28 February) were also favourable, especially the latter journal, which observed Susanna's abilities to reflect the picturesque in nature and the entertaining in human behaviour, emphasizing that, because she was a writer, 'her gifts brightened the pleasure enjoyed if they sharpened the pains suffered during a long term of harsh and heavy years, – and prevented her from sinking into that sluggish acquiescence in the drudgery of her lot ...'

With such favourable responses behind her Susanna could, perhaps, expect a second edition of the work and so she forwarded additional delayed chapters for inclusion. Bruce had, in any case, requested something on Canada of the present day and, therefore, Dunbar had written 'Canadian Sketches' to be included in the second edition, published on 9 November 1852. The other forwarded pieces, 'Jeanie Burns,' 'Lost Children,' and 'Michael Macbride' (sent earlier but suppressed by Susanna), were held by Bentley and eventually included in *Life in the Clearings*; 'Jeanie Burns' was also published in *Bentley's Miscellany* in October 1852.

The success of *Roughing It in the Bush* was attested to not only by the demand for a second English edition within a matter of months but also by the appearance of a pirated edition in the United States. G.P. Putnam brought the book out in his 'Library for Travellers and the Fireside,' in two parts, 1 and 15 July 1852. It was edited for American readers by C.F.B. (Charles Frederick Briggs), a New York writer and journalist who was closely associated with the Putnam organization and became the first editor of *Putnam's Magazine* in January 1853. Briggs excised poems and some sections of prose from the work, confidently arguing that 'the accomplished and heroic author will not, therefore, be disposed to complain that her work should have undergone a careful excision of certain passages of a purely personal or political character, which could have possessed no interest for the American reader, and the loss of which will be compensated by the gain of a larger audience than she could have otherwise hoped for.' Though his action may have been presumptuous, Briggs' editorial judgment was perspicacious. The American editions (there were at least five by Putnam and two more by De Witt and Davenport in a period of four years) made Susanna Moodie's name well known in the United States and Canada, and thus helped to create a market for her subsequent books. It is an interesting reflection of the cultural currents of the time that it was not until its American appearance that her book received much notice in the Canadian press. It was notice of which Susanna was often wont to complain.

Her discontent does not seem to be entirely warranted. Reviews in the *Globe* (7 August 1852), the *British Colonist* (9 July), and the *Anglo-American Magazine* in August, all of Toronto, commended the writing skills evident in the book as well as the character of the author, although the *Colonist* observed that she conveyed an unfavourable impression of Canada which was 'to be much regretted.' The reviewer for the *Commercial Advertiser* of Montreal showed no such reservations, but saw in her one who wrote truthfully and skilfully about her experiences in Canada:

She possesses the three great qualifications necessary to a successful novelist – the power to analize [*sic*] character, a lively descriptive style, and the faculty of constructing a plot.

Mrs. Moodie is a sincere writer, and never attempts to impose upon her readers by any of the tricks of authorship by which a fictitious interest may be excited. You feel that she is a good woman and resign yourself at once to the charms and witcheries of her narrative, feeling sure that she will amuse you to the end, and compensate you abundantly for the time you bestow upon her. Her comic powers are very remarkable for a woman, and her humorous characters are delightfully drawn.

It is probable that Susanna did not see this very positive response, for she makes no mention of it; but there were other, less kind reviews, focusing on her class-consciousness and attitudes towards Irish emigrants, that she saw and did not like.

Ironically, it was another British review, from the London *Observer*, reprinted in the Montreal *Pilot* of 27 March 1852, that began this line of attack and helped to form Susanna's impression that her book had not been well-received in Canada. The reviewer castigated her for her unjust and contradictory treatment of Irish character, charging her with describing Irish emigrants 'in terms which a reflective writer would scarcely apply to a pack of hounds,' and pointing out that such description was totally at odds with the fact 'that it was to the kindness, the charity, and the disinterested services of poor Irish emigrants and settlers that she and her family were indebted for, perhaps the only real benevolence she had encountered in Canada.' The only explanation the reviewer could find for such an anomaly was that Susanna had published in haste and had 'not had the opportunity of supervision as it [the book] went through the press ...' Susanna responded to this review in her conclusion to *Life in the Clearings*, making it plain there, as well as in her letters, that it was the Irish-Canadian reaction to *Roughing It in the Bush* that disturbed her most. It was probably an earlier review of her sketch of 'Michael Macbride' (*Literary Garland*, February 1851) in the Montreal *True Witness and Catholic Chronicle* on 21 February 1851 that led her to suppress the piece before it could be included as a chapter in the book, for the review sharply rebuked her for a Protestant bias against Catholicism and for a lack of knowledge of both Irish and Catholic character:

The lady is evidently ignorant of all the genuine characteristics of that fine people – their depth of feeling, their eccentric modes of thought, their shrewd and ready wit, their gratitude, their faithfulness: she draws them, it is plain, from the exaggerated accounts of those who love them not, and the consequence is, that they come from her hands distorted and unnatural ... No doubt Mrs. Moodie is a good Bible Christian, and may probably find consolation herself in reading the sacred volume; but we tell her that if it were read over from end to end to a dying Catholic – one trained in the Church of Christ – it would afford him small comfort, unless he could at the same time confess his sins to Christ's minister, who has received the power of loosening and binding here on earth ... For shame! Bible-reading authoress! – how could you get an unfortunate scape-grace who had been a Catholic, to believe that your reading of some select chapters could supply to his soul these tremendous wants?

Such commentary must have had a long-lasting effect on Susanna Moodie, and, when combined with harsh accusations of aristocratic condescension by Charles Lindsey of the Toronto *Examiner* (see Letter 50) and by the editor of the *United Empire*, brought about her conviction that most Canadians did not accept her views of colonial life.

Certainly she had no cause for complaint about the reception of *Roughing It in the Bush* in the United States, where it was universally acclaimed in leading magazines and provincial newspapers. An extensive review in the New York *Albion* of 10 July 1852 praised the book's 'obvious stamp of truth' and its usefulness and decorum in handling fictional elements often employed by lesser writers to arouse a merely 'piquant' charm. 'Ay, thanks,' added the reviewer, 'O honest and whole-souled woman, for showing that there may be a chivalry of feeling and there may be a tone of high-mindedness, even amidst the most depressing and demoralizing influences.' Other American reviews stressed the character of the book as a work of frontier literature, depicting life in 'the far west' or the 'wilds of Canada,' often observing its similarity to Caroline Kirkland's treatment of life in the backwoods of Michigan in *A New Home – Who'll Follow?* (1839). All gave favourable notice of the quality of the writing, the varied subject matter, the skill of character portrayal, and the strength and attainments of the author herself. In addition, some of the reviews, such as that in the *New York Weekly Tribune* (25 September 1852), noted Susanna's long experience as a writer and her relation to Agnes Strickland.

With the popular success of *Roughing It in the Bush* Susanna Moodie entered a period of intensive literary activity, during which she drew upon and expanded some of the serialized stories from the *Literary Garland*. She could offer Bentley sketches based on Suffolk life and history, gothic tales, historical romances, and her own New World adventures. The first of these was *Mark Hurdlestone* (1853) and for it she received fifty pounds advance against her share of profits, as she did for all of her works except *Matrimonial Speculations*. From 1852 to 1856 she earned upwards of £350 from this source, a sum that considerably helped to meet the Moodie family's medical and educational expenses.

While Susanna's preference was for recasting her earlier writing into book form, Bentley sought new material on Canadian life. On 29 June 1852 he wrote to her as follows: 'If you could render your picture of the state of society in the large towns and cities of Canada, interesting to the idle reader, at the same time you make it informing to those who are looking for facts it would be acceptable. Present them to the reader's eye as they were years ago and as they are now, and are still every year I imagine rapidly prospering it might form a good work as a pendant to "Roughing It in the Bush." I would if I like it, purchase the copyright of it and it should appear first in the Miscellany.'[4]

The result of this request was *Life in the Clearings* (1853), a work that did not meet with the same generally favourable reception as did *Roughing It in the Bush*. The *Athenaeum* (27 August 1853) observed 'the made-up tone and style' and suggested the book's main purpose was 'money getting.' The *Spectator* (13 August) acknowledged the usefulness of the information conveyed, but found the book wanting in spontaneity and dramatic character and containing 'too much of digression and disquisition.' Susanna was, of course, disappointed, particularly in the light of the positive reviews Samuel Strickland's *Twenty-seven Years in Canada West* (1853) had recently received: the *Spectator* (12 February) had found its 'reality, freshness, information, and that Robinson Crusoe character' admirable; *Bentley's Miscellany* had liked the 'rough, hearty, genuinely English tone about the work'; the *Athenaeum* had observed that the book compared favourably to John Galt's *Annals of the Parish* (1821). Susanna's irritation at the contrast between the reception of 'the Major's' book and *Life in the Clearings* sometimes shows in the letters. Another source of annoyance was the participation of her sisters, Eliza, Agnes, and Jane Margaret, in preparing Samuel's work. She may also have been annoyed that he received £100 per thousand copies of his book, considerably more than she had obtained for *Roughing It in the Bush* or for any of her books, and that for Samuel's book Agnes had been the chief negotiator. At any rate, the old antagonisms resurface both in the suspicion that Eliza, who had reviewed for the *Lady's Magazine* and the *Court Magazine and Monthly Critic*, was responsible for unfavourable reviews of *Life in the Clearings* and in the dispute with Agnes over the dedication to her that appeared in *Roughing It in the Bush*. It seems that Susanna's use of her sister's name as a way of assisting the work's public reception was unauthorized, and therefore an irritation to Agnes (see Letter 50); in response, Susanna requested the removal of the dedication from subsequent editions, a move that further irritated the unpredictable Agnes, although the dedication was not taken out until 1857.

If reviews of *Life in the Clearings* were not to Susanna's liking, neither were the English reviews of *Mark Hurdlestone*. She found herself increasingly discontented with the British response to her work as she added to her list *Flora Lyndsay, or Passages in an Eventful Life* (1854), *Matrimonial Speculations* (1854), and *The Moncktons* (1856), the latter book completing the major phase of her publishing connection with Richard Bentley. A version of each of these works had first appeared in the *Literary Garland*.

Actually, reviews of *Mark Hurdlestone* in Britain were mixed rather than wholly hostile. The *Spectator* (8 January 1853) found that the effects produced 'by extremes and startling contrasts' and 'characters ... either low or revolting, or at best disagreeable' might be suited to a colonial readership but not to a more experienced English one. Even this review, however, noted that 'the writing is good ... the mere delineation easy and powerful.' The *Athenaeum* review of 15 January expressed the view that Susanna's fiction filled a gap left by 'the cessation of' Mr. [G.P.R.] James's flow of fiction and that *Mark Hurdlestone* possessed 'the prolific romancer's easy conduct of story, [and] level fluency of language sometimes approaching to vividness in description and pathos in emotion ... ' Even though the characters and action seemed to be familiar, the reviewer observed, 'Mrs. Moodie makes us willing, somehow, to undertake the adventure once more ... ' It is possible that she had seen reviews of a more damaging kind, for she was certainly unhappy with the reception. *Flora*

Lyndsay and *Matrimonial Speculations* did not fare well, and with the publication of *The Moncktons* Susanna had to face the harsh truth that she was no longer writing with appeal to the modern reading public in England. The *Athenaeum* reviewer, for instance, saw the latter work as 'a foolish novel,' adding that 'the characters and the story appear to have been brought out of a dusty toy-box' (23 February 1856); and the *Spectator* on 9 February found the book totally conventional and commonplace, evidence of the fact that the author was simply ignoring the 'new current of human existence before her eyes.'

Susanna's consolation was that in North America the response to her books, especially the 1855 publication of *Geoffrey Moncton* (the American title of *The Moncktons*), was significantly better, thus bearing out the English view that such fiction was better suited to a colonial, or at least a less discriminating, society. A reviewer for the Hastings *Chronicle*, the Reform paper in Belleville, on 29 November 1855 found *Geoffrey Moncton* displaying an artistic plot with 'incidents, natural and striking' and characters 'all masterly conceptions and vivid portraits ... drawn to the life.' The efforts of De Witt and Davenport of New York to become Susanna's publishers offer further evidence of her popularity in North America. As early as 1853 they had sought to strike an arrangement directly with her. Bentley gave her the right to do so, but repeatedly she drew back, not wanting to jeopardize her connection with Bentley in any way, and being content with having him send advance sheets to the Americans. By June 1855 De Witt and Davenport reported that they had purchased the American rights to publish *Roughing It in the Bush* from Stringer and Townsend, a minor New York reprint publisher, although it is not clear how the latter firm had acquired the rights. To complement that acquisition De Witt and Davenport purchased *Geoffrey Moncton*, and with its publication in 1855 could claim to be Susanna's primary publishers. It was then the American firm's turn to send advance sheets to Bentley, who published the novel as *The Moncktons* the following year.

Although literary matters are the principal concern of the letters to Bentley (twenty of the thirty letters in this section are addressed to him), Susanna also reveals her sense of friendship by conveying to him aspects of the relationship between her writing and her domestic affairs. Naturally, family concerns are central as well to her correspondence with her sister Catharine. Foremost amongst these matters are the incidence of illness, the persistent financial difficulties resulting from Dunbar's position as sheriff, the movements of her children, and the close association between herself and Catharine.

A cross-written letter in Susanna Moodie's hand

Susanna's own illnesses in these years were one cause of financial exigency. In 1852 (see Letter 46) she was attended by two prominent Belleville doctors, James Lister and William Hope. Lister (1811–78), who was her regular doctor, had emigrated to Canada West in 1841 and was well known in the community for his generosity, kindness, and skill as a physician. Dr Hope (1815–94), who was called in on the case because of the seriousness of her illness, had lived in Canada from the age of seven and had received his medical training in Kingston, following which he had begun practising in Belleville in 1838. Hope was much involved in community activities and institutions and was, in fact, surgeon to the county gaol, a position that undoubtedly often brought him into contact with Dunbar; he served as mayor of Belleville in 1860 and, interestingly, himself became sheriff of the county in 1881 after resigning from active medical practice.

The letters also make apparent the usual needs of a growing family. Donald, the much-favoured second son of whom great things were expected, studied at McGill from 1853 to 1858 with intentions of becoming a doctor, but he never did complete his training and was a disappointment to his mother. Robert, the youngest, also attended school in Quebec, studying both at St Mary's College in Montreal and Bishop's College in Lennoxville in the later years of the decade. The need to support these studies was obviously a heavy financial obligation. The eldest son, Dunbar, was through much of the period seeking his own fortune in the goldfields of California and providing the Moodies with letters full of exotic tales and adventures.

The lives of the daughters followed a fairly normal course, including marriage and children, but here too there was cause for some distress. Agnes, the delicate and attractive second daughter, married Charles Thomas Fitzgibbon on 21 August 1850. He was a brother of William Fitzgibbon, who had replaced Edmund Murney, one of Dunbar's political foes, as clerk of the peace of Hastings in 1842, after Murney had been dismissed by Sir Charles Bagot for opposing the election of the attorney-general, Robert Baldwin, while Murney himself was a holder of government office. Fitzgibbon was also a son of the much celebrated Colonel James Fitzgibbon, who was in some accounts credited with saving Toronto from the rebel forces in 1837. Charles and Agnes lived in Toronto where he practised law and became registrar of the Court of Probate for Canada West, but his foolhardy speculations and gambling kept the young family financially uncertain. Clearly Agnes's situation was a constant concern to Susanna during these years, she fearing both for the health and financial welfare of her daughter and grandchildren.

Catherine Mary, the eldest daughter and Dunbar's favourite, married more successfully on 1 August 1855. Her husband, John Joseph Vickers, had emigrated from Dublin to New York in 1849 and worked there for a steamship company for two years, following which he farmed in the Belleville area. Farming, however, had convinced him he was best suited for business and he left the area to join the American Express Company; after two years he was able to form his own firm, the Vickers' Northern Express Company, in conjunction with the development of the Northern Railroad leading from Toronto into the northern parts of the province. The Vickers lived in Toronto, where John's success made Katie the most financially secure of all Susanna's children.

If family life was marked by ordinary concerns, it was also exceptional because of the literary proclivities and intellectual curiosity of Susanna and Dunbar. Despite their sometimes troubled circumstances, they kept abreast of current movements and events. The *Albion* of New York continued to be a favourite source of information on British political and cultural affairs, while Canadian papers from Toronto and Montreal, as well as the Belleville area, gave them a broad perspective on Canadian matters. Horace Greeley's *Tribune* (New York), in its weekly edition, was another vital source of information, particularly on American politics, states' rights, the anti-slavery movement, and cultural affairs. It is certain that Susanna knew the influential Greeley, although exactly how has not been determined. He had Belleville connections, but acquaintance may have come through his interest in her books (*Roughing It in the Bush* was extensively and favourably reviewed in the *Weekly Tribune*) or through a mutual interest in anti-slavery activities or spiritualism. The one reference to Greeley in Letter 69 is a fascinating hint that Susanna may have written to him on such matters.

She surely would have responded to Lydia Howard Sigourney (1791–1865), from whom she received a letter of praise. Sigourney was, before Longfellow, America's best known and most popular poet, one whose work the Strickland sisters would have been familiar with from the early stages of her career, for, like them, she contributed to the annual gift books and periodicals of the 1820s. She went on to write some sixty-seven sentimental volumes in addition to her autobiography, *Letters of Life* (1866). Her well-established popularity doubtless made her words on *Roughing It in the Bush* very valuable to Susanna.

In addition to such specific contacts with American writers, the letters disclose the wide range and contemporaneity of the Moodies' intellectual interests. Despite the traditional character into which Susanna's own writing fell, her perception of the work of others was both individual and astute. There is no evidence of 'cultural lag' with respect to her reading, for through newspapers and books she was able to form solid opinions of the latest works of Dickens, Thackeray, Longfellow, Tennyson, Emerson, and Margaret Fuller Ossoli, as well as to maintain her old interest in history through the works of John Doran, Thomas Babington Macaulay, and W.H. Prescott (see Letter 61). Richard Bentley was clearly the source of some of her reading matter, sending books by Doran and the novelist Charles Reade, but he was not the sole source. American publications arrived promptly in Canadian bookstores, such as those in Belleville owned by Duff and Harrison. The Moodies were frequent customers.

Concerning the Canadian scene and Susanna Moodie's place in it, the letters bear testimony to the validity of the assessments she offers in the 'Introduction' to *Mark Hurdlestone*. With the passing of the *Literary Garland* there was little market for her work in Canada. While she was enjoying success with the Bentley firm, offers from Thomas Maclear, Toronto bookseller and publisher of the *Anglo-American Magazine* (1852–5), and the Rev. Henry Hope, editor of the *Old Countryman*, did not interest her, though these were important publications for her sister Catharine. Few other opportunities remained. The newspapers were no longer the outlet she sought for her work, although they played a major role in Canadian cultural life, as she suggests in *Mark Hurdlestone*:

The standard literature of Canada must be looked for in her newspapers ... A Canadian newspaper is a strange *mélange* of politics, religion, abuse, and general information. It contains, in a condensed form, all the news of the Old and the New World, and informs its readers of what is passing on the great globe, from the North Pole to the gold mines of Australia and California. So much matter has to be contained in so small a space that no room remains for dulness, and should a spare column occur, it is always filled up by droll sayings and doings of brother Jonathan, or clever extracts and reviews of new works just issued from the ever-teeming American press.

It was the newspaper more than anything else that affected Susanna Moodie's attitude to the Canadian literary scene. Her sense of a hostile reception to her first book, the attacks on her because of her writing on Catholics and Irish-Canadians, led to disenchantment and a determination not to write on Canada beyond her trilogy of emigration and settlement, which was completed with *Flora Lyndsay* in 1854.

If Canadian literary affairs failed her during the decade, political and economic matters, both Canadian and international, were of great concern. Her early interest in the anti-slavery movement in England was reawakened by the developing crisis in the United States. The unrest resulting from the passage of the pro-slavery Kansas-Nebraska Bill in 1854, which effectively countered the Compromise of 1850 under which California entered the Union as a free state, was a subject she commented on to Bentley (Letter 64). In 1856 Kansas was declared to be in a state of insurrection, and it was feared that California would take the same course, or even secede. Susanna was most keenly interested in affairs on the west coast because her son Dunbar was writing to her about conditions in the goldfields and events such as the funeral of William R. King, the abolitionist vice-president who had been killed in 1853.

In Canada, too, there were dramatic economic and political changes that seemed to match the Moodies' own fortunes. The early 1850s were marked by prosperity emanating from the availability of British and American capital for the building of railroads, and the opening up of American markets for Canadian raw materials through the Reciprocity Treaty of 1854. A seven-year period of expansion paralleled the Moodies' relative prosperity as Susanna's publishing career supplemented Dunbar's earnings as sheriff. But by October 1857 an international financial crisis had brought a temporary end to the boom, and the political life of the colony had become fractious and unsettled. Coincidentally, the conditions of Dunbar Moodie's office had become increasingly difficult.

In politics Susanna remained firmly Reformist (see Letter 64). The liberal-conservative coalition governing the Canadas was struggling to maintain the union established in 1841 under the recommendations of the Durham Report. In Canada West the administration was under attack by the Grit reformers headed by George Brown. Susanna sympathized with their hopes to abolish the links between church and state, to establish the principle of representation by population, and to annex the western territories. She detested the governing coalition and longed for a reform victory, which came, in Canada West at least, in the election of November 1857.

But it was the detested liberal-conservatives who were largely responsible for the building of the Grand Trunk Railway, a feat that was celebrated in Belleville with the arrival of the first locomotive on 27 October 1856. Cities like Toronto and Montreal were now within a few hours travel, and a new era had begun, with a renewed sense of Belleville's status and place in the developing country.

For the Moodies it meant new friends like J.W. Tait, a civil engineer for the railroad, and an opportunity to travel much greater distances. The coaches, with their open platforms and hand-brakes, their stoves and kerosene wall lamps, ran to centres like Montreal at a speed of thirty-five miles per hour, and from Montreal excursioners of the day, the Moodies amongst them, could go on to the coast of Maine.

Both the arrival of the first locomotive and the trip to Maine nourished Susanna's fascination with machines. Years before, her 'Spirit of Motion' had appeared in *Enthusiasm*, as well as in the *Lady's Magazine* and the *Literary Garland*; an early expression of a continuing interest, it begins:

> Spirit of eternal motion!
> Ruler of the stormy ocean,
> Lifter of the restless waves,
> Rider of the blast that raves
> Hoarsely through yon lofty oak,
> Bending to thy mystic stroke;
> Man from age to age has sought
> Thy secret – but it baffles thought!

As she suggests in Letters 65 and 67, with such inventions she had the feeling that man was at last approaching the solution of the secret. Clearly her response to the locomotive is one of awe, the machine a thing of wonder, but at other times she was characteristically ambivalent about such creations. In *Life in the Clearings*, for instance, in response to news of American plans to harness the falls at Niagara into what she called 'motive power for turning machinery,' her paean ceases: 'Ye Gods! what next will the love of gain suggest to these gold-worshippers? The whole earth should enter into a protest against such an act of sacrilege – such a shameless desecration of one of the noblest works of God' (258). Here, as in her celebratory poem 'The Otonabee,'[5] her romantic enthusiasm for natural energy and rugged beauty is tempered by the inevitable harnessing of nature by machines.

In the face of her contrasting responses to machinery, it is not surprising to find her also sceptical and tentative about the phenomenon of spiritualism, the subject, apart from purely literary matters, to which she probably gives the most extended treatment in her letters to Richard Bentley. It was a subject, however, not totally foreign to her nature.

Her interest in spiritualism at this time seems to have stemmed from the publication of *Spiritualism* (New York 1853) by John W. Edmonds and George T. Dexter, although she had doubtless read reports in the New

York papers, the *Albion* and the *Tribune*, as well as in Canadian papers, that had piqued her curiosity. This book attracted much attention because of Edmonds' position as a judge in the Supreme Court of New York. While he was a great popularizer of the idea and proponent of the procedures of supposed communication with dwellers in the spirit world such as Francis Bacon and Emmanuel Swedenborg, his book was only one of many works, both supporting and detracting. Nearly all had as a starting point the celebrated 'Rochester rappings' and the Fox sisters, Margaret and Kate, two mediums through whom the spirits communicated. Most modern accounts also credit the Foxes with originating the social phenomenon and the new religion of spiritualism.[6] They were the daughters of John and Margaret Fox, who had moved to Hydesville, near Rochester, in late 1847. In the old house in which they resided, the mysterious rappings began early in 1848, always in association with the two girls, then aged thirteen and twelve, Kate being the younger. News of the odd noises excited the local community and, in the company of an elder sister, Leah Fish of Rochester, a means of interpretation was soon devised so the questions of numerous curiosity seekers concerning the spirit world could be answered. The testimony of witnesses, and the tests to which the girls were subjected, received such wide publicity that in 1850 they moved to New York for a time to appear as major attractions at Barnum's American Museum. In succeeding years they attracted a large following of converts, many of them prominent persons such as Judge Edmonds or literary figures of the day like James Fenimore Cooper, N.P. Willis, and George Bancroft.

For Susanna Moodie, the crucial factor in the Fox story was that the family had lived in the Belleville area before moving to New York State and the eldest sister, Elizabeth Ousterhout, remained a resident of Consecon, a nearby village. It was to visit Elizabeth that Kate and, reportedly, Margaret and their mother returned in the summers of 1854 and 1855, thus making possible the meeting between Susanna and the celebrated Kate Fox, which is the subject of Letter 59.

Although Susanna writes that she is sceptical of actual communication with spirits, even after this encounter, she was certainly intrigued enough to want to find out more, and the possibility of such communication was, in spite of her appeal to reason, fascinating. To explore the matter further, she continued to read the related literature. *The Healing of the Nations* (New York 1855), edited and introduced by Nathaniel Tallmadge, a former governor of Wisconsin and an American senator, with a text by Charles Linton, a young writing medium, found great favour with her, probably because of its aphoristic, proverbial seriousness, and a poetic quality that would appeal to her intuitive nature, but she was less impressed by Robert Hare's *Experimental Investigation of Spirit Manifestations, Demonstrating the Existence of Spirits and their Communion with Mortals* (New York 1855). Hare endeavours to provide a scientific approach to spiritual phenomena, including descriptions of apparatus for testing the validity of such phenomena, but the book is primarily a discourse on religious experience and treats spiritualism as the way to 'a new and better gospel' and Hare himself as a 'minister to earth's inhabitants.' E.W. Capron's book, *Modern Spiritualism: Its Facts and Fanaticisms, its Consistencies and Contradictions* (Boston and New York 1855), promised a comprehensive account, but despite the impartiality implied in the title it too gave her a defence of the movement.

Together with newspaper accounts, these books, and perhaps others, constituted a rather intensive reading in the subject of spiritual communication, a reading that belies Susanna's protestations of disbelief. Her exploration of the subject may have been the result of her relative prosperity at the time and a certain leisure and opportunity to do so, but it was also the result of a persistent interest in such elusive, mysterious experiences. The rationalist in her was always struggling with the romanticist, eager to test the powers of the mind; her early prose and poetry, as well as *Roughing It in the Bush*, give ample evidence of her experiments and interest in the occult and the irrational. The belief in 'sympathies,' which she declares to James Bird in Letter 4, is borne out in autobiographical facets of her Suffolk tales for *La Belle Assemblée* and especially in poems addressed to her close friend, Anna Laura Harral:

> Long I looked on the face of night,
>   At her hosts in glory shining:
> One lovely star shed a softer light,
>   To the rosy west declining;
> I gazed on its beam, and felt that thine eyes,
> Like my own, were bent on the glowing skies.
>
>
> Thy thoughts were with me in that silent hour;
>   Thy kindred heart was sighing;
> And owned at that moment the magic power
>   On my own dark spirit lying.
> We met in the shadowy world of thought,
> And dear was the meeting by fancy wrought.[7]

It is not surprising that in May 1856, when things were beginning to go badly, Susanna succumbed to the persistent persuasiveness of the occult and found comfort in the advice of those early 'father figures,' Thomas Pringle and Thomas Harral. The 'young man, old in the spirit world' of Letter 68 offers consolation and assurance to a Susanna Moodie suffering 'a year of great anxiety.' Perhaps one may even see in the resurfacing of old attachments and persons associated with early literary ambitions, another manifestation of discontent with her Canadian experience.

In the trials of her husband as sheriff of Hastings County she found ample cause for discontent towards the close of the decade and in the early 1860s. Dunbar Moodie's position had never been an easy one and its financial rewards were unpredictable. Serving writs on behalf of the courts often involved long journeys in bad weather, unfriendly welcomes, and time-consuming legal interventions. Changes in the procedure for the granting of writs and the loss of income involved in farming-out work to deputies or bailiffs forced him to take to the road often, an increasingly onerous task as he approached his sixties.

Even more troublesome, however, was the conviction that the sheriff and his family were the continuing victims of the machinations of unscrupulous and greedy lawyers, who did not pay their fees when duties were exercised on their behalf, and who carelessly or maliciously entangled him in legal snares. Such cause for complaint occurred in 1855 over the Cinq-Mars affair. At the fall assizes in November, D. E. Cinq-Mars brought an action against Moodie for having seized and sold his property to satisfy the creditors of his brother Peter, of Montreal; apparently the contentious issue was a deed to Belleville property claimed to be held by the latter. The plaintiff, however, contended that the deed had been mutually revoked and ought to have been destroyed. The Hastings *Chronicle* reported on 8 November that the case was a difficult one, but the decision went against Moodie and Cinq-Mars was awarded £36 3s. for damages. Letter 69 suggests the matter did not end there, and that Cinq-Mars brought a further execution against the sheriff, thus shaping another threat to the family's financial status.

The most exhausting and damaging turn in Dunbar Moodie's fortunes began in 1858 and ended with his resignation in 1863. Allan Ramsey Dougall, the nephew of Benjamin Dougall, a former political enemy, accused him of the 'farming of offices,' held to be 'one of the cardinal sins of the old system of patronage.'[8] The idea was that an influential man could secure more than one office, thus enabling him to sell an office to another man at a profit. Moodie had not done this. He had hired as deputy, in 1856, a man named Dunham Ockerman to relieve himself of certain of the office's burdens and to leave himself free for more leisure and travel. Dougall, however, persisted in his argument bringing formal suit against Moodie, despite unwillingness on the government's part to entertain the accusation. The suit was finally initiated in October 1859 and only at Dougall's expense; he was eventually successful not because of Moodie's actual guilt but because of the wording in the agreement Moodie's lawyer, W.H. Ponton, a long-standing friend, had drawn up between his client and Ockerman. The lawyer had omitted to include the words 'out of fees' to describe precisely how Ockerman was to be paid for his services. In December 1859 Moodie was found guilty at the Belleville assizes; in Toronto, in the spring of 1860, the verdict was upheld by the Court of the Queen's Bench. In the meantime, Moodie had found a new lawyer, the Hon. Lewis Wallbridge, Hastings' member of the Legislative Assembly, who initiated a formal appeal to the Court of Appeals before Chief Justice John Beverley Robinson. The appeal procedure took almost two years and necessitated more than one journey to Toronto, yet another drain on Moodie's time, health, and finances. Susanna was convinced that anxiety over his position caused the stroke on 28 July 1861 that paralysed his left side and left him partially disabled for the rest of his life. Characteristically, Dunbar saw his fate in much more complex terms, acknowledging in *Scenes and Adventures of a Soldier and Settler* (1868) that his condition had remote causes, perhaps the stress placed on his 'nervous system' by life in South Africa, as well as the more recent demands of his trial and the local management of the election of 1861.

Dunbar Moodie's case and its eventual outcome excited a good deal of interest in Belleville amongst both his supporters and detractors, and Susanna observes that the former far outnumbered the latter. As might be expected, she felt somewhat bitter towards those whose evidence had been damaging to her husband's defence, and she was convinced he had been deliberately betrayed by his lawyer and deputy. Sheriff Moodie, in his review of the case in *Scenes and Adventures*, made no public accusations of malicious intent, but the pro-Moodie Hastings *Chronicle* muddied Dunham Ockerman's name and declared his role in the affair to be villainous. In response, Ockerman stated his side of the controversy in the pages of the Belleville *Intelligencer*, the Tory paper, always a medium for Moodie's enemies. In letters published 10 April and 1 May 1863 he accused Moodie not only of farming the office to him at a rate of '300 [Pounds] cash quarterly in advance' but of deliberately obtaining the bond between them and burning it. This he claimed to have been proved in court. Ockerman saw

himself as the wronged party, 'a poor man in a lower state of life than the
Sheriff,' who lacked friends in court to protect his position and name. The
politically partisan involvement of the two local newspapers suggests that,
at the end as at the beginning of his long and sometimes precarious tenure
as sheriff, Dunbar Moodie was involved in a politically motivated dispute
not uncommon in a province in which party allegiances were both deep and
persistent. On 15 January 1863 he resigned his position as sheriff, a loss of
employment that signalled a very difficult period in the Moodies' lives.

1 Bentley Papers, Manuscript Room, British Library
2 *Ibid.*
3 *Blackwood's Magazine* (March 1852), 355–65
4 Bentley Papers, British Library
5 *Literary Garland* (May 1839), 275
6 See Earl Wesley Fornell, *The Unhappy Medium: Spiritualism and the Life of Margaret Fox*
  (Austin 1964); Howard Kerr, *Mediums, and Spirit Rappers, and Roaring Radicals* (Urbana
  1972); and Ronald Pearsall, *The Table Rappers* (London 1972).
7 'To __' in *La Belle Assemblée* (November 1827), 215
8 Audrey Y. Morris, *Gentle Pioneers* (1966), 229

---

44 To Richard Bentley

Belleville
County Hastings C.W.
Sir,   April 16th, 1852

The ill-health of my esteemed friend Mr. Bruce prevents me from trou-
bling him further with my literary matters; I therefore thought it best to
negotiate with you in my own name, for the sale of a new work. *Roughing
It in the Bush*, if I may judge from the reviews that have reached the
Colony, has met with a favorable reception in England; and this circumstance has induced me, to offer to you for publication a tale, entitled,
'Mark Hurdlestone, the Gold Worshipper,' being the *first*, of a series, that
employed my pen during the long winter evenings of 1838–9, that I
spent in the bush, during the absence of my husband on the frontier. The
very great popularity which some of these tales have enjoyed in this
Colony, and in the United States, as published in the Montreal *Literary
Garland*, leads me to hope, that as human nature is the same every
where, they may chance to meet with as much, or greater favor at home.

The MS. which I have just finished transcribing contains 300 closely
written pages, besides a long preface, in which I have dwelt at some

length on the state of literature in this noble country, and the great improvement in that respect which has taken place during the last ten
years.

I thought that this series of tales might aptly enough be styled 'Tales
of a Canadian Winter Hearth' although the scenes and characters described are not Canadian. Should you wish to see the MS. and could direct
me as to the safest and cheapest mode of transmitting it, to England, it
shall be sent to your order. The terms of publication or sale of MS. I must
leave to your *own liberality*. The first agreement you made with Mr.
Bruce for the copy right of *Roughing It in the Bush* was to me, far more
satisfactory than *the last*, with which I was indeed deeply disappointed; as I could have commanded far more liberal terms both in the States
and in the Colony.

Your answer upon this subject before the month of June, would greatly
oblige me; as in case of a refusal, a gentleman who is going to Edinburgh during that month, has offered to try and effect a sale for me with
the Mess'rs Blackwood, to whom he is personally known and who
publishes for my sister Agnes. But I thought it only fair to give my first
European publisher the choice in the matter.

Should the 'Gold Worshipper' prove successful it could be quickly fol-
lowed by tales of equal interest, each volume containing one story – or
two at the most. I have by me the following – 'Geoffrey Moncton, or
Memoirs of a Poor Relation' – 'The First Debt' – 'Monica, or Witchcraft' – 'The Royal Election, a tale of Ancient Poland' – 'Richard
Redpath' – 'Mildred Rosier' – 'Noah Cotton, a tale of Conscience' – 'Jane
Redgrave' – and a multitude of others, though shorter of equal interest
– 'A Vol. on Practical Jokes,' *illustrated* by real incidents both tragical and
comical – 'A Vol. of Essays' written by Mr. M. and myself. Of poetry I
say nothing, for no one reads poetry now.[1]

Prior to the publication of *Roughing It in the Bush*, Mr. Bruce wrote to
me, requesting me to add a concluding chapter to the work, upon the
present state of the country, and likewise to supply a chapter in the place
of 'Michael Macbride,' which I had supressed, on account of the Catholics, who considered that story as written against them, although in every
particular, *it was strictly true*. Mr. Moodie wrote a long and able
chapter, on the present condition of the Colony, and I sent a true and
pathetic narrative, entitled 'Jeanie Burns,' together with many interesting anecdotes of persons, who at sundry times, and under my own knowledge, had been lost in the woods. These chapters would have proved a
very useful, and almost necessary addition to the work, and Mr. M. and
myself regretted exceedingly, that they arrived too late for insertion.

Mr. Bruce has the Manuscripts with him; and should you wish to append them to a second edition of the work, if it should be so fortunate as to reach a second edition. We only ask of you the sum per sheet that you give to the contributors to your excellent *Miscellany*.[2]

My distance from England, and the necessity of being explicit, in order to save time, will I hope Sir, prove a sufficient excuse for the unceremonious manner in which I have addressed you.

I have the honor to be,
Your Obt. Servant,
Susanna Moodie

P.S. I have not yet seen a copy of the Canadian work; so that I cannot refer you to the page at which 'Jeanie Burns' should be introduced. But it ought to come in before the account of 'Uncle Joe and his Family.' Mr. Moodie's chapter should be the last in the volume. I am sure a cheap edition of the book would sell well on this side [of] the water, as numbers of persons are enquiring for it, but seem terrified at the large price of the work.[3]

1 All the tales mentioned had appeared in the *Literary Garland. The Moncktons: A Novel* was eventually published in two volumes by Bentley in 1856 after first being issued by De Witt and Davenport in 1855. 'Richard Redpath' became the third tale in *Matrimonial Speculations* (1854), and 'Noah Cotton' was reprinted as part of *Flora Lyndsay* (1854). Three of Susanna's stories entitled 'Practical Jokes' appeared in *Bentley's Miscellany* in 1853 and 1854.
2 Bentley paid ten pounds per sheet (sixteen pages) to *Miscellany* contributors.
3 The first edition of *Roughing It in the Bush* sold for a guinea per copy.

---

45 To Richard Bentley

Belleville
July 20, 1852

Dear Sir,

I hasten to reply to your letter of the 29th June, which I received by yesterday's mail. The liberal and gentlemanly tone it breathes, inspires me with a confidence towards you, which I feel certain, will never be abused.

I am perfectly satisfied with the terms of remuneration you propose for the MS, of 'Mark Hurdlestone,' which I consider fair and reasonable. I should like to receive from you, a regular draught of this agreement, as in case of anything happening to either of us; it might be made available for my children. I am the better pleased with this proposal, as it affords a chance of some provision for old age, should my writings be so fortunate, as to become popular.

The advance you offer, of fifty pounds on the profits, arising from the sale of the work will be of great service to me, just now; as I have promised my second son, a fine lad of sixteen, to assist him in going out to Australia; to which El Dorado, all his thoughts at present tend; and I am certain, that he will be more anxious for the *debut* of 'Mark Hurdlestone,' than I am myself.

I have not received a copy of *Roughing It in the Bush*, from Mr. Bruce, nor have I heard from that gentleman since I last wrote.

I have however, got a sight of the book. A son of Sir Robert Pigot, travelling through Canada presented me with his copy some weeks ago.[1] I have gone carefully over the work, and enclose you a few corrections, should the book ever go into a second edition. In such case – and you should deem it advisable, to insert the chapters we sent you; and which I think would add greatly to the general interest of the book, the Sketch of Jeanie Burns, should be placed between the VI and VII chapters of the first volume, and the portion written by my husband, should end the work.

From the publisher, of the American edition, of the work, Geo. P. Putnam, I received a few days ago, the following very polite offer, of sending me some of the *stolen brooms*.[2] Now I believe, in strict justice, that the *said brooms*, should belong to you, as the rightful owner of the work. However, I mean to take in good part, his splendid donation, of my own goods and chattels –

Mrs Susanna Moodie   10 Park Place
                                      New York

Dear Madam,

I have taken the liberty to send you, to the care of John Duff, Bookseller Kingston, 10 copies of your admirable work, *Roughing It in the Bush*. If the present state of copy right laws, had been such, as to give any suitable protection, I should have been glad to have made such arrangements with you, as would have served for you, a proper remuneration, for the American edition of your work

As it is, it has been printed at the lowest possible cost, selling in paper at 50 cents per copy, in order to be secure against a still cheaper edition. It will give

me the greatest pleasure to send you an additional number of copies of the edition,
if you can in any way make them available to yourself.

> With high respect,
> Madam
> Your most Obt. Ser
> Geo. P. Putnam –

P.S. I trust you will not be displeased with the liberties taken by the Editor,
if sins, they are sins of *omission* only.

A very decent letter, Mr. Geo P. Putnam, and I shall be glad of the
books, which I hear are lying at the wharf for me. Besides, I am very
curious to see the *Yankee omissions*. The New York *Albion*, has given us
a splendid review, the very best I have seen upon this continent. It will
tell well, as there is not a village in British North America, where the
Albion is not taken.

The American press speaks *most highly* of the work, while the majority
of the Canadian Anglo-Irish Editors, lo[ad] me with abuse. The work
bids fair to be as popul[ar] in the States, as I hear, it is at home. This will
no[t] [bring] any *pecuniary benefit*, on either you or me, but it may help
to win me a name, and in this way, serve us both.

I will think over the new Canadian work, but the little that I have said
of Canadian society has made me so unpopular with the natives, that I
believe it would be better to leave them alone for the future, if I would
hope to live in peace. Yet I have said nothing of them beyond the truth,
nor told half of what could, and ought to be said, of their unfaithful dealings, and utter disregard of all honorable feeling. Michael Ryan's letter,
in the preface to 'Mark Hurdlestone,' gives an admirable picture of them.
It is *God's truth* – I have been suffering much from ill health lately and
have been forced to relinquish the pen and apply to the Doctor. The
intense heat of this month has been even too much, for the Canadians
who are used to hot summers, it has almost killed me. I am busy with the
second tale of the series of which 'Mark Hurdlestone' forms one. I hope
to have it ready before Christmas, for Mr Robertson's next trip to Europe.
I am writing to you as to an old friend instead of to a stranger, but when
I read your truly kind letter I cannot consider you as such. Mr Moodie
unites with me in compliments, and believe me dear Sir

> Yours with grateful respect
> Susanna Moodie

1 Sir Robert Pigot (1720–96), a British army officer, distinguished himself in North America at Lexington and Bunker's Hill in 1775. Of his three sons, Susanna met either George, a major-general in the army, or Hugh, a captain in the Royal Navy.

2 Rather jauntily, Susanna explains the bold-faced pirating she encountered in receiving George Putnam's edition of *Roughing It in the Bush* (July 1852). In her 'Introduction' to *Mark Hurdlestone, the Gold Worshipper* she reworks the allusion to stolen brooms, this time in reference to the successful ways of American magazines of the 1840s and 1850s: 'American monthlies [e.g. *Harper's Magazine* and the *International*], got up in the first style, handsomely illustrated, and composed of the best articles, selected from European and American magazines, are sold at such a low rate that one or the other is to be found in almost every decent house in the province. It was utterly impossible for a colonial magazine to compete with them; for, like the boy mentioned by St. Pierre, they enjoyed the advantage of *stealing the brooms ready made.*'

---

46 To Richard Bentley

Belleville
C.W.
Nov 25, 1852

My dear Friend,

For such, I must call you, I have looked upon Death face to face, as it were, since I last wrote to you. That very night, I was taken alarmingly ill, and have been confined to my bed until a few days ago. I am able to sit up supported with pillows, but I am a sort of living skeleton, the very ghost of my former self. Thank God, my life has been spared and oh, how thankful I feel for this great mercy. Still I have the cold winter before me and am in a very precarious state.

I am attended by two very clever surgeons. Eminent men, for this country. My case it appears, has been a very singular one, and nature has thrown off without the aid of their dreadful knives, one of those painful internal complaints which are generally fatal to all attacked by them, and which was the cause of my long and obstinate illness during the whole of last summer. But the ordeal of suffering is past, and I feel very happy in my present relief from pain, inspite of my childlike weakness –

It will give me great pleasure, to try and meet your wishes with regard to another book on Canada, and I send you a few pages which I wrote the other day, as a sort of introduction to such a book to see if it would at all be the thing you required. My idea was, to describe as much of the country, as I could in my trip to Niagara, beginning with Belleville, and going through our lovely Bay, sketching the little villages along its shores, and introducing as many incidents and anecdotes illustrative of the *present state* of *Canada,* as I could collect or remember, to form a sort of apendix to *Roughing It in the Bush.* If it pleases you, and you insert it in the *Miscellany* I should like to retain the copyright, to be published hereafter between us on the same terms as you are now publishing, 'Mark Hurdlestone.' I hope the latter, may prove a favorite with the public; it is certainly an original thing –

I likewise send you two short sketches, which I thought might suit the Magazine. 'The Well in the Wilderness,' Is a real story. And its very truthfulness, gives it a horrid interest.[1]

The facts, on which this little sketch, was founded, were told me by a person who knew the younger members of the Steels family; and the story made such an impression on my mind, that during a severe attack of ague, I used to rave about it during the hot fit, and I wanted my daughter to write it down for me to get it out of my head. This *I did,* as soon as I recovered, but it would have been more effective as the *nightmare* of my fever. My dear child has copied it from my blotted M.S. and will copy another of the same stamp, in a few days. These short sketches I know are the most *useful* for a periodical but they *waste the powers of an author.*

Pray forgive all the blunders for I am very weak and this letter is the first that I have attempted since my illness ...

1 'The Well in the Wilderness' appeared in the *Miscellany* in 1853, having first been published by the Moodies in the *Victoria Magazine* (November 1847), 44–58.

---

47 To Richard Bentley   [late spring 1853][1]

... *the States.* It was the personal narrative that made the other so successful.'

This was probably the truth. Mr. Putnam's reprints, I think are generally the best we get. Harper's are very inferior though it is a great house.[2]

There is a want of *Individuality* in my writings, which I feel and lament, but I cannot remedy. In the phrenological development of my head these two organs were valleys, not bumps.[3] A scene or picture strikes me as a whole, but I never can enter into details. A carpet, must be very brilliant, the paper on a wall very remarkable before I should ever notice cither, while the absurd and the extravagant make lasting impressions, and I can remember a droll speech or a caracature face for years.

I do not think I will send you another sober tale like *Mark*, but a bundle of droll sketches of our adventures out to Canada and preparations for our emigration and all we met and saw on our voyage. This should have been the commencement of *Roughing It*, for it was written for it, and I took a freak of cutting it out of the MS. and beginning the work at Grosse Isle. This would make a volume, and might be termed 'Trifles from the Burthen of a Life.' Laughable as some of them are they proved to us *sober realities*.

If you determine upon publishing 'Life in the Clearings,' which perhaps might better be termed, as a companion to the other, 'The Clearings versus the Bush or Life in Canada,' – a Sequel to *Roughing It* etc. I should prefer our last terms of sharing profits, which seem to me to be the fairest for all parties. Should you like the work, I would most *thankfully* accept your kind offer of advance upon it. For though we contrive with rigid economy to make both ends meet, it is hard pinching. The money earned by the two works you have published has paid off a mortgage on our little estate of 18 acres,[4] and that alone saves the interest money of 15 £ per annum on a small mortgage of 150 pounds. Usurers thrive here. This is 10 percent but I have known 20 given upon loans.

The Shrievalty is so reduced of late years by handing over all writs once served by the Sheriff to the smaller courts, that the income is very small, not worth the fearful risks attached to it. *The lawyers never pay their fees*. Some have owed us for twelve years and will until the day of doom, and in this country, you cannot get one of them to sue another. They are a set of finished rascals and swarm every where.

Mr. Moodie is greatly beloved in the District, but he is so kind, that they all impose upon his benevolence. A nobler or an honester man never breathed, such seldom thrive here. M— is away during this bitter weather serving his spring assize jury in the back Townships. A dreadful journey but he cannot afford to give half the proceeds to his Bailiffs. The sorrows of a Canadian sheriff would not make a bad sketch.

I am really sorry that my brother's book[5] has had such little success at present. He is a dear good fellow, and if my sisters would have allowed him to write his own way, in his own frank natural language with the great experience he has had of the Colony his book must have been a very amusing clever one. But he told me that Jane who edited it for him insisted on turning out every thing that she considered vulgar, and this must have shorn the work of its identity. Rough Canadians don't use the fine language of an English drawing room; to make such people talk like a book would be ridiculous. I shall be delighted to see the copy for which I thank you much ...

1 Dated late spring (April/May) 1853 on the basis of the reference to Sherrif Moodie's spring assize duties. Susanna seems to be comparing the critical and popular reactions to *Roughing It in the Bush* and *Mark Hurdlestone* as the fragment begins, agreeing with some expressed view (likely English in origin) that the former succeeded better because of its 'personal narrative.'
2 Here she shifts attention to the general availability of English reprints in North America, the result of 'pirating' by houses like Putnam and Harper's.
3 Phrenological charts locate the area of Individuality as extending from the bridge of the nose between the eyes to the lower forehead.
4 This property, known as Moodie Cottage on Bridge Street West and Sinclair, was actually their second home in Belleville, the first having been damaged or destroyed by fire; the property was very much a country location at the time.
5 Samuel Strickland's *Twenty-seven Years in Canada West* was published by Richard Bentley early in 1853.

---

48 To Richard Bentley

Belleville
Sep. 3rd, 1853

My dear Mr. Bentley,

I have anxiously looked for a letter from you, by the last mails, but have been doomed to suffer disappointment. I hope illness is not the cause of your silence. Perhaps you are absent from home, in the search of health. May this find you convalescent.

I now send you by *Express*, the tale of 'Rachel Macgregor's Emigration.'[1] I trust it will prove a fortunate one for us both. The characters and incidents are drawn from life. The book is no fiction. Each page of the long paper on which it is written, contains 48 lines, and on an average from ten to twelve words in a line, being nearly equal to two pages of *Mark Hurdlestone*.

I would sell the copyright out and out, for £300. If you think this too high, and wish to publish it, we can do so, on the same terms as we have done the two last.[2]

I have still my heavy doctor's bills to settle; and to pay for my son's going down to the Montreal college, to pursue his medical studies, which will involve much outlay of our small means. Labour and attendance in sickness, costs so much here that my nurse claimed all the last remittance, received from you in June.

Mess'rs De Witt and Davenport offer me *200 dollars* for the *first chance* of republishing my next work; and they have written to me, to try and make some arrangement with you to secure to them that privilege. I enclose their letter. If the thing could be done, you would confer upon me a *great favor*, by allowing me this privilege.

Mark has a great run here and in the States, but I shall gain nothing by that, without you sold the right for us to Mess'rs Harper, who you will perceive, by their letter, sold it again to them.

This advertisement I copied from the *New York Tribune*, and I send a few of the many favourable notices of the work, from some of our best Colonial papers. The reviews in the *Canadian*, the Toronto *Globe*, and the Montreal *Pilot* were quite as flattering, beside a host of others. A vast number of copies have been sold in Belleville and Hastings alone, and I see by one of the Toronto papers, that the principal book-seller there, advertises, that he has got a fresh supply of this popular book.

I wish it had succeeded as well at home, but a re-action may take place in its favour. I am sorry we lost an additional fifty pounds from De Witt and Davenport. Their edition is a beautiful one, and astonishingly cheap. They have changed part of the title and omitted the preface. I likewise received a very flattering letter from Mrs. Sigourney, to whom I am an entire stranger, speaking in the highest terms of the work. This is a high compliment from a woman who stands at the head of the female writers of America. Another American friend writes to me from Boston, that the book is on every table, and spoken highly of in all circles there.

I shall feel greatly obliged by your letting me know as speedily as possible, of the safe arrival of the MSS. The poems and short tale are for the *Miscellany*,[3] if admissible. De Witt and Davenport are negotiating with me for a volume of sketches for the young. I think I shall get 400 dollars for it, with a certainty of success in the States, who have taken a fancy to my writings.

With kindest regards, in which all here join, believe me dear Mr. Bentley,

> Truly Yours,
> Susanna Moodie

The De Witt and Davenport letter is an amusing specimen of genuine Yankee correspondence. Pray restore it to me. I forgot to ask you if *Life in the Clearings* is out in London? I suppose it must be, by Mess'rs Stringer and Townsend's advertisement that the work is in press in New

York, and as I never made a copy of it, nor even mentioned the title to anyone, they could not obtain it through any channel, but direct from home.

My daughter FitzGibbon and her lovely babes have just left us after a long stay. I have been very lazy during the visit, feeling more pleasure in nursing the sweet engaging little pets, than in writing. I must make up now for lost time. We flattered ourselves from the coolness of July, that we were to have no *ultra* hot weather. Ye Gods! – August has paid us off – intense drought and 96 in the shade by the week together. Even now, the heat is killing and fatal fevers rife among us. This however can't last much longer.

Yours ever,
S.M.

1 Her manuscript title for *Flora Lyndsay*
2 Evidently, with knowledge of Samuel's contract with Bentley, Susanna sought to arrange better terms in her next contract, likely basing the £300 figure on the terms arrived at for Samuel's book.
3 Perhaps the 'Papers on Practical Jokes,' first published in the *Victoria Magazine* (February-April 1848); 'Practical Jokes: Lambeth Church' appeared in *Bentley's Miscellany* (1853), 299–303, followed by 'Practical Jokes: Ben Backstay' 410–16. Nothing is known about the poems.

---

49 To Richard Bentley

Belleville
U.C.

My dear Mr. Bentley,   Oct 8, 1853

I was truly glad to get your kind letter, by today's mail. I feared you had forgotten me altogether. The contents, as far as my literary matters are concerned are depressing enough, but, then, you are better, and I must set the good against the ill news.

So, *Life in the Clearings* is a failure? This seems strange, as it really is equal to *Roughing It* in every respect, that I can see. Had they made a *whole*, instead of separate works, we should have found it equally successful. My brother's book, is praised, by the English Press in the most flattering manner. Yet, you say that it does not sell. How is this? If the reviews entirely influence the reading public, it ought to be the most successful work of the year. But reviews are no criterion of the real merit of an Author. I have written reviews for literary papers myself before I left England, and I very well know, how little we can depend upon them. I really said what I thought of a book, but generally it did not please either the publisher or the Author. If my opinion happened to coincide with their interests, all well. If not, it was, to use a Canadian slang phrase, 'No go.'

I think it very probable that a certain influence may have been brought to bear against me in regard to the two last published books. But if they really do possess any merit, they will live in spite of the sneers of malice or the frowns of prejudice. The American press will do me justice, at any rate, where my name already ranks high as an author. Perhaps it would be better for me to publish in New York, as I fear you will be a loser by my writings. I think I might make a tolerable arrangement with some of their large publishing houses, which might ultimately become lucrative, and you would have the same right of republishing, which they claim from us. In a letter, which I received a few weeks ago from Mrs. Sigourney, a lady with whom I have no acquaintance, either personally or by letter, she is pleased to say, 'You will not think it strange, that one who has read with deep interest and sympathy your *Roughing It in the Bush*, should be moved to tell you so with the pen. Indeed ever since I hung over those pages with more enthusiasm than fiction creates I have felt a wish to know more of your history.' This is flattering from the pen of one of the first female American poets. These private testimonials of the merit of a book are more precious to me than a thousand reviews for they are real. I have many of these from strangers.

Mark has an immense sale in the States; I send you some of the reviews from the States papers. Now as the feelings of mankind are pretty general on these subjects, with some few exceptions I cannot help thinking that it has not got fair treatment in England. The difference of opinion could scarcely be so very great.

Do not hesitate to send me the bad reviews. They are more useful than good ones, as your enemies are more clever in discovering your defects; they would convey valuable hints for improvement, that might be turned to future account. Do send them. I can bear the castigation.

I have not seen a copy of *Clearings*. Did not even know that it was published. I have seen no notice of it here.

You have not sent me the return agreement to sign, or told me when, I could get the money, agreed upon on publication, viz. 50£ for I want it *very badly*. Alas, that one should have to work for money. But it cannot be helped, and I ought not to feel ashamed of turning the capacity God gave me to account, but ought rather to be grateful; still, it paralizes the mind having to tax it for daily supplies.

I trust you have by this time received the MS of 'Rachel Macgregor.' You must use your own judgment about it. I leave it entirely to you. I found it a very amusing book to write. But the public may not. After all, It shall be my last work on Canada. I am sick of the subject, and it awakens ill feelings in others.

I will employ the winter months in copying the tales and sketches, and send them, as soon as I can collect them together.[1] But if I have become so unpopular at home it appears to me rather a hopeless job.

I shall be most grateful for any work you may send me. I delight in the writings of Thackary. To me, he is the greatest satirist of the age, the most perfect anatomist of the human heart, and there is a touch of mercy in his severest castigations, that is almost sublime. By the by, He gives you a pretty good insight into the reviewing system in his inimitable *Pendennis*. I never read his books for the story. It is as a study of human nature. The minute examination of a wonderful picture.

We have had a very wet, cold, unhealthy fall, Typhus fever rife in our neighbourhood of the low, or ship fever kind. Many are sick and many have died of it.

The news of cholera having reached England is alarming. It will not fail to reach these shores in the spring, if such be the case.

Mr. Moodie is well and unites with me in kindest regards, and I remain

> Dear Mr. Bentley
> Yours truly
> Susanna Moodie

Perhaps the abuse of *Clearings* may increase its sales; some people are more crazy to read a condemned work than one that is highly praised, and they then make their own conclusions.

S.M.

1 Probably the tales for *Matrimonial Speculations*

50 To Richard Bentley [late autumn 1853][1]

... I will write to Mr. Armour[2] about the sale of copies of the book, but I fear the large number, will frighten him. He is a singular man, and I am told, drinks very hard. *Roughing It in the Bush*, keeps its popularity in the States. Several Americans have told me, that it sells nearly as well as Mrs Stowes *Uncle Tom*. What a pity that it is of no use to either of us in a remunerative point of view. Some of the Canadians are begining to retract their illnatured reviews. The Editor, of the *United Empire*, who gave me the worst, Says that he is very sorry for what he said. That he had never read the book, and took his review from passages quoted by *Blackwood*. That he did not like to retract what he had said, or he would write a very different one.

The Editor of the *Examiner* (the cleverest newspaper in the province) who is son-in-law to William L Mackenzie called me in his paper, 'An ape of the aristocracy. Too poor to lie on a sofa and too proud to work for my bread.' This sentence amused me very much; and if he could have seen how heartily I laughed over it, his spite would have received a severe mortification. But even *he* is repenting, and actually sends me American papers with his compliments, that contain excellent reviews of the very book that he condemned as a '*pernicious novel of the very worst kind –* '

I am really glad, that you have withdrawn the dedication to my sister. It was only her protest against the withdrawal that made me write to you as I did. She has wounded my feelings so severely about this dedication, that it is to me a perfect eye sore in front of my unfortunate book. Could I have forseen her reception of it, thousands would not have induced me to place it there.

And now let me thank you and most sincerely, both for the *Miscellany*, and the additional copies of *Roughing It in the Bush*. The latter are most acceptable as Mr. Bruce unfortunately lost the ones he had for me. They were forwarded to this country it seems, but never reached it. Having been mislaid at the office at home.

The tale of 'Jeanie Burns,' has been copied into American Magazines and papers not a few, but without my name or even telling where they stole it from. This is hardly fair of brother Jonathan, but it serves to show that the story has pleased the public. 'The South African Sketch' by my dear husband, which I send with my American one, is a great favorite of mine, and I really, *love* the pathetic little poem with which it closes.[3] He begs me to give his kindest regards to you. He has several short essays by him if they would be at all admissable in the Mag. I will send them. I have nearly the first volume copied of a work the size of *Mark* and hope to get it ready by the spring – 'Geoffrey Moncton, or the Memoirs of a poor relation.'

I rejoice in your restored health. May you long continue to enjoy it with every blessing –

Your gratefully obliged friend
Susanna Moodie

1 Dating here depends largely on the date of reviews of *Roughing It* in the *United Empire* and the *Examiner*, probably 1853 because the book 'keeps its popularity' and Susanna is sending Bentley an American tale ('The Well in the Wilderness') for the *Miscellany*.
2 Andrew H. Armour, a Montreal bookseller and publisher; see H. Pearson Gundy, *Book Publishing and Publishers in Canada before 1900* (Toronto: Bibliographical Society of Canada 1965).
3 Dunbar delivered two lectures on South Africa at the Belleville Mechanics' Institute that were later published as a series in the *Victoria Magazine* and again in *Scenes and Adventures as a Soldier and Settler, during Half a Century*. One of the parts in the former concludes with a short poem on the unknown potential of the human 'heart.' The sketches were not used in the *Miscellany*.

---

51 To Catharine Parr Traill   Belleville,
                                  Dec. 25, 1853

My dearest Catherine,[1]

I have delayed writing in the hope of having some home news to communicate, but mail after mail has arrived and no letter. Mr. Bentley seems to have forgotten me altogether. And from Reydon, I never hear, and suppose I never shall, as my correspondence is confined to the poor Mamma, whose will to write is perhaps beyond her power – I have nothing left but patience, which never was a sterling virtue of mine. Ours has been a dull quiet Christmas day, but the children have been superlatively happy, and I, happy seeing them so full of glee. I know not how it was, that Mary[2] and I, fancied all yesterday and today, that we should see her father walk in, and the little woman attended me like a familiar sprite watching me make mince pies and Christmas cake and pudding

talking all the while, of her own household Gods, and wondering what
Mamma and Papa, and all the brotherhood and sisterhood of home were
about – while Rob was wondering what old St. Claus would bring for
them – Poor dears! it was little Aunt had to give, but such as the good old
Patron of childhood brought, was received this morning, with extatic
delight, and Papa and I chatted a full hour over our bedroom fire last
night, Laughing as we filled the socks left very diffidently by our stove
pipe, and wondering what the children would say in the morning – what a
little swells to overflowing the gay glad heart of childhood. On Christmas morning – I always wish I was a child again. Jane[3] went out last night
and did not return until it was too late this morning for me to go to
church. But Papa went with the little ones and after dinner, took them a
long sleigh drive, and introduced Mary to a new world at Caniffs Mills
and Smithville[4] and they did not return until tea delighted with their
drive. They have now walked hand in hand to church and I sit down to
scribble to you. The holidays have commenced. The dreaded school ex-
aminations over, and the children have brought home books and slates
not to be idle during the holidays. Mary is making rapid progress in figures and is already in multiplication sums. She learns fast and if she
remains only a twelvemonth with me, she will attain a great deal of useful
knowledge. She is a darling good child, and I feel no difference in my
love to her than to my own. She and Robby love one another as all brothers and sisters should love. They have never had one word of difference, and are a great help and happiness to each other. You need not fear
my tiring of her. It is not my nature to tire of anyone I really value. My
obstinacy of purpose gives an obstinacy of affection. A good springing out
of evil – but still a good in its own peculiar way. She has fewer faults
than most children of her age, and her self denial and good feeling are very
great. The weather has now set in cold, but very pleasant. I have made
her two flannel jackets to wear next her skin and quilted her a good warm
petticoat, and keep her as comfortable as my present empty purse will
allow and she seems very contented and very happy. We see no company,
but it is as well for her as it does not take her away from her studies.
She occupies Katie's warm bed and room during her absence where she
and Rob sit in the sunny window sill and read alternately aloud for
hours together. We had another long letter from dear Dunbar. This was
however, written to Katie, dated the 8th of Nov – it was only five weeks
reaching us. The letter like most of his, full of amusing matter. By the by,
he tells us a queer thing if true – Three Americans were lately tried at
Nevada for murdering a Chinaman. It was a most interesting trial which

kept the court sitting for a fortnight. At first the judge refused the evidence of the poor injured pig tails, affirming that their evidence as uncivilized men was not worth taking. The chinamen indignant at this, affirmed that they were civilized and that they were the first discoverers of America, and built all those ruined cities which have filled the world with wonder. And they produced in court an historical book to that effect which was read by their interpreter proving what they said – which had the effect of convincing judge and jury, and ended in the murderers being sentenced to dance upon nothing. Dunbar is full of this discovery which he believes firmly. He had narrowly escaped with life from a frightful accident. In going up the mountain, he had to traverse a deep trench along the hill side made by the miners and jumping upon a large piece of rock about a ton weight in order to leap the ditch it gave way with him and he rolled down the mountainside about twenty yards, the stone rolling repeatedly over him, before he could free himself, bruising him terribly but without breaking his bones. A few feet farther from the spot where he was able to arrest its course would have carried him over a ledge and down a sheer descent of forty feet, which he says would have been certain death.

I was indignant at M'Clear wanting to cheat you out of your hard earned rights – 16 pages is a sheet of the *Anglo-American* – as any book or magazine of that size. Bentley's *Miscellany* is not so large, and I receive 10 guineas sterling for every such sheet I write. Don't put up with such a base fraud – for such it is. Your Mr. Hope has just written to Moodie to dun him for contributions from me – but really – I can't afford to write for the old twadler for nothing. He is going to publish a pamphlet containing Lord Ellsmere's[5] and your contributions and wants me to add my mite. As this is solely for his own benefit I shall do no such thing. There is a capital article in the last *Albion*, on table turning. Tell your Katie to read, mark, and inwardly digest it. I read it twice with infinite glee. I send the *Examiner* for though a radical paper it is one of the very best published in the Province. Though the Editor did call me an 'Ape of the Aristocracy – too poor to lie on a sofa, and too proud to work for my bread' – I was too much amused to be angry with him. I have as yet received no copies of my last book. I will try and send you a copy when they do come. I have not seen much of the Murneys lately. Mrs. M. 'is very weary looking out for land,' and I have been very busy with household duties. Rob was sick last week but is better. Excessive bleeding has left him very weak. All my boys are subject to this bleeding to excess. We heard of Donald but not from him, though I think we may get a

letter tomorrow. He was well and in high spirits studying hard to pass
his Latin examination in January and he hopes with success. Mr. Bains
one of the older students who lodges with him is instructing him for
love. Donald makes friends wherever he goes. He seems one of those
beings born for popularity, and is a finehearted noble boy. His last
letter to his father surprised me – it was written so well – so full of shrewd
remarks and life like pictures. Should God grant him life, I think he will
be a credit to us. God has been very good to us in our dear children. Tell
Annie[6] the bones to which Mary alludes were two skeletons that Donald has collected and put together and which he looks upon as his earthly
treasures to the cleaning and arranging of which he devotes all his
spare time. It will cost us one hundred pounds his seven months at college, and this for the four succeeding years. But I will work with more
zeal in the hope of serving my darling boy. He will remember my labor of
love when the hand that now writes is dust.

Katie leaves Peterboro for Toronto next week. She has been up to
Douro – Rather – I should say deeply disgusted with the education in
progress to the poor lads at the Agricultural College.[7] Her letter on the
subject is admirable so wise and just. You would like my Katie did you
know her more. She is to many proud and cold. But depths of tenderness
are in her heart. She is her father in women's guise. She will not show
her love like a true Scot, but she feels it – with her it is not on the lip, but
forms part of her being – Her true sisterly love for Donald is beautiful.
To us her affections are like living water refreshing the soul. I look up to
her with reverence, but Moodie idolizes her.

I have been reading Goethe's biography of his early years written by
himself. A very interesting book. Have been delighted with the memoirs
of Margaret Fuller Countess Ossoli. What a precious women. How little
one seems while reading the record left of such a mind. It is a noble
book. I am now reading Lorenzo Benoni's life, and am much pleased with
it.[8] As to writing, I am doing but little. I feel dispirited and lazy and
hate the mechanical task of copying but it must be done.

When I heard from my dear Addie she and my little ones were well.
Moodie is pretty well now. He was far from well for several weeks. He
is letting his beard grow. Beards are all the fashion. I am glad for it was
always a favourite hobby of mine. I have lived to see the day when men
are not ashamed of shewing their claims to manhood, and wearing this
kingly appendage to a fine face.

I must say goodbye. Mary will add a note to her dear Mother, and with
love to dear brother Traill and all the household of young hearts, and

wishing them many happy returns of the season, believe me ever thine in all affection

Susanna Moodie

1 Susanna spelled her sister's name variously, using either 'a' or 'e' as fifth letter. At this time Catharine was living on the farm she called 'Oaklands,' on the south shore of Rice Lake.
2 Mary, Catharine's youngest living daughter, was staying with the Moodies to attend school in Belleville. Susanna's mother, Elizabeth Strickland, was eighty-one.
3 Probably a servant, although Catharine in her journals mentions a cousin named Jane Allcock
4 Two hamlets north of Belleville in the Moira River valley, probably also known as Cannifton and Foxboro
5 Lord Ellsmere, Francis Egerton (d. 1857)
6 Catharine's second daughter
7 Samuel Strickland's Agricultural College (see contemporary account cited in Morris, *Gentle Pioneers*)
8 *Truth and Poetry from My Own Life; or, The Autobiography of Goethe* was published by several American firms at mid-century: Susanna may be referring to the edition published by Putnam in 1850, like others edited by Parke Godwin; *Memoirs of Margaret Fuller Ossoli*, 2 vols., ed. R.W. Emerson, W.H. Channing, and O.F. Clarke (Boston 1852); Giovanni Ruffini, *Lorenzo Benoni, or Passages in the Life of an Italian* (New York: Redfield 1853)

---

52 To Richard Bentley

Belleville
Dec. 30, 1853

My Dear Mr. Bentley,

Your letter of the 9th which I received this morning, has relieved my mind of much anxiety. I was afraid that your silence was caused by a fresh attack of your cruel complaint, and I am truly glad to find that you are in a fair way of recovering. Gout of all kinds – acute, rhumatic, chronic, and nuralgic, has been the tormentor of the Stricklands for the last century. Fortunately for me, I have only had two attacks of it. Once in my right foot, which I could not put to the ground for three weeks. One in my right hand. But these attacks strange to say, were in my early days. Few people are troubled with gout in this dry atmosphere, though *acute* rhumatism, is very common. My sister Traill is a martyr to the latter complaint. My husband was completely cured two winters ago, of a very severe attack of rhumatism in his right arm and shoulder by wearing a red flannel shirt lined *inside* with cotton wadding, the *fleecy part*, next his

skin. In a few days he recovered the entire use of his arm, and has
never had a touch of the disease since. He had been dosed with calchi-
cum, hensbane and all the other et ceterus given for those torturing
complaints without deriving the least benefit from them.

And now to business. Accept my grateful thanks for the remittance
which I suppose is for *Life in the Clearings.*[1] As the paper you sent me
was precisely the same as that for *Mark Hurdlestone.* The return dupli-
cate was never remitted. Will you be so good as to send it with the one
for 'Rachel' if you have determined to publish that on the same terms. I
still hope that a time will come, when *Life in the Clearings* will meet
with a better hearing. There are I know many things in it, which would
give great offence to *bigots* of all denominations, but as the substance
of it is strictly true, it may chance to make its way when more liberal
sentiments are popular in England. That period is coming fast. I feel
certain, that if published in the States, it will be popular there. I saw it
advertised some months ago. But I don't think it has been issued yet.
There are no copies in Canada at present. I hope you will send me some,
as I will send one to the *Albion*, and New York *Tribune*, to the *Canadian*, and *Globe*, our two most influential papers in Canada. A gentleman
of fortune whom my son met in the steamboat going to Toronto, who
was going to hunt in the Rocky Mountains with a large attendance of dogs
and servants, had three copies of the work, and promised to give Donald one. He spoke most highly of it and said that it was very popular
among all his friends.

I am rather curious to see it in print. With regard to 'Rachel Macgreg-
or,' I would not if I were you put – 'the Emigrants.' The ear of the
world, is tired of that word emigrant. Suppose you give simply the name of
the book, and add, 'Trifles from the Burthen of a Life.' The latter title is
at least a novelty. Were 'Practical jokes' ever inserted in the *Miscellany;*
or did the sketch entitled 'Matrimonial Speculations' answer? If you
thought two volumes would take with the *latter* title, I could soon copy for
you two tales longer than the preceeding for that purpose. All comic
enough, and all drawn from reality, if the public prefer laughter to tears
they ought to succeed. One of these stories I am now rewriting to send
you – Called 'Richard Redpath, or the Voluntary Slave.' – The incidents
of which, were related to me as *facts* by a West Indian Planter, whom I
met on board a Steam Boat in 1831.

I have not written another line of 'Geoffrey Moncton.' I feel so discouraged by the non success of *Mark* in England, that I had nearly come to
the determination never to write again. But our income is so limited, and

withal so precarious and hard to be collected from the lawyers – Many of whom owe us hundreds, and have never paid Mr. Moodie his fees for the last twelve years, that I am glad to lend what assistance I can to the general stock. The sum just received I hope will pay my two medical men for that long desperate illness which will remove a great weight from my mind. I have an *English* horror of being in debt, and cannot wear any article of clothing if it is unpaid for. You would laugh at all the poor Blue stocking's various daily employments. First, I rise at six, read a chapter to the children, with short appropriate prayers. Get breakfast ready with the assistance of one servant, all I can afford to keep. After that important business is discussed. I make my own bed and put my chamber neatly in order. Make bread, or pies as required. Give orders for dinner and sit down to write. By the time I have put down a few sentences on paper, the Irish help pops her head into the room, 'Please Mistress, you are wanted,' and this interruption is more or less continued until after dinner, when I get a little rest, take a walk, or sew *pro bono publico*. In the evening, I generally write until I go to bed as my eyes are not strong enough to sew by candle light. I have little time for reading, though I do continue to enjoy this luxury sometimes. When my eldest daughter is at home she generally helps me in the housekeeping. She also copies articles for me. But her health has been so delicate this Fall that I consented that she should first go for a visit to Mrs Sheriff Conger of Peterboro and from thence to Toronto to stay with my lovely Addie and her bonnie bairns. Katie is a noble looking handsome girl, very talented and as good as she looks. Our home is dull without her, who is the joy of all our hearts. My youngest son is the only one I have at home just now. He is an amiable boy of ten, and a little daughter of my sister Traill's, who I am sending to school. Donald is away at McGill College, Montreal attending medical lectures. This will cost us at least £100 out of our moderate means; and as the dear fellow looks to me to find him in the necessary evil, I am more anxious to see a book successful. He is so fond of me, that I know my labours of love, in his behalf, will be remembered when the hand that wrote, and the heart that vibrated, is dust. And he is worthy of every exertion on my part. Any Mother would be proud of this fine lad, with his handsome person and large brain. He has been very ill with Typhus fever in the hospital of the college, and his sickness will involve considerable additional expense. Thank God, he is still spared to me. To lose him would break my good husband's heart. There never was a man, more fondly attached to his family than Mr Moodie, or one more worthy of love and confidence.

I have been thinking over the plan of first selling M.S. in the United States, but after all, if you will always send the early proof sheets to 'De Witt and Davenport,' it may be the best to continue our present method. They have written a letter to me of overflowing thanks and tell me, that they will *certainly* remit 200 dollars to my order on the day of publication and *more* afterwards, if the work should be successful. If they keep good faith, and I do not mistrust them, I could scarcely do better. Besides, I should have to make two copies of every M.S. I could not do this. I have received several interesting letters from my eldest son in California but have not had leisure to copy them for you. In his last, he mentions a very curious circumstance.

It seems that three Americans lately murdered a Chinese. They were taken afterwards by the friends of the murdered man, and sent to Nevada City for trial. The court was sitting for 14 days and Dunbar says, that it was the most interesting trial that has taken place during his residence in the Country. The Judge it seems, refused to receive the evidence of the Chinese witnesses, on the plea, that they were uncivilized barbarians, who could swear away without any scruple the life of a white man. The China man in a great passion, swore that they were not only civilized, but that they were the *first discoverers of America*, and built all those ruined cities in South America which were now making such a noise in the world. In proof of which, he produced in Court, an ancient historical work in the Chinese tongue which was read by his interpreter, and which so thoroughly convinced both Judge and Jury, that they admitted the evidence and sentenced the murderer to be hung. If this should prove true, it is a very interesting fact. Dunbar, who was in Court during the trial, seems to entertain no doubts upon the subject.

I am exceedingly obliged to you for the new works you promised me. The fame of Mr. Reades[2] has already reached Canada. I have been reading the life of 'Margaret Fuller, Countess Ossoli.' It is an interesting record of a woman of great genius, though rather spoiled by its transcendentalism. Is not the womans' Rights movement, the most preposterous absurdity of the present day? If they would only let these ambitious masculines in petticoats, have their own way, the disease would soon cure itself; and the fair imbeciles regain their right senses and their proper position. Imagine a refined woman holding the plough, wielding the axe, or knocking down an ox. Faugh the idea is disgusting, worthy the wife of the old bug bear of our childhood, the giant Fee-faw-fum.

I'm afraid, that I am not *very* sorry for the non success of the Major's book. Between ourselves, the thing has no vitality, is in fact a *humbug*.

But it has got him a good berth in the Canada Company's service and the instruction of four hapless young Englishmen, in the mysteries of Canadian Agriculture, at the sum of £100 sterling each, per annum. I wish the limit of my papers would permit, to give you a picture which I lately received from my eldest daughter, who has been on a visit there; of the education in progress at the *Agricultural College*, as she calls it, and the gallant Major C[anadian] M[ilitia]'s method of tuition. It would shock all thinking people.

My *eldest sister*, is an extensive reviewer, and for many years followed it as a means of increasing her income. Hers is a *ready* and a *clever* pen. It is more than probable, that to her, both my brother and I, are indebted, he for the good, I for the bad reviews of our respective works. Could this be ascertained, and made known to the public, through some indifferent party, it would turn the tables upon the malevolent authors of these petty wrongs. It is however on a piece with all their conduct to me. My brother is dreadfully ridiculed by the Canadian press by adopting that absurd Major. One paper proclaims it snobbish another banters him on his love of titles, etc. And his book being entirely *one sided* has met with less favour than *Roughing It*. I have never heard from Reydon since the publication of the *latter* work.

Did you publish the work you had in contemplation by my sister A.?[3] I have never seen it advertised but then, I seldom get a sight of English papers. I saw one tolerably good review of *Clearings* not long ago in a London paper but I forget which. In pity to you, I must draw this long letter to a close. I meant to keep it within decent lengths, but have failed as usual. I will send 'Richard Redpath,' directly I get through with it. I am growing very lazy and hate the mechanical part of my task.

Mr Moodie unites with me in kindest and best wishes for your perfect restoration to health; and wishing that you, and all dear to you, may long enjoy together the kindly re unions of this festive season, believe me

Yours in all sincerity
Susanna Strickland [*sic*]

Dec. 30th – 1853 –

Received of Richard Bentley Esqre, Publisher in Ordinary to Her Majesty the Queen, the sum of Fifty Pounds Sterling, due to me on the publication of a work written by me, and published on shares by the said Richard

Bentley entitled *Life in the Clearings*. The said sum of fifty pounds fulfilling a part of the agreement determined upon, and drawn up between us.

> Susanna Moodie
> Belleville
> Upper Canada –

1 Susanna has received £50 half profits for *Life in the Clearings*, but presumably has not received her copy of the agreement of 10 June 1853; Bentley sent the requested copy, along with one for 'Flora,' on 10 February 1854.
2 Susanna had requested copies of Charles Reade's *Peg Woffington* (1853) and *Christie Johnstone* (1853).
3 'Lives of Royal and Celebrated Ladies' was the prospective title of a series Agnes was discussing with Bentley during 1853; the project was never brought to fruition.

---

53 To Dr Lister

Thursday evening
[January 1854]

Dear Doctor,

I should esteem it a great favour if you would send me your account for my illness last Oct. twelvemonth.[1] I may not perhaps be able to pay the whole, having been disappointed at present in the amount of money I expected to receive from London, and which has been delayed to my no small vexation from mail to mail until now. But I will give you all I can hoping for better luck next time. You *must not deny my request*. The debt of kindness I owe you, no money could pay. I only wish I had it in my power to repay it according to its desert, but I shall ever retain a grateful and affectionate remembrance of it. I know, that you wished to leave this to me. But that would be neither just to you nor me. Charge me what you think right, and I shall rejoice to send you the amount.

 With kindest regards and best wishes for the health and happiness of Mrs. Lister, the children, and all dear to you,

> I remain
> Yours most truly
> Susanna Moodie

1 Apparently the same illness reported to Bentley on 25 November 1852, thus dating this letter late 1853 or early 1854

54 To Richard Bentley

Jan. 30, 1854
Belleville

My Dear Mr. Bentley,   C.W.

I send you with this, the MS copy of a tale in one volume, entitled, 'Richard Redpath or the voluntary slave,' which I hope, may reach you in safety, and meet with your approval; and that of the public – of the *latter*, however, I feel very doubtful. When once a prejudice has arisen in the public mind, against a writer, it is very difficult for him, or her, to obtain fair play. The *Jew Editor*, is a true picture drawn from life, which so closely resembles the original, that it will be recognized by all who ever knew him, or fell under his lash. A man *detested* in his day and generation.

I likewise enclose for the *Miscellany* if admissable, two papers from the pen of my dear husband, and a sketch of my own.[1]

I likewise beg your acceptance of the last copy I possess, uncut, of a small volume of poems, published two months before I left England, on my own account. This little work, contains most of the poems written by me between the ages of 14 and 20. It was put to press by the particular request of some kind friends, who loved me well, and through whose influence, the edition of 500 copies, sold, paying its own expenses, and leaving me a profit of some 25 or 30 pounds. It was well reviewed by many of the best papers and magazines and I might have been tempted to try it again, had I not left England, and fallen into the troubles and trials which subsequently beset us. After my death these little poems may have an interest which at *present* they do *not possess*. They were the overflowing of a young warm heart, keenly alive to the beauties of creation, and to the sorrows of a very unhappy home. The latter influence, will account for the deep tone of melancholy that pervades most of them, for I wrote exactly as the spirit prompted me – as I felt.

You were pleased to say in one of your kind letters, that you liked my poems in *Roughing It*, and this led me to send you this long forgotten child of other, but not brighter years. As a wife and mother, I have been so blessed, that one day spent in the company of my dear white-haired husband, is worth all the joys and sorrows of those sad years of home.

I enclose the 'New Year's Address.'[2] You must know, that New Year's day is a great day in Canada. You must keep open house that day, and be dressed up to receive *all* who choose to come to eat cake and drink wine, tea or coffee with you. The gentlemen go round in their sleighs to wish the females in every house, (in their own class) the returns of the season. The bell and knockers are going from morning till night, and the bitterest enemies shake hands and meet on friendly terms. I like this custom. It is so hearty, and savours of the good old times. The Editors of all the papers have to furnish a 'New Year's Address' to their readers, in which the politics, characters, and actions of public men are very freely handled. Some of these New Year's addresses, are very amusing. My husband, in the one I send ...

1 Likely 'Practical Jokes: Wat Robinson,' in *Bentley's Miscellany* (1854), 393–9
2 This address, for 1 January 1854, must have appeared in the Hasting's *Chronicle* or Belleville *Intelligencer*, but neither is extant.

---

55 To Richard Bentley

Feb. 26, 1854
Belleville

My dear Sir,

You make me feel quite vain, by the flattering manner in which you are pleased to speak of my letters, and as I am not above the little weaknesses so common to my sex, I frankly confess, that your commendations so little deserved and so *unexpected*, gave me great pleasure.

It may be attended, however, with a very serious evil – by being the means of inflicting on your patience many more. I have long ceased to regard you as a man of business, and to value you as a friend, to whose kindness I have been indebted, to a far greater extent than I feel inclined to commit to paper. But enough of this. I write always what I think and feel, and it is a singular fact, that the little I have had to do with Gentlemen of your profession always ended in friendship, and my own experience of publishers, has greatly enhanced my estimate of them as men. To me, they have always acted honorably and generously, and I have little doubt that their good nature is severely tried by the suspicious vanity of some authors, and the overbearing pride of others.

Talking of the work you were negotiating with my sisters, has brought to my recollection, a scheme I contemplated long years ago, before I left England and when the research necessary to such an undertaking was in my power. This was to write a biographical work entitled 'The Memoirs of Royal Favorites.' What an interesting book it would be, if justice were done to such a subject.

Think of the strange vicissitudes of fortune, the tragic fate, the romantic situations, which the lives of these highly gifted but too often miserable pets of royalty would furnish. Several times, I wrote to both Agnes and Eliza Strickland, begging them to work out my idea, but they never deigned to notice the suggestion. With me, the thing is impossible. It would require reading and study, which it is out of my power, and at my age to give to it. But among the many unemployed men of genius in your great Metropolis, could you not find one to furnish such a biography? If well done, it ought to exceed in interest the most powerfully written fictions. 'What is so strong, so mournful as truth?'

The other day, my son sent to me a Canadian Newspaper, the half of which was occupied by long extracts from *Life in the Clearings*, copied from the Dublin *Warder*. They spoke well of it, and had continued their notice from a former paper, which I did not see, and ended by saying, 'We here close our long extracts from this shrewd and very agreeable volume.' Patience my dear Sir. We are struggling in deep water at present, but I feel a sort of conviction, that we shall swim yet. The next parcel I send by Express, I will copy my son's letters, and you can do what you please with them.

The *Major* has been staying with me for the last week. He is very sulky about his book, which he fancies from the many fine reviews upon it, must have an enormous sale. I did not undeceive him. He said that my sister A. had told him, that it was to be found on every table at home, and that its popularity was immense. His literary honours have sadly spoiled a naturally frank, goodnatured, but vain man, and made him pompous and arrogant, a sort of *he blue stocking*. In this country, I always *drop* the *profession*, and never allude to *authorship* ...

---

56 To Richard Bentley

My Dear Mr Bentley,

April 8, 1854
Belleville
U.C.

I trust the Bank business has been explained to the satisfaction of the parties in London, and that the blame, if there be any, rests entirely with the Bank of Upper Canada. You cannot imagine how vexed and annoyed I have been about it, lest you should think, that I could have done anything so dishonorable as to draw upon you for money without first acquainting you with the circumstance. But here let me assure you, that no sort of distress, not even starvation, (and thank God, at present there is no fear of that) would tempt me to do so. If I am proud at all, it is of that spirit of independence which has hitherto borne me through so many difficulties; and which can scarcely brook to ask a favour, however slight, from even a dear friend. It is this spirit, which makes me trust to the honour of those whom I esteem, with a child-like reliance, which the acute, wide-awake natives of this continent, can scarcely understand, and which to them, seems little short of folly. My dear husband, has teased me unmercifully about my distress on the Bank score; telling me, that he was sorry, that he had a warrant to take me to jail, for forgery, and then laughing unmercifully that I believed him.[1]

However, I am scribbling on as usual, without telling you the purport of my letter.

I received yesterday, a most *pathetic* letter, from Messrs De Witt and Davenport, entreating me to write to you, for the proof sheets of *Flora Lyndsay*, as they see that it is advertized for publication and they fear that some other American house will get the start of them, and what my dear Mr Bentley, more nearly concerns me, I shall lose the £50 they promised me. Now, between ourselves, I don't want to do this. My son being at College keeps me very poor, and this Yankee £50 would come very opportunely to pay his necessary expenses, so I hope that you will not disappoint the *Yankee gentlemen*, and your *humble petitioner will ever pray*, etc.

They have purchased from Putnam, (who by the by, is in difficulties;) the plates of *Roughing It*, and the right of publishing *Life in the Clearings*, from Messrs Stringer and Townsend, as they wish to be the sole publishers of my works in America.

I have not got the copies of the last work yet. My son called on Messrs Armour of Montreal, but the books had not arrived. He expected English books out soon, in three weeks, or a month. Perhaps mine will come with them. I have seen several good reviews of it in Canadian papers, and the Practical jokes are popular as Newspaper literature, both here, and in the States.[2]

I trust we shall succeed better by and by. I have finished another Story for 'Matrimonial Speculations,' and commenced the last and will send both, when concluded.

I think the two you have – 'Richard Redpath,' 'Rosamond Hartford, or Waiting for Dead Men's Shoes,' – and these two 'The Miss Greens' and 'Ariby Lockhart,' will make two good sized volumes. Perhaps three, as I hardly know to what length Ariby may run. 'The Miss Greens' – which is a true story, and a very laughable one, only takes 50, closely written foolscap pages. Ariby will not be less than 100.[3]

Perhaps these comic stories may please the public better, than the tragic ones. There is something in my character which always leads me to extremes. 'From the sublime to the ridiculous,' as Napolean truly said, 'is but a step.' I will not conclude this scrawl until I see if tomorrow's mail brings me a letter from you.

Saturday/ No mail from England yet, and I must not delay this, as I promised the New York Gentlemen to write to you.

May I request a little favour of you. If you have at any time, any Newspapers to spare, after reading them, they would be thankfully received; especially any, that said bad or good, of my poor works. The postage to the Colony is so trifling that I would joyfully pay it, to gratify my curiosity – *vanity* perhaps would be the truer word, but in this world of humbug people are afraid to speak the honest truth.

We have had a very mild winter, too mild for Canada. The spring, however, is long in coming. The ice still remains on the Bay. The Steamboats are generally running to and fro, to Kingston by the first of April. It will be the middle of the month before they start this year.

News of the war comes slowly. Most heartily I wish the Czar to be well beaten, yet, I have a sort of prophetic fear that the Turkish Empire totters to its fall. The spirit of Peace seems about to quit the earth for awhile and all nations are ready to start to arms.[4] It is a strange time this. I have been reading Judge Edmonds' strange book on the Spirit-rappings. There are some beautiful things in it, and some too absurd for a maniac with his eyes open to credit.

For instance. It is demanded of Lord Bacon, to describe a place of future punishment, and the spirit gets out of the horns of that dilemma saying, that as he never was there he can tell nothing about it. This is almost replied as if he told the Judge to go to __ and enquire for himself. For if he was as wise a spirit in the Spheres as he was while on earth, he must have felt some curiosity on such an important subject. Then he uses common Yankeeisms, such as '*Considerable* sick this evening,' 'I *guess*,' and oh, worse still, 'I feel *it some*.' Fye upon Lord B. And now farewell my dear friend, with kind regards to you and all dear to you, in which my dear husband heartily joins, I remain

Yours most truly
Susanna Moodie

I forgot to tender my best thanks for the trouble you took about my little books, for which indeed I feel greatly indebted.

1 On 10 February Bentley had written, advising her that his account with the bankers, Herries and Co., had been drawn on twice for the sum of £50 for *Life in the Clearings*, once on 29 December 1853 and again on 9 January, the first being duly signed by Susanna, the second appearing to be a forgery. A double processing or reproduction of the withdrawal voucher within the Bank of Upper Canada system seems to have caused the problem; one voucher was dated at Belleville, the other at Toronto.
2 *Flora Lyndsay* had been published only within the last two weeks, on 27 March, too soon to have been reviewed in Canadian papers. Susanna refers here to reviews of *Life in the Clearings*; she had not yet received her copies of the book itself.
3 'Ariby Lockhart' was likely not completed; *Matrimonial Speculations*, published as a single volume 28 October 1854, is comprised of 'Waiting for Dead Men's Shoes,' 'The Miss Greens,' and 'Richard Redpath.'
4 The Crimean War (1853–6): Russia recognized the Turkish-held states of Moldavia and Walachia in July 1853; Turkey declared war on Russia in October, and France and England entered the conflict on Turkey's side in March 1854.

---

57 To Catharine Parr Traill
Belleville,
April 23, 1854

My dear Sister

I have at last got my dear girl home,[1] but she looks very pale and thin, with a loud, dry harassing cough. Her illness during the winter has given her constitution such a shock that I fear she will hardly if ever get over it. Since her return she has rallied a little, and I will try and hope that with care she may yet be spared to us for a little. She left Addie somewhat better, and the little ones quite well and flourishing. Charles[2] has come in for some small property that belonged to his mother about a 1000 – or so; which will enable him to buy a house and furnish it, which will really add to the comfort of the dear child, as they have to pay 60£ per annum for the one they are in.

I got your letter this morning but was sorry to find that your spirits were still so low – I was hoping that you would have got at least 10£ for the butter prize. It was shabby pay. As to M'Clear, the type in which he printed your articles, being two sizes smaller than *the rest*, ought to have shown you, what confidence could be placed in his honor or honesty. Let us hope that the *Old Countryman* will pay you better. They say that his paper takes.[3] I never mean to write for Canadian paper or magazine again, after their unjust abuse of me.

Talking of magazines. I was earnestly entreated the other day in a most polite letter, signed William Morin, to write for a first class literary paper in *San Francisco* – promising liberal *payment*.

But how could I enforce it? I am by no means ambitious of spreading my name so far. However, I *gave* him a song for the Times, and asked him to send the paper, which indeed, I feel rather curious to see.

Talking of San Francisco, reminds me, that we have had two letters from dear Dunbar, one for me, and the other for Addy.

The poor fellow, has lost all the money he had made, and has to work hard to help pay up the Company's debts, to which he belongs, they having sunk in their last mining speculation, all their savings, and run in debt to the amount of 500$. He seems rather dejected and talks of leaving the hill mines, and going to *Oregon*. It seems, that one of their company, got a hint, from some quarter, that gold was to be found in large quantities there; and started, with forty dollars in his pocket and six months provision. They all thought he was going upon a wild goose chase; but a few days before Dunbar wrote to me they received a letter from their old comrade, informing them, that he had found the place, and had made from the first of last November until the first of December, 15,000 dollars.

That two half breeds, in that time had taken out 100 weight of gold. That for 100 miles north of the coast a man might earn from 50 to 100 dollars per day. He begged them to lose no time in following him, and he would give them his claims.

Dunbar and the rest were still unwilling to go without further evidence of the fact. However, one of their company, a fine young man of the name of Hathaway volunteered to go, and see if it was as the other stated, and if his account corresponds, they will all leave for Oregon – Dunbar says – That Hathaway is an honorable high minded fellow who scorns to utter a falsehood or do a mean thing. He would die rather than deceive them. Dunbar is keeping a journal of his adventures and will make notes of what he sees in that far off, and almost unexplored region. May God grant him success.

… speak for herself. Katie sends her love and begs me to say all sorts of kind things to Aunt Traill. Remember me to dear brother T. I was sorry to hear that he was suffering. He must come and see Belleville and his little girl soon to cheer him.[4] Adieu my dear Katie with affectionate love to yourself and all at home, believe me ever yours

Susanna

1 Katie
2 Charles Fitzgibbon

3 The Rev. Henry Hope: *The Canadian Settler's Guide* (Toronto: Old Countryman Office 1855), a new edition of *The Female Emigrant's Guide* published by Thomas Maclear in 1854
4 Mary Traill

58 To Richard Bentley

June 11th – 1855 –
Belleville

My dear Mr. Bentley,

U.C. –

Your letter of the 14th of Dec – reached me yesterday. It had been long and anxiously looked for. Accept my best thanks for it, and the permission granted to me, to draw upon you for the sum of 50 pounds due to me from the publication of *Flora Lyndsay*. This I did, this morning through the *Montreal* Bank, The Upper Canada Bank not discounting until the end of the month.

De Witt and Davenport, apprize me of the arrival of the advance sheets of *Matrimonial Speculations* some time ago. Not expecting the publication of the M.S. until we had come to some agreement as to the terms of publication, I had omitted making any arrangement with these Gentlemen for the reprint, as I was afraid of committing the name of the work to the American public before it had been advertised in London.[1]

They promise to act fairly and honourably by me; and I am inclined to trust to their promises; but it would have been more satisfactory to have it a regular business transaction in black and white.

They do not publish for some time as they do not wish to divert the public attention from *Life in the Clearings* just yet. It has a great sale, and has exceeded our expectations – 1500 copies have been sold in Montreal by Sadlier's, Armour's, and another house whose name I forget. One house in Belleville has sold over 200, and the American bookseller, here, in the like ratio. Now, supposing that Bytown, Brockville, Kingston, Cobourg, Peterborough, Toronto, Hamilton, Godrich, Guelph, and London, have had an equal sale, De Witt and Davenport, must have repaid themselves in Canada, alone, for the reproduction of the work. Particularly, as they paid me nothing for the right of publication, which they purchased from Stringer and Townsend, who bought it from Harper.

And now dear Mr Bentley, I must tell you the honest truth, that I never would have published any work on the bare chance of half profits. I have been told by many authors, that no money is ever realized by the writer on these terms, and I feel that my winter's work had been lost.

You will doubtless do your best to serve me, but as my works do not appear to please the English public, what chance have I of obtaining any profits? No, it will be far better for me, to try and sell copyright in the States, where I have a large reputation, and my books do sell, and sell well. Why even Canada would afford a better market.

I have not finished *Geoffrey* because I feel greatly discouraged; and I could not consent to publish it on a bare possibility of ever repaying myself for the time bestowed upon it.

It would really grieve me if our present literary connexion were dissolved (our *friendship*, I hope never will be) but if I could realize more from America than England I should consider it my duty to give the preference to the former, as long as my labours were necessary to the education, and well being of my family.

But I will not write longer on this subject, but turn to a more gracious one. You delight me with the accounts you give of your improved health, of the blessings you enjoy in such an excellent and promising *army* of sons; with society of wife and daughters, to add life and happiness to such a charming home. I see your gardens and lawns in my mind's eye.[2] The noble trees (Dear old English trees) reflected in those calm fish ponds, and can smell the violets in the grass, and delight in the – *'Wee modest crimson tipped flower*,' which spangles with living gems the green velvet turf.

You need not covet the anxiety and turmoil of business in such a paradise, but bless the Eternal Father, who has afforded you such a delicious retreat in the evening of life.

There are no plants or shrubs here, which are unknown to the gardener at home. Canada is not the land which Flora delights to crown with choice flowers. Our prettiest wild blossoms are violets, yellow, white, and blue. Beautiful in shape and color, but perfectly scentless. I would not give our charming little violet with its exquisite perfume for them all. There are some pretty shrubs and creepers in the woods, but they will not bear the transplanting into the native gardens. The shade, and the peculiar soil covered with dead leaves, seems indispensable to their life. I have found the wild Hepaticas, white and blue, do very well in the garden, but these flourish already in England in a high state of improvement, and are far more beautiful than here. The Cardinal flower, and French willow, as we call the same plant at home, are both wild here. The former adds great brilliancy to the shores of our lakes and rivers. The turk's cap and tiger lily, of two varieties, are wild flowers here. The exquisitely beautiful Mocasin plant, both yellow and white, I have often

transplanted, but without success, also the breeches plant, but they
will not grow out of their respective localities. The purple and white lych-
nadiaes they call *primroses* here, though nothing can be more unlike –
The Canadian flower, growing in bunches, on the top of a long stalk, and
in color of a vivid blue-lilac. The perfume is, however, very similar to
the darling of our mossy banks at home, and it is one of our first spring
blossoms, making glad the wilderness, and especially rejoicing in
swamps, where it literally covers the ground.

I never could procure the seeds of the native flowers, perhaps from not
knowing the proper time to gather them in. We have few ornamental
trees. The Rock Elm, is the most picturesque tree in the world, beautiful
and graceful in the extreme, and makes a fine object both in the landscape and, in the works of the artist, but it is of very *slow* growth. I
planted one in my little garden eight years ago, and though healthy and
flourishing it is still a mere switch, not so thick as my little finger. The
butter nut and hickory are handsome trees. The spruce, the hemlock
and the balsam, but you have all these in the nurseries at home. I could,
send you plenty of hickory and butternuts if you wish to rear them from
seed. And now while I am on the subject of trees, I must tell you, that
there is an Artist here, a Mr. Whitefield, who is going through the
country taking sketches on all our picturesque water.[3] His views are the
most truthful, and beautifully executed. He has several hundred of
them, with which he intends to make a pictorical work on the Canadas.
He asked me as a favor, when ...

1 For no apparent reason, De Witt and Davenport did not publish the book. *Matrimonial
  Speculations* was the only one of her books of the 1850s not printed in the United
  States.
2 In 1853, for reasons of health and failing eyesight, Richard Bentley retired with his wife to
  their retreat at Croydon to live, as the *Dictionary of National Biography* puts it, in
  'cultivated ease.' He still kept an active hand in the business, though in an irregular way,
  as is indicated by his interest in Susanna until his death.
3 Edwin Whitefield (1816–92), American painter, lithographer, and author, visited Canada
  in 1854 to make drawings and paintings of Canadian scenery from Niagara Falls to
  Tadoussac, en route visiting Toronto, Port Hope, Belleville, Montreal, and many other
  places. See J. Russell Harper, *Early Printers and Engravers in Canada* (Toronto:
  University of Toronto Press 1970).

---

59 To Richard Bentley   [autumn 1855]

Mr Doran's book has been very much cut up by the New York *Albion*.
(That is, his *Habits and Men*.) The other, is not yet out in America.

Messrs D[e Witt] and D[avenport] have just sent me an excellent work published by their house, *Scenes from the Practice of a New York Surgeon.*[1] I hope it may be popular. It deserves to be so. It is a terrible book, and contains terrible truths, though written by a merciful hand, and it should apply to many European females as practically, as it does to the fragile dark-eyed women of America.

Are they not lovely when very young? with those slender classical features. The dark lustrous eyes and delicate rose tinted cheeks and beautiful mouth. What a pity it is, they fade and fall so soon. The victims of fashion and frivolity not of climate or inherent organic disease. Our Canadian women of the second generation are just as delicate and short lived from the same cause. They turn night into day. Take no healthful exercise and eat the most unwholesome food and expect poor creatures to retain their vigor and good looks.

We have had a delightful Fall to repay us for our wet June and July. The country has been very healthy and though I suffered during the greater part of August with intermittent fever, there were few cases of sickness in the town and neighbourhood.

Since I last wrote you, I have had several visits from Miss Kate Fox the celebrated Spirit Rapper, who is a very lovely intellectual looking girl, with the most beautiful eyes I ever saw in a human head. Not black, but a sort of dark purple. She is certainly a witch, for you cannot help looking into the dreamy depths of those sweet violet eyes till you feel magnitized by them. The expression of her face is sad even to melancholy, but sweetly feminine. I do not believe that the raps are produced by spirits that have been of this world, but I cannot believe that she, with her pure spiritual face is capable of deceiving. She certainly does not procure these mysterious sounds by foot or hand, and though I cannot help thinking that they emanate from her mind and that she is herself the spirit, I believe she is perfectly unconscious of it herself. But to make you understand more about it, I had better describe the scene first prefacing it, with my being a great sceptic on the subject, and therefore as a consequence of my doubts anxious to investigate it to the bottom.

Miss Fox has near relatives in this place to whom Mr Moodie had expressed a wish to see the fair Kate should she again visit our town.

One morning about three weeks since, I was alone in the drawing room, when my servant girl announced Miss F and her cousin. I had seen her the summer before for a few minutes in the street, and was so much charmed with her face and her manners that it was with pleasure I met her again. After some conversation on the subject of the raps, she said, 'Would you like to hear them.' I said, 'yes, very much indeed, as it would confirm or do away with my doubts.' She then, asked the spirits if they would communicate with Mrs M__ which being replied to, by three loud raps upon the table, which in *spirit language* means yes, I was fairly introduced to these mysterious visitors.

Miss F. told me to write a list of names of dead and living friends, but neither to read them to her, nor to allow her to see them. I did this upon one side of a quire of paper, the whole thickness being between her and me; writing with her back to me.

She told me to run my pen along the list, and as a test the spirits would rap five times for every dead, and three times for every living, friend.

I inwardly smiled at this. Yet strange to say, they never once missed. I then wrote under the name of poor Anna Laura Harral, a daughter of Mr Thos. Harral who was for several years Editor of *La Belle Assemblée*, who had been one of the friends of my girlhood, 'Why did you not keep your promise.'

This promise having been a solemn compact made between us in the days of youth and romance, that the one who died first should appear if possible to the other. The answer to my unseen written question was immediately rapped out, 'I have often tried to make my presence known to you.' I was startled, but wrote again, 'if so rap out your name.' It was instantly done. Perhaps no one but myself on the whole American continent knew that such a person had ever existed.

I did not then ask more questions, Nor did Miss Fox know what I had asked. She told me to lay my hand upon the table and ask the spirit to rap under it. This I did. The table vibrated under my hand as if it was endowed with life. We then went to the door. Miss Fox, told me to open the door and stand so that I could see both sides at once. The raps were on the opposite side to my hand. The door shook and vibrated. Miss F. had one hand laid by mine on the door. I am certain that the sounds were not made by hands or feet. We then went into the garden. She made me stand on the earth. The raps were under my feet, distinct and loud. I then stood on a shallow rock under the window. The raps sounded hollow on the stone pavement under me. Her hand slightly pressed my arm. The strange vibrations of the knocks was to me the most unaccountable. It seemed as if a mysterious life was infused into the object from which the knocks proceeded. 'Are you still unbelieving.' 'I think these knocks are made by your spirit, and not by the dead.'

'You attribute more power to me than I possess. Would you believe if you heard that piano, closed as it is play a tune.'

'I should like to hear it –' I did not however, hear it that morning, but two nights after, in the same room. I heard the strings of that piano accompany Mr Moodie upon the flute, Miss Fox and I, standing by the piano, with a hand of each resting upon it. Now it is certain, that she could not have got within the case of the piano.

Mr Moodie had on a mourning ring with his grandmother's hair. On the inside of the ring was engraved her birth death etc. He asked the spirits to tell him what was inside that ring, and the date of birth and death were rapped out, he had to take off the ring, having forgotten the date himself, to see if it was correct and found it so.

I thought I would puzzle them, and asked for them to rap out my fathers name, The date of his birth and death, which was rather a singular one from the constant recurrence of one figure. He was born Dec. 8th. I did not know myself in what year, was 58 when he died, which happened the 18th of May of 1818, to my astonishment all this was rapped out. His name. The disease of which he died (gout in the stomach) and the city, (Norwich), where he died. The question being mental could not have been guessed by any person of common powers. But she may be Clairvoyant, and able to read unwritten thoughts. I have not time just now to give you more on this subject, and though still as great a sceptic as to the spiritual nature of the thing, the intelligence conveyed is unaccountable.

Can such a thing as witchcraft really exist? Or possession by evil spirits? I am bewildered and know not what to answer.

I saw the death of Mr Colborne in the papers. He did not behave very liberally to my sister I believe.[2] I never had any knowledge of him myself.

It is very late, the lights are all out, the town silent once more. Adieu my dear friend. God bless you good night. May the Lord prosper you is the sincere wish, of yours truly

Susanna Moodie

1 Autumn seems likely because of references to 'a delightful Fall' and to the death of Henry Colburn, 6 August 1855. John Doran's 'other' book is *Lives of the Queens of England of the House of Hanover*, 2 vols. (London: Richard Bentley 1855). *Scenes in the Practice of a New York Surgeon*, by Edward H. Dixon, MD (New York: De Witt and Davenport 1855); Dixon edited a literary medical journal, *The Scalpel*, and his book appears to be a compilation of sketches from it.
2 Originally profits on *Lives of the Queens of England* were to be shared equally; when, however, after publication of two volumes Agnes had received no payment, work was halted and Elizabeth Strickland renegotiated the agreement, with Colburn guaranteeing £150 per volume.

60 To Richard Bentley

My dear Friend,

Belleville
County Hastings
U.C.
Dec. 8th 1855

Owing to a misdirection in your last, it was some time travelling round to
its proper destination, and never reached me until the latter end of this
week. I was glad to see that you were able to write to me, and as you say
nothing respecting your health, I drew from it, a favourable augury,
that your health remained tolerably well.

I wish I could give you as good a bill of ours. My son Donald, has been
very ill with typhus fever, and I write this from his sick room, in which, I
have been a constant tenant night and day for the last month. Last night,
was the first night I have slept in my bed, and out of my clothes for that
period, and as no fire is allowed in his room, and the season is winter
here, you may form some estimate of the amount of fatigue I have
endured. But it is a poor Mother, who cannot nurse her own child, and my
invalid, although upwards of six feet in height, and as fine a young
man, as you could well see, has been as helpless as an infant in the
month. The dread of infection from these fevers is so great, that you
cannot get a servant to enter the room, or render you the least assistance.
The most menial offices must be performed by those who for love and
duty, dare all risks. Unfortunately, for me, my dear husband was ill, and
suffering from severe inflamation of the ears at the same time, and my
niece, Annie a daughter of my sister Traill's, who has been with me since
the marriage of Katie, was confined to her bed with Neuralgia in the
jaw, and had she been well, I would not have exposed the dear girl to
infection. It has pleased God to restore my dear boy to my prayers, and
he is sitting up for the first time today, but only a few paces from his bed. I
feel quite proud of my nurseling, and he, poor fellow, can scarcely bear
the 'old Mother' out of his sight. Many anxious hours have we spent
together for the last seven weeks, the term of his illness, and I trust it
will be for our mutual benefit. These afflictions though hard to bear, are
never sent to us in vain.

I hope all the works you are about to publish may prove to you a mine
of wealth. I suppose by this time, you have received the advance sheets
of *Geoffrey Moncton*. But if you should publish it, pray for my sake and in
the name of all good taste, repress the second title, *The Faithless Guardian*. Does it not savour of the old Minerva Press.[1] In the mean while,

Geoffrey has been highly spoken of in all the Canadian papers as *the best* of all my writings. I hope you will think so too, and that you will find it just the book you wanted me to write. 'The First Debt,'[2] which I have commenced transcribing is really a good story, but this illness had hindered all my literary work. I trust soon to be emancipated from a sick room and then I must take up the pen in earnest.

The works, you told me in a former letter, you had sent to me, of Dr. Doran's, have not reached me. *Habits and Men*, has been cut up in some of the American papers. I do not wonder at the success of Dickens. His beauties lie in exquisite touches of nature that go home to the heart. He finds these flowers of the heart scattered more plentifully along the dusty highways of life, and when he leaves the old broad track of humanity, for courtly halls and palaces, his descriptions lose all their touching truth and pathos. *Bleak House*, abounds in absurdities but it possesses a thousand redeeming beauties; and with all its faults, is a wonderful book. All his works abound in splendid portraits. People we all fancy that we have heard and seen. In these admirable delineations of every day life, lies the strength of Dickens as a writer. His fame like many of the great events in history, has been made up of trifles. His *Oliver Twist* is to me – the finest of his works. It is full of tragic interest. A Shakesperian power, that lives in the mind like reality, and leaves good fruit behind it. That book has done much good in the world, and every benevolent mind, must feel grateful to the author. Thackery, has more wit than Dickens. But his works never leave a happy memory behind them. You read and laugh. But the laugh is not that of mirth. It is a bitter satirical laugh against the faults of your neighbours, that they are so well hit off. But it does you no moral good, and you feel ashamed of yourself for being so much amused at the expense of others. I am angry with myself for enjoying Thackery so much. He is a literary giant, but one that makes you afraid.

What do you think of Tennyson's 'Maud'? Is it not (with only a few exceptions), a ridiculous rhapsody of affectation. Ye Gods! – No wonder poetry is out of fashion, when such Hurdy-Gurdy trash, passes current as such. I think the poet Laureate and Longfellow, should shake hands. But really *Hiawatha* is the most readable absurdity of the two. I must not tire your patience with all this tittle tattle about my betters, which will remind you of a gnat trying to sting an Eliphant – But draw this long hastily written letter to a conclusion. Do write and let me know your opinion of *Geoffrey Moncton*. I shall be very anxious to hear what you think of it.

Mr. Moodie unites with me in kind regards and all the compliments of the approaching festive season. I remain My dear Friend,

truly Yours

Susanna Moodie

1 William Lane (1738–1814) established at Leadenhall Street in London a successful publishing business he named the Minerva Press, specializing in Gothic romances.
2 'The First Debt. A Tale of Every Day,' another of the long stories she loosely called her 'Tales of a Canadian Winter Hearth,' appeared in the *Literary Garland* in eight instalments, April-November 1841.

---

61 To Richard Bentley

Belleville
Jan 22, 1856 –

My dear Friend,

Many happy and prosperous years to you and yours. May all the dark shadows of sorrow and trial flee before the sun of the present year, and leave the rest as a tale that is told.

I got your kind letter, by today's mail, and am really glad, that you are to be the English literary father of my *Geoffrey*. You have long ere this, got my last letter, written beside the sick bed of my poor boy. Thank God, he has restored, this fine promising lad once more to our hearts and hopes, and he has been able to return to his studies at McGill College. So the new year has dawned auspiciously for me, and the dead as it were, has been restored to me in life. This Donald, if he lives, will I hope, be somewhat in his native land. With great personal beauty, he unites that natural winning frankness of manner, which reaches all hearts. I never knew any one so popular with persons of all grades, and his talents are of a high order. My only fear, arises, from the attention and flattery he meets with every where. Which is enough to turn wiser heads than belong to boys of nineteen. The close attendance in his sick room, materially affected my own health, which is only now recovering from seven weeks of intense anxiety and bodily fatigue.

Geoffrey is selling magnificently in the States and in Canada. The reviews in both countries, have been unanimous in their opinion, that it is my best book. I enclose one from the New York *Tribune*, which I happen to have by me. Yet, it is far from the most flattering, that have been sent me. Mr De Witt, in his last letter, received the first of this month, says,

'*Monctons* has been splendidly noticed by the American press. It has only been out a month, and we have nearly sold the 5000 copies, and have every reason to expect, that it will greatly exceed that number.'

This is very gratifying to me, coming as it does, unsolicited from the publishers, who though rough men, seem liberal and true, as I have found all publishers with whom I have had any dealings. I only hope, that the English sale of the work, for both our sakes, may be as good. The work I am copying for De Witt and Davenport, though very different in its nature, is quite equal to *Geoffrey*. By many readers would be considered superior, it will be nearly 200 pages more.

And now dear Mr Bentley, let me thank you most sincerely for the pleasure you have afforded me, in sending me Dr Doran's books. They are the most amusing volumes I have read for a long while. It is quite a new idea, to write of Kings and Queens with as much familiarity as if they were commoners, and Dr. Doran, makes me bless my stars, that I belong to the latter class. We have little reason to be proud of this Hanoverian race, if all that he records of them, be true. What a mean contemptible wretch, he makes George the fourth. What an unfortunate vulgar woman his ill fated wife.[1] Well, Our Victoria is a great improvement on this selfish race. But the palmy days of crowned heads are on the wane. Yet, a few years, and all the earth will be republican. When you read Dr Doran's books, one is apt to exclaim, 'God hasten the time, If such heartless, brainless creatures are our rulers.' I have not seen Macawleys last volumes.[2] They have been a good deal cut up in the States. I read a splendid review of *Philip the II*. Long extracts were given, and the style struck me as perfection. I shall try and get it directly it is out in the States.[3] I have been reading one of the noblest books ever penned by a man, and which, I must believe, is written under *Divine inspiration*. It is called *The Healing of the Nations*, Edited by Gov. Tallmadge, with a short biography of the inspired author, a very young man. I am no friend of spiritualism, but I cannot doubt for a moment the truth of this wonderful book. Oh do get it, and read it, and tell me your opinion of it. I cannot describe the delight it has given me. I do not think that any person, who even thought upon the sublime subjects of which it treats, can read it with dry eyes, or an untouched heart. I have read Professor Hare's book. He reasons well, but ignores the truth of Revelation, in doing which, he is not aware that he is aiming a deadly blow, at the subject he so ably defends. What is hard to believe in Holy Writ is still harder to believe in these modern miracles. Hare's book has made a wonderful sensation in the States. Still greater than Judge Edmonds's and Capron's, both of which, are strangely fascinating books. But I cannot believe in them. Though in constant correspondence with Kate Fox, their great medium. She is a beautiful talented creature, and writes charming letters, and I cannot look into her gentle pure face, and believe her false. By the way, I can make the same raps, with my great toes, ancles, wrist joints and elbows. I found this out by accident. A girl, who has lived servant with me several years, tried it also, and she exceeds me in the loudness of these noises. Which so perfectly resembles those produced by the Mediums, that it has greatly surprised me. But I have run to the end of my paper, and tired your patience. Will you send me a few copies of *Geoffrey*, when published, and if you can spare it, A copy of *Roughing It*. I want one for my son in California. With best regards to you and yours, in which my dear husband joins, believe me

> Yours truly
> Susanna Moodie

PS There are a few verbal mistakes in *Geoffrey*, which your men of business will easily detect. I hope you will put out the second title and the third. One, is quite sufficient. I read a story last week in the *Albion* from some English Review called 'The Monktons of (some Abbey' – I have forgot the name),[4] so it would be as well to stick to *Geoffrey*. But I leave this entirely to you. My terms were £50 sterling when published and 50 if you realized the sale of 500 copies. You see, I was right, in my estimate of the sale of it, in the States where novels and excitement are as necessary to the people as meat and drink. I could not forbear a smile, when you called *Geoffrey* dramatic. My first attempts at authorship, were *all tragedies*. On one of these, Mr. Young, the tragedian,[5] pronounced a very high opinion, although I was but a child of 14. I was persuaded by foolish fanaticks, with whom I got entangled, to burn these MSS, it being they said unworthy of a christian to write for the stage. 'Henrie,' 'The Bride of Brittany,' and 'Bourbon' were, perhaps, the best things I ever wrote that perished in this auto da fe. The little headings in blank verse, that often occur in my books are snatches that memory retains of these tragedies. Nature certainly meant me for a dramatic writer, and having outlived my folly, I really regret the martyrdom of these vigourous children of my young brain. Don't *laugh at me*. That portion of my life, would make a strange revelation of sectarianism. But it may rest with my poor tragedies in oblivion. I do not wish it to meet with their firey dooms or the ridicule of the world.[6] Will you oblige me by sending a copy of *Geoffrey* to my dear friend Miss Gooding of Cromers, ditto to John Bruce Esqr. You can deduct them from the number you send to me. Is not Dr. Doran's *Habit and Men*, dedicated to the same Mr. Bruce?[7] I never hear from *Reydon*, now. They have ignored me and my books. My sister Traill, is publishing a juvenile work, with Hall and Virtue's establishment, for which she receives 25 pounds.[8] This is not much, with Agnes' weight in literature, to back her. How does the Major's book sell now? If fine reviews could sell a work, his should have brought a fortune.

Once more, adieu. Many happy years and successful, may providence have in store for you. I pity you the reading of this.

SM

What an odd thing is memory. I have just remembered the title of that book – 'The Monktons of Wincot Abbey.'

1 Queen Caroline, whom George IV had married in 1795 while regent, and whom he wished to divorce. Following the death of George III in 1820, the new king asked his ministers to begin divorce proceedings, seeking to charge Caroline with scandalous conduct. In the popular mind, however, the queen was considered wronged and she entered London in triumph in June 1820. Public inquiry into her conduct lasted from 17 August to early November, but the divorce bill failed to pass the Commons. She was, however, refused admission to the coronation of George IV.

2 T.B. Macaulay's *History of England from the Accession of James II*; volumes III and IV were published in London in 1855 by Longman's, and by Harper and Brothers in New York in 1855 and 1856.

3 W.H. Prescott's *History of the Reign of Philip II of Spain*, 2 vols. (Boston: Phillips, Sampson and Co. 1855); his work was published first in England by Bentley.

4 'The Monktons of Wincot Abbey,' edited by Wilkie Collins, appeared in the *Albion* in three parts: (22 December 1855), 603–5; (29 December), 615–17; and (5 January 1856), 3–4.

5 Charles Mayne Young (1777–1856), a nineteenth-century actor, first graced the London stage in 1801; he acted in Mitford's *Foscari* at Covent Garden in 1826.

6 The burning of manuscripts may have occurred earlier than her conversion in 1830 for there is nothing about Ritchie in the letters to suggest such hostility to literary endeavour on his part, nor any reference to writing for the stage in her correspondence with the Birds.

7 Doran's *Lives of the Queens of England of the House of Hanover* was dedicated to Bruce, *Habits and Men* to Henry Holden Frankum.

8 *Lady Mary and Her Nurse; or, a Peep into the Canadian Forest* (London: Hall, Virtue and Co. 1856)

62 To Charles Sangster

Belleville
July 28 /56

Sir,[1]

Accept my sincere thanks for the volume of beautiful poems with which you have favoured me. If the world receives them with as much pleasure as they have been read by me, your name will rank high among the gifted sons of song.

If a native of Canada, she may well be proud of her bard, who has sung in such lofty strains the natural beauties of her native land. Wishing you all the fame you so richly deserve, I subscribe myself your sincere admirer.

Susanna Moodie

1 Charles Sangster (1822–93): his first book was *The St. Lawrence and the Saguenay, and Other Poems* (Kingston: Creighton-Duff 1856).

63 To Catharine Parr Traill

Belleville,
July 30/56

My dear Catharine,

I have a few minutes to spare today and I seize upon them to write to you although too late for todays post – for I fear I should not be able to another day.

The tone of your letter was sad enough and came to a sad heart, for I knew my poor girl was weeping over the pale little thing that a few hours before was her loved and beautiful baby and my own heart mourned with her to whom the vision of death had become a terrible reality. The Saturday before poor little Eliza[1] died both babies were christened. Maria Tully and Mrs. Strickland[2] standing for Addies, Moodie as proxy for Dunbar. It was named Eliza Dunbar after Moodie's Mother. The little creature laughed and crowed all the time and patted its grandfather's white beard whose heart embraced the child and clung to it from the moment he saw it. Katie's babe was christened Georgina Eliza, after Dr. and Mrs. Beatty who were its sponsors. It seems to have been a happy day for all parties. They went home to lunch with Katie and her kind husband and the children's health was drank in lots of champagne. Addie's child was in perfect health up to three o clock on Monday afternoon when it was seized with violent vomittings which continued until six the next morning when it expired. The poor Mother thinking it was past all danger. Her grief, has been most painful to witness, and Katie seems to feel it as much as her sister, besides suffering a nervous terror lest she should lose her own child, which fear seems to have sickened both her and the baby.

For the dear baby I do not grieve. It is happy, it is blessed. But I know what poor Aggy suffers and it is for these sufferings I grieve. The death of the child may have been sent in mercy to save the life of the Mother who dared not wean it in the hot weather and to whom the nursing was death. Papa will grieve when he hears the death of his little grandchild, for he admired her so much. She died the very day she completed her 5th month. It is strange that I awoke at the very period of the childs death, with a horror of blood on my mind. I thought I was drenched with it, swimming in it. That the floor, the bed, everything around me was red with it. The maid just then brought in a glass of iced water, which I generally take at six, before I get up, my mouth always being so dry and parched and I, full of my terrible dream, asked her what it could mean. She said 'Death' – and so it proved for I got Charles' telegraph before six that evening.

Moodie being absent I have had to bear the load of sad thoughts, which crowd my mind, without his kind sympathy always so dear to poor old Susie's heart.

He had been so worn and worried with business, that I had prevailed upon him to take a little trip for the benefit of his health – in fact, for change of scene and faces. To this he reluctantly consented went up to be at the Christening. Left for New York by the way of Oswego the Sunday before the child died, at which place he arrived in safety on the Monday evening. Found Joe Linder out, who received him with open arms and bore him off in triumph to Brooklyn, where he was on the 25th. He is delighted with Joe and his family. Joe is now head of the firm of Linder and Kingsley, 22 Broadway N.Y. The head partner having perished in the Pacific on his passage out. Joe is rapidly making a fortune. Settling thousands of pounds worth of goods by wholesale every day. M. was going to start with him for Boston by the evening train. His brothers George and Homer, are in business there George – a very wealthy merchant. From Boston, Papa takes the sea steamer for Portland, and

then home by the railroad to Montreal. I hope to see him before the end
of next week. Time lengthens into ages while he is away. Will age never
diminish my love for this man – No, thanks to my organs of adhesion
and obstinacy.[3] No one can accuse me of being fickle to those I love – for
he is as dear to me after five and twenty years of intercourse as he was
when we first met. The kind darling sent me a beautiful gold locket and
chain containing a capital likeness of himself. You would laugh to see
me regarding that white bearded face with the devotion of old times. The
old romance of my nature is not quite dead. The poetry of life still
lingers about my heart.

My Rob is home. Much the better for his trip to Toronto. Moodie will
be pleased when he returns, to receive a charming letter from young
Robert Heddle who thinks of coming out with a 'dear young wife,' a
daughter of Dr. Duguid of Kirkwall, to settle in Canada – I have taken
quite a love for him from his beautiful letter. It is strange, that Moodie's
Nephews seem to be thinking of him at last.

I am glad that you are pleased with Mr. Thoms – Mr. Bruce spoke so
highly of the whole family that I felt quite interested in him. Moodie
was to see some natural son of Mr. Dunbar's, who came out this summer,
and is in Kingston, on his return. These natural sons are a disgrace to
Scotch gentry, and form very disagreeable links in families. I don't know
what Papa thought of the young John Dunbar or whether he will bring
him up here – I hope not. A man of the name of Donald Swanson brought
him out, and came here about him. I don't know what was the result of
the conference. Tell Mary that her constant and silent admirer Archy
sends his love to her, and talks of paying her a visit, while he is spending his fortnights holiday with his sister – Mrs. Sorley in Seymour. Give
my love to the dear Annie, to kind James, brother T. and all my young
relatives. Not forgetting kind regards to Mr. Thoms and with love to your
dear self I remain truly and affectionately yours

Susanna Moodie

I enquired here for Gray's botany of the Northern States[4] but neither Duff
nor Harrison had such a book or I would have sent it to you. My eyes
have improved ever since I discontinued cold water to my head. Everybody here are taking trips to Portland to the sea side. Ah don't I envy them
but I cannot afford to go. I will try and get up to see Agnes when Papa
comes home. Adieu dearest God bless and keep you safe under the
shadow of his love – Farewell

1 Addie's (Agnes's) third daughter, Eliza Dunbar Fitzgibbon, born 24 February 1856, died
   unexpectedly just two days after the joint christening in Toronto, on 12 July 1856
   according to *The Moodie Book*, a family genealogy by the Marquis of Ruvigny and Raine-
   val, privately printed in 1906, and often wrong on the dates of the Canadian family. If,
   as reported here, the baby died in the early morning hours, she in fact died on 15 July. The
   discrepancy is likely the fault of the genealogy rather than the grandmother.
2 Maria Tully, Samuel Strickland's daughter who had married the Toronto architect Kivas
   Tully, and Samuel's third wife, Katharine Rackham Strickland.
3 An allusion to phrenology: according to George Combe's *A System of Phrenology* (1836),
   the 'Affective' organs of Adhesiveness were located at the back of the skull.
4 Asa Gray, *A Manual of the Botany of the Northern States* (New York: Wiley and Putnam
   1848)

64 To Richard Bentley

Belleville
August 19 /56

My dear Mr Bentley,

Your letter gave me great pleasure, though it did dash some of the hopes I
had entertained of the success of *Geoffrey* to the ground. I must content myself with the praise it has received in the States, for I find that with
the British public, I can never hope to be a favorite. Yet, self flattery
apart, I do think, that many works possessing less interest have gained a
wide circulation. Even, in poor, tame Canada this book has a great
popularity, and is considered my best. I now send you one *totally different*.[1] So different, that it may perchance please better. It is more like
'Noah Cotton'[2] than the others, but contains some *exciting scenes* which
indeed, I know not, how to write a story without. It must have interest
to me or I could not write it. I am a most excitable creature, and my mind
dies out without something to interest and awaken alternate feelings of
love and terror, for both are necessary, and I enjoy a storm, with all its
fearful grandeur, quite as much as a day of unclouded Canadian
beauty.

It is difficult to write a work of fiction, placing the scene in Canada,
without rousing up the whole country against me. Whatever locality I
chose, the people would insist, that my characters were *really* natives of
the place. That I had a malicious motive in shewing them up, and every
local idiom I made use of, to render such characters true to nature, would
be considered a national insult. You don't know the touchy nature of
the people. Vindictive, treacherous and dishonest, they always impute to
your words and actions the worst motives, and no abuse is too coarse

to express in their public journals, their hatred and defiance. Have I not already run the gauntlet with them? Will they ever forgive me for writing *Roughing It?* They know that it was the truth, but have I not been a mark for every vulgar editor of a village journal, throughout the length and breadth of the land to hurl a stone at, and point out as the enemy to Canada. Had I gained a fortune by that book, it would have been dearly earned by the constant annoyance I have experienced since its publication. If I write about this country again, it shall never be published till my head is under the sod.

I cannot tell you, how welcome the remittance was. It enabled me to help one very dear to me, in sickness and sorrow, when I had no other means of doing so. My best thanks – I might add, my blessing is yours. It is strange. I had a presentiment of that letter, and of its contents, the very day it reached me. Some angel whispered, 'You will hear from Mr Bentley to day, and you will get money to help *her,*' and so it was – and my gratitude to God was blended with thankfulness to you, as his agent.

I do sincerely rejoice in your improved health and prosperity. May both abound more and more.

At my age, death is always near, and his aspect loses much of its imaginary terrors, and instead of the stern destroyer, he becomes the Angel of life, holding in his raised hand the key of heaven. But to the young and beautiful, the fondly loved and dearly cherished, he is always dreadful – Accept my best thanks for the home news. I am glad that the author of *Christie Johnstone,* is in the field again. I greatly admired his *Peg Woffington.* His last, *Susan Merton,*[3] I have not seen.

If you approve of the 'Linhopes,' you can publish it on the old terms on which *Mark Hurdlestone* and *Clearings* were published. If you wish to purchase copyright – Give what you think it honestly worth. I trust entirely to what you think best. It contains more writing than any of the others. The old title 'The First Debt,' tells too much of the nature of the story, but you will be the best Judge of that. I will send it by Express some time this week, when I have again glanced over it. Mr Moodie has just returned from a tour for the benefit of his health in Yankee land. First to New York, thence to Boston, and Newport, and lastly to Portland where he remained for two weeks rejoicing in the sight of dear old ocean once more after an absence of 25 years – He unites with me in kindest regards, and believe me dear Mr. Bentley your sincere and grateful friend

Susanna Moodie

R. Bentley Esqre –

P.S. I expect my son from California this winter, if the insurection in that Province does not draw him in another direction. He speaks of the 'Vigilence Committee,' as the only hope of the country. 60000 persons of all hues and countries, attended Mr. King to his grave. Such an expression of popular indignation has scarcely a parallel. The Californians talk boldly of a separation from the States. Such a course once adopted, would in all probability, lead to the separation of North and South. A storm is gathering over the destinies of the great Republic. Let her look at home. She will have need of all her cunning to save herself. Our own political horizon is cloudy enough. The Feud between the protestants and their Catholic fellow subjects grows stronger every hour. I fear, that we shall have a fearful struggle for power between these hostile parties before long. Every thing points that way. An Union of all the British North American Provinces is the only thing that would save us. At present the free industrious, British population of Upper Canada are kept in a minority by the Catholic votes of Lower Canada, which is most injurious to the general interest and prosperity of the Colony. I don't know how it will all end. A general election is at hand. Never was any ministry detested like the present. I query whether any coalition, ever was popular either here, or at home.

[Additional postcript to
19 August 1856][4]

It is a glorious thing, when the just man triumphs over the malice of his enemies. I have suffered much mental anxiety lately. My dear Agnes lost her youngest child about three weeks ago. It died very suddenly of mortification of the brain, and was only ill a few hours. The child was very lovely, and the poor young Mother inconsolable. Alas, poor girl, she has been aroused from the excessive indulgence of grief, by the stern message sent of old by the Prophet, 'Set thine house in order, for thou shalt surely die' – She is suffering from Bronchitis to an alarming extent, and the Dr gives us very slight hopes of her recovery. While her babe lived, she was too much engrossed by it, to take any notice of her own failing health until the warning appears to have come too late. Her eldest little girl has been with me since the winter,[5] and is the delight of her grandfather's heart, and the beautiful mother comes to us this week, if she is able to bear the fatigue of so long a journey. Perhaps, (I shudder as I write it) only to die. Our meeting will be a sad one. She is only just 23, and until lately was the mother of four children. Her second little daughter Geraldine[6] is in a very poor way, and my daughter Katie tells me, that it will hardly survive the summer. Ah thus it is with life. We bask for a few days in the warm sunshine of domestic happiness and awake one morning, to find the shadow of death resting upon our own threshold.

1 'The First Debt,' now retitled 'The Linhopes'
2 First appeared in the *Literary Garland* (September-December 1851), later in *Flora Lyndsay*, II, chapters 7–23
3 Charles Reade is the author.
4 This fragment seems to be part of this letter because it refers to the death of little Eliza and because in her letter of 27 November Susanna says she has not written to Bentley for three months.
5 Mary Agnes Fitzgibbon (1851–1915) became a writer herself; her work includes *A Trip to Manitoba, or Roughing It on the Line* (Toronto 1880) and *A Veteran of 1812* (Toronto 1895).
6 Geraldine Fitzgibbon, born 31 October 1854

---

65 To Richard Bentley

Belleville
Nov 27, 1856

Dear Mr Bentley

Many cares and anxieties have hindered me from turning a thought upon literary matters, but now that three months have elapsed, since I despatched to you, the M.S. of the 'Linhopes' without receiving a line, to inform me of its safe arrival, I begin to fear that it has been lost. This will be more unfortunate, as I have no complete copy of the original, and cannot recollect the portions of the tale that were added in the transcribing.[1] Did you ever send me any copies of *Geoffrey*. If so, they never have reached me. I should like a few copies of the English edition of the work.

When I last wrote to you, I was in great apprehension of losing my dear Agnes, and though she is still living, her health is very doubtful. We got her and the three dear little children down in August, that I might nurse her myself, and she only left me by train about a fortnight ago. She was so weak when she first came and with such a racking cough, that she could not walk unsupported across the room, and when she left me, she could walk a mile and back, without any great fatigue. I made her give up all her medicines, and take as much warm milk from the cow through the day as she could. It was astonishing what a miracle it wrought, both in her, and the little Geraldine, her now, youngest child. A beautiful delicate little sprite of a child, or *'frairy,'* as my Irish maids called her, who believed that she must be something super human as she was born at midnight, on All Hallow eve, and was so small and clever, and so lovely. I never saw such a tiny creature walking and talking, and with a face of such bright intelligence. When she came to us she was like the poor Mother, a fair but faded flower, and when she left us Madam Cherry, had rosy cheeks and sparkling eyes and was full of fun and frolic and vitality. The Doctor tells me, that Agnes *may* recover with *very great care*, but that complaint is so treacherous, that I have small hopes of it myself.

While she and the children remained with me, I had no time for anything but attending to her and them, and since she left us, a nephew of Mr. Moodies has come out to us with his wife and baby, intending to buy land and settle in Upper Canada.[2] They remain with us during the winter, which will hinder me from taking up my pen as a resource from ennui during the long hours that Mr. Moodie is absent at the office. I need not tell you how much I prefer the present state of things. I have grown weary of writing idle tales, and the public seems weary of them too and I begin to feel a mortifying certainty that my style does not suit the generality of readers. It belongs like me to *the past*. We have had a delightful cool healthy summer this year and though it is now late in the fall the weather continues mild and open without frost or snow.

The grand Trunk Railway, has been opened now for a month. The trafic upon it is immense. I hope it will pay, the shareholders as it will be of immense importance to the Colony.[3]

I never saw a Locomotive engine at work before. The sight filled me with awe. The spirit of man seemed at work in the wondrous machine, as the spirit of God works in us. What will not mind accomplish, when it can perform wonders like this. I have not ventured into one of the cars yet. They have gone up several times lately, freighted with [1]000 passengers, and make the journey from Montreal ...

1 'The Linhopes,' which had appeared in the *Literary Garland* as 'The First Debt,' had been transcribed by hand from what may have been a broken run of the story in that periodical. As was her wont, Susanna seldom copied without embellishing and expanding, especially when, as in this case, she was filling out a shorter tale to book length.
2 Robert and Jane (Duguid) Heddle; see letter 66 for a description of the visit.
3 On 27 October 1856, Belleville's citizenry gathered to welcome the arrival of the first railroad train.

66 To Catharine Parr Traill   [early 1857][1]

... he went to Pickering. They were at the house of a Scotch farmer of the name of Pollock, when R. H. suddenly declared that his thumb had grown a foot long and was increasing every moment. This announcement was received with shouts of laughter by all present when he said very gravely, 'This is very amusing to you, but is extremely painful to me.'

This was a strange fit of monomania from such a precise man. Can he be a little mad at times, which would account for all his excentricities causeless affronts and jealousies. If so, he is more to be pitied than censured – M. seems quite happy alone. He loved Jane and the baby very much. But R.H. he very much dislikes.

We are now quite alone. I teach Robert for two hours every morning, and Papa does a great deal of office writing at home, and he has no one to dispute his favorite theories, both he and Rob are quite well. I have little to complain of but occasional fits of cramp and rhumatism and dull headache, but at my age these are necessary consequences. The girls and Donald were well when we last heard from them and from Dunbar we have not heard since you left us. I was much pleased with dear Annie's letter. Mary[2] did not come down with R.H. Agnes had just put her to school, and did not like to pay the quarter for nothing. In this she was right. She will come to me in the holidays. I expect Charlotte Nickinson[3] to spend a few days with us, on her return from Kingston where she is at present performing, with the whole *troupe*.

So, dear James has sold his farm.[4] I hope it will prove of great advantage to him. The death of poor Joe Hutton, has left their fine farm to be rented for a term of years. Danton Hutton hired it at £100 per annum, but Miss Watson says they would lease it for 80. It has a good stone house, large and commodious with a lovely Bay view, good barns and all the etceteras and is one measured mile from Belleville on the Trent road. The market could constantly be supplied with meat potatoes, butter, eggs, and the town would buy milk, with which it is at present poorly supplied. It might be worth James' while to write to Mr. W. Hutton your old friend and hear his terms. As it is in the market, it will soon be caught up. I should like much to have dear James and Amelia for near neighbours as it is only a short walk from our place even for fat me.

I will try and learn the particulars of Danton Hutton when I see him.[5] Thank James much for his affectionate letter. I was much gratified by it, as I love him and prize his friendship. Wellington Murney wants to let or sell his farm on the Kingston road. A good farm, but it does not offer such advantages of situation as Huttons. If James wished for pupils from the old country he would have ample accommodation for them at Huttons and within a pleasant distance of churches lectures etc.

Mrs. Murney her husband and Isabel are off to a large party at W. Baldwin's den at Toronto. They will meet there the runaway bride Helen Dougall and Mr. Zurwood. Annie will remember both. I think Helen has made a good match but her father is perfectly frantic about it. He is supposed to be dying of consumption, but the Dr. ...

1 This fragment is dated early 1857 because it refers to the abbreviated visit of Robert and Jane Heddle who had been expected to spend the winter with the Moodies.
2 Anne Fotheringham Traill; Mary Agnes Fitzgibbon
3 The daughter of John Nickinson, manager of Toronto's Lyceum Theatre 1852–8, a popular young actress who later started her own company in Toronto
4 James George Traill had married Amelia Muchall in 1856 and started farming in the Rice Lake area.
5 William Hutton (1801–61) was one of Belleville's early settlers and prominent citizens; his sons, Joe and Danton, farmed in the Bay of Quinte region.

---

67 To Richard Bentley

Belleville
Dec. 2, 1857

My dear Mr Bentley

It is a very long time since I had the pleasure of receiving a line from you, and you will say, 'I had nothing pleasing to communicate and therefore did not write.' But you must not think me so selfish, as only to wish to hear from a kind friend when he has good news concerning myself alone, to write about. I should be glad to hear of your own health and welfare, independently of my poor literary matters, and I have not written for fear you should think that I only wanted to bother you about them. I have long ceased to anticipate any thing favourable, so I cannot be disappointed. The books you promised to send me, never arrived viz – Boswells letters[1] – and have shared the same fate with the others, and I have never got a single English copy of *Geoffrey Moncton*. I have not written one line for publication since I last wrote, my time, having been wholly occupied with other matters. The precarious health of my eldest daughter Mrs Vickers – '*Chronic Bronchitis*' only one name here, for consumption, made me too anxious to think of any thing else. It was necessary for her to go to the sea for change of air, and Mr Moodie and myself accompanied her to Portland, and from thence, to Cape Elizabeth – 'On the wild New England shore' – this was my first visit to the States. My first visit to the sea, after an absence of five and twenty years. The month was July. The weather on The Canadian side, glorious, as summer weather here always is. We went down to Kingston by the rail road. It was the first time I had ever been in the cars, and I felt very much inclined to shout with joy at their wondrous speed. It seemed to realize dreams I have had about flying. The sight of these great machines affects me strangely. I can never divest myself of the idea, that they possess a certain degree of intelligence. That the spirit of man is working in them the same as the spirit of God works in us. The perfect time they keep, the harmony of their motion is beautiful. The poetry of mechanism.

At Kingston, we joined my daughter and her good husband on board the Passport Steamer and proceeded to Montreal. I had not been this voyage since '32. Nature is little changed here. The noble river is still the same, with all its lovely islands and foaming headlong rapids. We accomplished however, in this trip, what never was dreamed of in '32. We shot all those glorious rapids, as the natives call passing through them. The Lachine rapids, the grandest, most formidable and exciting, we passed through at Sunset, and such a sunset. The boat was crowded with lads from the Toronto Colleges, going to spend their holidays. When the great vessel was tossed like a feather on the top of those long boiling surges, the boys flung up their caps and hurraed. It made even my blood effervese for the moment, and I could have joined in that glad wild cry with which youth and hope greet the accomplishment of any daring feat. But the soul is always young. It is only the mortal that grows weary, and I never remember my increasing years, amid scenes like this.

The heat at Montreal, that night, was intense. At 12 o clock the thermometer was 98, in the house.

The next morning, we crossed the river, and took the cars for Portland, on the other side, and travelled all day, through a splendid country. My dear girl, was quite knocked up, but my soul had gone into my eyes. I never felt the least tired. I was never weary of looking at the mountain scenery, The grand hills of Vermont and New Hampshire. The iron horses go with greater speed on the American side. We left two thunder storms among the mountains, behind us, and reached Portland at 7 in the evening. And there was the sea at last. The dear, old familiar sea, by whose side I had been bred and born, with whose every tone, and phase I was familiar in my English days. How my heart sprang to meet it. How I enjoyed the long forgotten smell of the salt brine, and the far off years rose up from the grave of time to stare me in the face, and recal to memory the days that had faded into the past. The sun and moon that had shone upon those blue waters long long ago. Sadness always will mingle with the deepest emotion, and is ever near us in moments of intense joy. Nay I believe that one can scarcely exist without the other, making that joy in grief, that Ossian[2] has so beautifully described.

Portland is a very picturesque city. A double row of noble elm trees shade all the principal thoroughfares, arcing over your head, and affording long arcades of living green, through which the rose bound portals of noble American mansions, are seen to great advantage. It is a land of flowers. I once more saw *real* gardens, full of well known flowers, dear to every English heart. Even the *sea fog*, had a sort of charm, in recalling the home scene of one's youth. The next day we proceeded to Port Elizabeth, and took up our quarters for the next month, at the Ocean House. A large solitary Hotel, which stands alone in its glory, on that rocky coast. If my paper and your time would admit, I would make you laugh over some of the scenes we witnessed here. But I enjoy the study of human character, and was greatly amused by all I heard and saw. I like Brother Jonathan[3] at home, and was agreeably disappointed. I found him *familiar*, but kind and attentive. *Inquisitive* but not rude. Less audacious than an Irishman, and more social and obliging than the English, with a certain dash of French politeness in his attention to your wants. The *servants*, were all *ladies* and *gentlemen*, and really one of the female waiters, a Spanish girl, Santina, was beautiful exceedingly, and more lady like than many of the visitors from the Canadian side. If music and singing were going on in the drawing room the servants came in, as a matter of course and formed part of the audience. At which no one took umbrage, as they ...

1 James Boswell, *Letters to Temple from Original MSS* (London: Bentley 1856)
2 The legendary Irish hero and bard of the third century whose poetry James Macpherson purportedly discovered and translated in the late eighteenth century.
3 A popular term not unlike Uncle Sam to identify Americans.

68 To Richard Bentley

May 2, 1858
Belleville
C.W.

My dear Mr. Bentley

I was truly glad to get a letter from you *at last*, having almost given up the hope of ever hearing from you again. To find that you were still in life, and combatting successfully with its many ills, was another source of pleasure, for which both of us may be sincerely thankful. The illness of your dear children being the only drawback, but God is a good and loving father, and these precious ones, also, may be given to your prayers.

This has been a year of great anxiety to us, both on our own account, and on that of others whose welfare is far dearer to us than our own. Money panics, and political changes, and roguery of all descriptions has placed us in continual jeopardy of losing all that we possessed in the world, and we have twice had all our effects under arrest, by the failure of parties from whom Mr M. had received indemnification, to sell the goods of iniquitous merchants, who make fortunes, by laying in a large stock of unpaid goods, and then going into fradulent bankruptcy, cheating their creditors, and retiring into comfort and independence with flying colors. At one time I hardly thought that we could extricate ourselves from these spider meshes of law and robbery. But God has fought the battle for us, and we are still afloat. At the very time when most needed, my pen failed to add its mite in the general trouble, and I felt in no spirits for the task. From Mr Routledge,[1] *I have never heard*, but think, that if any opportunity of getting back the MS. should occur, that I might get a sale for it in the States, now that the monetary crisis seems drawing to a close. I have a volume partly in progress, but do not know, whether it would meet your wishes, especially as its incidents are founded upon *magic* and *witchcraft*, but as both stories are pretty original, and strongly cast, they might awaken an interest in the reading world. I will try and send the MS. to you before the summer closes.[2]

Talking of magic, brings before me a subject, which inspite of the battling and opposition of a strong will, has forced itself upon my notice, until I stand astonished, and mentally exclaim – 'Can such things be?' – You know how often I have laughed in my letters to you, about *Spiritualism*. I was not only a sceptic, but a scorner. Yet, so many strange things have come under my own immediate knowledge, that though still doubtful on some points, I dare not now, exclaim, as I once confidently did, 'It is false. A mental puzzle. A delusion!' It is a mystery, strange, solemn and beautiful, and which I now believe, contains nothing more nor less than a new revelation from God to man. Not doing away with the old dispensation, but confirming it in every particular. As I know that every thinking mind, whether a believer or sceptic on this great question, must feel an interest in it, I shall not hesitate to give you some of my experience in these matters, and leave you to draw your own conclusions. I will not go back to my interviews with Miss K Fox, the celebrated rapping medium, for she left me as great a disbeliever as she found me, but confine myself to matters of a more recent date. A neighbor of ours, Mr J.W. Tate, one of the principal engineers upon the G T. Railway, had in his service a Scotch woman of the name of Mary Williamson, who was a very powerful Medium for physical manifestations, and as a great friendship existed between Mr M. and this gentleman, I had daily opportunities of testing the powers of this girl. I have seen a large heavy English dining table, rise in air repeatedly, without contact, have seen the leaf of the said table, fly up, and strike the snuffers out of my husband's hand, and put out the candles, have heard drums play, martial tunes where no instrument of the kind was to be found for miles, have been touched by unseen hands, and witnessed many curious phenomenon, which it is needless to my purpose, here to enumerate. Yet after the most diligent investigation, and an utter failure *in my part*, to discover the cheat, I still persisted in my vain unbelief. My husband had become an enthusiastic spiritualist and was much hurt by my obstinacy in refusing all the evidence offered to me, and we had several sharp mental conflicts on the subject, which grieved me much, and one evening last spring, after he had left me to go to the house of another spiritual friend, I went upstairs and wept very bitterly, over what I considered the unpardonable credulity of a man of his strong goodsense. As I was sitting alone by a little table, that had been given to my daughter Vickers, by a very talented young friend, long since dead, I suddenly laid my right hand upon the table, and feeling very angry in my own mind at all *spiritualists*, I said tauntingly, enough, 'If there be any truth in this doctrine, let the so called spirits move my hand against my will off from this table, and lay it down in my lap!' You would have laughed to have seen the determined energy, with which I held my hand down to the table, expecting the moon, that was then shining into the room, to leave her bright path in the heavens as soon, as that my hand should be lifted from that table. You may therefore guess my surprise, not to say, terror, when my hand became paralized, and the fingers were slowly wrenched up from the table, and the whole hand lifted and laid down in my lap. Not dropped nor jerked suddenly, but brought forward, as if held in a strong grasp and placed there.

I left the room and went downstairs into the diningroom. My servant had gone out for a walk and I was quite alone. My husband had contrived a very ingenious sort of Spiritoscope, A board running upon two smooth brass rods with an index that pointed to the alphabet in order to save the trouble of culling over the alphabet. I had always refused to put my hands upon this board, which would move for people under the influence and spell out letter by letter messages and names. But being alone, I placed my hands upon the board, and asked, 'Was it a spirit that lifted my hand?' and the board rolled forward and spelt out 'Yes.' 'What spirit?' 'A friend' 'What is your name?' 'Thomas Harral!' I must say that this startled me. Mr H, who for many years, was Editor of *La Belle Assemblée,* was the first literary man for whom I wrote, and I certainly had not thought of him for many years. I did not even know, whether he were dead or living, and I again asked, 'Why do you wish to communicate with me?' 'Because I felt an interest in you when upon earth.'

Knowing that he had been a great sceptic on religious matters, I said, 'Was yours a happy death?' The answer was so characteristic of the man, that it made me almost realize his presence – 'Susanna – Was mine a happy life?' 'Where did you die?' 'What matters it to you, where I died. If I were to tell you, what means have you of testing the truth?' 'Will you lift my hand again?' 'Tomorrow night at this hour.' This was done, and for many nights after. I then reversed the thing, and begged the spirit, to fix my hands down upon the table, so that I could not raise them. This too was done and so effectively, that my husband had to employ the reverse passes in mesmerism in order to break the spell.

Though, still unwilling to believe, imputing the whole matter to some new and undiscovered power of mind, I did at times consent to put my hands upon the spiritoscope and though at times I got no communication, the board never moving at all, and at other times, had my hands paralized and lifted up from the board, yet at other times it would move rapidly even with my eyes shut, Mr M taking the words down letter by letter, as pointed out by the index. The first I got in this manner, was from my dear friend Thomas Pringle the abolitionist, from whose house I was married, it runs as follows –

22 June 1857, Thomas Pringle

'You will not live to see the abolition of slavery in the United States. It will end in blood and great political changes must take place. The corruption of the Government will bring about a great moral reform, and the people will see the necessity of getting rid of the cause of so much crime. But it will not be in your day. A long struggle between the North and South, with the defection of California, Texas and Kansas, will set the poor Negro free, but this will take years to accomplish. God will prepare the mind of the slave, for the great moral change that awaits his condition. When God brings about a great National reform, He works slowly, and uses many instruments because many changes are affected by one. No more. Good night.' –

Since obtaining this communication I have watched with great interest the Kansas question. It would be running this communication to too great a length to give you some most curious and interesting communications which I have from time to time, received from a spirit, who calls himself my guardian angel but who will not give his name. I send you, however, the two first communications that we received from him.

June 30, 1857.

'A young man, old in the spirit world will communicate with you to night. Do not too readily give credence to all that mediums tell you. They are often deceived by their own thoughts mingling with the thoughts of the spirit that communicates. Only receive what looks like truth. All great truths are simple. The Circle, the most sublime symbol of Eternity, which is one name for God, is the most simple of forms, yet it is a problem which philosophers cannot solve. Such is God. All can behold his perfect beauty and the harmony that exists in his works, which love unites in the unbroken Circle of divine wisdom. Trust implicitly to Him. It is as easy to gain communications from his spirit, as from souls that have been stained with sins of earth. Pray for this divine influence and it will not be with held. It can neither lead astray nor deceive, for God is truth. Good night, my friends.' My husband asked, 'Will the spirit give his name?'

'I have a name in Heaven but not for your ears.'

On the 6th July, he gave us the following – 'God is a perfect Unity. The great circle and centre of existence. *Death*, is but the returning *wave of life* flowing back to Him. All created existence lives through and to Him, and no man lives for himself alone. He is a link in the chain of life, which would be broken without his ministration.

Hence, bad and good work together for the universal benefit of all.

There is no partiality or injustice in this dispensation. God makes no man bad, but their evil passions by forming the trials and temptations of others, bring out their virtues and fit souls for a higher state of existence, and educate them for Heaven. Thus they become ministering spirits to those who are tempted and tried on earth.'

Here follows a passage of a personal nature. My husband asked, 'Will you give us your name?'

'My name is unknown to you' –

'Can I distinguish you by any name?'

'You will know me by the nature of my communications. Rest satisfied. I wish you well – Good night.'

I have received some noble communications from this spirit, and if you wish to know more of him, I will give more, in my next letter. He is so unlike all the other communicants, that I know him from the first sentence he spells upon the board.

You, will perhaps think, as I too, have often thought, that the whole is an operation of my *own* mind, but my mind must be far cleverer than I, its owner have any idea of if it can spell letter by letter, whole pages of connected and often abstruse matter, without my knowing one word about it, for, it is not, until, Mr Moodie reads it over to me, after the communication is suspended that I know what it is about. My sister Mrs Traill, is a very powerful Medium for these communications, and gets them in foreign languages. Her spirits often abuse, and call her very ugly names. Had I time, I could surprise you with some that she has received, but could not surprise you so much as she has been surprised herself. She, who was quite as sceptical as me, has been rendered very happy by the intercourse of her dear children, which has quite overcome the fears of death that she till lately entertained. Now, do not think me mad or possessed by evil spirits, like that great Medium of old St. Pauls. I could wish you altogether possessed by such a glorious madness. You did not tell me, how I could get the books you have so kindly sent me, nor thrown any light upon the way in which the others have miscarried. I shall be delighted to hear from you, and if Mr Routledge buys 'The Linhopes' I should be very glad. Mr. Moodie is now in New York where I think he will see Judge Edmonds and several other notable spiritualists. I will report progress in my next, and with kindest regards to yourself and family circle, believe me my dear Mr. Bentley your sincere and obliged friend

Susanna Moodie

1 George Routledge was a reprint publisher to whom Bentley sometimes sold the rights to
  books; apparently he had also passed 'The Linhopes' to Routledge to consider for
  publication.
2 'Mildred Rosier. A Tale of the Ruined City' appeared in the *Literary Garland* in eleven
  instalments, February–December 1844, and 'Monica; or Witchcraft' in six instalments,
  January–June 1846.

---

69 To Catharine Parr Traill   Belleville
                                     Dec. 12th 1858

My Dearest Catherine

I will try and write if only a few lines, but my hand finds it almost impossible to manage a pen. The motion of my wrist being so painful, and when made so powerless – The difficulty of writing has alone kept me silent.

I saw dear James yesterday, he dined with us – looks very well and seems in very good spirits. He feels no fear, but that he shall overcome his present difficulties.

I wish I could feel as Confident about our own. I thought that we had got over that old Cinq Mars business, but there is an execution against lands and tenements on that score. And no time to be given –, and no mercy shown to the kind benevolent old man, who has had mercy on so many. He feels it very bitterly. It makes his sensitive nature keenly alive to the want of courtesy and the cruelty of such proceedings. There is likewise an execution of 50£ for some failure of security in the parties of the suit, of another case, and where the money is to come from I know not. Moodie has been obliged to recall Donald from Montreal, because he cannot raise money to keep him there, and this winter promises to be one of unusual sorrow and discomfort. Poor Aggie is penniless and I have not the means to help her, even with clothes of my own, for I am literally in rags – a misfortune which has seldom happened to me before. The Deputy cannot make his payments and we are in a *fix*. I am *glad* – yes, actually glad, that you cannot come to me just now. If I have to suffer – Let me do it alone. I am too proud, and selfreliant to tolerate sympathy.

I wish Moodie would consent to give up house keeping, and board, either at one of the respectable hotels, or with some private family. It would save us hundreds. We should not have the annoyance of finding a kitchen table, and paying high wages to servants.

In our present position, it would be wisdom to get rid of the cares and

expenses of house keeping. Jane is gone, and not before it was time –
but I have a very poor help in her place. Yet I pity the girl so much that I
don't know how to tell her to go.

She has been a spoilt adopted child, well educated, and possessing
very fair abilities but is indolent, desponding, discontented with a sub-
ordinate situation, and very destitute. She reads and writes well, can knit
sew and spin – but of all household work, she is lamentably ignorant,
and will not rouse herself to be instructed. To be a servant – is to her such
a dreadful disgrace, that life is worth nothing in such a situation. In
vain I reason with her and try to soothe her. Her only answer is – 'If I
think about these things I shall go mad.' Then, she is so dreadfully timid
that I cannot leave her alone in the house. Like the children in the dark,
she is afraid of something she does not know what. Her father was a
wealthy farmer, who owned last year 7000 dollars. Endorsing for others
has ruined him and the girls have to go out to seek their living. Now if
poor Joanne would only submit to unavoidable circumstances, she might
be very comfortable here, – but pride will not let her be at peace. While
these ghastly nervous fears rob her of sleep and paralize her mind, I
have to do half her work, and as I am very lame, it is not done as it should
be.

I expect poor Donald some day this next week. I dare say that he will
bring Allie with him for the Christmas holiday. Rob returns on the 21st
for a fortnight – whatever happens, I hope Papa will try to keep him at
school for this year. Mr. Capel writes of him in a very satisfactory
manner. He is coming to spend his Christmas holidays at the Filiters, and
brings Rob with him. His board at Mr. Smyth's would come to the
same money, as boys are allowed to travel to and fro to school by train at
half price – and I shall see my dear child again.[1] Your Willy looks very
well, is growing tall and handsome.[2] I am sorry dear Catherine that I
cannot ask Kate just now to stay with me. But Moodie in his present
troubles would not tolerate visitors. I am really hoping that D. will not
bring Allie until better times, but they will not feel the discomfort as
others would. But I am only talking of my own affairs – which is both
unkind and egotistical. I received my Nephew George's[3] wedding cards
and I wish him and the young bride much joy. By all accounts he has made
a wise choice and therefore stands a fair chance of much domestic
happiness. Pray give him Aunt Susannas love and kind wishes for their
future welfare – and congratulate my dear brother on the settlement of
another son. He is very fortunate to have them living so near him. I shall
be sorry when I hear of your leaving such comfortable quarters. I dread

your return to the cold comfortless house on the plains until the spring brings warm pleasant weather.[4] I can sympathize with you on the rejection of your MS. as Horace Bentley brought back mine, – which I had hoped would have afforded me the means of helping those I love. Horace Greeley has undertaken to sell it for me in the States, but in these ˙ times – people want bread more than books. Authors have but a poor chance of success. Horace Bentley told me that Didactic works were all the rage at home, and nothing but essays and biography and history would sell. I should have thought that your book would have just suited their house. I do not see the great advantage of boarding those young ladies. You can scarcely feed them for £25 each – besides the wear and tear of bedding, and the additional trouble, and the washing. In a town, it, would be impossible and you should make something by them, or you are better without the nuisance of inmates, who could claim attention and good food for their money. A young man, pays here 5 dollars a week for board and washing. It would be better to board one young gentleman on those terms than your two girls, who would expect a good room and decently furnished at their low terms. It is of no use having lodgers without you better your Condition by them. On a farm you might manage – but in a town it would be ruinous. Do think it well over before you commit yourself too far to recede. Your husband is not a very likely person to agree with any boarder, and I fear you would only increase your troubles without any ultimate benefit to yourself or others. Do you know anything about these girls and their dispositions or if they are likely to put up with any inconvenience, or any irritability in the temper of others. I tremble for your future peace of mind under probable circumstances – my dear sister. But I have a great want of faith, and am ever prone to consider the difficulties which surround our path of life, so do not be guided by me. My want of hope is as great a fault as your too sanguine expectations. But then I avoid much disappointment by the smallness of that organ.[5] James told you that we had heard from Dunbar. His letter was the most satisfactory of any that we have received from him for he was well in health, and making with 5 others, 200 dollars per diem (among them) – which he says, if it only lasts, will soon make him independent.

I think, we are as far off seeing him as ever now. Papa and I are longing to quit Belleville I only wish we could sell this property for what would support us elsewhere and we should not be long here. If Dunbar should settle in the Western States we have pretty much made up our minds to join him there with Robert.

I have not heard this week from my dear girls. They both forgot the old

Mother on her birthday. I was quite alone that day, Papa being at Montreal, and it passed so sadly and slowly away, that I almost wished it might be the last anniversary. I did not get your kind letter until three days after – The Western Mail having altered its hours – and coming at night instead of at twelve in the day.

Many thanks dear Katie for your kind solicitude on my behalf. May better and brighter days be in store for us both – and may we so improve the material present, that it may open the door of the dear spirit land to our weary longing souls. Moodie unites with me in kind love to yourself, to my brother, his excellent wife and to all the scions of the old stock, – believe me ever yours –

Susanna Moodie

1 Robert Baldwin Moodie, now fifteen years old, was likely attending Kingston Grammar School, a private institution headed by Mr Capel. In addition to fees, the Moodies had to pay his travel expenses and board with 'Mr Smyth' in Kingston.
2 William Edward Traill (1844–1917)
3 George Strickland (1834–90)
4 Catharine had been living with Samuel and his family since 'Oaklands,' her home on the Rice Lake plains, had burnt the previous August.
5 A reference to the phrenological belief that one's optimism or pessimism is determined by a bump in the upper central area of the cranium.

---

70 To Richard Bentley

Belleville
Feb. 12 / 59

My Dear Mr Bentley,

I have been long threatening you with one of my interminable letters, but I have had such a lame right hand, that for months my inability to guide a pen has saved you from the infliction. I still write with much pain and difficulty, but my anxiety to learn some tidings of Mr Horace makes me forget it. He promised when with us to let me know of his safe arrival at home, but as months have passed away, and we have not received a line from him, I begin to feel very anxious and uneasy about him. While with us, his amiable disposition and many estimable qualities, won a high place in our affections, and we parted with him with regret. I was much disappointed, that he did not take Belleville in his way home. He was certain of a hearty welcome, but some foolish European notions of giving trouble etc. kept him aloof from those who would have received him as a son.

I trust, that his trip proved beneficial to his health. I fancied that he looked stronger before he left us. What a glorious winter we are having. I wish my young friend could have stayed to witness it. The clear bright, bracing weather, would have done much to restore his shattered nerves. We have had two very severe days, when the Mercury was down to 40 below zero, but all the rest have been so beautiful. Nature dressed in a rich tissue of white and silver, and every twig enwreathed with pearls and diamonds. I am never tired of looking out of the window, the frost King works such miracles, and the sun lights up his doings with such a glory of dazzling brightness, that you wonder to find the world so cold when his beams are so bright.

The Bay[1] is a solid plain just now, traversed in all directions by sleighs and pedestrians. It is so safe after these iron frosts, that you quite forget the waters imprisoned beneath the coat of snow that covers them. I am always timid on this ice, but this year it would be silly to imagine the possibility of danger.

The Commercial prosperity of the country is just now at a stand still. The rail roads *do not pay*. Numbers of people are out of employment, and half the stores are shut up. The Colony is bankrupt, and cannot take the benefit of the insolvent act. Money is not to be had, and no one can live upon credit. What has occasioned this state of things can only be guessed at. For my *own* part, I believe it originates in the general love of dishonest speculation, which pervades all the mercantile ranks. They have ruined themselves and others in trying to grow rich at the expense of the country. A general gloom pervades all ranks and the certainty [of] the seat of Government becoming fixed at Ottawa, has put Toronto, Montreal, and Quebec, into the sulks. The decision of the Queen was so unexpected, so distasteful to the majority of the people, that the expressions of discontent almost amounted to treason, and the choice of Ottawa, was only carried in the house by a majority of *five*. A very few years will make Ottawa worthy of the royal favor. In natural beauty it far surpasses all its more wealthy rivals, and can be made a noble place with very little trouble. The Queen showed much taste in picking it, and I have no doubt, that the difficulty of deciding between the *three great rival cities* was one main object in her decision.

How is your health this winter? Is the book world prospering? I have heard nothing of literary matters since Horace left us. The only book I have read with interest, is Emmerson's, *Traits of English Character*.[2] I do

not think, he gives the English credit for the moral and intellectual
strength of ...

1 Bay of Quinte
2 Ralph Waldo Emerson, *English Traits* (Boston: Phillips, Sampson and Co. 1856)

---

71 To Catharine Parr Traill   Belleville
Nov. 28 '60

My dearest Catherine

I got your kind sympathizing letter this morning. James had carried it with
him to Madoc[1] or I should have replied to it before. I was certain of
your deep interest in our untoward destiny. It has been hanging over me
for years. The certainty of trouble. It has come at last, and God will
give us strength to bear it. There is still one forlorn hope. The sanction of
the judges, before whom the merits of the case will be tried tomorrow in
Toronto. Moodie is there awaiting their final decision. It may be in our
favor. The event is hardly probable, but God has so often defended us
in extremities as bad as this, and confounded the machinations of bad
men, that he may not desert us now. At all events, we shall soon know
the worst. I wish it were over in either case. Uncertainty is always worse
to bear than the pressure of sorrows known. When we know what we
have to expect, the mind rises to meet the emergencies of the case, and we
can mature plans for the future. If all is lost, we shall in all probability
collect the debts due to the office, which involve large sums, and emigrate
with Robert and Dunbar, to some distant land – California or the
Western States, to begin life afresh upon the verge of the grave. Here, I do
not wish to stay, and the change in our circumstances can be better
borne among strangers unacquainted with our former surroundings. I
have no ties to bind me to Belleville, beyond the dear home that has
sheltered us for so many years, and the trees I have with my own hands
planted, and last, not least the graves of my dear boys. I am ready to
act my part, to work unflinching while I have strength to work, and to bow
submissively to the will of that Divine Providence, who always acts for
the best, and in whose guiding wisdom I implicitly trust. So do not grieve
for me, my sister, my dear tried friend. I can bear, and am not ashamed
to labour for my bread. Many, many thanks for your kind offers of service.
Dunbar says, we shall never want while he has hands to work for us,
and he is firm and true, and will keep his promise. I feel most for poor

Donald. He is defficient in that energy which alone ensures success and will be left to struggle for his living without any help from those who love him. It may, however, be the best thing that ever happened to him, and he has shown much deep feeling and sincere kindness during this trying crisis. Should the judges award a new trial in the spring all these antici-pated changes may never take place. We should be almost certain of coming off victorious. They are all in our favour, and shocked at the treacherous manner in which M. has been betrayed into this snare by his professional advisers. The sympathy of the whole county hating the malignity of the men who have done this – is in his favor. They talk of petitioning parliament, and sending in an address signed by the most influential landholders in the District, but this may all end in mere words. It is wisdom to prepare for the worst – I too, am very sorry for poor James – for Dunbar – who as his father's deputy, would have been able to secure a good living for all. Fortunately, Papa settled two years ago, the house and ten acres of land upon me. This cannot be touched, without my consent and that I never will give, so, let the worst come – I shall still have a home, of which, they cannot deprive me, and I can live upon very little. The dear girls who are a great comfort to us, secure us some means as they pay 28 dollars per month, for their board, and their father, who returned last week to Jamaica, has left them with us until the spring. The dear Father, bears it much better than I expected. At first, the blow fell very severely, and I never saw him look so pale and worn, but he has rallied wonderfully, and when he left last Monday for Toronto, he was in better spirits than I had seen him for the last two months. I cannot enter into the particulars of the trial – Ockerman behaved like a consumate scoundrel and he, and Mr. W. Ponton *volunteered* their evidence against him. He had acted entirely by the advice of Mr. P., and he betrayed him in the most treacherous manner. Were you here, I could tell you all about it, but it is not safe to write about these people, as my natural indignation at their baseness, might carry me too far.

I have not been well for the last three or four months and am worn and weary, but this trouble has roused me from brooding over the symp-toms of approaching decay, and I am too much interested in the welfare of others, to think much of myself. Directly Katie heard of the issue of the trial, she came down with her baby to see us, and her shrewd sense, and hopeful disposition, did much to inspire her father with fresh courage to battle with his persecutors. The baby is a nice creature – The dear little Katie – A fair, fat sweet tempered creature, not pretty but *very nice*. It never cried the whole time it was here, but behaved in a most exemplary manner. It brought about a meeting, and a friendly one, between Don-

ald and his sister, an event for which I have prayed for years, so you see
dearest, there is some bright spots even in the darkest clouds. Rob has
behaved like a darling as he is. What a kind good fellow he is – a most
affectionate son and warm hearted friend. I don't know what we should
do without him. He carries on the whole business of the office during his
father's absence, with a judgement and decision, you could hardly expect from a boy of 17. But to turn from my own affairs. Mr. Tate told me,
that he met you and Mary on your return from the Lake.[2] He spoke in
great praise of the latter, and said that you were looking well. I hope that
this arrangement with Mr. V will turn out a fortunate one. I find my
boarders a great comfort to me. If I could only procure more on the same
terms, we might yet live very comfortably. Mr. Russell sent me the
present of a beautiful purse, and gold pencil. The former, seemed a luxury
little needed in our present circumstances, but dear Lizzy thinks it a
good omen. She is a daughter to me in my trouble and dear little Julia does
her best with her angelic voice to drive away care. They are both excellent young women, and seem to have been sent to us in the most providen-
tial manner to lighten our distress. Yes – these things are not acciden-
tal, they are foreseen and awarded to us as great and special
benefactions.

    Give my kindest love to dear Sam and his good Catherine. I am much
indebted to them for their kind sympathy. But a little while and all these
troubles will vanish away for ever. You know that I am too independent to
seek help from others as long as I can help myself. Katie kindly offered
us a home for life, but I must keep a home for myself (however homely) I
cannot eat the bread that others win for me. You must forgive this
hurried scrawl as I have all the work of the house to do today. I will write
as soon as the unfortunate affair is decided, until then believe me as
ever, in weal or woe

                                        Your affectionate and loving
                                        Susanna

Dunbar Donald and Robert unite in kind love to you and yours and to
dear Uncle and Aunt.
    Mr. Sisson has just brought me a letter from the dear husband. A writ
has been issued to show cause why a new trial may not be granted. So
there is still a hope to build on yet.

1 A town fifty kilometres north of Belleville and sixty east of Peterborough
2 Mary Traill and her mother were revisiting Rice Lake.

72 To Henry Morgan   Belleville
                                July 27, 1861

Sir,[1]

It was my intention to have answered your first application by return of
post. My mind was diverted from doing so, by matters of far more
importance to my family, and the subject of your communication was
forgotten altogether. Any ambition I once had for literary distinction is
so completely obliterated, by the sterner cares and trials of life, that I feel
no wish to see my name placed among your list of Canadian worthies.

By birth and education English I cannot have the least claim to the
honor you intend me. Wishing your undertaking all success. I remain
Sir,

> Yours truly
> Susanna Moodie

1 Henry Morgan (1842–1913) had written to ask Susanna's permission to include her in his
   Celebrated Canadians (Quebec 1862).

---

73 To Catharine Parr Traill   Dec. 28, 1862

My dearly beloved Sister,

I have wanted to write to you for a long while, but somehow or other lost
the opportunities. My heart, you well know, is often with you, and
during the many sleepless hours I spend of a night, my thoughts wander to
you continually. The time draws near, when I trust, we shall be no
more separated, but can hold sweet converse together, unfettered by time
or circumstances – making endless discoveries in the wonderful works
of the great Creator – deriving wisdom from the fountain of all wisdom,
and perfecting our being in his Divine Light. I feel very old and worn
just now. A great change in my physical woman. I do not suffer, as you do
my dear sister, with those horrible rhumatic tortures. My trouble, is all
in the stomach. A chronic settled pain and uneasiness, at the pit of the
stomach, sometimes extending itself into violent spasmotic pains,
which pull down my strength in a few hours, and which, only yield to large

doses of aspirin. Dr. Henry, told me plainly, that it arose from ulcer-
ation of the stomach. Dr. Lister, his partner, says, that it is from kidney
disease, which affects the organs of the stomach, but whatever the
cause, I think it will be ultimately, the fatal one. I have just got over a very
severe attack, which I really thought might terminate my life. It will, I
hope, serve for a warning to hold myself in readiness, for that great event,
which is for ever shrouded in the mists of eternity.

   You have doubtless heard of poor old Jenny's[1] death. It was a great
shock. I had a dread upon my mind, from the time that she made her
unexpected advent to Belleville, that she would never leave us again. Her
stay, always put us to much inconvenience, as the other servants would
not sleep with her, and she occupied a room I could ill spare and bedding
required for the family. She was, however, in excellent health, with a
most ravenous appetite. A thing most unusual with her. She sometimes
talked of going home but, then, she told the maids, that she meant to
stay all the winter, as she enjoyed herself best where she was. She had to
be petted to keep her in good humour, and always expected a glass of
whiskey before she went to bed. Her whole time was spent in wandering
from my house to Mrs. Dunbar's,[2] from there to Mrs. J. Traills,[3] or
down the street to see Mrs. Lyons, old Burkes daughter. She was, however, extending her acquaintance, as her curiosity and love of gossip had
increased with age and leisure, and she knew almost every one upon our
hill, and their most private business, while of a night, she stole after
Bridget and Margaret, to see if they met their sweethearts – a system of
espionage, of which, they by no means approved. About six weeks ago,
she complained one day of a pain about her heart, but she said, that she
had often had it before, it was only a little cauld she had taken. In the
evening, some friends of Margaret's came to see her, and the old lady
seemed very merry, laughing and funning from the chimney corner.
About 10 o'clock, she suddenly rose and went into the inner kitchen,
where she fell heavily. I was upstairs with Rob talking over with him
some private matter, Donald taking his piano lesson in the drawing room.
Hearing the fall, I said, 'D. is too heavy, he has overturned the music
stool,' but hearing a confused noise, Rob said, 'Let us go down. It may be
Father.' A deadly fear crept over me. In the kitchen we found Father
and Donald, supporting poor Jenny, who had been struck down with
paralysis as if she had received a stroke of electricity. The boys carried
her up to bed, and I, and Margaret undressed her. She had lost the use of
her right arm, and her speech, though incessant, was inarticulate. The
tongue was paralized. She suffered, she told me afterwards, no pain, a

numb chill, crept up her back and over her arms, and she weakened and fell. For about a fortnight, she remained perfectly helpless. I had to feed her with a spoon like a baby, and as she had grown very fat, I found turning and helping her in and out of bed, a great trial. Bridget had left me, about a fortnight before, and Margaret, though a good servant, is a selfish woman and did very little for me. She could not stand the bad odour from Jenny. It was horrible, I must confess. Could I have gotten the poor soul into a bath, the trouble would have been nothing, but that 'Smell!,' as Margaret said, 'was sickening.' It was not of disease, but of concentrated dirt. The unwashed secretions of the body, accumulated for years. I no longer wondered at the girls refusing to sleep with her.

The Doctor, who came immediately after the seisure, told me that she might get over this attack with care. The next would be fatal.

Well, I did all I could for the poor old …

1 The same, faithful, eccentric old Jenny Buchanan of *Roughing It in the Bush*; she accompanied the Moodies to Belleville and continued in their service for several years before retiring to Lakefield or Dummer.
2 Dunbar Moodie's wife Elizabeth
3 Amelia Traill

1863~1869

'The frowns of
an untoward fortune'

THE 1860S WERE DIFFICULT YEARS for Susanna Moodie. Early in the decade, disappointment and bitterness accompanied her husband's resignation as sheriff of Hastings County. The letters she wrote after this event frequently mention illnesses, the frailties of old age, tensions in family relationships, and the constant threat of poverty, reflecting her response to much changed circumstances. But, characteristically, her moods varied considerably. There is a feeling, too, of returning strength, energy, even a certain *joie de vivre*, particularly beginning in the fall of 1866. It is almost as if Susanna needed to feel the full weight of defeat, loss, and hopelessness in order to test and marshal her strength. One imagines the elderly couple, both now in their sixties, Susanna very much in control, enduring their lessened estate in a small, rented cottage near the Bay of Quinte, dispossessed of much that had been theirs but cheered by a sense of independence regained and by the satisfaction of sharing their struggle with an 'untoward fortune.'

After Susanna's heady success in the early 1850s, first in England and then through the agency of De Witt and Davenport in the United States, the popularity of her work had begun to flag. As a result, she found herself early in the 1860s without a publisher to whom she could turn in England, the United States, or Canada. It was the first time she had been without some sort of outlet since she had begun nearly forty years ago in Suffolk to write for *La Belle Assemblée* and to entertain, with some seriousness, romantic and youthful aspirations of literary fame. Equally significant, however, was her own inertia. The humiliation and indignation she felt over the prolonged lawsuit her husband had to endure seems to have had the effect of cooling, even paralysing, her initiative as a writer. The fact that she apparently allowed her sympathetic communications with Richard Bentley to lapse for a period prior to March 1865 suggests this state of mind, as does her reply to Henry Morgan in July 1861 (Letter 72) in which she justifies her lack of interest in her reputation with the remark that her attention was given over to 'matters of far more importance to my family.' To her sister Catharine she confessed, in January 1864 (Letter 76): 'I really feel, that I am growing [a literary fossil] myself and often say, I am beginning to petrify. Ideas will no longer come. I seek, but do not find. Solomon said truly – there is a time, for all things under the sun. There is a time to write and a time to refrain from writing. I feel that the latter season has come for me.'

Yet even feeling so, it was difficult to forsake what had been an important source of family income, especially when circumstances made writing an important means of survival. A year before she wrote her despairing words to Catharine, Dunbar Moodie had voluntarily resigned from the sheriff's post on 15 January 1863, thus relieving the Appeal Court of its disagreeable legal obligation of finding against him. No new position was immediately forthcoming, but there had been suggestions and promises from influential quarters that had spurred him to retire from office when he did and in a manner agreeable to his sense of personal dignity. With his official retirement in March, the Grand Jury of Hastings assizes had given him a highly complimentary 'Presentment,' which read in part: 'it is our belief that he retires from office with few enemies, and the warm sympathy of many friends. We also believe that he unwittingly transgressed the law in the transaction that has caused his retirement from the position he so long occupied, and being innocent of intentional wrong, we think this should not militate against his appointment to the discharge of duties of any other office in the gift of the Crown, and we have reason to believe that his appointment to some other office would give general satisfaction to the inhabitants of the County.' For its part, the supportive Hastings *Chronicle* had commended the sheriff's work, noting the 'universal esteem and respect' felt for him and deploring 'the cruel and vindictive prosecution which occasioned his retirement from office.'[1]

In the spirit of such goodwill the Moodies waited, patiently at first, for word from the capital, Quebec City, concerning a new position. However, bureaucratic delays and changes in government combined, it seems, to seal the fate of the ageing, somewhat incapacitated, ex-sheriff.[2] Dunbar's youngest son Robert had in effect run the sheriff's office over the final years of his father's tenure and the family was still able to draw upon unpaid notes and accounts due to him even after he had officially resigned. But prospects were dim so far as a regular source of income was concerned.

Thus, the offer early in 1863 to write for the Toronto-based *British American Magazine* must have seemed a blessing. Susanna had not had a Canadian outlet, let alone one that paid, since the *Literary Garland* ceased publication the year after John Gibson's death in 1850. She was also impressed by the reputation of the editor, Henry Youle Hind (1823–1908), a University of Toronto professor who had gained prominence not only for his scientific writings but also for his important government expeditions to Rupert's Land in the late 1850s.[3] Under Hind's direction, the magazine made a professional and presentable start. Susanna complied by providing for the May 1863 issue her evocative reminiscence of Thomas Cheesman, 'My Cousin Tom – A Sketch from Life.' The second sketch mentioned in Letter 74 seems not to have been used by the magazine, though Catharine Parr Traill's 'Flowers and Their Moral Meaning' also appeared in that first issue. In January and February 1864 Susanna contributed a two-part children's story, 'The Accuser and the Accused' (published in Scotland as *George Leatrim* in 1875). She had just begun to write a novel called 'Dorothy Chance,' the first chapter of which appeared in the April 1864 issue, the last before the *British American Magazine* folded.

Though disappointed by this failure, so characteristic of the fate of worthwhile commercial magazines in Canada during her writing years, Susanna was quick to find another home for 'Dorothy Chance.' Her old friend John Lovell accepted it for serialization in 1867 in his new Montreal paper, the *Daily News*.[4] She then avoided the painfully dull routine of copying by sending the newspaper text to Richard Bentley, who, perhaps as much out of kindness for an old friend in need as from interest in the manuscript, published it in 1867 as the three-volume novel *The World Before Them*. Bentley had less luck in placing her shorter pieces, 'The Race for Royalty,' 'The True Histories of Mrs. Moodie's Racoons, Jenny and Ned,' 'Arminius,' and 'Will She Forget?' all of which he returned after a long delay. All but 'Arminius,' which had been previously published, are now lost.[5]

But if Bentley failed her in this regard, he used his influence otherwise in a way that deeply touched her. Stirred by her letter of March 1865, he set in motion the process whereby, as a tribute to her literary contributions over the years, she received a most timely grant from the Royal Literary Fund. A long-standing director of the fund, Bentley thus occasioned the only formal recognition – in England or in Canada – that Susanna Moodie was to receive during her lifetime. In requiring an account of her work to present to the directors (Letter 78), he drew from her what is today a most useful record, complete with information about her early dabbling in pseudonyms, though the inevitable errors and omissions of memory are also evident.

As diligently as Susanna kept to her writing, at least in the mid-1860s, her real interest was shifting to painting, a skill she had developed as a pupil of the wife of Andrew Ritchie of Wrentham. This skill she had encouraged in her daughter Agnes Fitzgibbon, who, with her own daughters, had undertaken the monumental task of painting by hand all the illustrations for *Canadian Wild Flowers* (Lovell 1868), the text of which was written by Catharine Parr Traill. Susanna's work was both less ambitious and less rigorous, though no less capable. Her watercolour flower studies found buyers in Belleville, Toronto, Montreal, and even in Ipswich, mostly among friends sympathetic to her situation and interested in her talent. Her delight at the positive response she found among certain customers of Samuel Dawson's bookstore in Montreal (see Letter 85) does not mask the fact that the income from such work made its contribution to the Moodies' meagre income during these years.

For his part, Dunbar also turned to writing. While Susanna completed her 'Dorothy Chance' story, he collected many of his previously published essays and poems, for which he provided a personal reminiscence, and went about the onerous business of arranging buyers by subscription. The volume, *Scenes and Adventures of a Soldier and Settler during Half a Century* (1866), while marked by the plaintive self-justification of its introduction, constituted a demanding effort not only in its preparation but also in the contacting of prospective purchasers. Something of that effort is evident in the Moodies' brief trip to Montreal in November 1866 (see Letter 85). Dunbar was there to make final arrangements for his book and to sit for his frontispiece portrait in the studio of William Notman (1836–91), by then achieving recognition as Canada's leading photographer.[6] He also sold subscriptions to his book, while Susanna arranged sales of her paintings and turned 'Dorothy Chance' over to their old friend John Lovell.

During these years, Susanna renewed acquaintance with one old correspondent and found a new one. The reappearance in her life of Allen Ransome, her old Quaker friend from Ipswich, proved a great pleasure and comfort to her. Widowed and wealthy, he wrote to her after some thirty-five years of silence, eager to know more of her fortunes beyond what he had read of her life in *Roughing It in the Bush*. Since their Suffolk days, when they often met through their mutual friend James Bird, Ransome had gone on to business success in his family's Ipswich-based agricultural implements factory, the Orwell works.[7] The young man Susanna had described in *Flora Lyndsay* as 'a handsome, talented man' of 'joyous disposition and mirthful humour' (she called him 'Adam Mansel' there, with tongue in cheek) kindled old feelings and warm memories as the decade drew to a close.

While it is evident that Susanna wrote to Ransome over several years, another correspondent, Anna Ricketson, is regrettably represented here by a single letter. This is particularly frustrating because Letters 91, 93, 95, and 133 confirm that both Susanna and her husband were often in contact with Anna's father, Daniel Ricketson (1813–98), a gentle-spirited Quaker and abolitionist of New Bedford, Massachusetts, and acquaintance of Henry David Thoreau, Bronson Alcott, Ralph Waldo Emerson, and other New England writers and intellectuals. It may well have been Ricketson who wrote the unsigned but highly favourable review of *Roughing It in the Bush* in the New Bedford *Mercury* of 9 July 1852. Certainly he knew

J. Allen Ransome of Ipswich

Dunbar, likely as a result of the latter's occasional trips to the United States, and he often wrote to the Moodies. As Susanna told Ransome in November 1869 (Letter 93), Ricketson's 'delightful letters and poems have been a great solace to me and my husband.'[8]

In the late sixties, family matters increasingly preoccupied Susanna. Her brother Samuel, a victim of diabetes that emerged late in his life, failed rapidly after his last trip back to England in 1866 and he died in Lakefield in January 1867. Her sister Catharine, residing in Lakefield, continued to suffer from ailments and complaints but spent much time in Belleville and Toronto during 1865 and 1866 visiting and trying desperately to make arrangements with various publishers. Her schemes, which seem to have come to nothing until she teamed up with Agnes Fitzgibbon, were pragmatic efforts to relieve the financial constraints that troubled her greatly during these years. At the same time, she was much concerned about her Belleville-based children, Mary Muchall, whose husband Tom had a drinking problem, and James Traill, who, much weakened by what was likely recurring tuberculosis, died in 1867. Susanna knew Mary and James well and was solicitous of their struggles and well-being. But she also had concerns of her own, in particular the problems of her two oldest sons. As Catharine observed in a letter to her daughter Annie on 9 April 1868: 'Your poor aunt is doomed to suffer through her children; it makes me sad to think of her trials in that way.'

John Alexander Dunbar Moodie, the eldest son, who had followed the gold rush to California and Nevada in the 1850s, had returned home and in 1862, at the age of twenty-eight, married Elizabeth (Eliza) Roberta Russell, the eldest daughter of the Hon. Robert Russell. Russell, a colonial administrator in the British West Indies, had visited Belleville in the late 1850s, possibly seeking a more 'English' environment for his two daughters, for when he returned to Jamaica he left them as boarders in the Moodie household, thus occasioning the meeting with Dunbar. The young couple continued to live near the Moodies after their marriage and had two children in Belleville.[9] However, some four years later, Susanna's relationship with her daughter-in-law began to deteriorate. According to Letter 81, the Moodies made the ownership of the stone cottage on Sinclair Street over to their son 'in the hope,' as Susanna phrased it, 'of securing a home for us, in our old age.' The younger couple subsequently sold it in order to emigrate to the United States. A combination of factors made a split inevitable. There was, in the first place, a feeling of loss upon the sale of their old home. Susanna had been ill and her husband's health was weakening; moreover, she was distressed at the arrogant manner of Eliza once the younger woman felt she was in charge. Eliza and Dunbar used most of the money from the sale of the house to purchase a farm near Camden, Delaware, where in August 1866 their third child was born. They had invited the elder Moodies to join them, but the prospect of living with Eliza apparently caused Susanna and Dunbar to reject the scheme to emigrate so late in life. Left behind with little and feeling hard done by, the elder Moodies rented a small cottage near the Bay of Quinte, where they lived for the next few years. So great was Susanna's exasperation with Eliza that in Letter 81 she indulges in racial slurs somewhat surprising in a woman so taken up with the cause of abolishing slavery. Clearly, such a contradictory tendency was not common either in her or in her husband. As late as 26 March 1862, in the *Christian Guardian*, Dunbar had published an anti-slavery poem, 'Stand Your Ground,' and had pursued his anti-slavery interests in visits to the United States. Such outbursts serve to remind us, however, that for many Victorians of an idealistic cast of mind the strength of family feeling often clashed with high-minded principles.

Donald Moodie presented problems of a different order. An attractive youth of considerable potential, he had been much doted upon by his mother. He had, however, failed in all his endeavours: his medical studies in Montreal in the 1850s, his subsequent law studies, and his work as a law student with the Belleville firm of Ross and Bell in the early 1860s. A report in the Belleville *Intelligencer* on 26 December 1862 mentions Donald's participation in a tavern brawl, an early hint of his subsequent alcoholism. His marriage to Julia Anna Russell, Eliza's sister, in February 1866 in Brooklyn, New York, was apparently undertaken without his parents' knowledge or approval, but seems at least temporarily to have awakened in him some sense of responsibility. Two years later, however, he had lost his job with the Inman Steamship Company and seems to have disappeared for a time;[10] in the 1870s he would increasingly fall victim to alcoholism, as later letters reveal.

By contrast, the youngest son, Robert, was reliable and of all the children remained closest to his parents in their later years. After attending several educational institutions in the 1850s, he served as his father's deputy until 1863, then acted as assistant to Dunbar's successor, Sheriff George Taylor, until 1865. He married Sarah Ellen (Nellie) Russell (not related to the Jamaican Russells) in Belleville in June 1863 and their first child, Bessie, was born the following April. For a period in the late 1860s, he was forced to leave his family in Belleville while he sought work in the United States, working briefly in Brooklyn (reporting to his parents on Donald's work with the Inman firm in 1866), before returning to Canada.

Susanna and Dunbar Moodie with Julia or Eliza Russell

He served in the Hastings militia, worked briefly as captain of the Lake Ontario schooner, the *Alert*, and then entered the service of the Grand Trunk Railway as a freight clerk in the southwestern Ontario town of Seaforth. Robert's progress was slow but steady and he seems never to have lapsed in his affection for his parents. Little wonder, then, that Susanna described him fondly to Allen Ransome (Letter 93) as 'His dear Father's best and most beloved son.'

Agnes Fitzgibbon, the first child born in Canada, also faced serious difficulties during this period. Despite his legal abilities and his political prominence, Charles Fitzgibbon was troubled by illness and his precarious financial situation led to additional uncertainties. He died on 22 February 1865, leaving his wife with six children, two of whom, John Wedderburn Dunbar, age five, and William Winder, age four (the Billy of Letter 85), also died within eighteen months. Much grieved by her losses, Agnes, whose own health was always delicate, had neither the time to visit nor the means to aid her struggling parents.[11] Her eldest daughter, Mary Agnes, born in Belleville in 1851 and referred to by Susanna as 'Maime' or 'Mamy,' did, however, occasionally come to stay during these years. She became a favourite granddaughter and Susanna did what she could, within her own limited means, to promote these visits, both as a consolation for herself and as relief for Agnes. It is Mamy whose presence is the subject of Susanna's note (Letter 90) to a Belleville friend, Mrs Kersterman.

While Agnes's troubles were of deep concern, Susanna was also puzzled and upset by the silence of her eldest daughter, Katie Vickers, who was living comfortably in Toronto with her husband and their six children. By 1864 John Vickers had established himself as a well-known businessman and influential Tory; he was a captain in the sedentary militia, and from 1864 to 1879 served as alderman for St George's Ward, taking the lead in the movement to construct a new waterworks for the city.

The silence that so disturbed the Moodies (see Letter 84) was the result of John Vickers's strong disapproval of Moodie senior's decision to allow his son to sell the stone cottage. Likely, Vickers, who had provided some financial aid to the Moodies, felt he was in a position to offer sounder advice about what was, after all, their major capital investment. On the basis of available letters (see Letter 103), it seems the estrangement continued until Moodie's death, when John Vickers attended the funeral thereby reopening the lines of communication between mother and daughter.

During his years of retirement, Moodie's health, which had always worried Susanna, declined markedly. The partial paralysis that resulted from a stroke in 1861 seems to have increased to the point where he was unable to leave his bed without assistance. Nevertheless, Susanna describes their last few years together as happy and contented. He died on 22 October 1869 at the age of seventy-two. Her account of his death in a letter to Allen Ransome on 9 November is a moving tribute to the love and companionship that had sustained them both through thirty-eight often difficult years.

1 J.W.D. Moodie, *Scenes and Adventures of a Soldier and Settler during Half a Century* (Montreal: Lovell 1866), xvi. The 'Presentment,' signed by Grand Jury foreman George Neilson, was printed in both the Belleville *Intelligencer* (7 March 1863) and the Hastings *Chronicle*.

2 The 'Presentment' was brought to the attention of the provincial secretary with the support of Mr Justice Hagerty. On 16 April 1863, the *Intelligencer* printed an encouraging reply from Assistant Secretary E.A. Meredith that 'the subject will receive the consideration of the government.' But on 15 May 1863 the government fell. Even though the subsequent election returned John Sandfield Macdonald and A.A. Dorion to power, the ministry was significantly altered. Elected on an anti-British platform, opposed to the colonial patronage system, these men were not the most encouraging source of appeal for the Moodies.

3 See W.L. Morton, *Henry Youle Hind, 1823–1908* (Toronto 1980).

4 John Lovell's 'new' paper, referred to in Letter 87, was the Montreal *Daily News*. Extant copies of its 1867 running of 'Dorothy Chance' have not been located.

5 The 'Arminius' referred to here is the poem Susanna had published in the 1830s.

6 A Scot by birth, Notman came to Montreal in 1856, expanding his business to various cities in Canada and the United States and gaining a reputation for the medals he won at international exhibitions. The first volume of his impressive *Portraits of British Americans* was printed in 1865.

7 See *The Victoria History of the Counties of England: Suffolk*, ed. William Page (London 1911), and J. Allen Ransome, *The Implements of Agriculture* (London 1843).

8 There are no known letters from or to the Moodies among the much broken holdings of Ricketson's papers in archival and private collections. Nor is any mention made of them in the two published collections of Ricketson material, edited by his son and daughter, Walter and Anna, *Daniel Ricketson and His Friends* (Boston 1902) and *Daniel Ricketson: Autobiographic and Miscellaneous* (New Bedford 1910).

9 Robert W. Moodie, 'The Moodie Family of Melsetter and Cocklaw in America' (1976), Public Archives of Canada, MG25 G274

10 In a letter to her daughter Annie Atwood, 9 April 1868, Catharine Parr Traill writes: 'Donald has disappeared having lost his situation and aunt is in a great state of anxiety about him. She has only heard this from someone in B[elleville] who has been in New York.' (PAC, Traill Family Collection)

11 Having visited Agnes in Toronto after her husband's death, Catharine observed in a letter of 2 March 1865 that '[she] will not be badly off. She will have enough to live on with comfort if careful.' George Rose's *A Cyclopedia of Canadian Biography: Being Chiefly Men of the Time* (Toronto 1886) includes interesting sketches of John Vickers and Robert Moodie.

74 To the publishers of the *British American Magazine*

Belleville
March 4th 1863

Sir,

I did not reply to your letter, until I was certain, that I could comply with your request. I have written two Sketches, which I think may interest your readers.[1]

Truth is always more interesting than fiction, and both are drawn from life.

Should these find favor in the eyes of your Editor,[2] I shall be able to furnish more of the same stamp.

I gladly accept your promise of remuneration. Mr. Moodie having resigned his situation, we are just now under the dark cloud of adversity, and every honorable means of earning bread, I consider a blessing.

You ask for my dear sister Traill's address. It is as follows –

Mrs. Traill
To the Care of Sam'l Strickland, Esqre
North Douro, C.W.

Will you kindly take care of the MSS. if they are inadmissable, as I cannot spare precious time to make copies. Writing to an old woman of sixty, is a hard task

Yours truly
Susanna Moodie –

I will send the Sketches by Express, to the care of Mrs. Vickers.

1 Only one of Susanna's autobiographical sketches, 'My Cousin Tom – A Sketch from Life,' appeared in this year, in May. The newly established *British American Magazine*, a monthly periodical, aimed to replace the *Literary Garland* as a cultural voice and to present to the public scientific information written in familiar language.
2 Professor Henry Youle Hind, MA, FRGS, who regularly contributed scientific sketches and editorials to the magazine

75 To Catharine Parr Traill   [late May 1863][1]

... Jane. She says, 'I am delighted with James Traill. He is not so handsome as his mother, but he is very like her, and his Uncle Tom, but
much better looking than Tom ever was.' Agnes was from home on a visit
in Suffolk, but she expected her return before James left. I pray that this
visit may be productive of good to you all. Jane wrote kinder than is her
wont to me, and as I did not write by James, I felt grateful for the
friendly feeling her letter displayed. Our dear old Mother was quite well –
had got through the winter splendidly. Jane was complaining as usual.
Of Eliza and Sarah she made no mention at all. Tom had been to see them
since his return, and sailed again for New York the day she wrote. He
had his daughter Diana with him, for change of scene and air, as the
breaking off of her marriage with some one, whom she does not name,
on account of money matters was the cause of her Mother's death.[2] Jane
expresses a hope that Sam would meet his brother at New York, and
introduce Diana to her aunts and cousins. Poor Jane seems to think that
New York is a very little distance from Douro. I should like to see dear
Tom very much, it seems cruelly tantalizing for him to visit this continent,
and not be able to meet. Poverty has few things more distasteful in its
bitter cup than this separation of friends. Harry has been and is gone, he
looks very well, and seems cheerful and hopeful.[3] Mary was still at Rice
Lake. I saw Amelia yesterday and the two fine boys. The little Tom still
takes me for his grandmother, and I do not attempt to undeceive him,
he is a very nice little fellow. The boys appear very fond of each other.[4]
With regard to our own affairs, everything looks dismal enough. With
this ministry all hope of obtaining another situation expires, and Father
has been in very ...

1 Date assigned because of reference in the fragment to James Traill's visit to England and
  the allusion to a general election that took place on or near 26 May 1863.
2 After his first wife, Anne Thompson, died, Tom Strickland married a woman named
  Margaretta (about whom little is known). They had six children: Walter, Julia, Mary,
  Diana, Adela, and Elizabeth. Diana married a Mr Patrickson; other than the evidence of
  this letter, nothing is known of the failed marriage or of Mrs Tom Strickland's death.
3 Thomas Henry Traill (1837–70), Catharine's second son, was farming at Rice Lake and
  courting Lilias Grant MacLean of Belleville.
4 James and Amelia Traill, who lived in Belleville, had two young sons, Richard Henry
  (born 1858) and Thomas Edward Strickland (1859).

76 To Catharine Parr Traill   Belleville
Jan. 6th, 1864

My Very dear Sister,

I return you all the good wishes, you so kindly send me, with interest. God
grant that this new year, may bring health and prosperity to you and
yours, especially to the good Mary who has gone from the home nest, to
build for herself a new home in the world.[1] She deserves all the good
that this world can bestow, which may be comprised in the short sentence
– domestic happiness – and she is deserving of this, in no small degree.
Moodie, told me on Monday that she was home from Brockville and I
went down in the afternoon to see her. I found her looking well, and
very cheerful and happy. It was a pleasure to look into the dear sunny
affectionate face. I was indeed glad to see her, glad to have her so near
me, and I will do all that I can, to give her the advice about household
matters that you desire.

I know that she loves me, and I hope that she will make a motherly
substitute of me, in the absence of her own dear Mother. I like her
husband, he seems a kind sensible man. I prefer him to all the Muchalls
that I have seen, and I believe that he will make a good affectionate
husband, to his excellent young wife. They have a very nice house, comfortably furnished, and Mary is too prudent to run into any unnecessary
expense. She has promised to come up and see us tomorrow when I shall
hear all about the wedding, and the dear Douro friends. Father came
home from Toronto in a very delicate state of health, but he has rallied
since, and though not so well as I could wish, has much improved since
his return. Our affairs, remain just in the same state as before. Mr. Wallbridge promises to get the government to do something for him, but I
build very little upon these promises. I wish the dear husband would cease
to hope, and resign himself to the probability of disappointment. The
anxiety and uncertainty of his position is killing him by inches. He left the
girls and their children in Toronto, quite well. Dunbar and Lizzie are
well, but the dear little baby[2] was dangerously ill for some weeks with
dropsy caused by scarlett fever turning into the system. She was swol-
len all over from head to foot, and for some time Dr. Lister thought there
was no hope of her recovery. It was a very trying time for the poor
Mother, who had the fever likewise. The dear little thing is getting quite
strong again and has cut six teeth, and more nearly through. It is a very
sweet tempered intelligent child, Grandpa's darling, and she knows him

so well, and is so fond of him. She can say a good many words, and imitates every sound she hears.

Dunbar is talking of going down to the lower Province in the spring to try his chance of mining once more. I shall miss them very much when they go. But many changes may take place before then. I have found it best, not to look too far ahead. The future we are so apt to dread may never be ours. I have not seen Harry; Mary tells me that he is going back tomorrow. James is looking better. Boysey,[3] has a very mild sort of whooping cough and Tom is flourishing. Robert, and his dear little wife are quite well. She expects a baby in the spring. I think Mary and Nellie would be great friends as they are girls of the same stamp – generous warm hearted and affectionate – I am very fond of my dear little daughter.[4] They have a nice cottage and are very comfortable, though they keep no servants and live very economically. Her Mother helps them a great deal, and is very fond of Rob.

It is a hard trial for you dear Katie to part with your girls, they are such a comfort to the Mother, but it is the law of nature, a sorrow for which there is but one remedy, the satisfaction of knowing that they have a home of their own when we are gone. This has always consoled me for the lonely years that I have past, without female love and sympathy, with no loving child to comfort you in sickness or advise and strengthen you in times of trouble and anxiety. Strangers may be kind, but you cannot repose your mind upon them, with the perfect confidence you feel in a loving child. Katie will feel her sister's loss very much, and you say truly of Mary, that she is devoid of selfishness. I see your *friend* Mr. McCarrol has lost his situation. Agnes shewed me his letter to you. It was worthy of him.[5] I could not help laughing at the, *'literary fossil,'* for I really feel, that I am growing one myself and often say, I am beginning to petrify. Ideas will no longer come. I seek, but do not find. Solomon said truly – There is a time, for all things under the sun. There is a time to write and a time to refrain from writing. I feel that the latter season has come for me. By the way, McLear[6] wrote to me to know, what was the lowest sum I could take for writing for their Magazine. I named 2/6 per page. It was a miserable pittance, but was eagerly accepted. Perhaps they wait for you to reduce your terms. He said, that most of their contributions they received gratis, and they couldn't afford to pay much for the very best articles. I feel very much inclined not to write at all, for my mind is neither so lively nor so elastic as formerly, and then, I shrink from the mechanical part of the business, even the writing of a letter tires me. You will perhaps get this on your birthday. May you live to see many returns of it, my beloved sister. I hope we may live to meet again, and have many a pleasant chat, over the past.

You will always be an honored and welcome guest as long as I have a home of my own in the which to receive you. I have not heard from Reydon since I last wrote. On Christmas day, I wrote a long letter to the dear old Mother, though she may not be able to read it, she may be pleased that I did so. Donald is with us just now, he has been ill for the last week, and is seldom well many days together.

How I wish I had a photograph of Uncle like the vignette one that Mary shewed me.[7] He looks beautiful in that, but the sitting one, he sent me, is not like him. I did not even recognize him in it. I should like one of you the same size. I would gladly pay for it. Here, they charge only three dollars a dozen for them, or a quarter a piece. But if you come, I will have one, it would be such a treasure to me. Alwred Goddart called here the other day. How time flies. He is a grey-haired middleaged man. He shewed me a photograph of his brother Cyprian, my old favorite. He too, bears the brand of coming age. I can hardly realize these changes. They seem so odd. I am certain that dear Sam, did every thing he could for Mary. He has been a dear generous brother to you, and I feel proud of him. Give our united love to him and his dear wife. May every happiness be theirs, both in time and eternity, and don't forget Aunt Susys love to all the nephews and nieces young and old. The weather here is *cruel* cold, with hurricanes of wind. It reminds me of the first year we came to Belleville. Mary is to enclose a note in this, so I must cut my yarn short. Julia sends her love to Jenny,[8] and begs her remembrances to Mr. and Mrs. Strickland. Good night my dear sister. God bless you ever.

Your loving sister,
Susanna Moodie

Julia will write to Jenny soon.

1 Mary Traill married Thomas Muchall in December 1863, and after a wedding trip to Brockville the couple settled in Belleville.
2 A daughter, Agnes Strickland Dunbar Moodie, born 11 February 1863
3 Richard Henry Traill's childhood nickname
4 Robert's wife, Nellie
5 James McCarrol (1815–96), a teacher, journalist, and poet who lived in Douro for several years; editor and proprietor of the Peterborough *Chronicle* and the Newcastle *Courier* during the 1840s; later established a humourous weekly, *The Latchkey*
6 Thomas Maclear was connected with the *British American Magazine*.
7 A 'head and shoulders' photograph of Samuel Strickland, Mary's uncle
8 Julia Russell and Jane Strickland, Sam's eldest daughter

77 To Richard Bentley

Belleville
[early] March [1865][1]

My Dear Mr. Bentley,

I can offer no excuse, for suffering your last kind letter making over to me, the copyrights of the works you have published for me, (saving *Roughing It in the Bush*) long ago. I have been so harrassed by cares and sorrows, that I had no heart to write, even to thank *you*, for your generous gift. You have known much of this worlds troubles, and will I know, forgive me. Mr. Nelson returned to England, without visiting Toronto, and I did not avail myself of your liberality.[2]

The horrid and fratricidal war, still carried on in the States, has closed that market to Canadian Literature, and has so crippled the commerce of Canada, that the greatest distress prevails on every side. People have neither time to read books, nor money to buy them, if they had. They would not even support a very clever Magazine carried on by Professor Hinds, of the Upper Canada College, and let it drop to the ground to the great loss of the proprietors.

[The go]vernment have done nothing for [my de]ar husband, though many offices which he could have filled have fallen to their disposal. They always speak fair, but do nothing. I find this living upon hope a very sorry indigestible sort of diet, which does not at all agree with my natural independence of character. I would gladly work for my own living, could I only get work to do, but there lies the difficulty. I have entered upon my sixty first year, and the cares and anxieties of the last four years have made me very old and feeble. I feel indeed, that my strength is failing me fast, that but a short time may elapse before I gain the coveted quiet of the grave. But while I live, I want to help those I love, and earn bread for myself. If you could only assist me in getting some employment in England, which would bring even a small sum it would be a great favor, and help to keep the gaunt wolf poverty from the door. I send for your inspection a manuscript entitled, 'The Race for Royalty and who won.' It is not the worst thing I ever wrote, and has at least the merit of originality. It would have made a capital play had I time to arrange it for the stage as it is highly dramatic, and the interest does not flag to the end, but gains strength as the story goes on. It was written many years ago when my heart was full of the dreams and hopes of youth, ere the cares of the world and the frowns of an untoward fortune, had calmed my aspirations, and worn down the energy of my spirit. My sisters Agnes and Eliza, used to say, it was the best thing I ever wrote. It has lain by

me, for many a long year, and should you think it worth publication, I
should be glad to sell the MS. out and out, for whatever sum you
deem it honestly worth, only reserving to myself, the right of republication
from the advanced sheets in the States. The story is founded on an old
legend, which I found in a very ancient Geography and History of Europe,
in my father's library. Whether worthy of historical credence I don't
know, and the name of the old book, which I have no means of referring
to, and which I have not seen for forty years, I have forgotten. The
legend pleased me, suited my purpose and I wove from it, the tale you
have before you. It would afford many picturesque subjects for illustra-
tion had I the pencil or the talent for supplying them. I am now employed
upon a story, which promises to be good – 'Dorothy Chance, or the
fortunes of the Foundlin[g].' When completed, would you like to see it? If
you could help me to dispose of it, You do not know what an act of
kindness it would be. The dark clouds of adversity have gathered so thick-
ly over me, that I can see no bright lining to their stormy edges. My
dear husband is well nigh heart-broken, and the infirmities of age are
upon him. He has been cruelly treated, after having served the country
so faithfu[lly] for so many years. It seems hard to be called upon to endure
greater privations at the close of life, than we did in the Bush, we no
longer have the strength and buoyant hopes of youth, to help us out of our
present difficulties. To add to our many sorrows, my dear daughter
Agnes, has within a few weeks, lost her husband, and been left with six
small children, the youngest only two years and a half old, without any
means to support them. Her husband, had the place of Clerk of the Surro-
gate court, which brought him an income of four hundred a year, but an
improvident Irishman, who always lived beyond his means. His sudden
death, has left his family destitute, and what is to become of them, I do
not know. We have *no income*, and are barely living upon what debts we
can collect from Mr. M's late office. But, even this, scanty maintenance
cannot last long. My eldest daughter, does all she can to help us, but she
has a large young family, and it is with deep regret, that we are obliged
to take from them a part of their living. Two of my three sons, are married, but their means are *very limited*, and in these, *the dark days of
Canada*, they can barely support their families. Help from them is impossible. My second son, has never succeeded in keeping himself; and his
heedless extravagance has been a sore burthen and trial to us. With fine
person, excellent manners and good abilities, he has failed in every
instance to establish himself, either as a medical man or in the law, both
professions he has studied, but relinquished for sheer want of application, and a proper spirit of independence. It is a shame to burthen you my

dear old friend, with this long catalogue of domestic troubles, and I
would not attempt it, did I not feel certain of your kind sympathy. And
now about yourself. I hope you are enjoying a healthy old age, surrounded by a happy and prosperous family. How is our young friend, Mr.
Horace? Has he commenced his clerical career? Pray remember us most
kindly to him. Many changes have taken place since he was among us.
Many faces he then saw, the world will see no more. Belleville is enlarg-
ing its bounds on every side, and promises soon to be city. Another English church has been built by the river, on the west end of the town.
And a very large one indeed, belonging to the Wesle[y]an Methodists,
fronting the English church on the hill, and handsome dwelling houses in
abundance, but the spirit of gloom hangs over all. The doing away of the
reciprocity treaty, between Canada and the States, has destroyed the
lumber trade, one of the great sources of our national wealth; and nearly
destroyed all the important mercantile transactions between us and the
Northern States, while the constant influx of Southern refugees, and their
plots concocted here,[3] have drawn upon us, the hatred and suspicion of
the North, who look upon us, as enemies. The great drought of last summer, destroyed the harvest all over the country, and most of the farmers are ruined in consequence. Inspite of the great scarcity, they have to
sell their scanty produce, at ruinous low prices, and the best of it goes
to the States. We live in hope that if the federation of the British North
American provinces, c[an] be carried through; a better state o[f th]ings
may take place. Lower and [U]pper Canada are agreed, a[n]d New
Brunswick seems fa[v]orably disposed for such an union; but Nova Scotia
and Prince Edward offer factious opposition, on very low and selfish
grounds. They will not see, that union will alone save them from the
felonious grasp of the [No]rth, and even loyal men, fear [t]hat if their arms
were turned against Canada, she must fall before such overwhelming
odds. It would be impossible, for a handful of raw militia, who have never
smelt gunpowder to stand against their huge well-diciplined armies.
May God in his mercy, avert from us the horror of such a war. The one
now carried on across the border is unparrallelled in the annals of
history for its blood-thirsty and savage love of slaughter. It seems to me as
if the curse of God rested upon the land; as if it were undergoing a
fearful punishment for its sins. I must hasten to [co]nclude this long epistle. Mr. Moodie unites wi[th] me, in kind regards, and hope[s] that the
MS. I send by the same [ma]il, may find favor in your eye[s.] I remain,

> My dear Mr. Bentley,
> Your grateful and sincere friend
> Susanna Moodie

1 Dated 1865 for several internal reasons: the death of the Moodies' son-in-law, Charles Fitzgibbon; the death of young John Fitzgibbon on 16 March 1865; and the demise of the *British American Magazine*.
2 Likely William Nelson, son of Thomas Nelson, who entered his father's Edinburgh publishing business in 1835 and travelled regularly as the firm's chief agent promoting sales.
3 An allusion to the brief invasion from the Eastern Townships of St Albans, Vermont, on 19 October 1864. The raid, led by a score of commissioned Confederate officers, was ineffectual but had the effect, in Donald Creighton's words in 'The 1860s,' *The Canadians*, ed. J.M.S. Careless and R. Craig Brown (Toronto 1968), 26, of 'rous[ing] the Northern Americans to a state of fury against the Province of Canada.' Considering Canada guilty of a violation of neutrality, Americans talked increasingly of invasion and of arming the Great Lakes.

---

78 To Richard Bentley

Belleville
April 24 / 65

My Dear Mr Bentley,

The contents of your letter brought the tears to my eyes. I have read and reread it many times, and fervently thanked our heavenly Father, for raising me up a true friend, in the hour of grief. God bless you, for your goodness, and reward you an *hundred* fold. I find words very inadequate to express all I feel upon the subject. I prize your kind sympathy, even more than your generous offers of service, it has soothed and comforted my heart. I never imagined, that any writings of mine, could deserve assistance for the author from the Government, or from any literary society, and I never made any application, for such relief.[1]

The Canadian Government, does not *encourage literary* talent. I never heard of it granting a pension to any author, and I did not make any application to it – for assistance. One of their public men, Dr Rolph[2] – long since dead – used to say, that Mrs. Moodie, deserved a pension from the British Government for the good that her patriotic songs, did, during the rebellion of – /37. I hold perhaps, the first place among the female authors residing within the Colony; and my contributions to their periodical literature, has always enjoyed great popularity. But this has not made them, more ready to give my dear husband a small place under the government, to keep us from the Author's fate – A dry crust and the garret. My husband is now in Toronto, whither he has gone, to *mortgage* the few acres we possess, to raise the money to pay off the execution brought against us, by the government Attorneys, to settle the law costs, in that most unrighteous suit; which deprived an honest good man of his

office, and his family of bread. When he returns, we will fill the literary
fund schedule, and return it to you, with the necessary documents. I am
a babe in such matters. I really don't know how to set about it, and I leave
entirely to you, the *memorial* to the *government*. I am sure, it will be
done so much better, than I can do it. I am gifted, with *too many words*.
Shall say *too much*, and do not know the propper form of words to use.
An annual pension, however, *small*,[3] would be a great mercy, if it only
enabled us to pay the interest, (of 10 percent), on these horrid mortgag-
es. We have no *income* in the world, and are living on the few small debts,
that Mr Moodie, now and then, gets paid, for work done while in the
office. Would you believe it? Lawyers, whose dues to us, embraced hundreds of pounds, and in one instance £1000, have pleaded the '*statute
of limitations*' and thus escaped from paying their just debts. I will now
turn to your letter, and answer the queries.
1st. I hope the 'Race for Royalty,' may please you. It does not want for
a certain degree of wit, and possesses much dramatic effect, and it
could be made into a lively acting play. But somehow, I do not care for
theatricals. I believe, I had a natural talent that way, but I have never
encouraged it. The moral of my story, is the certainty of good always
triumphing over evil, in the end, and Lectius is a fine manly fellow.
Honest and independent, without cant.

I am not very extravagant in my expectations. If you like it, give me
what you can afford to pay for it. I shall be thankful for a small sum. 2d.
If Mr Nelson, be inclined to purchase the Copyrights, I leave the terms
entirely to you. I know that you will do better for me, than I can do for
myself. I shall be gratefully satisfied, by any arrangement that you can
make.

I send you by this mail, the copy of a volume of poems, published by
me, and printed by Messrs Smith and Elder.[4] It paid its expenses, and
£20 to boot, though published by subscription, and was very well reviewed, both in England and Scotland. The volume, is rather dilapidat-
ed, and has long been out of print. Of its moral tendency, there can be no
doubt. Mr Nelson might, perhaps, purchase the copyright. I have many
poems, superior to some of these, (which were mostly written when very
young) – which might supply the place of others, of which he did not
approve.

If it be necessary, to send a copy to the Literary fund, of all the books
and papers, I have written, it is not in my power, for most of the
Magazines, were burnt in the fire, and nearly all my private papers.[5]

I have only one copy of *Roughing It*, ditto of *Clearings*, of *Flora Lind-*

say, of *Matrimonial Speculations*, of *Mark Hurdlestone*. I never had one of the English edition of *Geoffrey Moncton*, and I should be sorry to part with the copies of the books I have.

The first time, I ever appeared in print, was in a small volume, called *Spartacus or the Slave's Struggle for freedom*. It was written at thirteen years of age.[6] James Black, of Covent garden, who for years was printer to the house of Commons (whom perhaps, you knew) was an old friend and brother Mason of my father's,[7] came down to pay us a visit at Reydon. My Mother shewed him the MS. as a literary curiosity, turning to me, he said, 'Suzy I shall keep this.' How great was my surprise, when some months after, he sent me 10 pounds and *Spartacus, my Spartacus*, in a pretty little bound volume.

I had no idea of writing to make books, in those days. It seemed to me a dream, that I held a book written by myself, in my hand. *Spartacus*, of which I have no copy, was published by *Lane*, I think of the *Ave Maria firm*, but the little book, though bearing upon every page, the mark of a child's hand, went through many editions.[8]

My next literary efforts were a series of childrens tales. *Precept and Practice, or the Vicar's Tales*,[9] were published by Dean and Munday of Threadneedle Street. Also, *Hugh Latimer, Rowland Massingham* and *The Little Prisoner*.[10] Maunder, of Newgate Street, who was always a kind friend, published *Josiah Shirley, the little Quaker*, and 'Mamma's fairy tales in rhyme,' both of these, he told me, had a great sale.[11] *Hugh Latimer*, has gone through many editions, and is still being published under the title of *The Soldier's Orphan*.[12] I wrote for several years, for *La Belle Assemble*, while Tho[s] Harral was editor, and gained very flattering notices of my articles. I wrote under the signature of ZZ in *Friendship's Offering*, and as Sophia Sandys, in the *Athenaem*. For *Ackerman's Juvenile Forget-Me-Not*, under my own name. My tale of the 'Son of Arminius,' was noticed by some of the journals of the day, as one of his best contributions.[13] I then published the book, I send you, just as I was leaving for Canada, leaving my poor literary babe, like an orphan to its fate.

While in Canada, I wrote a few poems for Dr Bartlett's *Albion* and had I accepted his kind offer to come to New York, and become one of his regular contributors,[14] I should have been better off than toiling in the Bush for so many hopeless years.

I contributed for seven years, to the *Literary Garland* published by Mr Lovell of Montreal. *Roughing It in the Bush*, appeared in its pages, as 'Canadian Sketches,' *Mark Hurdlestone* as the 'Miser and his Son,'

Geoffrey Moncton, The Memoirs of a poor Relation. ('The First Debt'), the MS. you returned to me, was the most popular story I wrote for it. 'Jane Redgrave,' 'Mildred Rosier,' and 'Monica, or Witchcraft,' three novels, have never been republished.[15] 'Monica,' and 'Jane Redgrave,' might, perhaps please the English public. I could send you the bound volumes that contain them, for your inspection. I wrote for a short time for the *North American Quarterly*, published in Philadelphia, and edited by the poet Fairfield – Whose remarkable poem, *'The last Nights of Pompeii'* was published before Bulwer's work, and sent to him, by the author, it bears a striking resemblance to that beautiful production. Fairfield wrote me the whole tale of his wrongs, whether real or imaginary, I cannot say. As he told his story, it looked ugly enough. Only I think it more likely for the American to rob Bulwer, than the latter to steal from him.

Last year I wrote several papers for the *British North American Magazine*, for the poor sum of 2/6 per page, and they wanted to give me only half of that, and left *unpaid*, one article. To be sure, they paid none of their contributors, but me. In the year '48, Mr M and myself, edited a Mag. called the *Victoria Magazine*, but got nothing for our labor, though the Mag. was a success, having obtained the first year 500 subscribers, who *all paid in advance*, and who were ready to subscribe again, if we would continue to conduct it. The proprietor was such a dishonest fellow, that we declined it altogether. You see my dear friend, that I have been dabbling in ink from my childhood, though I have not gained much by my authorship. I lost a great many unpublished papers in our fire in Belleville, and could not re-write from memory. I think I can safely say, that I never wrote anything, but in the hope of its doing some good or forming some useful lesson. But I conscientiously believe, that I do *not deserve*, half the credit for talent, that the world, especially the American world, has bestowed upon me. The Canadians will never forgive me for disclosing the secrets of that rural prison-house the Bush. I have no doubt, they consider our present distress a just punishment for telling the truth ...

---

1 Bentley had been for years a director of the Royal Literary Fund, designed particularly to help impoverished or ailing writers.
2 Dr John Rolph (1793–1870), politician, lawyer, physician, and teacher of medicine at Victoria College
3 Bentley had likely asked her to choose between a lump-sum gift or an annual pension.
4 *Enthusiasm, and Other Poems.* Eleven years earlier Moodie had sent Bentley the same book (see Letter 54).
5 'In the December of 1840 we had the misfortune to be burnt out, and lost a great part of our furniture, clothing, and winter stores.' *Life in the Clearings*, 13

6 *Spartacus*, which has at least two variant subtitles – 'A Roman Story' and 'The Slave's Struggle for Freedom' – was published by A.K. Newman in London in 1822. Susanna was then eighteen or nineteen.

7 James Black is an interesting figure in the Stricklands' background. Not only did he take an interest in the family after the death of his close friend, Thomas Strickland, but he later left his position as printer – under some sort of cloud, according to Samuel in *Twenty-Seven Years in Canada West* – and emigrated to Canada, settling in the Darlington area on Lake Ontario west of Cobourg. It was on Black's suggestion in 1825 that Samuel emigrated and it was Black's daughter Emma whom he married. Emma died in childbirth in the spring of 1826; Samuel's son by that marriage lived only three years. It may well have been the Blacks whose letters provided Catharine with much of the material for her children's book, *The Young Emigrants; or, Pictures of Canada* (London: Harvey and Darton 1826). Black was later appointed to the Bench and was made a militia colonel.

8 A.K. Newman had taken over John Lane's Minerva Press, originally located in London in Ave Maria Lane.

9 Also printed under variant titles *Practice and Profession* and *Profession and Principle*

10 Dean and Munday published *Rowland Massingham; or, I Will Be My Own Master*, but no copy has been found to verify publication in the 1820s. *Hugh Latimer; or the School-Boy's Friendship* was published by both A.K. Newman and Dean and Munday, its frontispiece carrying the date 1828. *The Little Prisoner; or, Passion and Patience* was published by itself and in combination with Catharine Parr Strickland's *Amendment*; the *English Catalogue of Books* describes it as published by Newman in 1829.

11 *Josiah Shirley, the Little Quaker* or *The Little Quaker; or, the Triumph of Virtue* are variant titles. The copy held by the Osborne Collection has the latter title and was published by William Cole of London (firm started 1825) but without a date. No trace of *Mamma's Fairy Tales in Rhyme* has been found.

12 The British Library catalogue lists *The Soldier's Orphan; or Hugh Latimer and Something More about the Soldier's Orphan, or the Further Adventures of Hugh Latimer*, 2 parts (London: Thomas Dean and Son 1853); the story was printed in two forms, complete in one book and as two separate parts. The frontispiece of *Hugh Latimer* carries the date 1828.

13 Actually she published poetry in several annuals under the signature of Z.Z. Two poems in the *Athenaeum* early in 1830 are signed Sophia Sandys: 'Stanzas: Thou Wilt Think of Me Love' (23 January), 42, and 'To Water Lilies' (6 March), 136. For 'Son of Arminius,' see Letter 11, note 2.

14 There is no evidence of this offer, though Bartlett published several of her poems in the *Albion*.

15 In fact, Susanna wrote for the *Literary Garland* for twelve years. The 'Canadian Sketches' appeared in 1847, the 'Miser and His Son' in 1842, 'Geoffrey Moncton' in 1839–40, and 'The First Debt. A Tale of Today' in 1841. 'Jane Redgrave' was serialized in 1848, 'Mildred Rosier' in 1844, and 'Monica; or, Witchcraft' in 1846.

79 To Richard Bentley   July 10, 1865

My Dear Mr Bentley

How shall I thank you for your kindness. May God bless and reward you
as you deserve. I must ever remain your debtor. I was on a visit to my
brother at North Douro, and did not get your letters till to day. Or I
should have replied to them by return mail. Mr Macnider, The manager of the Bank of Montreal, in this town, paid me over the sum of 60£
Sterling this morning, and I have written to thank the committee of the
R.L.F. for their most liberal donation. Not knowing how to address the
letter, I enclose it to you. Will you add to the many obligations I owe
you, by forwarding it in the right channel. I was afraid that you were ill,
when I did not hear from you, before. I trust that the cause of your
suffering has been removed, and that you are once more enjoying the
blessing of health. I have got the first volume of 'Dorothy Chance'
done, but so many cares have oppressed and harrassed me, that the work
progresses very slowly. I must try and make an effort to finish it. You
say nothing about the 'Race for Royalty.' I wish I had the talent to make
designs for it. If some artist good at pourtraying character would illustrate it, I still think, that it would make a taking gift book for Christmas.
Age, alas, quenches the fire of the spirit, the infirmities of the flesh,
close around it with walls of adamant, and it is useless battling against
the common doom.

How rapidly the face of this country changes. I left the woods of North
Douro, 26 years ago. Only three houses all composed of logs and of the
smallest dimensions were to be found within three miles of us. Now, my
brother, who may be termed the Father and founder of the village of
Lakefield, has a handsome commodious house and a beautiful garden
which would amply satisfy the taste of any gentleman of moderate
fortune, four of his five lads are married and settled near him.[1] A neat
village consisting of pretty well built houses, has sprung up like magic,
where the lovely falls once foamed and thundered in the heart of the
forest. The hand of industry has curbed the wild torrent and made it
subservient to the wants of man. The stumps are almost all gone, and
tasteful gardens full of bright flowers meet the eye in every direction.
The place has already four churches, and they are busy building a very
handsome new Episcopal church. The old one raised 12 years ago, is

not half large enough to contain its worshippers. My Uncle's son Walter is the architect, a young man of much taste and talent.[2] To keep even, the balance of good and evil, there are as many taverns as churches. A post office, a daily stage to and fro from Peterboro, a fine town, now, 10 miles distant, three stores, a bakery, 2 large saw mills and many pretty villas belonging to the gentlemen settlers. I was charmed with the lovely scenery, with the air of comfort and general improvement that pervades the place. The people are all kind and friendly. And why. No lawyer has as yet shewed the cloven foot among them. And the hilly country is so healthy that the one doctor barely ekes out a living. My sister Traill lives in a neat cottage, on the banks of the river, devoting herself to her favorite pursuit of botany.[3] She has written a very interesting work on the wild plants of Canada, which my poor widowed Agnes, who paints flowers delightfully *is illustrating*. Would such a work sell at home, and who would be likely to publish such an one? My brother talks of visiting England some time next month. Would you like to see a specimen of the work with the illustrations? She could easily send it by him. I was struck most during my visit, by the alteration of persons I had known, when living there, who were then in the very prime of youth. I took them all for their fathers while they in return, could scarcely believe that the stout grey haired old woman could be Mrs. Moodie, was once so slight and active.

'Why should man be proud –'

Yet, I do not remember, that I ever spent a happier or more enjoyable fortnight in my whole life, than the one I spent in the woods. The woods no longer. 'Old things are done away with, behold all things are new.' I did not recognize a feature of the once familiar landscape. My old home is lost and gone.[4] I did not know the place. My brother, I am sorry to say, is in miserable health. This cruel Diabetes is wasting him away, eating him up, as it were. The exhaustion and faintness he feels all the time, is worse than pain. It is happy for him, that his wife is the best of women, and is ever near to comfort and assist him.

My dear old husband forgot for a few days, his cares, and enjoyed himself as much as I did. I caught a bad cold in the ears and my head is dull and confused to day, so you must expect a dull letter in consequence. I dare not indulge a hope about the pension.[5] It is too good to happen to me, who have not been among fortune's favorites. I am only too thankful for a relief from some very pressing difficulties, and if I can only earn bread and butter and tea for the future I shall be very thankful both to our merciful God and to you, my dear friend whom he has made instrumental in helping me in our sore difficulties.

I have written to day to Mr Cassel's the Cashier of the Bank of Upper Canada about the £5.10. Shall most likely get his reply before I post this. I feel certain, that this is not due to me, but is a donation of your own. As such, I receive it. Accept my grateful thanks.

Yours truly
Susanna Moodie

Mr Moodie desires his kind regards

1 Samuel Strickland was a justice of the peace, a county councillor, and eventually acquired the honorary title of 'colonel' for his militia activities. He and his second wife, Mary Reid, had eleven children, most of whom married and settled in the Lakefield area as farmers or in business with either family.
2 In 1853 Sam had raised the money to build Christ Church (Anglican) in Lakefield; its architect was Kivas Tully, who had married Sam's daughter Maria, the first service being held on Christmas Day 1854. However, the small limestone building could only accommodate a hundred parishoners, and so in 1864 work was begun across the street on St John the Baptist Church, designed by Sam's son, Walter Reginald Strickland, and completed by October 1866.
3 After Thomas Traill's death in 1859, Catharine received a grant of £100 from the British government 'as an acknowledgement of her botanical and literary contributions.' With this, and Sam's help, she had 'Westove,' a small frame cottage, built on the west bank of the Otonabee at Lakefield, just before the river widens into Lake Katchewanook.
4 See Letter 34. The Moodies' bush property was primarily cedar swamp that would quickly regenerate if not kept cleared; similarly, a rough log cabin on an earth foundation would not survive without constant attention. The only evidence of habitation on the site today is the remains of a dug well.
5 Apparently the donation she refers to at the beginning of this letter did not preclude the granting of a pension as well by the Royal Literary Fund.

---

80 To Catharine Parr Traill   [December 1865][1]

... my dear son is concerned. I have good news too, of poor Donald. I sent him 40 dollars to get him from Toronto, to New York. Never was money better bestowed. I had a long kind letter from him on my birthday. J. Linder has got him a first rate berth as Check Clerk to the Inman Steam Company. He has eight hundred dollars a year and his board – worth five hundred more – and excellent fare – on board the great steamers. He checks all the parcels with the custom house officers, and though he has to sit up all night when ships arrive or leave, he gets 10 dollars for every night – *extra*. His employer is so well pleased with him, that he presented him with a handsome patent English lever watch,[2] with the remark, 'A dog could do as well without a tail as a man of business without a watch.' The poor fellow says, 'It is quite *enjoyable*, to be at work and paid so well, after such hopeless idleness.' Then Rob and he, are excellent friends. Rob's salary has been increased to 14 dollars per week, and he hopes to be able to send for the wife, and the two babies in the Spring.[3] So you see dear Katie, there is a bright gleam on my dark cloud, for my anxiety about Donald was killing me. The boys both wish us to go to Delaware. You ask where J__ R__ is. Here. She has been here since she left Toronto. E__[4] and I were quite happy till she came, yet without any words on either side, all seems changed, ...

1 This letter appears to fall just prior to Donald Moodie's marriage to Julia Russell (16 February 1866) in Brooklyn; the reference to her birthday implies December of the previous year.
2 A popular pocket watch of the period, with a lever escapement having a vibrating lever to connect the action of the escape wheel with that of the balance.
3 Nellie, whose second child (named after her) was born on 17 September 1865, was waiting in Belleville.
4 Julia and Elizabeth Russell

---

81 To Richard Bentley   Feb. 21 / 66 (Belleville)

My Dear Mr Bentley,

Since I last wrote to you in the beginning of January, I have been confined to the house, and during the greater part of the time to my bed, with severe illness. Inflamation of the stomach, liver and kidneys, succeeded by Typhoid fever. My sufferings were *great* and I fully experienced what amount of pain, nature in her agonies can inflict. My disease, the Dr says, was entirely brought on by mental anxiety, of which, during the last *two* months, I have had my full share. He has forbidden me to go to Delaware, for he says I am too weak to bear such a journey, that the fatigue would in all probability bring on a fresh attack, and I might die upon the road. So here I am still, and am likely to remain in dear old Canada, where I hope to live and die a British subject. I never did like the idea of turning Yankee in my old age, or of living a miserable dependent, I might truly say, a servant of all work, to my son's West Indian wife, A selfish, cold hearted arogant Quadroon, a woman of *little intellect*, and who dispises it in others. Since Mr Moodie, gave up his little property to his son, in the hope of securing a home for us, in our old age; her conduct has been *so cruel*, that you would imagine we were beggars depending upon her bounty, instead of the obligation being *all the other way*.[1] It is impossible for us to live together; and though the separation, will leave us without a home or means beyond the interest derived from 200 pounds sterling; unfortunately invested in mortgage, and so beyond our living upon the principal; yet we shall be *free* – and I believe, the gracious Providence that has hitherto always provided for our wants, will not desert us in our worst need. I look upon my illness, though it brought it me face to face with death; as a merciful interposition in our favor, and bless God, even for my sufferings. My son and his family, are still living with us, but the house will be sold either this week or the next, when they leave for the States, and we must look up some cheap lodging, and hope for better days. In my sixty-third year, I cannot reasonably expect to be long here. I am only anxious to remain on my dear husband's account; as he grows feebler every day and requires a loving wife, to sympathize in his sorrows; and assist him in his increasing weakness.

My dear Mr Bentley, you have always been such a kind friend, that I do not hesitate to confide to you my present troubles. I am now about to ask of you a very *great favour*. With this letter, you will receive, a small MS. It is a work for the *juveniles*, and I want you, to give it your powerful recommendation to some of the publishers in that line. I can hardly ask you to read such a trifling performance, and yet, I believe, that *well illustrated*, it is quite as good *in its way*, as *Roughing It in the Bush*, and calculated to be as popular. It is called, 'The True History of Mrs Moodie's Racoons Ned and Jenny' – by the author of *Roughing It in the Bush*, and contains besides all their droll adventures, the natural history of those diverting creatures drawn from observation, during a period of eight years.[2] I feel certain that it will be a favorite with all the boys and girls, for most young people are fond of natural history and anecdotes about cats and dogs. I think, if you glance over the MS. it will please you. Perhaps *Mr Nelson* might be induced to buy it. I do not expect more than 25 pounds for the copyright, and would *take less*, for I have a heavy Doctors bill to pay, and no funds to meet it. I see by the papers, that the *Temple Bar Magazine*; has passed into your hands.[3] Could you give me any employment in that quarter? If you hold out any hope, I will transcribe a tale, which I think might be successful. You have given me no answer about the 'Race for Royalty'; would it be admissible in the pages of a magazine?

You see, what a bold beggar I have become, but indeed, I have lost all faith in my literary powers, now that I must depend upon them, for my bread; and hard as this fate is, thousands of better and cleverer people, have been reduced to the same alternative. 'Such is the fate of genius upon earth' – I hope, that your own health is improved since I last had the pleasure of hearing from you; and that your dear girl, has been restored to you, to gladden your heart and cheer your home with her presence. You must give my kind regards to Mr Horace, tell him, that his friends here often ask after him, and that I should be delighted to hear from him, whenever he can spare a leisure hour to write to me. Any letter or parcel, will still find me directed to Mrs Susanna Moodie, Belleville. The other day I saw a notice of a work by my sister Agnes published by you.[4] I hope it may prove a success. My brother Col. Strickland, is now in England, but I have not heard from him since he left. He has been suffering for years, from *Diabetes*, and looked very weak and ill last summer. He will have an opportunity of consulting some of your eminent physicians on his case. He will not return until next June.

I enclose with this, the first of a series of Historical Sketches if you can spare a page of the Mag. for it,[5] and it should find favor with the public, I have [more] of the same class –

Mr Moodie unites with me, in best wishes and kind regards to yourself and family. Believe me dear Mr Bentley

ever yours most truly
Susanna Moodie

1 A reference to her eldest son, Dunbar, and his wife, Eliza, who, with their two children, had been staying with the Moodies in Belleville.
2 There is no trace of either the manuscript or publication of this work.
3 The Bentleys acquired *Temple Bar* in January 1866, and it was edited by George Bentley from 1868 to 1895; it became one of the firm's most valuable properties, but nothing by Susanna appeared in it.
4 *How Will it End?* 3 vols. (1865). This was Samuel Strickland's third trip to England.
5 She enclosed a manuscript copy of 'Arminius,' one of five 'Historical Sketches' in verse that had been published in the *Literary Garland* and, in some cases, in other literary periodicals as early as the 1820s.

82 To Richard Bentley

Belleville
March 5, 1866

My Dear Mr. Bentley,

You remember the Story of Simbad the Sailor and his celebrated old man.
I begin to fear, lest you should think a strong resemblance exists between me, and that world renowned individual.[1] Only with this difference,
that an old woman is always a less interesting personage than a man. I
would not however trouble you so often, if I was not urged to do so by
imperious necessity.

You told me last summer to send you the story I was writing. Now I
have been too much overwhelmed with trouble and anxiety to continue
it, but I have sent you one, which I think may please you;[2] if not the taste
of your general readers, you might perhaps, induce Mr. Nelson or
Rutlege to become the purchasers of the copyright. That Doctor's bill lies
on my conscience for I have no available means of liquidating the debt,
and being far from strong, I am very apprehensive lest I may fall ill again. I
only wish that the M.S. may suit you. It will not make more than one
volume, so that I do not expect so much for it, though in real merit and
moral worth it may be far superior. If not suitable to publish as a whole
it might be appreciated in a magazine. I sent you my little 'History of the
Racoons' the 22 of February which can hardly have reached you.

J.A. Macdonald our premier, has done nothing for us. I have no hope in
that quarter. The men in power reserve all the situations under their
control for their own satelites, or leave to the members of the different
counties the privilege of filling up vacancies from among their constitu-
ents. So without a place falls vacant, that you could fill which is not often
the case, your chance of obtaining one is small indeed.

My son has not yet left for Delaware, and if he does not go soon, he
will lose all chance of securing a crop this year. Unfortunately, I lent
him the little money I had on mortgage, which is the reason my hands are
so tied, but for this, we could have lived for two or three years upon the
principal of our little means by restricting our expenses to 50£ a year. Like
the poor Macorbers[3] I am hoping for something to turn up that may
break this galling yoke from off our necks. My heart has been nearly
broken. I often wonder that I am alive. I am naturally frank and open,
and too generous for my own interest, and I can't understand these dark,
secretive, avaricious people, still less the low spite and malice that is
used by them against those to whom they owe the very bread they eat.

My dear husband is not very well, low-spirited and anxious[;] for his sake more than my own, I wish I could obtain employment in the great world of literature. By the by, I was greatly delighted by a volume of poems by a new writer, Jean Ingelow.[4] 'They are beautiful exceedingly.' When I closed the book after a third perusal I felt grateful to her for the great pleasure she had afforded me. I could hardly keep from writing to her to tell her so. The great charm of the book is in being so natural, such a truthful transcript of the beautiful that is a living presence. Not the far off *ideal*, which belongs to another world and is often too high and spiritual for the practical realities of this.

You seem in England to be rather scared about the Fenians.[5] We care very little about them here, resting upon the sure foundation laid down by the blessed Master – 'A house divided against itself, Cannot stand.' These people never could unite as one man in any of their revolutions but always betrayed each other.

The same spirit is at work now. The O'Mahony and Stevens and Sweeney are more likely to go to loggerheads with one another than attack a powerful enemy like England. If they invade Canada, the case may be different, as they have plenty of partizans to help them here and if success attended their first invasion of the Colony thousands of Irishmen would join them who we now consider loyal to the British government. I am surprised that they did not attack us in the winter, when help from the mother country, could not be obtained, beyond the few troops she has in Canada. These, even with the aid of the militia would scarcely repel so large a force as the Fenians could bring against us aided by rebels secretly existing in our midst. Annexation would be almost sure to follow such an invasion.

Your cattle plague appears to me a more terrible calamity, than all the threats of these bloodthirsty would-be liberators of Ireland. It almost looks like the 'Great Tribulation' of Dr. Cummings about to take place.[6] So much easier is it, to fight against man tha[n] God who from the most insignificant causes apparently to us, can produce such awful effects.[7] Our cities are preparing for the visitation of Cholera.[8] May God in his mercy avert it from our shores, or with the fearful scourge reveal a sufficient remedy.

Hoping to hear from you soon, and with kind regards to yourself, Mr. Horace and the rest of the family

> believe me, dear Mr. Bentley,
> Yours Most truly
> Susanna Moodie

Mr. Moodie sends his best wishes –

1 On his fifth voyage, Simbad (a variant of Sinbad or Sindbad) offers assistance to the Old
   Man of the Sea; the latter, however, becomes such a persistent and tenacious burden
   that Simbad is forced to destroy him.
2 'The Race for Royalty'
3 The Macawbers of Charles Dickens's *David Copperfield*, first published in book form by
   Chapman and Hall in 1850.
4 (1820–97), an English poetess and novelist whose first two books of poetry, *The Round of
   Days* (1861) and *Poems* (1862), had appeared prior to this letter.
5 The Fenian Brotherhood, a transatlantic Irish organization, was active in Britain, Canada, and the United States throughout this period. The unsuccessful 'Movement of '65'
   to strike at English installations in Ireland was followed by a series of plots to invade
   'British' Canada. Attempted invasions in 1866 and 1870, launched from American soil,
   turned out to be little more than skirmishes along the border. James Stephens, General
   John O'Mahony, and General T.W. Sweeney were leaders of various factions within
   the Fenian army. Susanna's complacency at this time is interesting in that the Canadian
   government was so convinced of a serious Fenian attack in 1866 that it ordered out
   10,000 militia volunteers on 7 March. The great fear, as she points out, was annexation by
   the United States in the event of Canada's inability to defend her borders. See Captain
   John A. Macdonald, *Troublous Times in Canada: a History of the Fenian Raids of 1866
   and 1870* (Toronto 1910).
6 John Cumming (1807–81), a Scottish divine who prophesied the Apocalypse in his books
   published between 1848 and 1870; his *The Great Tribulation, or Things Coming on the
   Earth* had appeared in 1859.
7 This difficult sentence seems to mean that man is inclined to fight against man rather than
   to heed the awful consequences of God's power.
8 After its first terrible visitation in 1832, cholera recurred intermittently during the next
   forty years; by 1866 warnings of new epidemics caused civic authorities to alert the
   populace to the latest theories of prevention and hygiene.

---

83 To Mary Muchall

Belleville,
August 6, '66

My Dear Mary,

It was an unexpected pleasure hearing from you so soon. I didn't expect to
be remembered among so many friends whom you had not seen for so
long; and when you had so much to hear and tell. You are a very good
May and Auntie is much obliged to you for the kind letter. After such a
long catalogue of disasters it is well that you and the darling boy got home
safe at last.[1]

Little has happened here since you went away to interest you. I am
better, but feel weak and weary all day. But I have got rid of the little

Scotch nuisance[2] and my dear old Margaret is as careful over me and
Uncle, as if we were her father and Mother. I have not seen your dear
Tom nor any of the family since you left. I am too weak to walk as far as
the store, and have only been twice to market since, and then – 'dear
knows' – as Margaret says – I was so tired, I had to sit down on the long
side walk that leads to the Mill to rest. I begin to wish that we were
nearer to the town for Father's sake, as well as my own.[3] I like the cottage
very much, but the long way to town knocks us both up completely.
Robert has got the command of a schooner, and sails her for Robert
Evans, to and from Oswego taking out lumber, and bringing back
coals. He has fifty dollars a month and his keep on board. He has just
returned from his first voyage and sails again tomorrow. I watch the
schooners come and go with more interest now. His black eyed baby has
been very sick with teething and bowel complaint. This wet cold weather is very bad for that.[4]

Mrs. Howard had her baby nine days ago. A little girl. I have not seen
it, but she had a capital time and is doing very well. Mrs. J. Ponton
likewise has a daughter, but I have not heard how she is. But if anything
was wrong, Mr. Jones who was here the other day, would have told
me. Mrs. Rous and Mrs. Crang have been up several times to see me. As
kind as ever. They never come empty handed, and I feel ashamed of
receiving so many benefits. Mrs. Baker on the hill, sent me a large basket
full of nice vegetables, and Mrs. Flint came on Friday afternoon and
took me a long ride up the Trent road with her nice ponies. She ordered a
painting of me, besides, and sent me yesterday, a lot of onions, carrots,
beans, and cucumbers, so that I am well provided for a week to come. She
is going to the sea side tomorrow for five weeks, but on her return, she
means to take me out often. Truly all these people are very kind to me.[5] I
had a letter from dear Mamy yesterday, to let me know, that she is
coming tomorrow to spend a month with the old grandmother. I got her
little room all ready, and I feel so glad that I shall see my darling child
once more. I hoped to have been able to have sent her the carriage money
but I had to pay Annie three dollars and had only 2 left out of the money
I got for my paintings to send the poor dear, but I hope I may be able to
earn more before she goes home.

Monday morning – I could not finish my letter last night. Father was so
sadly. I did not dare to go to sleep until near morning. He looks a little
better since breakfast. I hope he will rally again. I feel anxious and sorrowful. I hope the coming of the dear child will rouse him up a bit. It is
so dull for him. I wish we had more friends to come and chat with him.

Dear Mary, I shall be glad when you come back. This, I know is very
selfish, but old age *is* selfish. It covets companionship, which the young
too much immersed in the pleasures and hopes of their happy prime,
have no time or inclination to give, and when your own nestlings are all
flown, the lonely hours hang heavily on your hands and the shadows
lengthen in the dark valley as you totter slowly and sadly on.

I shall be much obliged to you dear child, to bring my parcel, though to
tell you the simple truth, I almost feel a horror of it coming into the
house. The thought of wearing the clothes of the dead, and of a Mother I
can't entertain for a moment. I would as soon make a dress out of a
shroud. But I may be able to give them in lieu of wages, to those who
would not feel such objections. Absurd perhaps, but we cannot help
these prejudices, no more than we can help refusing some fruit or vegeta-
ble that created disgust or nausea. You must give my love to the dear
Mother, whose kind letter refreshed my heart. I cannot write to day but
will do so soon, when I hope to have more cheery news to communicate. Annie has written to Mrs. Dunbar to send for her. I am sorry, for the
girl has told such things about herself and him, to the people next door,
that I fear her advent in Delaware will be followed by some domestic
tragedy, and her mistress will find what a dreadful girl she is.

If I were to state the facts to them, I should not be believed. They must
just take their own way in the matter, and as she has stated some
things which I know to be downright lies, this may be so also. We have not
heard from them, Donald nor Katie. The latter has not written to me
since the early part of winter.

Give our united love to darling Kate, to dear little Alice. I will give
Mamy her letter when she comes, and now dear I must go down town.
So good bye

Your faithful loving Aunt
Susanna Moodie

1 Mary and her son Hargrave (born 1865) had been visiting Catharine at 'Westove.'
2 A servant girl known in the letters only as Annie, who had decided to follow Dunbar and
   his wife to Delaware. Margaret is an older servant, again known only by her first
   name.
3 The little cottage, 'about a mile from Belleville' (Letter 84), was the Moodies' third and
   last home in the town.
4 Robert's position as schooner captain under Robert Evans was shortlived. His second
   child, Nellie Moodie, was born 17 September 1865. Susanna's concern reflects a Victorian notion that many infants suffered gravely and often died from the effects of teething;
   likely, in such cases, the teething coincided with internal and undiagnosed ailments.

5 The wife of James Ponton was the former Anna Hutton, daughter of William Hutton (1801–61), an influential Belleville farmer, teacher, and government official. See Gerald E. Boyce's *Hutton of Hastings* (Belleville 1872). The Pontons lived on the Hutton estate, 'Sidney,' west of the village of Belleville. Another daughter, Eliza Bruce, married Rev. Septimus Jones, a well-known Anglican clergyman. Bella Flint was the MLA for Hastings in the late 1840s and early 1850s. The Rouses were Quaker friends of the Moodies, Frederick Rous being the inspector of schools at the time.

84 To Richard Bentley

Belleville
Sep. 4th, 1866

My Dear Mr. Bentley,

I am almost ashamed of writing so often. You must begin to realize in my pertinacity, the story of Simbad's 'old man of the sea,' but I feel so certain, that nothing but illness or domestic affliction has been the cause of your long silence, that I no longer hesitate in writing once more. It is just 14 months since I received your last valued letter. In that letter, you told me, that you would let me know your decision respecting the 'Race for Royalty' by the next mail. Some time in March,[1] I can't recall the exact date, I sent you a MS. for the juveniles, requesting your kind services to recommend it to some publisher who dealt in such small wares.

The title of the said small affair was 'A True History of Mrs. Moodie's Racoons Jenny and Ned.' Perhaps I was too sanguine in expecting the public to think as highly of my pets as I did. I think Mr. Horace knew one of them, *The lady Coon.*

In April I sent you another MS entitled 'Will She Forget?' Not a very taking title, but I could not hit upon a better.[2] Whether these two MSS. ever reached you I do not know, as I have never heard from you since. I sent both by mail and the postage was paid, both of the MSS., and the letters which accompanied them. If the last, or both of these, should not have suited you, will you be so good as to transmit them to Mr. Nelson of Edinburg. It is just possible that they might suit him. I am very anxious to get a purchaser for either, and shall not be very particular as to terms, even a *small sum would be acceptable.*

I have suffered much during the last eight months from inflamation of the stomach and kidneys. Yes, agonies, and every fresh attack brings me nearer to the grave. From the last seizure in June, I never expected to recover, nor did my medical attendant give me the least hope.

My dear husband too has been ill and grows weaker every day, his term of life I fear is fast drawing to a close, and this prospect to me is peculiarly sad and dreary. I before told you, my dear friend, that we had determined not to accompany my son and his wife to Delaware. Mr. Moodie had given up all his property to him under a bond that he was to maintain us during our lives. But his wife treated us after she took possession of my dear old home in so cruel a manner that we found it would be impossible to live with her, and so at the risk of starvation we determined to remain in Canada. Imagine my scrubbing floors and doing all the menial work in my once comfortable home while she kept a servant on my means to wait upon her. Well, he sold the place and furniture and left us fifty pounds, I suppose all we shall get for our property, and left us in May, to do the best we were able, but this was better than dying of broken hearts.

It was a sad trial to me to leave my home, but I was free, and I tried to look all the difficulties of my position calmly in the face; but my health and spirits had been so broken down by sorrows and sickness, that I felt how little able I was, in my sixty third year, to contend with a hard world for bread. We removed to a small cottage about a mile from Belleville, rent 2 pounds per annum, with a cow, the only thing we possessed, to do the best we could upon our scanty means, and we have enjoyed more real comfort during the last three or four months than I have known for the last six years. God has been very good to us, and raised up many kind friends, who sympathize with us in our misfortunes. The two children who could have helped us, were so enraged at their Father's unfortunate disposal of his property, that they have withdrawn themselves entirely from us.[3] My poor, widowed daughter, who is left with five young children to maintain and educate, would help us if she could, and Robert my best, and youngest son, will do so, the moment that he can get employment – he too has a wife and two babies to support. But I want to get my own living as long as I can work; and as I am not a popular author I employ myself in painting groups of flowers, which pay me from a dollar, to three dollars a group. I am fast improving this long neglected talent, but my poor eyes suffer more than I like to let my dear husband know. This is a sad history, but I thought you would feel interested in it. Sympathy is so precious to the suffering heart.

I do want to hear how you are. I fear you are not well – if unable to answer this long egotistical scrawl, will you get some one to write a few lines to assure me of your welfare. My brother Col. Strickland has returned to Canada, I fear only *to die*. I wish much that I could go up to

Douro to see him. He is dreadfully weak, and unable to rise to breakfast. He seems quite aware of that approaching change, and happily for him, is prepared to meet it. His large family are all prospering and his loss will be severely felt by them, by whom he is greatly beloved.

My dear husband is publishing a book upon subscription.[4] A very good readable book it will be. He has over four hundred subscribers which will pay Mr. Lovell's printing expences but we must double these before it will pay us. However we have only canvassed Belleville and Toronto at present, and we hope to obtain many in Montreal, Quebec, Ottawa, Hamilton and London West. He has been too ill of late to prosecute this himself. And now dear Mr. Bentley, hoping that this will find you and all dear to you enjoying health and prosperity believe me, yours most faithfully

Susanna Moodie

My dear husband desires his kind regards to you and Mr. Horace. Tell the latter he has my best wishes.

1 She sent it on 22 February.
2 A one-volume work Bentley chose not to publish, returning it to her finally in September 1867
3 Donald, then in the United States, and Katie Vickers in Toronto
4 *Scenes and Adventures of a Soldier and Settler during Half a Century*

---

85 To Catharine Parr Traill   Belleville
Nov. 18, 1866

My Dearest Catherine,

You are quite right that my silence arose from no want of affection, or even deep interest in your welfare, but many things hindered me from writing, which I need not here stop to name, but will employ my paper in telling you what I can without taking it all up with excuses. I heard of the death of Aggie's poor little Billy[1], and the illness of Mamy, before I knew anything of our dear brother's alarming sickness. All these things combined to make me very sad and anxious, especially as I had only just got over one of my dangerous attacks. I fear, that we must prepare our minds to part with the dear brother before many months are gone. His gain – will be a severe loss to us all – especially to you dear Kate, to whom he has always been such a kind friend. I owe him a great debt of kindness for his goodness to you. May God bless him, and may he find the Saviour's love his exceeding great reward. It will not be long dear sister before we must all tread the same path. Happy for us if it leads to Heaven – I have always had the idea that my father's younger children who were born when he was so infirm, would be the first to die: but when the family link is once broken, a few years will swallow them all –

I was ill at the time of your dangerous attack, which was one cause of my not writing at the time, but I heard from dear Mary how you were. I know what evils to the body arise from anxiety of mind, and I have no doubt, that to it, may be attributed your alarming seizure. If it is possible for you to keep your mind at rest, I have no doubt you would overcome the disease. But how you are to do so, *in your case*, I don't know. I could never find out a remedy for myself. To rest entirely on God is the only efficacious medicine for crushing care, and heart sorrow – I have done this for the last half year, with unwavering trust, and all my wants have been almost miraculously supplied, and now I feel no fears for the future. He will give me the daily bread. You want to hear of my visit to Montreal. It was far from my wishes to go, but Mrs. Rous – , one of our best friends, pressed so strongly upon me, the weak state of my husband's health, and the absolute necessity of my accepting Mr. Lovell's invitation, that my own selfish scruples had to give way. We left here by the St. Helen Steamboat on the 1st of October, Mrs. Murney kindly getting Mr. McCuaigh, the proprietor of the boat,[2] to give us a pass to and fro, meals Cabin and all included. We did not run the rapids, but had a glorious view of them, especially of the Long Sault rapids, from the canal. We had pleasant company on board and beautiful weather, and reached Montreal on Wednesday the 3, at three in the afternoon. From Mrs. Lovell and her husband we received the kindest welcome. They live in a large stone house in one of the best squares in the city, and are surrounded with every comfort and convenience. During the summer I had continued to pay my servant by painting groups of flowers, for which I got a ready sale at 3 dollars each. I took one of these down for Mrs. Lovell and she went with me, to Mr. Dawson, the great bookseller,[3] to know what he would give for such. He admired it much, but said, that no money would pay for so much work, that it was killing. But if I would paint him a spray of Canadian flowers, with my autograph, he would see what he could do for me. Not much encouraged, yet having some time on my hands, I painted a spray of my darling dwarf Canadian roses, such as used to cover the lawn in June at the old house. Father left it at Dawson's, two days after he met M. and said, 'I have sold that painting for five dollars – Mrs. M may go to work and do as many as she pleases.' I invested the five dollars in card board and colors, but I have not sent him any more yet – and why? – Father sold 150 copies of his book in Montreal, and paid Mr. Lovell 100 dollars on account and took 60 dollars to pay Notman for the Photographs. Mr. Notman, a handsome clever young Scotchman, would only take 35. But said, 'if Mrs. Moodie would paint him a group of flowers with her autograph it would pay for the other 500 Copies.' Was not this generous – to value my poor little drawing so highly. I sent off the picture, last Thursday. It was a group of crimson, white, yellow, and pink roses, and really it did look very nice.

This was why I have done nothing since my return for Mr. Dawson, but mean to do so. It has opened up a new way of making a little money. You have no idea how I have improved. If I had only a few lessons I believe, I should yet make a good artist. I allow one dollar percentage out of five, and this is better for me, as it will give Mr. Dawson an interest in selling, while the pictures cost him nothing.

I met with several very kind people in Montreal, especially dear Mrs. Cross, who came to see us directly she heard we were there, and sold 10 copies of the book, and took 20 more to sell – and a Mrs. Ross[4] – a clever Scotch writer who sold 10 copies for father, and told me that she would sell pictures for me without my losing the percentage. Montreal is a very fine city, and ought to be the capital, but the men are wholly mercantile, without much appreciation of talent. Mr. Lovell is an excellent kind man, and very anxious to serve us. The book will cost us 500 dollars independent of the photographs. Father has paid 300 of the debt, and the artist – but not one penny will come to us untill the whole is paid. It is very fatigueing to poor father delivering the books, but it is the only means of ensuring success. It has given great satisfaction, and I have no doubt that he will sell the 1000 copies, and more if he had them. He went to Kingston last week and delivered there, and will go to Northport[5] by boat tomorrow, but will have to wait for a fresh supply from Montreal before he goes West –

I had a letter from Agnes and one from Mamy on friday last. Poor Agnes seems to grieve much for her baby, as she calls Billy. Mamy is coming to me for the winter for change of air. She is afraid of the damp walls of the new house endangering the dear girl's health. I shall be happy enough to have her with me to share our bread and butter, especially as Moodie will be a good deal from home. We have got through the summer pretty well. Our Cow Mrs. Powers, has found us in milk and

Butter and bread – the latter – from the sale of flat and butter milk. A dozen hens gave us eggs, and a good many nice eating chickens. The bit of ground – for garden, I cannot call it – loads of Cabbages Pumpkins, beans and potatoes. The latter, however, though a great crop, have the disease which is very common all over the country. We don't buy much meat, or sugar. Tea is an article that we cannot do without. I have presents of apples sent me, and many other nice things. The kindness of the Belleville people is beyond all praise. From Donald I never have heard since his marriage, but I often hear of him. He is now *head receiving clerk* on the great Inman line. Is well and prospering. Is quite steady, and a wonderful favorite with his employers and with every one. Mr. Fox our parson saw him last week and was quite fascinated by his manners and beauty. He enquired for us very affectionately, it is only that horrid woman who keeps him silent.

I cannot write to him, to have her turn and twist everything I say into mischief, and with such as her, let you be ever so guarded, they can always find a way to make strife. From Dunbar, I have heard three times since he left us. Poor fellow, he does not seem to be very prosperous. She had another daughter on the 24th of last August, and had neither a nurse nor servant in the house. He had to be a doctor and nurse himself. He wrote last week. They are still without a servant, but she and the child are strong and well. Mannie had been so ill for two months, that when he sat down, they had to lift him up again, he was too weak to rise.[6] Aggie, he says, is growing very like me. Poor little dear I hope not, it would not increase her Mother's love for her. He says not a word about the looks of the new baby, though he talks of the beauty of Mannie. I fancy that it is not a pretty child, or that something may look niggerish about it. He talks of having to raise money on the place to get through until after next harvest. Poor fellow. He went very cheap to have to cook and nurse children and work in the fields. Few men could stand it. But he is a very goodtempered fellow and most kind to women and children. I am sure he was sorry for her base conduct to the dear old father, but he could not show it. He writes, however, very kindly. It will be useless expecting any aid from that quarter, but if Father sells his books we shall not require it for the next year. From Katie Vickers I never hear, though I often write to her. The reason of her silence to me I cannot tell – I, who loved her so much – I fancy it proceeds from some difference between M. and her husband about the property. Her alienation wounds me to the heart, for I have not deserved it. She, however, Mamy tells me, is well and has been very kind to them in their recent trouble, for which I feel grateful. My dear Robert, after shouldering lumber for awhile, and help[ing] load vessels, at a dollar and a half a day, rather than be idle, has got a good berth on the railroad, at a station called Seaforth, between Goderich and Detroit; he is getting a good salary and gives great satisfaction. The long distance is a great trial to me, as seeing the good boy occasionally, cheered both the father and me, but I must not repine at that, which will enable him to get bread for his wife and children. He is an honest industrious fellow, and deserves to succeed. I was so glad that your dear Walter and Willie were prospering; they will most likely realize a comfortable independence in that far land,[7] and the certainty of their being well situated must be one cause for anxiety off your mind. I met your dear James in the market on Saturday. He looks very thin, but said, that he felt better. Mary too looks thin, but there is a natural cause for her pale cheeks and sunken eyes. She is a darling child and I look upon her as a daughter. Her fine boy is looking bright and blooming, and she bears her painful position with heroic fortitude, re-spected by everyone whose esteem is worth having. I hope Tom may get something to do in Belleville, for I would be so sorry to miss her.[8] Mr. Lovell is going to make out an estimate of what Aggy's proposed book of Canadian flowers would cost. The painting of the plates alone, would come to 1500 dollars, that is 500 copies of the book – and if she paints them all herself it will well nigh kill her. I know what a weary job it was, Eliza and I painting the Canadian Floraensis – think of 500 copies of one flower – and that repeated 25 times as she proposes to have 25 plates in the volume. Mr. Lovell sent me last night a page printed of your letter press, to shew type. It is too large to enclose in this. It looks well and reads better – but I much fear either of you embarking in such a hazardous enterprise which if it did not succeed would be utter ruin. If Agnes went about herself and canvassed the country with a specimen copy of the work and did the painting herself, it might perhaps succeed. I have written till my shoulders ake. Give my love to the dear Kate and to all my nephews and nieces great and small, and believe me dear sister, ever your own affectionate

Susy –

Moodie sends his best love and many thanks for the names for his book. It is likely that he may visit Peterborough with books to canvass the town. In such case he would most likely visit Lakefield.

1 William Winder Fitzgibbon (12 April 1862 – 18 October 1866)
2 P.F. McCuaig, owner of the St Helen Steamboat that travelled between Belleville and Montreal
3 Samuel E. Dawson (1833–1916) and his brother Charles ran a highly respected Montreal publishing firm, chosen by Mark Twain for his Canadian editions; in 1891 Samuel left the firm to become Queen's Printer in Ottawa.
4 Ellen (McGregor) Ross (died 1892) also wrote for John Lovell: *Violet Keith* (1868) and *The Wreck of the White Bear, East Indiaman* (1870).
5 A small village near Sophiasburg, on Marsh Front, Bay of Quinte
6 By this time Dunbar and his wife had three children: Agnes Strickland Dunbar (Aggie) born 11 February 1863, Robert Russell (Mannie) 28 November 1864, and Elizabeth Dunbar (the new baby mentioned in this letter) born 24 August 1866 at Camden, Delaware.
7 Catharine's two youngest sons, William Edward (born 1844) and Walter John Strickland (1847), had migrated to the Northwest Territories in July 1866 and initially established themselves with the Hudson's Bay Company at Lesser Slave Lake.
8 Tom Muchall was frequently ill and out of work; concern about the Muchalls' well-being is a constant theme in Catharine's letters at this time.

---

86 To George Bentley

Belleville
May 7th, 1867

George Bentley Esqre –
Dear Sir,

Though a stranger, I shall make no apology in venturing to address you; as the son of an esteemed and generous friend. Your Father's silence to my repeated communications makes me apprehensive of the cause – illness or death. Most sincerely I hope that my surmises are unfounded, and it would be almost as painful to imagine, that I have in any way offended him, or lost the kind sympathy he has always expressed in my fortunes.

The last letter I had the pleasure of receiving from him, together with the result of his generous application to the Literary Fund in our behalf, was in July, 1865. In this letter he promised to give me an answer by the next mail, respecting a MS. then in his hands – 'The Race for Royalty.' I never heard from him again. In the March of 1866, I sent him the MS. of a juvenile work entitled, 'The True History Mrs Moodies Racoons, Jenny and Ned,' hoping that he might obtain for it a purchaser among the publishers who deal in such small wares, and in the April of the same year, a tale in one Vol. 'Will She Forget,' which I thought might be suitable to the pages of *Temple Bar*, which I saw by the papers, had passed into his hands. I paid the postage and carriage, of these parcels and the letters that accompanied them. Not receiving any notice of their safe arrival, I wrote to my valued friend, in September last, requesting an answer, and that he would return these MSS, if not suitable for publication. Unfortunately, I have no copies of the two last, and a publisher in Toronto, is very anxious to see them, especially that of the Racoons, and you would confer upon me a very *great favor indeed*, by returning them to my address at Belleville. If your dear Father be still living present to him my kindest regards, with every earnest wish for his health, happiness and prosperity. His kindness to me, and the generous sympathy, he extended to us in our misfortunes, are amongst the most treasured memories of the past, and which I can never forget. God has been very good to us, and with the pencil and pen, we have been enabled to baffle the evil genius of poverty, but we have no other source on which to depend.

Hoping that you will excuse the liberty I have taken in addressing you, I remain

> Dear Sir
> with much respect
> Yours truly
> Susanna Moodie.

---

87 To Richard Bentley

Belleville
July 17, 1867

My Dear Mr Bentley,

By this mail, I send you the MS of 'Dorothy Chance,' as I wish you much to see it before I venture to print it on my own account.

If I could *dispose* of the copyright, I would much prefer it, to the trouble of, canvassing the *Dominion*, though I believe, the latter plan would ensure a larger return. I have sent you the printed sheets, to save the trouble of making a new copy, and as offering greater facility to reading or reprinting from. I think in my last, I told you all about this M.S. that Mr Lovell had given me 100 dollars for allowing it to be printed in his new paper,[1] but the Copyright, you will perceive by the first page is secured to me.

I *do so wish* you to read this book, for I think you would like it better than those that have appeared in England. I think it might be as well to *drop my name*, and merely substitute the initials – D.C (of our new Dominion).

If it should happen to take I have several other long stories, which might take also, but I do so hate the task of copying, that I let them lie idle to be published after my death. Let me know as soon as convenient, if you take the MS., as in case of your rejection, I must make some arrangement to bring it out here, or in the States. We are having an intensely hot summer after our long cold wet spring, but the crops promise a fair average.

My very heart has bled for that murdered Maximilian. What a set of untamed ferocious savages those mexicans must be. I think, however, Mr Seward most to blame, one word of menace from him would have saved the unfortunate prince.[2] His memory has become a sacred thing. He will live for ever in the sy[m]pathy of all noble hearts. I hope my dear friend you still continue to enjoy health. Pray remember me most kindly to Mr. George and Horace. Mr. Moodie unites with me in affectionate regards, and believe me ever,

Yours truly and gratefully
Susanna Moodie

1 Montreal *Daily News*
2 Maximillian, archduke of Austria, was supported as emperor of Mexico by Napoleon III; arriving in 1864, he pleased neither conservative nor liberal elements; nor did he please American interests because his presence along with French troops contravened the Monroe Doctrine condemning European influence in American affairs. When the French troops withdrew at the end of the American Civil War, Maximillian, left to lead his own army, was defeated by Mexican rebels and shot. William Henry Seward, secretary of state in Lincoln's cabinet, helped bring an end to the reign.

---

88 To Richard Bentley

Belleville
Sep. 26, 1867

My Dear Mr Bentley,

I have still to thank you, for your most kind and welcome letter of the 24th of July. A letter which I have read many many times and prize most highly. Your expressions of generous sympathy went warm to my heart. I shall never forget them.

I should have replied to them sooner had I not despatched my MS. of 'Dorothy Chance,' through the post office here, July 16th, registered and paid to your house of business, and I thought it better to wait until I received news of its safe arrival, and your intentions with regard to it. So long a period has elapsed, that I begin to fear that it never reached its destination. So thought it best to make some enquiries respecting it. The three returned MSS. arrived perfectly safe, and I have sent the 'Racoons' to Mr Maclear of Toronto, who wished to see it.[1] I hope it may meet with his views, but I have been so unfortunate of late, that I have lost all faith in my power to interest the public.

I return you my warmest thanks for the trouble you took about these MSS. It was so good of you, that I hardly know how to express the deep gratitude I feel. The books you mention as having sent to me, have never arrived. Through what channel were they sent?

If you will give me the necessary direction, I will enquire for them. The pleasure I felt, in finding that you were still living and well, was the best news contained in your truly valuable letter. May you long be spared to your family and friends, among the latter, I shall always feel proud to find a place.

This dreadfully hot summer is at last waning into the fall; and the weather is cool and pleasant, after such a long continuance of burning cloudless days. It has been the most beautiful Canadian summer I ever remember and the harvests are abundant everywhere. During June, July and August, up to the middle of the present month, we had only three showers, but they were abundant, accompanied by stunning thunder. My dear husband felt the heat very severely, and for several days was so dangerously ill, that his medical attendant, bade me prepare for the worst. It pleased God to spare him to me, yet, a little longer. Isolated and lonely as our position now is, it would have been almost insupportable without him. He sends you with his kind regards, a copy of his book upon the proceeds of which, we have been living for the last nine months. I cannot say much in praise of the manner in which my friend John Lovell, got it up. The size, the paper, and the typography, are all against it, and I often marvel that a small volume of such inferior outward pretensions should have sold so well. An American house would have produced a handsome volume for the price, 7/6 Halifax currency.

Though I cannot boast much of my own health; my family are all quite well. My son in Delaware, does not find it such an Eldorado as he expected. Provisions, clothing and taxes in the United States are so high, that he finds it very hard to get his own living, and this year at any rate, will be unable to assist us. From my second son, I never hear. Robert has got an appointment on the Grand Trunk, but the salary is only £100 per annum, little enough to keep a wife and two children, but he is a dear good boy, and will help us as soon as he can.

So you see up to this present time, we have received no help from our children, and excepting Robert and Mrs Fitzgibbon I have not even seen one of them since we were left to struggle on by ourselves. God has been very good to us, and has hitherto blessed our honest endeavours to help ourselves, and I hope the daily bread for which we pray, may never he withheld. Not only the bread that nourishes the body, but that which gives life to the soul.

I hope my dear friend you will be gratified by your son's success in the ministry. He reads so well that one cannot imagine him incapable of delivering a sermon, but after all, there is more than that needed in a faithful minister of the gospel, and if Mr Horace, has any doubts upon the subject, I must respect such scruples of conscience. To take charge of the souls of men is an awful responsibility, which will make a wise man pause and think deeply, before he undertakes it. Without he feels himself led by the Holy Spirit, to make such a choice, it is better to give it up altogether. Pray remember us most kindly to him. Great changes have taken place in Belleville, since he was here. The young ladies he met, are all wives and mothers, and death too, has done its work. Nature however, leaves no blanks, and the coming generation steps into the vacancies as fast as they occur.

The English are sending us out arms and troops, but very little fears are entertained of a Fenian Raid. Should England engage in a European war, there might be some danger. I cannot but think, that America is at the bottom of the movement, and her likely alliance with Russia, might throw us into her hands. I feel some doubts as to the ultimate success of the Dominion. The hostility of Nova Scotia is much against it.[2] The Government has secured most of the members in the late elections, and George Brown's influence in politics is over.[3]

Hoping soon to hear from you, and of the safe arrival of 'Dorothy Chance.'

> I remain,
> my dear friend
> Yours most truly
> Susanna Moodie

My best compliments to Mr George. He writes so like yourself that I fancy he must greatly resemble you. I trust he has quite got over his accident.

1 No trace of this manuscript has been uncovered; presumably Maclear did not publish it.
2 The Atlantic provinces offered the strongest resistance to Confederation. Prince Edward Island and Newfoundland refused to join, but when A.J. Smith's anti-Confederation government in New Brunswick failed to develop an American railway connection and the Reciprocity Treaty ended in 1866, Samuel Leonard Tilley was re-elected and both New Brunswick and Nova Scotia were gradually won over.
3 Here she laments the loss of Reformist impact in the recent elections, seeing the Grit defeat as symbolic of Brown's loss of political influence.

---

89 To Allen Ransome

Belleville Ontario –
Dominion of Canada
December 26, 1868

Dear Friend Allen,

You will not recognize my handwriting after the lapse of so many years – 35 I think, since we last shook hands and parted by the shores of the stormy sea on which we had been tossing for so many long hours in pouring rain and tempest. But the friendships formed in youth survive all changes and *mine* has always burnt warmly in my heart for you, bringing often back to memory the many pleasant hours spent in your company at the house of our mutual friend James Bird – a bright genial spirit long since passed into the better land.[1]

A letter received from my sister Mrs. Gwillym informed me that you had applied to my sister Jane for my address and that you wished to renew our old friendship and I could not wait to hear from you first, but gladly seized the opportunity afforded by a few leisure hours to give you a few words of sisterly and affectionate greeting.

Her letter informed me of your sad bereavement. I wish Dear Allen it was in my power to console you for the very heavy loss. Alas human words are in vain, they cannot pour balm into the wounds of the bleeding heart. He who has reclaimed your crown of life can alone restore you to peace and happiness. He wounds but to heal, and out of much sorrow can still bring forth the abiding joy. May his divine peace and blessing rest upon you for ever.

Do not mourn for your beloved partner as dead. She still lives for God is a God of the living and all live to Him. What he has taken he can again restore in marvellous power and beauty. But even now she still lives and is ever near you, shining like a pure and steady light in the inner world of memory. After the first anguish of the blow is softened down every lovely and tender recollection of the dear one will kindle in your breast a calm and holy joy. For joy is born of sorrow, and love receives its baptism in tears ... *Deeply* do I sympathize with you dear friend for I have felt that these separations from those with whom our own being is so closely entwined constitute the most severe trials in our mortal pilgrimage. Keenly have I felt that desolation of the soul when it speaks but can no longer find the object of its fond idolatry. There is nothing sinful in this, or Christ would not have wept at the grave of his friend Lazarus ... What tears I shed over the pale form of a beautiful and talented boy (taken from me by the cruel waters) who was the pride and joy of my heart ... I never thought it possible that time could reconcile me to my grief – that my hungry aching heart could outlive its passionate regret. I now rejoice that my dear boy was taken to a better home in his lovely innocence and secured from the snares and temptations of this evil world.

You have perhaps read *Roughing It in the Bush*. A true picture of our life and experience while residing among the grand old woods. But sorrows have deepened upon us since then, that have been much *harder to combat*. For nearly 24 years my dear and honored husband held the post of Sheriff of this County (Hastings of which Belleville is the Capital, a town containing a population of 8000) with honor to himself and held in much esteem for his integrity. We possessed a handsome and comfortable home, and enjoyed many of the luxuries of life or such as are considered so in the Provinces. Of course summer friends were not wanting in our prosperity they always abound when the sun shines upon you. We should have been happy and comfortable but for a set of *legal thieves* who literally swarm in Canadian towns and cities, called *gentlemen of the bar*. In this small place we count some thirty of these landsharks, and the sheriff who is poorly protected by the laws is generally the victim of their underhand villainies. They kept us from the larger emoluments of the office by never paying their accounts and by bringing constantly vexatious suits against my husband in the name of parties who were unable to pay their costs, which though he always *won*, yet in the end was out of pocket by having to pay for the defence. This was one of their ways of filling their own pockets to his cost. This kept Mr. Moodie too poor to keep a clerk and he did all the work of the office for many years himself. In 1857 his health was so much affected by the constant persecutions of these men, that he was advised to take a short trip to the sea side for its improvement and he consulted his legal advisor, a Scotchman of good talents, who had always professed for him the warmest friendship if instead of paying his deputy he could command his services by a yearly salary to be paid *out of the fees of the office*, while he continued to perform all the important duties himself. Mr. P.[2] assured him, that it was not only legal but perfectly safe, and was a plan adopted by all the Sheriffs in the Province. This *latter statement was true* and is still common. Assured by this my dear husband ordered a bond to be drawn up to that effect but the wily lawyer, who was afterward an applicant for the office of Sheriff, purposely omitted the four words that would have made it legal – to be paid *out* of the fees and M., quite unsuspicious of the treachery practiced against him, unfortunately never examined the document till it was too late. Mr. P. was the man who informed the Government that he was farming the office which led to our investigation, which ended in his resigning the office to the great indignation of the whole district. This base conspiracy, for it was nothing less, was headed in secret by the very barrister, a member for the County who defended the trial and Mr. P. went into the box as the chief witness against Mr. M., while the other legal gentlemen gave the office to a friend[3] who could hardly sign his own name and my youngest son Robert, who had been in his father's office and was continued in it for a year after, had to write all his letters for him.

The Government which was tory at the time, my husband having always been a reformer, completed his ruin by charging him with the costs of the Prosecution which was an unprecedented thing and this together with the heavy expenses of appeal involved us in irreparable loss. The great mental anxiety brought on a stroke of paralysis, which deprived my husband of the use of his left hand and partially of the whole of his left side from which he still suffers. But proudly conscious of all intention to do aught against the laws, he bore up bravely, *paid every debt he had in the world,* and left his difficult and dangerous position with the character even from his enemies of a just and honest man. But little remained to us when all this was done. The wreck of his property did not realize more than 2000 dollars for it was sold to great disadvantage and he gave this to his eldest son Dunbar, on the condition that he was to give us a home during the rest of our lives. D., who is a clever practical man, decided to buy a farm in the state of Delaware U.S., thinking that Father would prefer removing to the States, to remaining in Canada goaded by the recollection of intolerable wrong, but his wife, a proud selfish West Indian, treated us so unkindly that after everything was prepared for our journey we both concluded it was the best and wisest course to remain behind and work for our own living. D. gave us 200 dollars out of the sale of the furniture, the rest of the property

having been invested in the purchase of a Farm in the States, and we
were left to our own mental resources. My other sons Donald and Robert
were not in a position to help us. Both were married, in poor circumstances, and fighting hard to support their families. Agnes my second
daughter a clever and most beautiful woman had just lost her husband
and was left to support a family of six young children on very small means.
Katie the baby of the book, who was *well* off, was so much displeased
with the disposal of the property to D. that she stood aloof.

Well, dear Allen, we had been poor before and trusted in God, who
had brought us through all our troubles in the bush and we confided our
cause to him once more confident in his help, and calmly and cheerfully
descended into *the valley of humiliation*. We had the esteem and sympathy of all the worthy people in the town and in fact in the whole province and several worthy gentlemen anonymously rendered us much
kind assistance through the Agency of a generous Quaker friend.[4] But we
did not wish to be burdensome to anyone. My husband wrote the little
work I send with this, on which he realized about 600 dollars, I another
The World Before Them, published by Bentley in London, the proceeds
of both yielding us 40 pounds a year. On this humble income we contrive
to live with the aid of my pencil for I have become quite an adept in an
art, for which I had when young a taste, but neglected, little thinking that
by it I should one day be enabled to keep the wolf from the door. I am
grateful to God for all his mercies, especially that I am not left to struggle
on alone but still have the company of my dear and honored husband to
sympathise and assist me. I wish you could see him as he is now sitting
before me a beautiful specimen of old age. Though feeble, still in the
possession of his fine intellect and so cheerful and uncomplaining, feeling
the reverse of fortune, more on my account than on his own. I regard
neither age nor poverty among the greatest evils of life. The one is tranquil
and even enjoyable, the other one of God's good angels in homely guise
from whom, if we listen to her stern teachings aright, we derive many
valuable and heaven-given instructions.

So here we are – living in a little cottage with just room enough to hold
us, but beautifully situated on the edge of our lovely bay, with a fine
common in front covered with noble trees through which we see the spires
of Belleville about a mile distant, and for which we pay a rent of 12
pounds per annum and the rates[5] 10 dollars. My servant Margaret's
wages 12 pounds more for I am too old, now 65, for hard work and am
able to earn the money that pays her wages. She is a good and faithful

woman though *Irish* and a *Catholic*, and lived with us in our prosperity and will not leave us in age and poverty, and whom I regard as a tried and valued friend.

Then I have a faithful Skye terrier who is known by the name of Quiz, very ugly and small, but full of almost human intelligence and much more love than generally belongs to the dominant human race. A steel kitten Grim, who is dear M's especial pet. A perfect incarnation of mischief very common to the Maltese race. 24 hens who help furnish our larder, who come to me to be fed at the sound of a small handbell. I had a favorite cow – y'clept Mrs. Powers but I was too poor to keep her, and had to sell her though the milk was a great comfort, M. living so much upon it. I have no garden – and I dearly love flowers and tending them, but I have learned like dear St. Paul to be content with little or to abound. Now I think I have given you my dear old friend a picture of our life and I shall not apologize for this long epistle. If you are the same Allen Ransome I once knew and so highly esteemed you will tolerate the garrulity of an old grey haired woman. My dear husband unites with me in offering you our best wishes at this festive season. May you yet live to enjoy many happy returns of the year is the sincere prayer of your faithful friend

Susanna Moodie

... I have 19 living grand children and 5 in heaven. Oh you would never recognize the Susy Strickland of old, in the stout, care-worn matron, but my heart is still young ... Excuse the bad writing for I have very dim sight and at times scarcely can see what I write. Painting tries them so much even with powerful spectacles.

1 In *Flora Lyndsay*, Mansel (Ransome) and his friend Mr Hawks (James Bird) see the young Moodie family off on the first stage of their voyage to the New World.
2 William Ponton
3 Allen Ramsay Dougall was apparently instrumental in the appointment of George Taylor to replace Moodie as sheriff.
4 Likely Frederick H. Rous, a close Belleville friend.
5 The British term for property or municipal taxes

90 To Mrs Kersterman   Friday Afternoon.

My dear Mrs Kersterman[1]

My Grand daughter, has just walked down to town with the *guid man*,[2] and as he travels slowly, may not be back before dusk.

I am sure she will be very glad to accept your kind invitation, if not too tired.

But as that may be the case, as she was out last night, do not expect her till she comes.

Yours affectionately
Susanna Moodie

1 A Belleville friend. This letter, likely written in Belleville during the 1860s, was found pasted inside the cover of a first edition of *Roughing It in the Bush* held at the National Library in Ottawa.
2 The Scottish 'guid' meaning 'good' – an affectionate reference to her husband

91 To Anna Ricketson   Belleville
                               Sept 4 1869

My dear young Friend[1]

I feel quite proud of your graceful little letter, and receive the lovely ferns as symbols of yourself. Ah, how sweet they look traced by the hand of the inimitable Artist, Mother Nature. I could almost fancy the spot where they grew. We have many pretty ferns in Canada, and I expect our flowers are mostly of the same class as we have all the charming 'wildings,' you mention in your letter.

How kind it was, your wishing to send me the daisies. I should have prized them much, but their not being real denizens of the soil, diminishes my disappointment. 'Our wee crimson tipped flower,' is much larger than any of the emigrant daisies, I have seen in Canada that all look in the last stages of consumption, as if they were pining to death for the salt

breezes, and moist climate of England. They always make me sad to
look at them. It reminds me of my own heartsickness, to return and die
upon my native soil.

All true lovers of Nature, are lovers of flowers. To me flowers and
birds, are among the fairest of the creations of God. The one delights
and refreshes the soul, with their sweet melodies; The others are so pure
and spiritual, they cheer and refresh the heart with their rich perfumes,
exquisite coloring and forms of grace and beauty. I always recall our large
gardens at home, with a sad regret, and the want of flowers is to me a
sad privation, very hard to be borne. I have no flowers round our small
cottage, and the house being only a slight frame, hinders me from
keeping a few in the windows. In my old house, which was of stone every
window was full of flowers, and I tended them with a mother's care.
This is not a land of flowers. They have no perfume, at home you could
inhale the perfume of our roses and violets long before you came in
sight of the gardens. The very furze filled the air with delicious fragrance.
We have few birds, and I miss the rich notes of the nightingales, black-
bird, lark and thrush, the sweet piping of the robin, linnet and woodlark,
whose united chorus from our own long plantation, and the lofty greenness of Reydon wood, that fronted the old hall; filled the whole air with
their matin and vesper hymns. Hawthorne has truly said, that the
English do not sufficiently appreciate their delightful spring and summer.

Like you, dear Anna, I greatly admire the poetry of Bryant. I remember
copying into my scrap book forty years ago, his beautiful lines to a
'Waterfowl' – which is an exquisite gem from the unfathomable mine of
genius. You have many fine poets. Longfellow, I prefer to our much
admired Tennison, Whitier is a grand poet, whose poems I often read
with ever increasing admiration and pleasure.[2]

I send you the music with this letter. Mr. Moodie, laments that he is no
longer able to copy music so well as he once did. To the flute players,
the simple airs will be sufficient; The accompaniments were written by a
dear young American friend, long since passed into the spiritual land.
The words of 'Lachlan with the Raven hair,' my husband adapted to a
wild Highland wail that bears that title. I think I had better write the
words of the songs separately, they will be more easily read than with the
music. 'Through the Deep Woods,' was written the first year we were
in Canada, 'Welcome welcome thou little bark,' was written before we left
England, and were living in a sweet little cottage on a cliff that over-
hung the sea. There was an old Norwegian Pilot – Peter Hurrli 90 years of

age, who used to go off to ships in distress. He had a very pretty granddaughter, who was engaged to a handsome young sailor who always accompanied the old man in his boat. It was during a heavy storm, and I watched the young girl as she stood upon the beach in the driving rain, her fair hair floating in the wind watching with intense anxiety the returning boat, which gave the idea of the song. It has always been a great favourite with my husband, and he set it to music –

'Oh Can you leave your native land,' was suggested by our own emigration. But to me, 'The Magic Spell,' by the dear old Norseman, is the gem of the collection. He was an excellent musician, and this love of music and song, was a great solace to him in his heavy misfortunes, and it is a source of regret to us both that he can no longer play upon his favourite instrument.[3]

My son Donald has an exquisite tenor voice, and a great ear for music, but strange to say, has never cultivated these two noble gifts, by which he could have earned a handsome living.

Now you must tell me, what 'That Grand old tune,' is – of which your dear father writes so eloquently for I am very curious to know. I should have liked much to have witnessed the festivities of that memorable night, in the old homestead, but he has told the story so graphically that I can see it all – even the old dog and cat. Your dear little note reminds me so of the good father of whom you may well be justly proud. His gentle hospitalities to the poor wandering tramps in that old barn, shows so much genuine kindness and benevolence it almost drew tears from my eyes. I feel so happy in being able to call him friend, which I consider no small privilege –

I want to know more about your dear Mother, and the little children, who rejoice in such grandparents. Of course they are great pets with Aunt Anna. Are they girls or boys, or one of either sex? It is an old woman's privilege to ask questions and I hope you will not deem me too inquisitive. I have 20 grandchildren, and five in heaven. Mrs. Fitzgibbon's eldest daughter Mary Agnes, is just eighteen years of age. She is a dear gentle loving clever creature, but *very fragile* – and my own especial darling – She is not beautiful like her Mother, but very graceful and ladylike, and writes me charming letters. In short, we perfectly understand each other, and our love is mutual. Cherry (or Geraldine) the second, is a very lovely girl, and has a great genius for painting, and greatly helps her Mother in this department. Alice is a pretty, lively bright-eyed thing, full of frolic and glee, and James, who comes between

Mary and Cherry, a fine lad full of talent. But I have come to the end of my paper, and must say goodnight, for I am tired, and *far from well.*

Thanking you much, dear girl, for your kind thoughts of me, I remain, with sincere interest,

Yours most truly
Susanna Moodie

1 Anna Ricketson was probably writing to Susanna because of her knowledge of her activity as a floral painter and her familiarity with Agnes Fitzgibbon's artwork in *Canadian Wild Flowers* (1868).
2 One such scrapbook or copybook by Susanna is held in the Norwich Records Office, but it does not contain the Bryant poem, which was published in 1818. Catharine Parr Traill quotes lines from 'To a Waterfowl' in *The Backwoods of Canada.*
3 This letter was accompanied by copies of the several poems mentioned, and by a short note from Dunbar telling of his paralysis and apologizing for the music he sends with the poems.

---

92 To the County Council of Hastings

Belleville
Oct. 26, 1869

Gentlemen,

My grief for the loss of my good and honored husband, has been greatly cheered by the kind sympathy you express for my bereavement,[1] which I assure you, is very gratifying to my feelings.

I have *indeed*, lost an excellent husband, endeared to me by his many domestic virtues, and a *just*, *honest* man, has passed away from your midst. A man of fine literary tastes and talent, he never felt that he was too old to acquire fresh knowledge; and to the last day of his long and checkered life he found a solace for his many sorrows in his books; expressing the deepest interest in every fresh discovery in arts and science.

He bore his heavy reverses with a calm unshaken fortitude, entrusting the future to the goodness of God, on whose mercies, he relied with the simplicity of a child, and looked forward to his release from the burdens of the flesh, as the happiest moment of his life.

To the many worthy kind men, who knew and appreciated his worth, and who contributed so largely to his comfort in a manner so delicate as

not to wound his sensitive feelings he felt deeply grateful, and to whom I
take this opportunity of tendering my heartfelt thanks.

> Gentlemen, I remain
> Your obedient servant,
> Susanna Moodie

1 The letter of condolence has not survived.

---

93 To Allen Ransome

Seaforth, Ontario D.C.[1]
November 9th, 1869

My Dear Friend Allen,

Your most kind and welcome letter reached me at a moment of intense
affliction. The shaft of the death angel had smitten my house and my
beloved husband had been suddenly removed to another and I fully hope
to him a better world. Oh Allen what sorrow is equal to this sorrow.
The very *esse* of my life seems gone. I am no longer my former self,
bearing in my bosom a twofold life, every thought centered to one
point. It is a strange new feeling to feel so desolate and alone. I ought to
be glad. I ought to rejoice that his exit was so easy and painless, that he
had for months looked forward to death with pleasure, that the merciful
Father saved him from what he most dreaded, a long lingering death of
helplessness and suffering. But my dear friend we are human and nature
asserts the supremacy of her physical laws and though I have blessed
God from my very heart in releasing my loved one from a life of privation
and sorrow, I still must mourn as a wife for my bereavement …
    My husband died October 22nd at 6 in the morning. He went to bed
cheerful and apparently in good health, saving his usual infirmity, and
when I assisted him to undress he said to me 'My dear Susy, I give you a
great deal of trouble.' 'Trouble,' I said. 'I thank God that I have been
spared to help you.' 'Ah,' he replied, 'it will not be for long.' When I had
arranged his pillows and seen that he was comfortably fixed for the
night, I kissed the hard noble brow and bade God bless my darling husband and give him a good night's rest. He drew me down to him and
held me against his breast, 'May he bless you my dear dear old wife.' And
so we parted and though I was with him till the last, and held the dear
hand long after it was cold, he never was able to say words of love or

tenderness to me again. I slept on a couch near him and had done so for 16 years, as he often required my help during the night. But though I was awake at the usual hours he slept tranquilly. At the first early dawn before it was light a voice rang through the room like a trumpet, '*Mother*' I was at his side in a moment. 'Are you ill, John, what is the matter?' He seemed to awake and said, 'What *is* the matter?' I was trembling from head to foot. 'You called so loud I thought you were ill.' 'Susy, I did not call you, but I am very thirsty and my breath comes up like fire. Have you any water?' I always had water, matches, and a lamp ready. I lit my lamp and gave him some water, but he could not drink it, but he begged me to open the window and get him over the bed as he wanted air. This difficulty of breathing lasted about half an hour when he closed his eyes and died as peacefully as a child. I begged him to speak to me, to send some word to the children, but he waved his hand solemnly in farewell, the power of speech was gone. The Doctor for whom I had sent came just after his departure. He died of paralysis of the heart and breathing organs, he said, a painless death. I cannot dwell on the dark hours that succeeded ... He completed his 72 birthday on the 7th of Oct. and had never enjoyed so much peace of mind and happiness as he had done during the last year in the little cottage. He was so gentle, so kind and so sweet that I loved him better than I had done in our more youthful days. Being quite alone he was my Care, the chief object of my thoughts, and I did all I could to make him as comfortable as our reduced circumstances would permit. For him I painted, for him I wrote, and I now feel that my occupation is gone. That poor Susy is alone – has no motive to live for herself.

Time will wear down this blow. What will not time wear down. His two sons Donald and Dunbar were unable to attend the funeral. Katie was not well, and Robert, Agnes and my son-in-law Mr. Vickers came immediately and kind friends gathered round to help me in my hour of need. Robert is a noble honest young man, and is fully worthy of his father. He has a fine face too, full of goodness. Though his features are Moodie's, his hair and beard are dark chestnut, but I can always see his father in him. His dear Father's best and most beloved son. He would take no denial that I was to live with him and though Moodie had always wished me to remain in the Cottage as long as I was able to earn my living I could not withstand the dear son's prayers and tears. His circumstances at present are but limited, and he has a dear young wife and 3 small children to maintain on a very small salary. He is freight agent at this place on the G.T.R. and has given much satisfaction to the great men of the road and if your good friend, *the dearest of Toms*, could speak a word in his favor it might help him forward.

And now my dear friend let me revert to your letter which was a gleam of sunshine on the dark cloud of my sorrow. How delighted Moodie would have been with your recollection of him for you always [held] a very prominent place in his regard ... It has been my fate to bear all the storms and crosses of life often in deep poverty and in much affliction. But God mercifully fitted me to the burthen laid upon me. I never shrank from my allotted task, working and hoping on, never forgetting the soul in the fierce battle of life. My spirit has been brought very low, but it has never yielded to despair. I have learned to regard my youthful aspirations for fame as a dream, which if realized on earth never brings happiness or satisfies the heart. The lust for wealth *I never felt*. I never wished to be rich. I care not for rank or station and can truly say with Abe Lincoln, 'Why should man be proud.' I am afraid my friend Allen you would think me a terrible radical, did I tell you all my thoughts on this great subject ... Dear Allen I wish I could send you the sketches you wish but I never *tried* to draw a landscape in my life, but I will send you two flower sketches, one of our *Wild Marsh Iris*, the other is a Rose that grew at my cottage door, and is a good likeness ... Your magnificent remuneration for these trifles (in England scarcely worth a cent) came most acceptably to help pay the decent funeral expenses for my dear husband. Generous kind friend, I take it as it was meant and thank you with my whole heart ... Your delightful letter gave me interesting accounts of the changes that have taken place in my old neighbourhood. Are the good Ritchies of Wrentham all gone?[2] I have not heard from them for years and I loved the dear old man and his family passing well. I wish our dear old friend Mrs. Bird would allow my daughter Agnes to copy that picture you mention. It should be faithfully returned to her but my children have such a wish to see the old care-worn Mother as she looked when young that it would be a great pleasure to gratify them. Do you think you could prevail upon my dear old friend to grant my request ... [3]

I send you with my poor pictures my daughter's book 'The Wild Flowers of Canada.'[4] The sketches are her own, the letter press by your old friend Catharine P. Traill. Dear Kate, she has had like myself a troubled walk along the hard dusty high way of life, but has borne a severe lot with the same cheerful loveable serenity which marked her youth. She is in poor health and I fear will not be long here. But the exchange for her will be a blessed one. She has two very fine lads in the Hudson's Bay Company service who are much respected and doing well. Her daughters

Annie and Mary are married with families. Kate the eldest [is] still single but a good high minded woman. Mary is very clever but is not very fortunate in the choice of a husband. The curse of Canada, whiskey, desolates many a home. I have 20 grand children ... In my own family I had five boys and two girls, only 3 of the former reached maturity. I look and feel a very old woman and since my heavy loss I look ten years older. You would not know the wild Suffolk girl so full of romance in me ... I have a dear Quaker friend in Massachusetts whose delightful letters and poems have been a great solace to me and my husband ... Frederic Rous of this town,[5] the brother I think of the lady to whom you allude in your letter, has been the best of friends to me in my adversity.

> Farewell dear friend
> Yours faithfully
> S. Moodie

1 From the home of her son Robert
2 In 1882 James Ewing Ritchie, Andrew Ritchie's son, visited Canada and later published his impressions of Catharine and Susanna as 'octogenarians' in *To Canada with Emigrants* (London 1884).
3 According to Una Pope-Hennessy's biography of Agnes Strickland, Thomas Cheesman, a Strickland cousin and London engraver, visited Reydon Hall about 1828, when he seems to have drawn a set of miniatures of the young sisters. Susanna's apparently belonged to Emma Bird at the date of this letter. Ransome did send it (see Letter 99) and it was copied, possibly several times. At some point the other miniatures were also copied for Canadian relatives since one partial group still exists in the home of a descendant.
4 The published title is *Canadian Wild Flowers*.
5 Newly settled at Seaforth, Susanna errs in saying 'of this town,' when she means Belleville.

1869~1882

'The soul is always young'

D URING THE LAST SIXTEEN YEARS of her life, Susanna Moodie experienced loneliness and physical deterioration. Nevertheless, she was well cared for by her children, especially Katie Vickers and Robert Moodie, and to a lesser extent Agnes Fitzgibbon Chamberlin. Her letters from late in 1869 to 1882, the majority written to her sister Catharine, are full of news about children and grandchildren and numerous nieces and nephews; yet her thoughts turn frequently to memories of her own generation, to her youth in England and to her early years in Canada. Her delight in the birth of a new grandchild is accompanied by pleasure at the baby's resemblance to its deceased grandfather, just as her response to events in the lives of older members of the family is tempered by a sense of what her husband's reaction would have been. Her grief at Dunbar's death gives way gradually as the years progress to the mental and physical restrictions of old age. She finds herself frustrated with a body that cannot keep up with her mental energy (see Letter 111); on another occasion, she acknowledges the difficulty of keeping her thoughts organized: 'I had no idea that age was such a ruthless destroyer of the senses and so perfectly obliterate[s] the past, by mingling it up with the present' (Letter 137).

Susanna's writing days were clearly over. The loss of her husband's intellectual companionship, the physical discomfort of sitting at a desk for long periods, left little inclination to compose new manuscripts. However, when George Maclean Rose (1829–98) of the Toronto publishing firm of Hunter, Rose and Company approached her in the spring of 1871 with the idea of giving her books Canadian publication, she seems to have rallied briefly: she prepared a new introduction for *Roughing It in the Bush* and contemplated rewriting *Flora Lyndsay*; as well, she began to review her husband's papers in hopes of seeing them published.

Of all these plans, the first Canadian edition of *Roughing It in the Bush* was the sole result. She made a number of textual emendations to the Bentley edition and eliminated much of her husband's material (certain poems and his sketches 'The Village Hotel,' 'The Land Jobber,' and the two-part 'Canadian Sketches'), keeping only 'The Ould Dragoon,' a humorous caricature most like her own writing. Her new introduction, 'Canada: A Contrast,' reflects the spirit of her remarks to Richard Bentley (Letter 107) that the country was 'rapidly rising in wealth and importance and at no distant period, must become one of the great centres of civilization.'

The contract with Rose was negotiated by her son-in-law John Vickers. Only Canadian printing rights for the revised text were purchased, not the copyright; in return she received $200, a promise of a royalty of four cents on each copy beyond an initial run of 2500, and ten complimentary copies of the new edition. The book was distributed by Thomas Maclear (see Letter 112) and met with a much more favourable reception than it had received in Canada in its original 1852 edition. The *Canadian Monthly and National Review* of February 1872 (182), another Hunter, Rose and Company venture, initiated the generally more objective attention to its literary qualities, which the book has continued to receive: 'It is an extremely lively book, full of incident and character. Although its primary object was to give warning by means of an example, it is by no means a jeremiad. On the contrary, we almost lose sight of the immigrants' troubles in the ludicrous phases of human character which present themselves to view in rapid succession.'

John Vickers attended his father-in-law's funeral in October 1869 without his wife, Katie. He persuaded Susanna to accompany him back to Toronto, to the Vickers home at 152 Adelaide Street, and helped arrange her prompt departure from Belleville. Within a year, after a final experience with unscrupulous lawyers resulted in the loss of a small investment she had made on her own, Vickers became her official representative in all business and legal dealings. Indeed, John and Katie ensured Susanna's material well-being for the rest of her life, in spite of her insistence that she was extremely poor during her last years (in her will, executed by Vickers, she left an estate of $4700).

Now on her own, Susanna resisted Katie's wish that she settle permanently with the Vickers in Toronto, fearing to hurt her son Robert who had earlier invited her to live in his more humble household. Her reconciliation with her daughter was tempered by knowledge of her strong will and her realization that this was 'not my Katie of old,' as she observed to Catharine (Letter 96). Their new relationship ripened in affection and mutual admiration as the years passed, but when she was unable to live on her own in lodgings Susanna seemed to prefer being with Robert, punctuated by short visits with the Vickers or the Chamberlins, and long sojourns with Catharine at Lakefield. As long as she could, she clung to her independence.

The household Susanna arrived at little more than a month after her husband's death consisted of Robert, his wife Nellie, her mother Mrs Esther (Ham) Russell of Belleville, and three young children. The family was in the throes of moving into the accommodation provided with Robert's recent promotion to station agent. (John Vickers's concern for his wife's family seems to have extended to assisting Robert Moodie's fortunes, first

Susanna Moodie, age 63, photograph by William Notman

with promotions within the Grand Trunk Railway, later by hiring him as office manager for the Vickers Express Company in Toronto in 1878.) To Catharine (Letter 96) and her old friend Allen Ransome (Letter 99), Susanna describes the town and her rather trying circumstances during the first six months of her widowhood. Because of Nellie's precarious health, Mrs Russell ran the household. Susanna was not impressed with her counterpart's 'moral' care of their mutual grandchildren.

In this cramped and uncomfortable situation, Susanna expressed her gratitude to relatives and friends in England, South Africa, and Canada for condolences they had sent. Among these were Mrs Mary Moodie of London, the wife of Dunbar's Cocklaw cousin[1] and mother of young Major John Douglas Moodie. Old Mrs Moodie's poem 'In Memoriam to J.W.D. Moodie' was apparently published in the Hastings *Chronicle* early in 1870. Another old friend, Daniel Ricketson, in an obituary on 6 November 1869 in the *National Anti-Slavery Standard*, described Dunbar as 'a gentleman of literary taste, and a good poet' and commented on his books and his work on behalf of the 'oppressed slaves of South Africa': 'the writer who had the honor of being his friend and correspondent, can add, that he was of a most friendly spirit, and of the most generous and noble impulses, one of those whose memory must ever remain green and beautiful with all who knew him.' Ricketson continued to write Susanna 'sentimental love letters' until his remarriage in 1880 (see Letter 133). She also heard from Jane Heddle, who had visited the Moodies in 1856, and of course from her sisters in England. While she was grateful to receive sympathetic letters from Agnes and Jane, she felt most drawn to Sarah, with whom she shared recent widowhood, Canon Gwillym having died in 1868.

In June 1870, Susanna travelled to Toronto to attend her daughter Agnes's wedding to Lieutenant-Colonel Brown Chamberlin (1827–97), a member of Parliament for his home riding of Missisquoi in the Eastern Townships of Quebec. Agnes had met her fiancé while canvassing in Ottawa for subscriptions to *Canadian Wild Flowers*. Early in 1870 Chamberlin had been appointed Queen's Printer, which may have prompted his marriage plans. He was active in the militia and took part in quelling the Fenians at Eccles Hill in May 1870,[2] but the wedding took place as planned on 14 June. Susanna's compassion for Agnes's difficult life seems to have taken a less sympathetic turn after this marriage and her letters frequently complain about her daughter's handling of financial matters and her failure to provide for her children by Fitzgibbon. In fact, Susanna's concerns for her Fitzgibbon grandchildren proved largely unjustified. Her favourite, Maime, after an early unhappy love affair, travelled extensively and built her own modest literary career, which included publication in 1880 of *A Trip to Manitoba, or Roughing It on the Line* by the Bentley firm. In 1877 Geraldine and in 1878 Charlotte Alice began long visits with their aunt Sarah Gwillym in England before making good marriages and settling in western Canada. Their brother James seems to have got himself well established in Toronto by the time he married in 1880. Agnes herself, residing in Ottawa, gave birth to her last child, Agnes Gertrude Mary Chamberlin, on 7 April 1871, and despite living the busy life of an Ottawa socialite assisted Catharine Parr Traill as the illustrator of *Studies of Plant Life in Canada* (1885). Whatever Susanna's reservations about Agnes's new state, they did not prevent her from visiting Ottawa in 1873 (Letter 116) or longing for her daughter's infrequent letters.

The prospect of returning to Seaforth and old Mrs Russell's unholy management of Robert's household, coupled with constant yearnings to return to familiar surroundings, led Susanna to take up independent lodgings in Belleville on 1 October 1870. She rented a room from her old friends, Mr and Mrs Frederick Rous. Frederick Rous, Sr, had been Belleville's inspector of schools during the early 1860s. Another of the Moodies' Quaker friends, by 1870 he had adapted his beliefs to accord with those of Theodore Parker (1810–60), the founder of Unitarianism; at the same time, he became interested in Nathaniel Meeker's plans, actively encouraged by Horace Greeley, for an experimental agricultural community that would be established in the Cache la Poudre Valley of Colorado early in 1871. By March the elder Rouses had left for Colorado and Susanna was forced to take up new lodgings with Mrs John Dougall, 'corner of Church and Dundas Street, Belleville' where she remained until she began an extended visit to Lakefield in the early summer of 1872. She maintained her ties with her Belleville friends: Letters 114 and 115 are addressed to the Rouses' daughter Maggie and there are many references in her letters to Murneys, Breakenridges, Baldwins, Ridleys, Davys, and Wallbridges.

When the Rouses arrived in Colorado they found that the Moodies' eldest son had also been attracted to Greeley's colony. Although their farm in Delaware was beginning to reap good harvests, Dunbar and Eliza sold their property in Camden and took their five young children west. News of them was scant except for occasional reports of their progress (see Letters 121 and 127), announcements of the births of two more grandchildren, and the tragic content of Letter 136 shortly before the death of Eliza Moodie herself.

There was even more cause for worry about Donald Moodie in these years. After the birth of his third child, on 1 January 1872, he and his wife

Julia appear to have separated for a time, probably because of his alcohol problem. At any event, he endured a period of suffering and extreme poverty, prompting Susanna to send money from her own limited resources. After a short-lived reconciliation in 1874–5, Julia seems to have returned to her father's home in Jamaica while Donald disappeared for a time before turning up in Ottawa at the Chamberlins'. In the spring of 1879, however, Susanna again sent him money, this time for clothes and his fare to Chicago, where he underwent treatment enabling him to hold down a job and effect another reconciliation with his wife.

In her letters Susanna worries a great deal about the health and fortunes of her children and takes pride in the promise and accomplishments of her growing grandchildren. John Vickers had a stroke in 1872, which caused Susanna great concern; he apparently recovered sufficiently to continue his successful career. Nellie Moodie's mental collapse in 1871, on the other hand, was severe enough to require hospitalization in the Toronto Asylum, where she was treated by Dr Joseph Workman (1805–94) during the last few years of his distinguished service there. She regained her health, returned to her family in mid-1874, and later gave birth to three more children.

Susanna's youngest grandchildren were born during these years, the last being Robert and Nellie's daughter Catherine Agnes, who was born on 13 December 1881. At the same time, the oldest grandchildren were beginning to work and to raise their own families. Susanna was proud of such matches as Georgina Eliza Vickers' marriage to Edward Philip Leacock (Stephen Leacock's 'remarkable' uncle) in 1881 and young Katie Moodie Vickers' marriage to James Playfair McMurrich, son of the Hon. John McMurrich, a prominent Toronto businessman, in 1882. She was also delighted at the marriage of Geraldine Fitzgibbon to Major John Douglas Moodie of London in the summer of 1878, a match that united the two branches of the old Orkney Moodie family and produced in England her first great-grandchild, Melville Mary Moodie, on 3 March 1879. She was greatly interested too in the lives of her Traill and Strickland nieces and nephews and their large families. The charming little letter (120) to young Katie Traill, Catharine's granddaughter, and the teasing poem (119) to her own grandson Billy Vickers when he was a schoolboy at Upper Canada College attest to her special relationships with young children. According to her great nephew Hargreave Muchall, she gave to children, and received from them, a quite genuine love and respect. When he was nearly eighty, his memories of Susanna at Lakefield in the early 1870s were recorded in the Toronto *Telegram* (17 May 1952):

we grew to be great friends and she always came to my rescue when I happened to be in trouble, which was often enough.

Aunt Moodie liked to fish, so in the summer time on many occasions she would take her fishing tackle and go down to the banks of the Otonabee River hard by, and I always went with her to put the worms on the hook. She had a horror of doing this, due to her aversion to worms which grew to an enormous size in and about Lakefield and to her, were repulsive. This assistance on my part cemented our friendship to such a degree that I became her favourite grand-nephew.

The letters also record the passing of the older generation. After a long break in her correspondence with Richard Bentley, she wrote at least two letters to him during the last few months of his life. He died on 10 September 1871. Allen Ransome died in 1875. On 13 July 1874 Agnes Strickland died, occasioning an obituary in the Toronto *Globe* that Susanna, in the old spirit of family solidarity, promptly corrected (Letter 117). Their brother Thomas died a few months later, followed by Eliza Strickland in 1875. Jane Margaret, who lived in semi-retirement in Southwold writing her *Life of Agnes Strickland* (1887), outlived Susanna by three years. Sarah Gwillym, however, lived longer than all her brothers and sisters except Catharine: after her husband's death in 1868 she resided at Abbot's Lodge, the fine house left to her in Tilford, Surrey, by her sister Eliza; in spite of the failure of some investments in a company that had insured many of the buildings destroyed in the Chicago fire of October 1871 (see Letter 113), she was able to send financial and other gifts to her Canadian relatives and delighted in the transatlantic visits of her great nieces and nephews.

The loss of her English correspondents had the effect of drastically reducing Susanna's comments on public affairs in Canada. However, in writing to Catharine in December 1869 (Letter 96) she does mention briefly the Red River Rebellion and the possible union of Manitoba with eastern Canada as she worries about Catharine's sons, William and Walter, who were working for the Hudson's Bay Company in the area at the time. And in October 1878 (Letter 124) she describes the torchlight parade and celebrations held in Toronto for Lord and Lady Dufferin, the departing vice-regents (it is amusing to note that Catharine named her cat after the Marquis of Lorne, who succeeded Dufferin as governor-general). But apart from sketches of Seaforth and descriptions of the Toronto homes she lived in, suggesting something of the growth and appearance of the city in the 1870s, she recorded little of the world outside her own immediate environment.

Watercolour floral painting by Susanna Moodie

Between 1872, when she gave up her Belleville lodgings, and 1877, when she seems to have become a permanent member of Robert Moodie's household (which had by then moved to Toronto), she spent most of her time in Lakefield either at 'Westove,' Catharine's cottage on the Otonabee, or boarding at a nearby house. Though she frequently suffered from bronchial ailments and a chronic abdominal complaint – Catharine's letters from this period often remark that Susanna has not been able to leave her bed – she clearly enjoyed being with old friends and participating in a limited way in the lives of her Traill and Strickland nieces and nephews and their offspring. She was also able to undertake short visits to her daughters in Ottawa and Toronto, though she often mentioned the fact, probably not really the case, that her lack of money made more frequent visits impossible. (It is conceivable that John Vickers, while more than willing to ensure her needs, sent her little extra cash for fear she would simply send it to the ever penurious Donald.) In any event, her five years at Lakefield were filled with the joys and sorrows of family and friends that she had always observed so closely.

She sympathized with Catharine over the sad lives of most of the Traill children. James had left his young widow, Amelia, with four young children in 1867. Harry, a guard at the Kingston Penitentiary, was murdered in 1870, leaving his widow, Lily, with two young sons and Catharine's three-year-old namesake 'Katie 3,' as she was called after she became the constant charge of Catharine and her eldest daughter Kate. Annie and Clinton Atwood continued to farm near Rice Lake but money was often scarce and jobs hard to come by as the lumber industry in the area began to decline. Mary and her rather irresponsible husband, Tom Muchall, seem to have suffered even more than the others from accidents, illness, and poverty, in spite of Mary's efforts as a writer and teacher in Lakefield and Peterborough. Willie and Walter, in the service of the Hudson's Bay Company, were far away and in apparent danger because of the Riel Rebellions in 1870 and 1885, but both made good marriages, enjoyed life in the west, and appear to have been financially secure.

The Stricklands, too, had their problems. Samuel's widow, Katherine Rackham, a great friend to both Catharine and Susanna, suffered the misfortune of seeing the 'Homestead,' the Strickland family residence, severely damaged by fire in the early 1870s. Many of the business concerns left by Samuel to his children in 1867 began to fail as a result of the general decline in the economy during the second half of the 1870s. Among the Strickland great nieces and nephews, Charlotte, the eldest daughter of Robert Alexander Strickland, was a particular favourite with her aunts; she was a young evangelist whose regular meetings in Lakefield became so well known that she began to speak in more distant places such as Toronto and Brantford until her marriage to the Rev. John Charles Taylor in 1879. Another Strickland often mentioned in the letters is Maria Tully, Samuel's oldest daughter who had married Kivas Tully, a prominent young architect, in 1852. The Tullys lived in a large house in Brockton, a small village near the intersection of Dundas Street and Spadina Avenue before Toronto's development in the last two decades of the century swallowed it up. Susanna was fond of the Tully family, particularly the daughters, Louisa and Agnes LeFevre.

A new Strickland relative settled in Lakefield in 1869. Adela Wigg, the beautiful and talented daughter of Tom Strickland, had married a lackadaisical husband in England. After several years of poverty they decided to try their luck in Canada. However, the family's fortunes improved very little in spite of Adela's popularity as a pianist and music teacher in Lakefield.

In 1879, Susanna's niece Cherrie (Fitzgibbon) Moodie returned to Canada from England with her husband John Moodie, a new baby, and her elderly father-in-law. In 1881 the young family decided to join their Traill cousins in Manitoba (see Letters 132 and 136), where Major Moodie joined the North-West Mounted Police.

News of all these young relatives and dozens of Lakefield friends fills the pages of Susanna's last letters; it is often confusing to follow them, requiring constant reference to the family genealogies and earlier letters. After she settled in with Robert in 1877 she kept up with all their comings and goings through her correspondence with Catharine and obviously enjoyed their visits to her in Toronto.

Her physical health deteriorated more rapidly during her final years, necessitating regular care by her physicians, Dr C.B. Hall (1816–80) and Dr William Canniff (1830–1910), who had begun his notable career in Belleville as a physician and later became a professor of medicine and a historian. But her health, while it reduced her participation in social events as she aged, did not prevent her from meeting many members of Toronto's literary and academic community. Among these were Daniel Wilson (1818–92), a poet and historian who served as president of the University of Toronto, and Dr Edward Chapman (1821–1904), the author of several books of poetry (see Letter 130).

In 1882 the visit to Canada by James Ewing Ritchie, rekindled old Suffolk memories. Ritchie was amazed to find in the elderly woman 'a mental vigour and active memory rare in one so aged. She told me anecdotes of myself when a boy that I had quite forgotten, and retains in old age the enthusiasm for which she was remarkable when young.'[3]

The final letters in this section, addressed to Catharine, affirm the sisters' abiding affection for each other. As the last surviving members of their generation in Canada, now in their eighties, they shared memories of their youth in Suffolk and understood each other's physical sufferings and family worries. They also shared an intellectual world as avid readers and writers and spiritual companionship in a common Christian faith.

1 In the seventeenth century, the Orkney Moodie family split into two branches, the Moodies of Melsetter and the Moodies of Cocklaw.

2 See Rose's *Cyclopedia of Canadian Biography*, 555.

3 James Ewing Ritchie, *To Canada with Emigrants* (London, 1884), 94. See also the interview with her in the Toronto *Globe* on 10 May 1884.

94 To John Vickers

Seaforth Ontario
11 November, 1869

My dear John,

I ought to have written before this, but as Robert had telegraphed you of our safe arrival, and as I took a bad cold on the journey I have not felt able before today. We did not reach our destination until past four o'clock in the morning, and altogether it was the most miserable railroad journey I ever had in my life, but, then my experience is very small. We went merrily till we reached Brampton, and I was delighted with the country, but here we came to a stand still that lasted six long hours. A previous train was off the track, some miles ahead of us, and the road had to be cleared of the *debris*. A great many plans were proposed, at last after two hours, it was determined to put us into an empty car and take us as near the wreck as possible while our luggage was being shifted to the waiting passenger car. In being lifted bodily, from one car to the other I lost the package of sandwiches dear Katie made for me and the nice box of grapes. In these cars we stayed four hours. The next move was to lift us all (women and children) body and bones out again, and guide us by the light of a lantern round the broken cars, *through* mud and wet grass, stumbling at every step. We had they said not more than a hundred yards to walk, but half a mile was more near the mark. The worst of our troubles was being crammed into the already crowded car, and getting a seat any where we could find one. The heat was dreadful, a large fire had been made for the benefit of the poor little starving children, who were going to Illinois with their tired parents. The windows and doors, were all open. The heat and draught combined gave me this bad cold. I was hungry and thirsty. But there was no cup, to drink out of, and so, slowly, wearily, and sad at heart I travelled on, to Stratford, and there we changed these odious cars, and Rob met us, and took me into the Seaforth car, which was comfortable and well ventilated, but it was nearly daylight when we reached here. Dear Nellie and Mrs. Mather who had been expecting us all night fed and warmed me and did every thing in their power to make me feel comfortable.

I miss the dear fair faces of your sweet children very much. Kiss them all for poor old Grandmamma. With dear love to my own Katie and thanks for all hers and your own kindness. God bless you and yours dear John and believe me yours ever most affectionately

Susanna Moodie

95 To Katie Vickers

Seaforth
Nov 25 1869

My dearest Katie

Your kind letter gave me great pleasure. I felt dull and sad and very homesick, but I have no longer a home, and must rest contented waiting patiently for the deep rest of the last and best home, beside my lost darling. We have been in the muddle and mess of moving [in] this horrid weather, but this is of course only a temporary inconvenience. Rob is obliged by his new appointment to be nearer the trains. Two extra rooms are being built for me, and until they are finished I am boarding at the Hotel which is exactly opposite, and I feel far from well and very weary. Robert and his family are very grateful to dear John for the valuable assistance he has given in attaining the desired position. Robert's greatly increased salary, will make them very comfortable when things at the house are settled.

The children are both good and pretty, more like their mothers family than their fathers. I am writing this sitting on a low box with a chair for a table, which must be the excuse for the horrid writing. Painting and writing I shall have to give up altogether for want of space, and both occupations would relieve the monotony of my present life. A good many people have been to see me but I cannot return visits. All I want is to be alone and quiet.

After three weeks of mush and snow, we have fine bright weather at last and I can see a little of the town, which extends over a large flat surface. Nothing in the shape of a rise is visible, it is *intensely new*, treeless and unpicturesque, without creek or river to diversify the scene. The town is built entirely of wood, and pleasantly located in a swamp full of ugly stumps. In spite of the immense fall of snow it is not cold. I suffer from the heat of the coal stoves kept burning night and day. You would think that the good folks were Salamanders. They have lots of fine stores here, and dry goods are cheap. There is only a narrow path between the station house, and the railroad which runs through the upper end of the street. The little ones could fall from the door step, under the wheels. I shall have to keep a good watch over them. I often think of you and the dear children. Those girls are all lovely, Katie, as beautiful as an angel. You must kiss them all for me and tell them that I found my dear dog Quiz, and Grim the Maltese cat quite comfortably settled at Uncle Roberts when I got there. Quiz is now lying under the chair looking at me with his beautiful earnest eyes. We cannot persuade Grim to leave Robert's house, and come to the station. I will go and try if I can coax him down today as he will starve out there. How I miss your dear Father, miss our dear cottage home, our quiet happy evenings and the calm grand face, that made the light of my life. Never, never, can I hope to be so happy again. I have so many kind letters to answer, but I cannot do it yet. I have not even had courage to write to your father's friends at the Cape to tell them of his death. Mr. Ricketson wrote a beautiful notice of him in the New York *Anti-Slavery Herald*, in which he did ample justice to my dear husband's literary talents, and his beautiful letter to me cheered me a good deal. I have not heard from England yet, but there has hardly been time. [A] dear Quaker friend has invited me to come to Montreal to them for a long visit. This you know dear is not possible but it is very kind. Dear Minnie Chisley (Mrs. Macdonald) wrote to me begging me to come to Ottawa, and spend the winter with them. If I live till spring I will take a trip to Belleville during the summer months, with Nellie, who has friends there also. We will spend a short time with you, and dear Agnes, on our way down. I am building on this trip already. My heart lies buried in Belleville. I want to commune with it and be still. Give my love to dear John. Thank him for all his kindness to dear Robert and me,

Your loving Mother,
Susanna Moodie

96 To Catharine Parr Traill

Seaforth Station, Ont.
Dec. 21st, 1869

My Beloved Sister,

Your letter was a treasure *dearly prized*, I wish, however, that it gave me a better account of your health. I suffer too, but it is from the bladder and womb, but as I have never had much of *rhumatism*, one of the most hideous offsprings of sin and death, I ought to be very thankful. My internal complaint, whatever it is, is more sickening and miserable than painful. A tight contraction which seems to draw me up inwardly like a tight string tied round the lower part of the body, which makes common evacuations at times, very difficult and painful.

I shall not doctor for it, but leave it to nature. I have little faith in the physicians skill, but great confidence in that of the Surgeon, which is not guess work, but practical scientific skill guided by experience and truth.

I hope my dearest Katie, that your valuable life may be spared yet awhile to us all.

I have wanted to write to you for a long time, but until very lately, I could not get a chance. We have been in all the muddle and discomfort of moving, from a handsome commodious house to one no bigger than a nutshell, and in horrible weather too. You perhaps have heard that the Station agent Mr Broughton, has been removed to Brantford on an increased salary and that dear Robert has been promoted to the Station. The requisition to the Directors of the G.T.R., was signed by every professional man and freeholder in the place, and his nomination received with acclamations. He has an increase of 200 dollars on his salary and the house (such as it is) rent-free, and all his wood, coal, oil, (don't laugh) and brooms and matches found him. The wood cut and his water brought to him, which gives him an income of about 800 dollars. This, poor dear, will set him free from many difficulties, and he bears such a high character, that Vickers told me that he was now on the high road to advancement. But the dear kind fellow has a shocking cough which hourly reminds me of poor James, and is very thin and delicate. Nothing can exceed his kindness to me. I have the best room in the cabin, well-carpeted, but there is only room for a small iron single bed, one chair, and one table at which I am now writing and which I had made to serve me for wash stand, drawing, and writing. It corresponds with the dimensions of the room. The window, fortunately is due south, and nearly half the size of the room which is on the ground floor. As are the 3 other apartments. Rob had to put up a kitchen, and a bed room for Mrs. Russell and the two little girls, at his own expense, so you may imagine what a mess we were in. The place filled up with trunks and packages, with no room to move in. I went over and boarded at the hotel for a week, until I could get a place to sleep in. I could have written to relieve the intense weariness, but my trunks were at the other house, which contained all my writing materials, and I could not get at them. I have had so many letters to write since I returned here. To dear M's friends at the Cape, to Mrs. Moodie of London. To my sisters at home, to Jane Heddle, to Allen Ransome, and a host of business letters, and worse still, letters of compliment which, though meant kindly, tear open afresh the deep wounds of the heart and cause them to bleed uselessly. But it cannot be helped, we are bound to receive thankfully what is meant kindly. I hope this ordeal is over. But the postages cost a little fortune. I pay dear Robert 100 dollars a year for my board. It is very little, and he don't want me to pay anything, but you know I could not feel happy at all, if I were dependent, and I can help him in many ways, to make it up to him, for he has a large family to support.

His wife and I get on *very well* together. She is really a good darling, very fond of him and very industrious. The mother, however, takes the active management of the house. She works like a tiger, but without order or economy. Is alternately petting the children or punishing them with injudicious *violence*. The consequence is utter disobedience to her commands, and this miserable system, is in constant operation. Of course, I cannot interfere. I do all I can by kindness to the little delinquents to counteract the pernicious effects of such folly, by trying to teach them moral duties, and I teach the eldest, who is making rapid progress in the art of reading and sewing. She stays with me, more than half the day, and already there is a great improvement in her. She is a fine generous, clever girl, nearly six years of age, and with *proper* training, would make a noble woman. I must be patient, in the hope of leading these poor lambs to the good Shepherd. She is very fond of me, and really wishes to be good.

Ah, my dear sister, there are times, when I feel the loss of my dear companion, and the treasurers of his fine mind as a direful calamity. Those mental treats that ever afforded me such delight, are lost to me now entirely. My poor, sore heart, is so *empty*, aches so, for companionship such as it has been used to. The days seem so sad and long. The blessed night, though it brings fond tears and sad regrets, also brings prayer and sacred study, and then I feel that my grief is better than the occupations and pursuits, of the noisy day, and I think of the beloved and sleep in peace, thinking of that blessed rest beside him in his lowly grave. Sometimes I think myself ungrateful, to these poor women, who do all they can to make my lot brighter, especially as one, I am certain, is not accountable for her temper, and dear kind Nellie, is really *very sweet*. I believe God has placed me here, for some wise purpose, and I will not relinquish the situation. Do not, dearest, allude to any remark of mine, or shew this letter to others.

How did you hear of Allen Ransome, having remembered his old friend? He wrote me a long charming letter, and sent me his photograph, which shews him to be as handsome an old man, as he was, as a young one. He kindly sent me a draft on the Montreal bank, for 10 pounds sterling, to be paid for by two groups of flowers, which are ready, but not yet sent to him. He speaks most affectionately of you, and desires his love to dear amiable Kate. He is a paralytic like father, but makes light of it, and suffers from gout and rhumatism. Which, only he says, impedes his loco-motion, in other respects, he is contented and happy.

Jane Heddle sent me an Orkney *Herald* with a long notice of the dear husband,[1] and my excellent friend, Dan'l Ricketson of Massachusetts, wrote a beautiful obituary of him in the New York *Antislavery Herald.* I have not been able to write a word about him, but I hope when the cold recedes, to collect all his sweet poems into a small volume, and give a slight memoir of him.

I have received most kind letters from dear Sarah, Agnes, and Jane, which were very comforting to my heart. Dear Sarah, seems a most holy excellent christian woman, but she always was a sweet creature. Jane's letter is really charming. Time and the influence of the blessed spirit, seem to be fast ripening her for heaven.

Yes, beloved sister, this union of kindred hearts, after such years of separation, is a most blessed thing, for which I daily thank the blessed Mediator who can alone perform these miracles, and subdue the hard rebellious heart of sinful man. To Him, be all the glory and the praise.

I have thought much about your dear boys, since those revolutionary movements at the Red River settlement. How will it all end? I fear there will be no union with Canada.

You ask about Dunbar. He wrote to me very kindly, on receiving the news from Donald of his Father's death, and said that I *must* come to him, as it was with him I had to make my home. I answered him as soon as I was able, and gave him a full account of his father's death. But he wrote to me on my birthday. A very disagreeable letter, speaking most cruelly of his good brother, and going over all the old troubles. It was a sad affair altogether. I wrote to him in reply kindly and firmly, and refuted many things that I knew to be false, but he seems mad with jealousy that I preferred living with a younger brother to him. That letter upset me a good deal, for I have so truly repaid him good for evil, that it cut me to the heart, that he could write in such a strain to me, at such a time. But there must ever be a thorn in the flesh to keep us watchful, and I will not give him up yet. Donald and Julia wrote both very kindly, but have not written since my reply.

I hope a perfect reconciliation has taken place between Vickers and Katie and I. I never thought John was in the wrong, nor do I think so now. Katie, like her father, took deep prejudices and saw the actions of others often in a wrong light and nothing could dispossess her mind of these convictions when once formed. Katie is greatly changed. I should never have known her. The cares of the world and the deceitfulness of riches, seem to have closed up her heart to all, but her own.

She was kind and hospitable, but not my Katie of old. Her children are darlings. Her Katie Moodie the loveliest of human creatures, and they all seem gentle and obedient. Happy in being loved. Not like my poor babes here thrashed for nothing all day.

Well darling I would tell you more about the place, etc., but my hands are freezing with cold. I will write soon again. Give my love to our dear sister Katherine. I hope she will forgive me not writing, which I have often done mentally at night when in bed. Give my love to the dear girls, and believe me ever your faithfully attached Sister

Susie

1 On 11 December 1870 the *Huron Expositor*, Seaforth, reprinted this obituary tribute from the Orkney *Herald*.

---

97 To Katie Vickers

Feb 17 1870
Seaforth

Dearest Katie

I was so glad to get your dear letter. It cheered me, for [I] have been far from well, many things reminding of [how] short may be my sojourn here. Besides, I love to hear all about the dear children and their ways and doings. It brings them all vividly before me, and in fancy I hear their happy young voices. I am glad that they are all well and have not forgotten the poor widowed Grandmother. I often feel very sad and lonely, thinking of the *dear* father, who *is dearer* to me than ever now. I feel that I can see the noble venerable face no more on earth. My life without him seems so dreary and aimless, its objects and occupations alike gone, and seldom a night passes that my pillow is not drenched with tears.

> Ah human love thy trusting Heart.
> In all things vainly true.
> How stamps upon thy wasted past
> Its passionate adieu.

My dear little daughter-in-law will be the bearer of this. She goes down with some friends for a little trip. They wished her to go to the Hotel

with them, but I knew that you would not like that. And I know that she
will enjoy herself more with you. I am sure that you will like her for
she is a sweet lady like girl, sings and plays well, and is very lively and
pleasant. I wish that I was going with her, but my cold is too bad.

Nellie will tell you all the Seaforth news. How dear Rob is getting
along, in his new berth, and how the old woman your respected Mother
is progressing. One day here is the fact simile of the last. We breakfast at
seven. I put my room in order and sit down to paint, knit, or write. I
cannot stand the heat of the sitting rooms and prefer the cool and quiet of
my own room. We dine at twelve and the same routine continues till five
when we take tea, and I go back to my room and read till nine or ten,
when I go to bed, to think, often for hours of the dear father, and of the
absent ones, who have become doubly dear since he left me. This daily
life is sad and dreary enough, but I find in my dear old Bible a solace, and
seek to find a better life in the future. Every one is kind and good to me
especially dear Robert, who does all he can to make me forget my grief,
but he cannot recall the lost, or supply, the companionship of so many
years – The treasures of your fathers intellect I miss more than any thing
else. I have no one to talk over the books we used to read together of an
evening, and to speculate on subjects which interested us. My mind seems
quite a blank without him. Poor dear Donald's beautiful boy, has been
at the point of death with Scarlett fever. I am very anxious but hope that it
has pleased God to restore him to his parents, who love him so dearly –
Every one who has seen the child, have told me of his loveliness and how
proud dear Donald is of him. I received very kind letters from home this
week. Agnes, Jane, and Sarah all wrote to me. Sarah's letters are always
so kind and sympathizing. Since a widow herself, she knows exactly
how I grieve. I must stop now as dear Nellie is down, and ready for the
train. With fondest love from the old Mother to all the darlings.

Susanna Moodie

---

98 To Katie Vickers   March 4th 1870

My dearest Katie

I got dear John's telegram with the glad tidings, of the arrival of your little
daughter. May she prove a happy gift to you and her dear kind father.

Kiss her for her old Grandmother. Today is the birthday of my 'two little doves.' I think that I told you, that on the morning of the 4th March, 1868, I dreamed that I went out to the chicken house to look for fresh eggs but there were none, but in the pidgeon house I found two eggs which I put in my bosom and came in to the kitchen, to give them to Margaret to cook for father's breakfast. When I took the eggs out, to give to her, the shells were broken and two lovely little doves flew out. When I awoke I told Father, and he laughed at me. Just as we sat down to breakfast, I got two telegrams, one, from John telling me of little Ethel's birth, the other from Rob, with the joyful news, that they had a son. Now was it not a queer dream? I always call those children 'my doves.' Our boy here is a very fine active child, but don't talk so plainly as darling golden haired Ethel.

I have had letters from all my children this week. Agnes is quite well and still in Montreal staying with her kind friends the Mulhollands. She then goes on a visit to Ottawa. She has sold 280 copies of Mr. Corelyn's book, and is in very good spirits. Donald's boy, is quite well again. Your dear Aunt Traill has been ill but is better. She writes such loving letters, and is so anxious that I should go to see her in the spring. I had also a long kind letter from your father's friend Mrs. Moodie of London. She has transferred her correspondence to me. She is a clever warm-hearted woman. She sent me a fine poem 'In Memoriam of J.W.D. Moodie.' I sent it, at her request to the Belleville *Chronicle*[1] and will send you a copy of the paper. She was a great friend, to dear Father. Mrs. Michaud is a distant cousin. Mrs. Moodie's letters were a source of great pleasure to him. She wishes me to write a memoir of him and publish [it] with his poems, and send it to her, and she will try to find a publisher. My kind friend Mr. Ricketson of Massachusets is an enthusiastic admirer of your father's poetry and has written several fine notices of him in American papers. Oh! does he know how much we all value and think of him? I must send this to post or miss todays mail. Hoping this letter will find you and the dear babe doing well. With fond love to all from your affectionate Mother

S. Moodie

---

1 The Hastings *Chronicle*

99 To Allen Ransome

Dear Friend Allen

Seaforth Station
Ontario
May 6th 1870

On my return home from Stratford (not of Shakespeare notoriety) I found your most kind and welcome letter ... The winter has been long and dreary. Nature will grieve for the loved and lost, but now that I have realized in spirit that he still lives I have gathered myself up from the dust and ashes of grief and try to be hopeful and contented – Robert's prospects too have brightened a little. [I]n December he was appointed to the Station here by a requisition signed by all the respectable Merchants in the place and his appointment received with acclamations. If ever a young [man] strove earnestly and honestly for the good of his employers he is the man. His salary now amounts to 600 dollars per annum and the house rent free, a great advance on $300 on which he could barely buy bread for his family.

But oh such a droll little house. It is all on the ground floor, and the kitchen, parlor and two 8 by 6 bedrooms could all be contained in one tolerably sized room. R. had to build a bed room at his own cost for his wife's Mother and the two eldest little girls, ditto kitchen, for the old one neither kept out the rain, nor snow, and was free to all the winds of heaven. I was domiciled in the *state cabin*, as I call the room in which I am writing to you in which I read and paint, think and pray, but I feel terribly cribbed, cabined and confined, but still very glad to be tenant at will. You would wonder how a man, three women, and three children could be accomodated in such a narrow space. There is no room for a servant so we do without. I take charge of my cabin and the wee parlor, the other two ladies doing the rest. The worst of it is that we have no privacy. The parlor door opening directly into the rail road which is only separated from us by a narrow board pavement, and trains are rushing to and fro all day shaking the wall and stunning our ears with the [a]larum. The house is mistaken for the waiting room half the time, and as the two little bed closets open into the parlor my door is often opened by some strange person enquiring for 'the Station Master' and not long ago my daughter-in-law found a tipsy man in her room and had to go on to the platform to get some of the employees to get him out. All this is droll enough but it is annoying too. However, we make the best of it, and are very thankful that the darling Robert is lifted out of the rugged valley of unceasing toil and grinding poverty. His cough too is better for he gets more to eat and the cruel load of care is removed from his shoulders. I begin to hope that he may outlive his consumptive tendencies.

He is so pleased with the idea of seeing what I looked like when young. It was so kind of you dear Allen sending the picture. I will get Agnes to copy for the others. She while in Ottawa canvassing for the 2nd edition of the 'Wild Flowers of Canada' met with the *dearest of Toms* ... I am going shortly to stay with her a few weeks during the hot months (for this stifling little place would kill me during the intense heat of July and August) ... My little sketches are only curious as being performed with the unsteady eye and hand of 66 years.

Here we are almost in the woods and I have paid several visits to them to be a child again among the flowers and recal[l] many a rural scene of my first settlement in the forest land ... I had a severe attack of inflammation of the lungs during the winter, which fortunately diminished the burthen of the flesh and has reduced me into tolerable proportions. I feel however age coming on with rapid steps, but it does not trouble me. I would not be young again if I could. I have found age the happiest period of my life. Though I have been sorely tried, my heart and mind are as fresh as ever, they feel no decay and certainly have received lessons of wisdom in the hard school of adversity that I trust will ripen to eternity. I feel that my spiritual nature has progressed and is progressing, that in patience I am learning to possess my soul, and the more I cherish this calm spirit, the more I can endure.

I was not a little surprised in hearing from my dear Agnes that she is to be married again and from what I hear of the talents of her intended, he is a man of great literary attainments and the best speaker in the [H]ouse. An Author, an Editor, and President of several of our best societies, but not over rich, as such men seldom are ... I am afraid that she will be removed far from me as Colonel Chamberlain is a lower Canadian by birth and resides in the County he represents in Parliament.

Well although my child, she is a beautiful clever charming creature, sweet-tempered and lovely, both in mind and disposition ... I have often wondered when looking at Agnes and Donald how a woman so plain, could be the mother of two such splendid specimens of humanity. I think I owe it to my intense love of the beautiful.

How vividly I recalled while reading your letter, the many places over which we had strolled together in dear Yoxford and that visit to Mr. Jessup and the episode with the ungallant butcher, who refused a seat in his cart, to little Emma Bird and me, during the pouring shower on the plea that he had 'a Calf in the Cart and no room for two Lambs.' How you laughed when I related gravely the circumstance at our friend's hospitable board, as if I did not recognize the man who sat facing me as the identical Butcher, and how dear old Jessup gave us both a *little* lecture, after he went away, upon our levity ...

All here are very kind to me and Robert's young wife, a very pretty creature I might truly call the *dearest of Nells*. I have earned some dollars in painting and have several orders to fill, and as my physical wants are very few I am easily satisfied. Poverty and Grief are the two much abused Angels that lead us to God ...

> Yours most truly
> Susanna Moodie

Robert desires me to present his kind regards and grateful thanks.

---

100 To Allen Ransome

June 13th 1870
Toronto

My dear old friend,

... I am here to witness the marriage of my dear Agnes to Col. Chamberlain, who has so gallantly repulsed the Fenian Robbers from our shores ...

Few persons have ever experienced greater trials than have fallen to my lot, yet the love of one good noble man repaid me for all ... How I miss him. This famine of the soul is very hard to bear, but every day brings us nearer to each other ...

I have not been well since I came here. We have had hot summer weather in the Huron district since the snow went, and here it is positively cold. I have had to resume all my winter wraps ... Farewell, I cannot write more until all the excitement is over ...

> Susanna Moodie

101 To Catharine Parr Traill Toronto
July 9th, 1870

My Dear dear Sister,

I know not how to write to you, or what consolation to offer, in your great sorrow. We only learned the sad tidings of your dear boy's untimely end last night, through the papers. It has haunted me ever since. You and the poor wife seem constantly before me, and I picture your terrible grief. Oh dear, dear Katie, you have my fullest, deepest sympathy, but He who took him away, can alone comfort and restore you to peace. The poor wife will feel it most, for in the course of Nature, you and I will soon join our dear ones again, but she poor thing has a long sad life of widowhood before her, and must toil to support her little ones. I pray for their sakes, she may be sustained in this terrible hour. Last night, I prayed long and fervently for you all. The dear girls too, who must feel this sudden wrench most keenly. Dear Mary, I hope her trial was over, and that she will not be physically injured and her little one by this sad news. Every person here feels for you, and sympathizes with you, my beloved sister, and *it is* a comfort in our grief to know that other hearts partake of our sorrow.

I know that you will seek help from the only source from which it can be obtained, and that the blessed Physician of souls, will pour oil and wine into this bleeding wound. But oh, these ties are so strong. They hold us so fast, that when suddenly wrenched apart, we seem to die with them, and the burthen of life becomes for awhile intollerable. Only a few days ago, I received a heart-broken letter from Donald's wife, wailing over the death of her youngest son. In want and sorrow, sick both in mind and body, her husband ill and out of employ, without a friend to help them in that vast city of 'splendor and of wretchedness.' I think a sadder description of human suffering, was never penned by a human hand. It wrung me to the very heart. I had no means at hand to help them, nor could I obtain any before October. I sent them half of the contents of my purse (10 dollars) which I am glad that they received safely. 10 dollars is but a drop in the bucket, but even a drop will moisten the lips of one dying of thirst, and I have written to a friend to see if he can give him anything to do on the G.T.R.

Alas, that ill-starred marriage. What sorrow has it not occasioned. But the poor wife has been punished heavily for her imprudence. I pray that the Saviour, to whom she clings in her dire adversity, will give her that

peace, which she seems so earnestly to crave. All my dislike to her has
vanished in her misery. Her little son appears to have died from want of
proper nourishment. He could run about and talk and by her description appears to have been a beautiful winning creature, but is it not a real
blessing, the sweet child being removed so early from this world of sad
vissisitudes, and safely folded with the lambs of the good Shepherd's
flock. I shed no tears for little Walter, but the misery of the poor parents, fills me with sorrow and dread. Like all exciteable people, reverses
plunge Donald into despair. Julia says he is terribly cast down, but she
hopes that the death of his darling will be the means of bringing him to
God, and then, much as she laments the loss of the child she would for
ever bless the hand that took him from her. Poor thing. You could not,
darling sister, read the reccord of their sufferings without tears. It is too
sad. I fully meant to have paid you a short visit before I returned to
Toronto, but I had to send them the money that I needed for the journey. Much as I regret not seeing you, I know that you would have done the
same, in my case.

I have thought much last night and to day, that you, will miss dear Mrs.
Strickland's kind Christian sympathy in your great affliction. I have an
unfortunate reserve on these subjects. I feel them deeply but I cannot
clothe my thoughts in words of practical utility that would afford consolation to the mourner.

Mr. Vickers told me, that he was talking the *other* day with a gentleman from the Red River, who had *very lately* seen both your sons, of
whom he spoke in the highest terms, and said that they were getting on
well, and esteemed by all who knew them. I hope that this will console
you dear Katie a little. You have still two dear, honest noble-minded sons
to love and care for you, and dear Harry has left a charming boy to fill
his place. Even my dear husband, whose admiration for children, was a
good deal confined to his own, when H and his wife, brought him to see
us last summer, said that he was a noble child, a born gentleman and
looked as clever as he was handsome.

Harry too, looked strong and handsome. I almost marvel how he could
be overcome by two ordinary men. It is certain that our lives are hid
with God. That no precautions on our part can arrest the shaft of Death.
My dear Nephew died in the performance of his duty. The same thing
happens to thousands on the battle field, of whom we take no account, but
not one of them falls to the ground without the Heavenly Sanction. My
own individual idea of Death, has long been, that it is the angel of life and
mostly to all, A Messenger of Mercy. Whenever, lately, I visited my

dear husband's grave, it appeared to me, such a blessed haven of rest, that I longed with an intense longing, to lie down beside him. Poor darling, the hare bells and Ox-eyes were growing upon his lowly bed, and the robins hopping from branch to branch, discoursed to me sweet music in that early morning hour, before any one was stirring, that I chose daily to hold sweet communion with the beloved. I left Belleville with regret. I seemed so near to him there.

My darling sister, I have said little of what is in my heart. I cannot, but you will feel it all. Do get some kind hand to tell me how you are. How dear Mary and Kate are, for I shall pine to know. All friends here send kindest love to you all, and believe me ever, in joy and sorrow,

Your own attached
Suzie

---

102 To Catharine Parr Traill   Nov. 18, 1870
Belleville

My Dearest Catherine,

A long, a very long time has elapsed since I wrote to you, and I feel quite ashamed of it; but the mechanical part of writing has become quite a task, as I begin to think it does to all people, as age dims the eye, stiffens the fingers and dulls the brain. While on the other hand, it revives all the dear old memories and affections of the past, leading us back insensibly to our youth and making us children again. Now, you are very seldom long absent from my thoughts, and I make up in mental talks what my hand and tongue are so deficient in. I hardly know who wrote last. You or me, but that does not matter. I owe you many letters I am sure, but I feel just now very anxious to have some tidings of you. I had long held to the hope of being able to go up to Lakefield and spend a few days with you before the cold winter set i[n], but my money matters had got into such an inextricable muddle, that I was quite deficient in the necessary means. If it had not been for the kindness of John Vickers, who took them into his hands, I believe I should have lost everything. As every investment was made in the lawyer's name instead of in mine. I shall lose a good part of this year's income at any rate, and will only be too thankful to get the larger part of the small sum, on which I have to depend, back again.

After dear Agnes and the family left for Ottawa, I spent the month of September with Katie, who took the tenderest care of me. I was so worn and thin, you would never have known me, harrassed in mind, and well nigh done up in body, also. If she had not nursed me so kindly, I don't think I should have been alive now.

The children are perfect darlings. *Real* children, sweet-tempered and confiding, and all tried to do their best to make poor old Grandma happy. Such a contrast to those poor neglected violent little things at Robert's, who would be fine clever creatures away from the influence, certainly not a moral one, of Mrs. R__. I felt it impossible to go back to Seaforth, to be under her control, and had almost determined to remain with dear Katie, when Mrs. Rous wrote to me, making me the offer of boarding with her. The terms were liberal, only two dollars and a half a week, and I was to find my own bedding. Upon consulting with Vickers, he thought that I would be able to pay this, and any deficiency he would make up for me, both in clothes and board. After due reflexion, I thought it might be for the happiness of all parties, and remove any jealous feeling of preference being shown more to one, than the other, if I boarded with friends, who were independent of my family, and who knew and loved me, and had been tried in the poverty and affliction from which my beloved partner had escaped. So I made arrangements with Mrs. Rous and came here the 1st of October, and so far, I have no reason to regret the step. I have a large, nicely furnished bedroom with a stove in it, and carpeted floor and every thing comfortable and handy. I can remain in my own room or join the family when I like, and then, I am independent. My own absolute mistress, and to me this is life. A palace would be a prison if entirely dependent upon the will of another. Nothing can exceed the kindness of dear Mrs. Rous and the whole family and I am near to the dear husband. A couple of minutes walk brings me to his grave, and every fine day, I go alone and spend some time in communion with the dear spirit, who seems to meet me on that spot.

Katie, dear soul, took every care of my outward woman and helped make up with her own hands, a suit of very handsome mourning, bought me boots and shoes enough to last me half a life, and no less, than four excellent widows caps, and told me anything I wanted just to write without scruple to her and it would be furnished. She only wished me to be comfortable and happy. Ah, poor Katie, I fear she has been blamed for what she never deserved. She is a fine honorable woman and I believe would have saved her father, if he would only have listened to a practical solution of his difficulties. I think before he died, he had seen her

conduct and his own, in their true light, and felt very sorry for the
estrangement, but like her, was too proud to yield. She is so wonderfully
like him in temperament, and turn of mind. The baby is perfectly lovely.
It is called Henrietta Moodie.

Agnes seems comfortably settled in Ottawa among the big wigs. I am
only fearful lest the company that unavoidably she must keep should
involve her in difficulties. He is not a rich man, and has to provide for
three old maiden sisters and though his situation is a good one, 2000
dollars salary, yet house rent and every thing is so dear there, in consequence of the great fires, that she will find it hard to live in any style.

Maime is staying in Dunham,[1] at his old homestead with his sisters,
and the bracing mountain air will I hope restore her to health.

Poor dear, when she left Brockden[2] she looked in the last stage of
consumption. Alice is staying in Montreal, with Mrs. Lowe, the Col.'[s]
sister, and is learning French and Music, and Aggy says is wonderfully
improved. Cherry is with Mamma, and much pleased with the change.
She is a sweet girl. I grew to love her very much, for she is a lady both in
mind and manners. Agnes writes rather desponding about the book.
However, Mrs. Ross, (Our sister of Montreal)[3] has made some offer for
the edition, and she hopes to dispose of it. I helped the girls color some
of the plates. I could soon learn to do that sort of painting well.

Dunbar has another little daughter. He wrote to me kindly at last to tell
me of the event. This makes his fourth girl – it is to be called Alice – I
don't care much for the name. The last was Jessie. No prospect of any
more in Robert or Donald's households. Agnes expects to be confined
the end of April, and complains a good deal of her weight and unwieldi-
ness. The Colonel is in extacies. By what she says, I fear she may give
him two instead of one. She has lost no time. Mrs. H. Traill called upon
me on her way down to Kingston. Poor thing, my heart ached for her.
She had a pretty delicate baby in her arms, very like, what the 'Tiny man[']
was at the same age. I have seen Mrs. James Traill several times, and
two of her boys. Herbert whom she thought so like herself, is the image of
his father with blue eyes the color of yours. He is a very fine boy. The
poor Duponts are in the greatest sorrow for the death of Henry who was
drowned with the crew of the unfortunate *Jessie*.

I have heard no news from England since the middle of summer. But
the return of Robert Strickland must have brought you tidings of the
whole family and I hope, something more substantial. How is dear Mary
and her bairnie's three. What is she about in the way of writing? Give
her my kindest love. Also to dear Katie. When does she go to England?

You will find it hard to part with her, but it might make her independent, if the climate should happen to agree with her. Aunt seemed very much set on having her with her. Poor dear, I daresay that she feels lonely in her old age, dependant entirely upon servants. What of dear Mrs. Strickland? Will she return to Canada? You must miss her so very much. Dear Maria Tully was very kind to me during my stay at Brockden. Her girls are all very pretty. I liked Brockton, it is a very sociable little place, and I think Agnes's girls must have left it with regret. Col. R. Denniston was always talking about you, and never forgot to tell me, that I was not sociable like Mrs. Traill, because I never went out. I can't help it. I never want to, when I cannot return hospitalities. I am best content at home. I have not taken a cup of tea out for five years. I liked the old Colonel. He was a handsome jolly old fellow enough. William Ponton was married last week to Miss Hanwell, but that nine days wonder is over. The Filliters are all out again and come to live quite near to us.

All here send best love, darling, to you and yours. Have you published a book lately? I read a harmony extract[4] in the Ontario paper, on the Indian Summer from Settlers in Canada. I must say good bye, dearest Katie. I hope that this will meet you well, and I promise to be a better correspondent in future.

Your loving Sister
Susanna Moodie

Love to all my nephews and nieces, and to Mrs. Atwood and her family.
Tell dear Mary that Septimus Jones[5] has accepted a church in Yorkville, and is gone. His wife is daily expecting another. She seems to regret leaving Belleville.

1 Located in the township of Missisquoi, southeast of Montreal
2 Brockton; the place is frequently misspelled.
3 Ellen Ross, the authoress (see Letter 85)
4 Part of an assembly of items on a particular theme or subject, for newspaper publication. 'Settlers in Canada' is Catharine's *The Canadian Emigrant's Guide* (1855). 'Indian Summer' is a short descriptive essay in the book.
5 (1830–1915), an Anglican clergyman who followed his appointment in Belleville with a notable career in Toronto as chaplain of Upper Canada College

103 To Allen Ransome

Dec. 15th 1870
Belleville

My Dear Friend Allen,

Another year is drawing to its close and I have not written to thank you for sending out the picture though I do not feel less the obligation. It was indeed kind of you to send it and Robert is so pleased with his old Mother's face. I was not at home when Mr. Northcott called with it at Seaforth, a circumstance which I much regret, nor have I even seen the picture which is framed and hanging beside the dear husband ...

I had to go to Belleville on business. The lawyer who had the charge of my little property invested it in his own name and if my son-in-law John Vickers had not come to the rescue I should have lost the little I had, though it only brings me £40 a year currency. It was my all. I had a better opinion of this young man than of most of his tribe and I was really grieved to give up my confidence in his integrity. These lawyers of Canada are a Curse to the Community. Peter the Great would have hung them all and freed the Colony at once. We have 32 of them in this small town of less than 9000 inhabitants and they prey upon the Community ...

In September I went for a long visit to Katie and her family – This was not only a very pleasant sojourn, but brought about a perfect explanation of events which has always seemed to me quite inexplicable. The estrangement after all was no fault of hers. She made every effort to save her father from ruin, as far as her husband would allow, and acting in obedience to the latter in which she only performed her duty, drew upon herself unmerited obloquy My dear could not comprehend, that a wife must love her husband above every other tie, and she poor thing suffered great anguish of heart at this strange misconception of her conduct. He never told me the real state of the case, or it would have saved me great mental misery ... Kate has a very comfortable, even a luxurious home and a charming young family of beautiful children, eight in all. She was very anxious for me to live with her but had I done so poor Robert would have felt hurt at my leaving him, so I thought it best upon due consideration to return to Belleville, where I should be near the grave of the beloved and where I spent some of the happiest as well as the most sorrowful years of my life.

I am boarding with Mr. and Mrs. Rous, old and valued friends ... Mr. Rous has withdrawn from the Society of Friends and belongs to that wide church that Theodore Parker founded, or rather I should say to the philosophy he taught. I do not agree with him in his views, but he is a very intellectual pure-minded man. The family are very kind to me and I am quietly comfortable. I spend my time chiefly in my own room. Reading, painting and knitting my principal employments. I never go out visiting, but often go to the Churchyard at the back of the house to hold spiritual communion with the loved and the lost ... To tell you the truth this grave is the great attraction to me. I cannot live away from it. My home is there ... I have not seen poor Robert since I left Seaforth. He has had a good deal of sickness in his family this summer. I am busy looking over dear Moodie's papers and letters, a sad task that keeps my eyes weak and watery. Looking over letters that I wrote to him in the Bush, when he was away from me for two long years in the rebellion brings everything so vividly back to me ... My dear sister Traill has been in great affliction. The Murder of her second son Henry, by an escaped convict, was a terrible blow and her daughter Mrs. Atwood is threatened with consumption. She bears these things with real Christian fortitude. Hers is a lovely character. She has been tried in every way. Death, poverty and sickness have only strengthened her trust in the Divine Father and added fresh lustre to her cheerful hopeful disposition ...

Susanna Moodie

---

104 To Catharine Parr Traill   Belleville
Jan 6, 1871

My own dear Katie,

Monday will be your birthday, and if I do not write tonight, my letter will not reach you in time to wish you many happy returns of the day. So to make sure of the slippery old Gent, I have caught him by the forelock. Ah, my poor darling, the last year was a sad one for us both. But doubly so, perhaps for you. May the present bring with it a blessing for you and yours, to compensate for all the sickness and sorrow. I have much to be thankful for, and yet, I feel profoundly sad, and spend most of my time in my own room, only going down to meals. I have grown a solitary silent creature, wrapping my soul up in the past, clinging with passionate love to the long long ago.

To an independent creature like me, the want of a home is terrible, and I cannot feel at home anywhere else. I pine and sigh for liberty to do just as I please, and I have no doubt that I make a very poor inmate. I ought to be very happy and comfortable here, for Mr. and Mrs. R. are very kind to me, as well as Maggie the eldest girl, who I am growing fond of. The rest are very commonplace. The second, very *disagreeable* and not over civil. However, I take no notice of her airs. She has a horrid temper, which is trying to the whole house. A sort of Jane, without her talent.[1] It is strange, that in most families there is one, that always is a trial to all the rest, and who get their own way by merely insisting upon it. Who are selfish, indolent and conceited, and fancy themselves the genius of the family. I carefully conceal my dislike to this young lady, but I feel that she does not like me, and knows by that resistance that flows from the magnetism of two antagonistic natures that I do not like her. She is at times pretty, but a sinister cast in the eye, and a dubious expression, does not make her face a pleasant one. The men in her class think her pretty and she has several admirers.

Her father is greatly influenced by her likes and dislikes. He is not so cordial as he was, which I think is her doing. We rise at six in the morning, breakfast at seven, dine at 12, and get tea at six. This is a pleasant arrangement for me, as it gives me a long day to paint and work in, and I go to bed when I like, as I always go back to my room when meals are over, where I have my own lamp and a fire and where I am writing at this moment. I was so glad to get your last letter. I did answer the last you wrote to me in Toronto, but the letters from Addie's house were always sent to the post by neighbors, so I expect that mine got lost. I am glad that you are going to spend some time with dear Annie, it will do good to you both. I hope that she will yet rally and get well and strong. Pray give my kindest love to her. I am told that her children are very charming.

My dear May,[2] seems quite lost to me now, but her hands are so full, poor child, that I am not so selfish as to expect her to write to me.

I had a letter from dear Sarah just before Christmas. Very kind, but no particular news. Agnes was better, Jane quite well, Tom failing, but steady. She sent a folded paper within her letter, which she said contained her photograph taken from the likeness that Cheesman took of her. I clutched the paper. But alas, she had forgotten the photograph. How surprised she will be to find it unsent.

She does not mention your dear Kate in this letter. I hope she will be able to go, because it might be a comfortable provision for life. The dear good Kate is worthy of good fortune. I wish I could see her and you. Perhaps I may be able to run up and see you all in the spring, if God grants me life.

My Katie, sent me a box full of good things by old Santa Claus – a nice winsey dress, 6 yds of grey fine flannel very *good*, for bloomers, card board, paper, pens, envelopes, colors. A fine Christmas cake, 2 great Lake Superior salmon, 6 boxes of sardines, 2 of choice figs, 3 large glass jars of Lemon preserve, 6 packets of Epps chocolate, 3 bottles of good wine, and a lot of packets of corn starch and arrowroot. All very nice and acceptable. The larger eatables like the salmon and cake I share with my friends in the house. The dress has made me a most warm and comfortable house gown and I have it on now. Katie has been most kind to me, and I can go to her whenever I get tired of living here. I heard from Mrs. Chamberlin, and her dear girls last week. Maime was still in Montreal with Mrs. Lowe, her aunt by the new father's side. Her health is in a very precarious state. Dr. Chamberlin does not give much hopes of her ultimate recovery, but she may linger for awhile. My poor pet, I always dreaded this, and the anguish she suffered mentally in parting with her lover, has hastened her doom.

I do not think that he was a man calculated to make her happy, but young people are always ready to risk the future, for the present. Agnes expects her confinement, the latter part of April. She writes in great spirits and seems more in love than ever. He certainly is a very delightful companion and has a charming temper. The Council have at last decided to give her, 2000 dollars, which will pay all her debts and leave the house in Brocton free from Mortgage. I hope that she will settle this remnant of poor Charley's property, on her children by him. Cherry seems quite delighted with the change of residence, and they move now in the best society. But this, if an advantage, brings with it many expenses and additional cares.

That Mrs. Ross, The *sister* of *ours*, is in treaty I think for the last edition of the Wild Flowers. She seems a good generous creature. She ordered two paintings of me, and sent me 12 dollars for them, besides ordering another. I have now three orders to fill. Truly my darling these pictures pay better than the pen. If I was at Lakefield, I could teach you to make lovely copies of your ferns and mosses, equal to any painting and the drawing as perfect as a photograph and more beautiful.

Some of my last flowers are very nice. Mrs. Lowe of Montreal says, that I don't ask half enough for them. My Aggy is always very chary of her praise. Rather *Addisonian* in its way but most people like them.

I spent a very enjoyable Christmas day with dear Mrs. Murney.[3] She sent the sleigh for me, and sent me home at 12 at night. It was the first evening I have spent out since I was alone. All the family but Minnie Ridley were there.

The old lady [is] very childish but quite well and as sweet as a little child. She is well taken care of. I have left off smoking for the last three months. I miss it, but do not mean to go back. If I had a place of my own it would be all very well, but it is a nuisance to those who do not smoke themselves.

I have not seen Amelia since I got your letter, or any of them, but Boysey who is growing a fine tall handsome boy. The image of poor James. Mr. Burdon says the cleverest boy he ever had in his school. I hope he will get a good education, for I fancy that he is a real genius. The little one, who was like his mother, is now a handsome likeness of James. A perfect Traill.

I have had a sad time of sorting all father's papers, which has kept my eyes dim and watery. I burnt *hundreds* of *letters*. I have not destroyed any of yours, and they would fill volumes. I thought of giving them to Mary.[4] As a most lovely memoir of you could be compiled from them, and these letters so admirably written, would prove the best monument to your memory. Her loving hand could cull all that was excellent and interesting. I would not have them burnt for the world.

Well, I finished my sad task, before New Year's day. I did not find any of my dear husband's letters to friends previous to his marriage. He must have destroyed them himself. I must have had 1000 weight of letters and old bills and militia papers alone. They kept my fire going for a week. I had a letter from Robert to day, with a photograph of him. He says that he has gained 15 pounds of flesh lately, and never was so well in his life. He is expecting a lift in his business, but will let me know in a few days. I wanted some good news for I felt very low. I suffer so from dyspepsia. Our diet is chiefly composed of stews and hashes, which never did agree with me, when I made them well. But these are fat and greasy, every thing but nice. But of course, I cannot expect very good diet for three dollars per week, and I never object to them but often prefer a cup of tea and a bit of toast. It is quite a misfortune to have been a good cook. It makes one very dainty, but I can't help it. I don't care for luxuries. Plain food cooked well is a luxury, if only porridge. I must say goodbye. God bless you darling, wishing you all joy and peace in the beloved, and with love and good wishes to the dear girls I remain your own loving

Old Susy

Burn this. Birds of the air will carry a small matter.

1 Jane Margaret Strickland
2 Mary (Traill) Muchall
3 The elderly widow of Dunbar Moodie's old political foe, Edmund Murney
4 Mary Muchall's poetry and children's stories had begun to appear in print.

---

105 To Richard Bentley

June 29, 1871
Toronto

Dear Mr. Bentley,

A long time has elapsed, since I had the pleasure of addressing you. I ought long ago to have written to thank you for the copies of *The World Before Them*, sent to me through my kind friend Mrs. Moodie of London. They arrived a few days before the death of my beloved husband, and so many sad trials and misfortunes have fallen to my lot since, that I had neither the spirits, nor the time to write. My dear husband's end was short and peaceful, without pain or even struggle. Only one hour elapsed between his waking comparatively well, and his passing away. He had always wished that such might be his end, and a kind Providence granted his request.

I was alone with him during this sudden, and to me, unexpected event. His hand clasped in mine, but he had no power of speech granted to bid me a last farewell. I do not think that he was conscious of his danger, and looked beautiful even in death. It was so early in the morning, that the Dr. arrived just as he passed away. Paralysis had touched a vital organ and released a great and noble soul from its earthly prison. Oh, how I miss the dear companionship. My partner for nearly forty years. But I cannot dwell upon this subject. My God alone knows what I have lost in him.

Nothing was ever done by the government for either him or me. A small pension would have been a great help as I was left almost destitute on the charity of my friends. From my son-in-law Mr. Vickers, at whose house I am now on a visit, I have received much valuable assistance. My sons are far distant and unable to help me, but you know my old indomitable spirit of independence. As long as I am able, I must help myself.

You my dear friend, could do me a very great service, *If it does not interfere with your own business*. I have a prospect of publishing a Canadian Edition of all my works, in a series, or library. And you most kindly restored to me all the Copyrights of those works published by your house but that of *Roughing It in the Bush*, and *The World Before Them*. But these two, are just the ones most required for the speculation. Could you grant me the privilege of using these, strictly confining the sale of the books to the Dominion, I should be greatly indebted to you for this great favor, though I feel that it is too much to ask of you. Yet, the proceeds which we expect from the intended publication would place me beyond that chilling grasp of poverty.

It is a singular thing, that in looking over Mr. Moodie's papers, I found a large portion of a work on Canada,[1] written in his very best style, and during the stirring events which led to the Rebellion here, which he foretells as a certain result of the conduct of the people then in power. It is valuable as a perfect picture of the Colony of that period. I am surprised, that he never communicated to me, that he had commenced such a work, and yet there must be in this fragment, matter enough to fill a good-sized Octavo volume. To which might be added many interesting letters written to me during his absence on the Frontier. The whole corroborates all my previous statements, in *Roughing It*, which so many persons have thought fit to call in question, and which he, who was the soul of honor, would never have assented to if they had been false. Would you like to see these MSS? ...

1 The manuscript was apparently lost.

---

106 To Allen Ransome

Toronto
July 12th, 1871

My Dear Friend Allen,

... For nearly two years before my dear husband left me he could [not] manage to write his name distinctly and had to get me to answer all his letters. It was a great privation for he wrote a capital letter and was fond of it ... My friend Mr. Rous and his family left Belleville the 4th of March and joined my son Dunbar in Horace Greeley's New Colony in Colorado ...

After my friend left Belleville, or rather I should say the week before their departure I had to seek out another home. I found no small difficulty in obtaining suitable quarters. At length a widow lady residing in the Kingston road, with a single daughter, consented to board me, but at a higher rate than I had paid with my dear friends. I felt low enough and sad enough in parting with them to sojourn with comparative strangers, but

have had no reason to complain. I have fallen into good Christian hands.
Like me they are very poor and have known better days and can sympathize with my isolated position. Indeed [they] have grown so fond of me
that they regret my absence on a temporary visit to my daughter and wish
me back again. They are devoted Adherents to the Church of England and
have always family worship night and morning, and as I still read
distinctly I have to act as Chaplain. Our life though rather monotonous is
peaceful and quiet and I have every reason to be thankful ...

Since my arrival in Toronto I have been called upon to experience a
great sorrow which is to me far more painful than the *cross* of poverty
... the 8th of last May, my dear Robert's young wife presented him with a
fine young son, but has never been well since. Her illness has culminated in *raving madness*, and her afflicted husband had to bring her here last
week to place her in the Asylum ... I promised him I would go as often
as I could to see her and I have been twice since he left and spent a good
part of both days with her. With me she is as gentle as a lamb ... She is
a beautiful pianist and has always helped out Robert's slender means by
teaching ... I return to Belleville at the end of the month, or the beginning of next. Any letter directed to me at Belleville, to the care of Mrs.
John Dougall, Corner of Church and Dundas Streets, Ontario, D.C, will
be sure to meet me.

Susanna Moodie

---

107 To Richard Bentley

Toronto
August 10th, 1871

Dear Mr Bentley

I can scarcely find words to express my thanks for the very great favor you
have so generously conferred upon me.[1] May God reward you an hundred fold. I submitted my request to the great disposer of human events,
before I made it to you, and your gracious reply is an answer to my
request. Whether it remains successful or otherwise my gratitude and
thankfulness to you will remain the same.

I had not heard, my kind friend, of the death of your dear partner when
I wrote to you. I was in a painful state of doubt, as to your being alive
yourself, and, was delighted to get an answer from your own heart.

It is only those who have realized the breaking assunder of that dearest
of all earthly ties, that can at all imagine the extent of such an irrepara-

ble loss. The want of the dear companionship. The sharer in all our joys and sorrows, the very life of your life. But there really is no death in the case, they live in our hearts and memories for ever. My dear noble husband is more intensely alive to me now than when he stood beside me in our once happy home –

> 'E'en from his grave the voice of Nature cries
> E'en in his ashes live their wonted fires.'

I have no doubt that he is ever near to me and knows all my sorrows and trials since he stepped out of my sight into the beautiful world of spirits. At our age, it is a consolation to know that the separation cannot last long. It was however, a great pleasure for me to find that you were still a denizen of this world, and long may your valuable life be spared to your friends and family. I have had another severe trial since I wrote to you. My son Robert has been obliged to place his pretty young wife in the Asylum here under Dr Workman's care. I was with him when he parted with her. I never wish to witness such a heartbreaking scene. His agony was something terrible to see. He loves her so much and clung desperately to hope, until that broken reed seemed to enter his very soul.

I promised to go and see '*His poor little thing*', whenever I could, but it is a terrible shock to my nerves, which makes me not only doubt my own sanity, but the sanity of everyone else.

Her baby, a fine boy of eight weeks old, has to be put out to nurse and the expence of keeping her in the lady's ward, will cost three parts of his small income. I don't know how he will get on at all, and to carry about to his daily work that sad breaking heart. Dr. W. says, that at her age 24, she may get over it, but I doubt it very much. She has every care and comfort in that 'paradise of the lost,' as she calls that beautiful place. But I will turn from so sad a theme, and tell you about the new edition of my works.

Mess. Rose and Hunter, the parties who wish to bring it out for this Country, are not booksellers or publishers, but worthy intelligent Scotchmen, who print the works of others. They have a very large business, and have the credit of being honest independent men, of considerable wealth and good standing in the city. They want to try publishing my works as a sort of experiment. Of course, I hope they may be successful. They do not purchase copyright, but only the right of issuing so many copies of each book they want. Say 2000 copies, for which they are to give me, 200 dollars. If a new edition is called for, they pay in the same rates. The sum is given before the books are brought out, so that I can lose nothing by this arrangement, and may secure 200 dollars per annum which will make me quite comfortable in a small way. You see my dear friend how much, I shall be indebted to your generous kindness, if our plan should take effect. I have several stories that have never been published in book form, but Mr Rose wishes to commence with *Roughing It*, as that has received the sanction of the public. The rest will follow in course. I will send you copies as they come out, as a matter of curiosity for you to see how we do these things in Canada.

Directly this business is settled I will write a short memoir of my dear husband, by way of preface and arrange the papers on Canada he left unfinished, and send the MSS for your perusal.

His contributions to *Roughing It*, would come in better in this work entirely his own, which will bring our Dominion copy within the compass of an octaval volume. *Flora Lyndsay* ought by rights to precede this, as it contains our voyage to Canada, and was written prior to it.

Such a great change has taken place in this Colony, that it bears no resemblance to the Canada of 1832, but is rapidly rising in wealth and importance, and at no distant period, must become one of the great centres of civilization. The population has more than trebled, and the wide extent of cleared lands, has pushed the wooded wilderness nearly out of sight.

Belleville is almost a city. Your son would scarcely recognize it, and Toronto is a noble city, full of fine public buildings, and can boast of merchant princes and millionaires. All the new streets are built of brick and stone, and planted with fine trees, forming beautiful vistas terminated by the blue waters of Ontario.

Its wharves are thronged with steamboats and shipping, and new buildings are going up every where.

We ought to feel proud of our beautiful free country. We enjoy the best government in the world. A healthy climate and exemption from the petty persecutions of religion and caste. What more do we require? The unsettled state of Europe will give the best answer.

Even in the matter of books. A very intelligent bookseller assured me the other day, that a great change had taken place during the last few years, that where he formerly sold a few copies of popular works, he sells hundreds now. The sale of Mark Twain's vulgar books is almost incredible. Every shop boy buys a copy.[2]

I shall leave Toronto, I think next Saturday for Belleville, but do not know how long I may remain there. If my son's mother-in-law, who lives with him and has taken charge of his four little ones, should go to live with *her* son, I may have to take her place, but if you will allow me the privilege, I will from time to time write and let you know my whereabouts, and what I am doing.

Pray remember me most kindly to Mr George, my esteemed correspondent, and to Mr Horace.[3] I should like to hear him preach, he reads very well. Mr and Mrs Vickers desire their kind regards, and with every feeling of affectionate esteem

> I remain
> Dear Mr Bentley
> Your faithful own friend
> Susanna Moodie.

The books will be most acceptable. Any letter or parcel directed to the care of John J. Vickers Esquire, Northern Express Office Toronto Ontario, will meet wherever I may be.

1 The copyright to *Roughing It in the Bush* (see Letter 105)
2 Twain's *The Celebrated Frog of Calaveras County* (1867) and *The Innocents Abroad* (1869) were before the Canadian public in 1870, in cheap pirated editions reprinted without Twain's approval. See Gordon Roper, 'Mark Twain and His Canadian Publishers,' *The American Book Collector* (June 1960), 13–29
3 Susanna had written George Bentley in May 1867 and had entertained Horace during his 1858 visit to Canada. George had taken over the business in 1867.

---

108 To Katie Vickers

Belleville
August 13, '71

My Darling Katie,

Here I am safe at the old stand, and found all my friends well and glad to see me. But to day, I feel far from well – the jiggling of the cars has brought on a rather severe billious attack, and I have been obliged to have recourse to friend Ayre's Pills to get rid of the sickness at stomach and swimming in my head, where the cars seem joggling still. I hope tomorrow will find me all right. We had a fine run down and no stoppage by the way, and came to Belleville before eleven.

Not a soul on board I knew, so I never opened my lips during the whole journey. I bought a *Telegraph* to read, by the way,[1] and when I finished all I cared for, we were past Bowmanville. It was quite cool too, and no fog so I enjoyed the ride very much. At the station I met Minnie Ridley, her husband Fred R. and dear Arthur Baldwin, and got a hearty kind welcome. Arthur got my luggage all right and they went home to Mrs. Dougall's with me in the omnibus. Here I got another very kind reception. Mrs. W. Murney, Miss Gifford and May Dolier were packing up to go away which they did after dinner. May is a very handsome black-eyed girl, and I never saw Mrs. W.M. look so well in all my life. May was going home with her to Bowmanville. I found my room all ready for me, and everything right. Hester as kind as ever and the good old lady glad to see me.

Old Mrs. Coleman is dead. Mrs. Crang not expected to live and prayed for in the church. It seems to be very unhealthy here just now for old people. Mrs. Breakenridge was only a week ailing and gradually sunk to sleep. She had a stroke of paralysis before she died but knew them all again before she went.

The weather is just as dry here as it was at Toronto, but no smoke, and there is a cool breeze from the Bay. The fields were all full of sheaves as we came along, and the yield looked good. Tomatoes are as scarce here as with you, dried up by the intense drought. 9 cents per lb. I have felt too poorly to go out, and, would you believe it, took a cup of tea in bed and did not rise until dinner time. I feel a little better, just now, and hope to get right soon. I found the enclosed letter from Mrs. Ross, staring me in the face. I wish that she had sent me back the paintings. I could have sold them to Mrs. Strickland, but from the date of her letter, she must have left Montreal last week. I shall commence upon *Roughing It in the Bush,* if I am able tomorrow but can do no business to day. I don't think Mrs. Ross means to do anything about my books. My proposal of 100 dollars for every 1000 copies must have [illegible] read about them. I am glad to get quit of her at any rate. Mr. Rose may do as he thinks best. I leave dear John to do the best he can for me, and will abide by his decision whatever it may be.

I miss you all *so much.* The merry voices of the little ones, all seems receeding from me in the distance. I hope dear Vic's wounded head is better, and that darling baby is recovering. Tell dear Georgie, that Miss Corbett has been staying with Mrs. Cochrane some time, and has been looking out for her coming to stay in Belleville. Mrs. Dougall and Hester send kind love to you all. If Georgie had come with me, she would have been dearly welcome, but I hope to see her yet. I suppose dear John and Katie and Billy will have started before you get this. If not, give my best

love to them, and good wishes for their prosperous journey and safe
return,[2] and remember me to dear Mrs. Strickland and Maria,[3] and all
friends, and believe me dearest, your affectionate and grateful Mother,

[signature cut out]

You had better give Mr. Rose my address, in case he should want to
communicate with me – Mrs. Susanna Moodie at Mrs. John Dougalls
Corner of Dundas and Church Streets Belleville
    God bless you all

1 The Toronto *Telegraph* (1866–72), published by John Ross Robertson and James Cook
2 John Vickers planned to take his children, Katie (age 11) and Billy (9), on a trip to Fort
   William, where he had mining interests.
3 Katherine (Rackham) Strickland was visiting Maria Tully at Brockton.

---

109 To Katie Vickers

Belleville
August 15, 1871

My darling Katie

Supposing dear John to be on his voyage to Fort William, I enclose the two
books for Mr. Rose under cover to you, that no delay may occur in his
getting them to make up his mind upon the subject of printing.

    I have been seriously ill since I wrote. Had to send for Dr. Hope late on
Sunday night, so you may be sure, that I felt pretty bad, with those
violent spasms in my stomach. This is the first time that I have been up,
but I feel weak, and giddy, and purblind with the bile, and my side
aches all the time, but as I am out of torture I can bear all the rest. I shall
have to get my liver put into order, before I shall be able to go out, or
feel steady on my feet. I looked over the books yesterday lying in my bed
and I have drawn my pencil through many objectionable passages. As
this edition is for the D.C., we need not arouse their anger by a repetition of
them. I cannot tell how kind dear Hester and the old lady have been to
me. I fear I have given them a good deal of trouble.

    I heard to day that dear Georgie was coming down on Saturday. I hope
I shall be well enough to go down to the train and meet her. If she will
send me a card to let me know by which train she comes. I am anxious to
know how the darling baby is, and if Victor is quite well from the blow
on his head. I think a great deal of you all as I lie in my bed.

I have had a parcel with two books from Ottawa directed in Maime's hand but no letter. It was Mr. Reade's book[1] which G. Barnham gave me, and 'Cometh up as a flower.'

I, of course, have seen no one as yet. Miss Cassie Howard was married yesterday to Mr. Green, and Henry Walbridge's baby boy was buried in the evening. Miss Cobbett is staying with Mrs. C. Walbridge.

You must help me with matter for the Canadian Preface. I forget all the subjects dear John told me to write about on the present state and prospects of Canada – a little memorandum would help to jog up my memory.

Oh what a vile scratchy pen, how I detest these fine nibbed ones. I must get some M pens before I begin to edit father's book. I am fit for nothing just now. We had rain last night, only enough to lay the dust. With kind love to dear John if at home and all the dear ones, believe me ever

> Your own
> affectionate old mother
> Susanna Moodie

I hear, that an account of Dunbar's illness, went the rounds of the Belleville papers. I have not seen it, however. I suppose Fred Rous supplied the matter.

Mrs. Dougall and Hester send love. *I am quite safe in their hands.*

I leave my letter to Mr. Rose open that you may see what I have written to him. The book cannot be more curtailed than it is now without spoiling it. Love to dear Mrs. Strickland and the kind Tullys, to Mr. and Mrs. Hull and Mrs. Morrison. I am sorry that I couldn't bid the two latter parties good bye.

1 Charles Reade's *A Terrible Temptation*, published in 1871

---

110 To Katie Vickers   August 16, 1871

My own dear Katie

You will think that I am bothering you with letters with a vengeance, but I cannot write to dear John, as I suppose that he is away at Fort William, and this business has to be attended to, and I do not wish to do *anything* without your knowledge and concurrence. I send you Mr. Rose's letter and offer for the new Edition, which I think liberal enough, and dear John can accept for me, if it pleases him. I also send you my letter to the firm, for your inspection, and if dear Jack[1] can copy it for me, I will give him a copy of the work when published with my precious *old autograph* attached. Perhaps he has a machine for copying at the office. We must keep Rose's letter.

Will you send me your copy of *Roughing It* by Georgie, and replace it with mine, as I may want to refer to the work while it is going through the press. The pencil marks in the one I sent to Mr. Rose, can easily be rubbed out when he returns the volumes.

I feel horribly weak to day, and the weather is very sultry. I cannot begin that introductory chapter, till I have a better bone in my back to write with, and less confusion of head to think with.

I hope to get good accounts of the dear baby and Victor, and all of you, and remain my own darling, with much love to all, your loving

old mother
Susanna Moodie

1 Susanna's thirteen-year-old grandson, John Alexander Dunbar Vickers

---

111 To Allen Ransome

Belleville
Oct. 17th, 1871

My Dear Friend Allen,

What must you have thought of me for not acknowledging the receipt of your most kind letter and the generous gift for my dear Robert before? Your letter found me apparently upon a death bed, from which I have only just been raised by the merciful providence of God. This is the first time I have left it since the 12th of August. I can hardly steady my poor skeleton hands to write, but I was so anxious to do so that you must forgive the bad work I make. I tried several times to write in pencil in bed, but had to give it up. Robert was here last week and he looked ill and worn, had been to see his hapless wife and the meeting had been one of great grief to him ... Katie and her good husband have been here too and supplied me with every comfort. I want for nothing and am as contented and happy as I can expect to be. I have suffered awful agonies from inflammation of the stomach and bowels and frightful haemorrhage which has reduced me to a bag of bones …

I see by the papers that a kind friend of mine has come to his reward. Richard Bentley the great London Publisher. Almost one of his last acts was to write a letter and such a kind one – to me giving me the right of republishing *Roughing It in the Bush* in the Dominion of Canada. Rose and Hunter of Toronto give me 200 dollars for the publication of 2500 copies and a Royalty of 4 cents on every copy they may require over the above number. Thus has God provided most unexpectedly the means of my paying for the expenses of this long illness … I must send you a copy just to show how our new Country can get up books. I have written an introductory chapter contrasting Canada, as it was 40 years ago and what it is now. My booksellers are Scotchmen, and good honest fellows and wealthy withal … I am so glad you like my poor little sketches. I have improved since, but Dr. Hope my kind medical attendant has forbidden all stooping to paint for the future. I am sorry, but must, I suppose, submit. My worst physical enemy is an undying energy which will urge me to work beyond my age and now feeble powers.

All you tell me about Yoxford and the dear old scenes in which we were so happy is very precious. England does not change like Canada. When I came here to Belleville in the year '40, it was on the very edge of the wilderness. Its principal streets were woods then. No one who saw it then could recognize it now. A fine large handsome town full of fine buildings, though I loved it best in its infancy among the gleaming waters and the grand old woods. Allen, the poetic spirit, the love of dear Mother Nature will never die out of my heart. I am just the same enthusiast I ever was and often forget white hairs and wrinkles when my heart swells and my eyes fill with tears at the beauty of some lovely spot that glows from the hand of the great Master.

My dear sister Catharine is as amiable and loveable as ever. A truly noble Christian woman. We still love with the old love through weal or woe. Like myself she is fast going down into the vale of years but hearts that love are always young. She has worn better than I have. Her calm placid spirit can better resist the rude shocks of the waves of thought that beat me to pieces … The murder of her son Henry was a terrible blow but she had the moral courage to comfort the mother of the murderer and forgive her wretched son.

Susanna Moodie

112 To John Vickers

Belleville
Dec. 31st 1871

My Dear Son John,

It is the last day of the old year, and I will use it in writing to you, to whose kindness I owe so much, during its course. And first, let me wish all peace and happiness to you and yours for the coming year, and may you all live to enjoy many returns of it in the fear and love of God. May His blessing rest upon you and the dear wife and children and all that are near and dear to you. I pray that you may be kept from all evil and realize both for time and eternity the precious promise of salvation in our Lord and Saviour Jesus Christ which is the first great end of our being.

I return you many thanks for your most kind letter. I have every thing I want. You have supplied me with so many comforts, that I have nothing to ask. One thing, however, would give me much pleasure, if you think I can do without it. If we could absolve poor Robert of the debt he owes me of the 200 dollars and the interest thereof. But this I leave entirely to you. If you think I have enough without it, write to him, and set him free from the obligation for ever. I shall soon be able to set to work and try to earn more. I feel as if I should do better if the consciousness of his owing me anything but love was off my mind. I hardly know what to go to work on next, or if Rose would be willing to undertake another work. If so, I had better prepare *Flora Lyndsay* for him, as it is Canadian, and the real commencement of *Roughing It*. By re-writing I could make it much better.

By the way, I received a letter from Mr. Maclear enclosing a postal card from his agent here. A Miss Cambell, complaining that I have sold the book to *great numbers* of people in the town, and taken her work out of her hands. Now I have just sold five copies, neither more nor less of the *great number* and given 4 copies away – as presentation copies, which could not affect the general sale of the work. I just wrote to Maclear and told him the plain truth. But as to call upon Miss Cambell and offer any apology to her, I will not. I exchanged with Van Norman three copies for stationary that I wanted.[1]

The old man seemed very exacting. Why did they give me the copies if I was not to make use of them? If I had thought that the selling of a few copies was wrong, I should have been the last to do so. The next work I will avoid the temptation; by asking but one copy for my own use, and buying for my friends.

Had we not better put the 200 dollars into the Savings Bank on interest, or the Building Society.[2] I shall not want any funds before the middle of next month as I have enough to pay my board in advance on the 12th and to buy and have cut another cord of wood. I shall want funds after that for washing, etc. Thank God I feel much better, except a little rhumatism in my knees and finger joints which latter makes me write very shaky.

Your dear good boy Jack, I have not seen since last Thursday when he called with Mrs. Gordon to take me up in the sleigh to see Mrs. Murney. It was a bitter cold day, and we only found *Isabel* at home. I gave her your message. She said, 'I have no objection to kiss him, especially as he is so handsome.' But poor Jack blushed up to the roots of his hair like a girl, and dared not to advance one step. I guess his father would not have been asked twice. But really it showed the innate modesty of the dear boy and I admired him for it. So Isabel lost the kiss, and without she breaks the ice herself I am sure Jack will not. How much he has grown, and is so kind and gentle every one seems to be drawn to him at first sight. I expect that he will call in this afternoon. On Christmas morning he left with Mrs. Dougall a can of Oysters for a Santa Clause for Grandmamma. God bless the dear fellow, it was a pity to spend his money on me, but it was so kind. I had a jolly Christmas with the Murneys, and Mrs M. sent me home at night. I have not seen Mrs. Wilkins for some time. She has been busy, Nelly's intended being there on a visit. You need not tell me to kiss Jack for *you*, for I always kiss him for *myself*, and for his Mother and you. I got a very kind letter from Agnes and her husband, though as usual past time. They have all been ill with a sort of fever, James[3] and all, he was at a party at the parson's, and fainted dead away when taken with it. James it seems, has bought me a camp chair for a Christmas box. A useful present in a house where chairs are rather scarce. Agnes did not tell me that she had sold her B.V. lots but I met G. Bull, who did, and said that he had paid her 1300 dollars for them. Not so bad after all. She has made money out of the despised lots. If all was put together she got as much or more than Dunbar did.[4]

She wants me to say if there is any thing I would like that she could send me, as a Christmas gift, but really I do not want anything, and if I did, would scarcely ask for it, but her letter is kinder than usual.

I heard from dear Rob, he has heard that Nellie is better, and seems full of hope. Mr. Dickson the old member for Huron, went to the Asylum to see his son, and saw Nellie and the Dr. said she was much quieter. Allair has got a good berth with a Jeweller at Galt. A good honest man who

considers him an excellent workman and pays him 9 dollars a week. Poor
things, they want something to cheer them. Did you read in the *Globe*
the article about Allen Ransome and his workmen.[5] It was very interesting
to me and so like him. I think I would like to change the *Globe* for a
paper less political. The *Express* seems a very chatty nice paper and is
cheaper, but Van Norman does not take it. The new Magazine looks
dull enough with all its puffing. What has become of the old one, the
Canadian Journal?[6] Is that dead so soon? They give a list of the Rose
publications but never mention my book. It will never be popular in
Canada.

I must say goodbye, dear John with a happy New Year to you all

> Your affectionate Mother
> Susanna Moodie

I will add a line if Jack comes to let you know how he is.

1 Van Norman and Miss Campbell were Belleville booksellers.
2 A co-operative savings and mortgage lending institution
3 James Gerald Fitzgibbon, born 1853
4 Letter 113 reveals that these lots were in Belleville, probably property left to her by her
  father.
5 'A Pleasant Incident at Ipswich,' reprinted from the London *Spectator* in the *Globe*, 5
  December 1871
6 The *Canadian Literary Magazine* in which Susanna's sketch, 'Washing the Black-a-Moor
  White,' appeared in 1871 (163–5). The periodical ran until May 1871, then became the
  Canadian Magazine from July 1871 to January 1872. The new magazine is probably the
  Canadian Monthly and National Review, which commenced in January 1872.

---

113 To Catharine Parr Traill   [January 1872]

I enclose a photo, of the picture cousin Cheesman took of me.[1] Is it not like
all your girls, especially Kate. I was astonished at the resemblance. I
sent one to dear sister Sarah, who seems so pleased with it. Have you
heard from her lately? She [is] well, as are all my sisters and poor Tom,
but she, poor dear seems to have met with a great pecuniary loss by the
burning of Chicago. It seems strange that it should affect her in any
way, but she says, 'I draw the greater part of my income from many 1000
shares in the London and Liverpool royal Insurance Company and they
are the greatest sufferers in the Chicago fire, having already paid upwards

of £400,000 Sterling to it. I shall not be able to draw any income this year or perhaps next either. My instalment to be paid next March was £584. I do not fret about it, I have suffered so much deeper sorrow. I only regret that it will shorten my hands to help others. However, I have not anticipated my income and with economy have enough to live upon for a year and to give poor Tom his usual allowance.' What a noble woman she is – A real christian. No literary reputation is equal to this.

How have you borne this strange winter? – some days so warm, and then so intensely, almost unbearably, cold. It is very trying to old people. I have a very large cold bed room with 3 large cranky windows and 3 cold drafty doors, and though I keep a good fire, I can scarcely keep myself warm. I have had to buy wood at $8 per cord and give $1 more for having it cut and piled.

I heard last week from dear Robert. His old cough has returned, and he seems ill and dejected. Poor hapless Nell, is no better. When her mother went to take her new winter clothes last week she kicked them about the floor, and would have torn them to pieces, if the keepers and nurses had not interfered. My good Katie is very kind to Robert and the children and gives them many necessary comforts.

I heard from Agnes last week, and dear James sent me the present of a handsome camp chair. They had all been suffering from fever but the baby, who seems quite a jolly little soul. Agnes had sold the remainder of the B.V. lots for 1300 dollars which I hope will get her out of all her difficulties. All her property seems to have been swallowed up in the expences of her marriage. Not one cent will remain for the poor girls. I think her publishing has not been profitable in the long run. The last unfinished edition will most likely be a dead loss. I wanted her to have brought out a second volume of the flowers, as most people who bought the first would have taken the 2nd, but she would not listen to my advice.

If I gain little by my book, I lose nothing.

You must give my kindest love to dear Mrs. Strickland and wish her for me many New Years of tranquil christian peace and comfort, and give my love and affectionate regards to all my nephews and nieces and their families. May the New Year bring them many blessings. I hope dear May is well, and her little ones, and that they are getting on in their new vocation.

That my dear Kate is happy and flourishing, a comfort to all who know and love her for her worth. I wish I could step in and kiss you all round, especially the dear old face, that seems looking at me through the dim mist of years in its youthful bloom. So may we see each other when we meet in that better world. Farewell my beloved one, and believe me ever

Your own affectionate
Loving Susie –

Love to Mrs. Atwood and all the good wishes of the season. I hope before the year again draws round that you will see dear Walter.

1 The date is suggested by the New Year greetings and the reference to the Chicago fire, 8–9 October 1871. Cheesman's miniatures of the sisters seem to have come to Canada at different times (see Letters 99 and 104); here Susanna has apparently had her own miniature photographed, though she had suggested in Letter 99 that Agnes Chamberlin would copy it.

---

114 To Maggie Rous

Lakefield
North Douro Ont.
June 22 72

My Dear Maggie,

I promised to write to you, before I left B.V. You must have thought that I took a long time in fulfilling my promise. But I have had many things to employ my mind, and render me too anxious to write to anyone. Mr. Vickers' dangerous illness, which was expected to end fatally; and from which he is only now slowly recovering, put everything else out of my head. But now that it has pleased God to spare his life, I begin to feel more cheerful and like my old self.

This second attack of paralysis was more dangerous than the first, and he was unable for several weeks to move his left arm and leg, during the last few days, he has been able to sit up and move them a little, and the medical men consider that all danger is over for the present. My Katie who is such a loving wife and mother, has had a sad time of it, watching by the sickbed of her dear husband.

One good thing has resulted from this domestic trouble. Mr. V. has induced Robert to give up the station at Seaforth, and take the situation of Superintendent of his office, on a salary of 100 dollars per month. This will place R. in a very comfortable position, without the hard drudgery of his present office, and he will be near his poor wife, and good schools for his children, and will enjoy the society of friends who truly love him and wish him well. It will be so nice, to see him and his children when I go to stay with Mrs. V.

Now you will want to know my dear Maggie, how I like Lakefield – I only wish you were with me to enjoy the lovely country scenery. My sisters cottage is very charming. It stands on the banks of the beautiful river which is pouring its tumultuous white crested waves just below my window, filling the air with the burthen of its mournful music. The green steep slope to the water is a natural grove of forest trees, and Aunts lovely garden is full of flowers and flowering shrubs, in which the bright winged birds and butterflies disport themselves all day. I sit in a dreamy sort of rapture communing with nature and my own soul half a day. We are about ten minutes walk to the village, but I am so happy here I seldom walk into it. All my nephews and their wives come to see me, and I have met with great kindness and attention from many people. But do not imagine that I have forgotten my dear Maggie's sunny face, or Fred's grave kindness. Seldom a day passes but I think of you both, and feel anxious to hear that you are well, and sometimes remember the old friend. I have not heard from your dear Mother, or from any of Dunbar's people. If you write, give my love to your dear parents, and ask your Mamma, if she got my letter written in May. I forget the exact date. We had a grand party last Tuesday week up to Julian's landing in Stoney lake.[1] We went up in the small steamer, the Chippewa, that starts from here, landing just on the opposite side of the river. The day was very hot, but 'beautiful exceedingly,' and we had on board, our parson Vincent Clementi,[2] his wife and niece – A young lady just out from England. Mr. and Mrs. Robert Strickland, and their two pretty daughters, of 15 and 16, who look like twins. Mrs. Traill and my niece Kate, Mrs. Roland S. and her husband. Mr. George and Percy S. Mr. C. Boker, old Isaac Garbiot and *Auld Mistress Moodie*, besides a Miss Sheraze Macdonald – A very pretty girl, born in Greece.

The sail was quite enjoyable, and the wild rocky islands of Stoney lake still in the wilderness, very beautiful. 1200 of these islands have been surveyed, without counting numbers of bare granite rocks that rear their red heads above the water uncovered with grass or lichens, that look like the bare bones of some former world. We reached our destination about 3 o'clock and dined on board. A capital picnic dinner, the gentlemen having provided us with quite a feast of good things. After dinner, we all went ashore to look for flowers in the woods, but the sun was so hot and the paths so steep, and the moskitoes and black-

flies so savage to have a picnic at our expense, that we were glad to
return to the boat. I scared up a great snake, which scared me, though
Mr. Clementi said, that he was a beauty. To me, he looked as ugly as
sin, and I was glad to give him a wide berth. This Stoney lake, is a very
grand place, and will one day be as popular as the English Lakes to
the sight seers. Few persons have any idea that such a lovely spot lies
within the compass of a day's journey. I was puzzled to think, how the
steersman could find his way among all that labyrinth of islands without
bumping us upon some of the many rocks. We got home just in time
to escape the heavy drenching of a thunder shower. The storm returned
again at midnight, and gave us a grand bombardment. The angry
roar of our tumbling waters, filled up the pauses between the awful
thunder claps, with its deep melancholy diapason.

We have had oceans of rain for the last three weeks, and nothing can
exceed the greenness of the fields and woods. I have painted some wild
flowers, and several pieces of flowering shrubs, that are among my best
efforts in this way, but I don't expect to get much call for them here.
Money in the woods is rather a scarce comodity, but the life here is
natural and pleasant. The village is twice the size it was seven years
ago. I often amuse myself by fishing in the evening, and have been
tolerably successful. But the black flies have prevented me this week.
But they will soon leave us now. My face has been in a state approaching to inflammation from their venomous bites. You must tell me how
you are all getting on at B.V. Give my love to Angus McFee, and tell him
of Robert's promotion to a better berth. To dear Mrs. Davy, to whom
I will write soon, in fact to any of my B.V. friends who think me worth a
thought, but though absent they are all very dear to me. And don't
forget *dear Ruth*, tell her, that I live in the hope of seeing her one day
and if not, she will ever form one of my pleasant memories.

If I should go up to Toronto this fall, I will try and take B.V. in my way.
My heart ever yearns towards that green mound in the churchyard,
as my real home, in which my life's best treasure lies hidden.

I had some ague chills after coming here, and my dear niece Katie,
had a severe week of ague, but is better now, but is at all times very
delicate. She is an excellent girl and we get on splendidly together. I love
her very much. Mary is looking well. She lives at Peterboro, but it
only takes 40 minutes to reach this place, the fare 30 cents or 40 to go
and come. Mary has been up several times to see us. Her children are
pretty creatures. My sister went down this evening to stay with her until
Wednesday, and we have a pretty black eyed Miss Reid staying with

us, and wee Katie, poor Harry's little orphan. A clever amusing little elf, who adds a good deal to the comfort of the house, by her merry ways. Now surely, Maggie darling, I have tired out your patience. You will hardly want a second infliction in the way of a letter for a month to come. If you see Miss Dougall give my love to her and to the old lady. I wrote a long letter to her, some time ago, but have got no answer.

With love to dear Frederic, and much for your dear self believe me ever

Your loving old friend
Susanna Moodie

How is the dog!

1 Now called Mt Julian, the spot was a natural landing place on Stoney Lake's north shore. Though in this case on a steamer rather than in a canoe, Susanna is duplicating her 'A Trip to Stoney Lake' from *Roughing It in the Bush*, travelling from Lakefield via Young's Point to Stoney Lake.
2 The Anglican minister in Lakefield

---

115 To Maggie Rous

My Dearest Maggie,

Lakefield
North Douro
Dec. 30 1872

I do not deserve your kind letter, and the charming little drawing which accompanied it. I have said a thousand times to myself, I will write to dear Maggie this week, nothing shall hinder me, and so it has gone on day after day and all my good resolves melted into thin air. But your packet of undeserved remembrances, has pricked my conscience, and I am determined to write this very night to you and answer all your kind queries. I got through the beautiful summer much to my own satisfaction. The nice garden, the trees and rapid water, lending a constant charm to a scene that Nature has made very charming, the society of dear friends and relatives making it rich in social blessings. I have been quiet peaceful and as happy as I could expect to be. Mrs. Chamberlin, Alice and the dear baby came and spent six weeks with us. Unfortunately we had three children in the house with whooping cough and little Agnes took it and was so ill that her Mother thought it best to return to Ottawa for better advice. The child is quite recovered now Maime writes me, but we had a poor time for several weeks with the sick children. The last week in November, I went up to Toronto, with Mr. and Mrs. Robert Strickland and their two dear girls, Agnes and Charlotte. We left Lakefield by train at 2 o'clock P.M. and got to Port Hope at six the same evening. Here we were delayed by the non arrival of the train West, till 12 P.M., when Robert voted, a good supper and bed. I was tired, and not sorry for the rest. Oh, Maggie, you would have laughed, at the grand oration the Hotel Keeper made me. I wish people would hold their tongues and let me and my book slide into oblivion. I am afraid, that I received all the fine compliments very ungraciously. I dared not look at Robert for fear I should laugh out. We were up before 5 next morning, think of that, and got into Toronto at half past eight. Mrs. Vickers expected me at night. However, *My Robert*, came to see if I was on the train and carried me off in triumph. Well, I enjoyed my visit very much. I had promised my dear nephew to return with his two young daughters in ten days, or most likely I should still be in Toronto. Baby Arthur is a darling pet – very like his grandfather Moodie – the best natured little fellow in the world. I found Mr. V. much better, and as cheerful as ever though he walks lame like my dear husband. All the children had grown almost out of knowledge – Jack is six feet high, and a handsome lad. My Georgie a lovely girl. Katie almost as tall as her sister. They all made much of me, and made me many nice presents.

The children all sing, and it is very pretty to hear little Henrietta, who was the baby when I was last there singing like a lark. Well, the time sped too fast away. All dear Robert's children are greatly improved. John Wedderburn Dunbar, is a splendid fellow, and Bess and Nellie are very pretty clever girls. I did not see little Ned. They were in all the trouble of moving, and it was too far for me to walk. I went out to the Asylum to see dear Nellie. She is much better, but Dr. Workman says – *Not to be trusted* – She will be quite sane for a week or two, and then as wild as ever. She looks fat and well, and was very glad to see me. She amuses herself with embroidery which she does beautifully – Poor dear child, my heart ached for her, but she says, that she is happy with some nice new lady boarders – Well for her –

> Wishing you dear Maggie
> many many happy new years,
> believe me ever your
> loving old friend,
> Susanna Moodie

116 To Katie Vickers

My Dearest Katie

Lakefield
North Douro
Jan 18th 1874

Our last letters *crossed*, I sent mine on the Monday, and got yours on
Tuesday, and I had nothing left to tell you, so put off writing. The weather
has been so *iron cold*, that the ink froze, and everything liquid in my room
all last week, and this severe weather, always takes away my breath,
and makes me very inert. Lady Dufferin had sent to Agnes for my autograph and I felt so lazy and chilly, I could hardly summon up courage to
write my letter to A. with the desired Autograph. Then a queer man from
New Bedford, who wrote to me while I was at Ottawa for my Autograph and my sister Agnes, wrote again, and I had to answer. I had sent
him mine from Ottawa, with a promise, that I would send him one of
my sister's when I returned to Lakefield. But he might have to wait some
weeks first. Well, I forgot all about him, when on Saturday he wrote
quite in a huff – 'Supposing I was home, and must have forgotten my
promise; and he wanted the Autograph *so much*, that he hoped I would
make *haste and find it.*' He enclosed a dirty shin plaster of 10 cents, to pay
the post.[1] Now, I did not like his curt, ungentlemanly letter, and the
odious plaster – so I found a good Autograph of poor dear Agnes's, and
enclosed it, with the blue abomination without a word, not even my
signature, which will give him a hint the next time, how to write to a lady.
This was last Sunday, but I had to overlook a vast pile of family letters
to get the autograph, and fell areading them, not without tears. I had no
idea, that I had so many, and such long letters from Agnes, and until my
unlucky book was published, so full of affection. I could almost write her
literary career, from these letters, and it would be by herself. I will leave
these letter in tac, for you, when I am gone, as they might be of use
hereafter if Billy took to writing or lecturing, which I feel sure he will.
Mrs. Traill, seemed quite *astonished*, that Agnes had written *such letters
to me*! The elder sister, comes out very strong at times, and the sense of
superiority in every way. So my day slipped away over these records of
the past, and I did not write. I had to send Cherrie's photo to Aunt
Sarah, and write a long letter, not having written since last September,
and Oh, my dearest child, I do dread a long batch of letter writing now.
But enough of excuses. I was *rejoiced* to get your letter this evening –
delighted with your charming present, the two handsome Photos, of the
dear boys – I like the thoughtful look on Billy's brow. He will be a great

thinker. I hope a great, good Christian man. A moral leader in the
stirring times just ahead of us. A *man* both for time and eternity. I am so
sorry for your poor useful fingers. Have the Doctors ever tried electricity for them. It is a cruel pain, that horrid rhumatic, or flying gout, but
people often live to be very old with it. Your Grandfather Strickland[2]
was a martyr to it, yet lived to be 81 – and the lock of lovely auburn hair,
my father cut off his head after his death has not a gray hair in it. I keep
it as a curiosity. It is the colour of Dunbar's. No word from Dunbar yet. I
sent off two letters to the States today – One for him and one for
Donald. I felt, as it were, compelled to write to them.

Oh, I am so glad about dear Robert. A thousand thanks for the good
news – Rob *can* – and *will work well*, but all the responsibility must
rest upon himself. He will always make a better, cleverer master, than a
man. In this he partakes of my spirit. I cannot even persist if anyone
looks over me. I hope his dark days are over, for the dear fellow has had
little sympathy, and has been sorely tired. I have never ceased to bear
him on my heart and pray for him – I know him better [than he knows
himself]. He sent me not long ago, a very sweet photo of little Ned. If he
is stationed on the direct line of the G.T.R.[3] I may live perhaps to pay him a
visit. I do so long to see him again. The Steam Ship from England that
has Fred Barlee on board, has not been telegraphed yet, and poor Emma
is very anxious about him. We expect news of Aunt Eliza by her.

Poor Robert Casement, our Post Master is dying tonight.[4] He has been
speechless since Saturday. It was only the week before that he presented me with a nice drawing pencil and talked over the times when he
used to carry you and Agnes down to Mrs. Wolseley's in his arms for
me – and what dear little girls you were. He looked poor fellow the picture
of death while he spoke, but remarked that he never could feel or
believe that he was old. [It is certain] he is going to leave us – he brings
back the memory of those old stirring times. The poor Boltons have
another death in their family. Agnes Bolton died this morning of heart
disease at Cobourg, making five deaths in the family since the Major
married last year. This is very unlucky for poor Mrs. Wigg[5] who was with
us since Friday, getting out the placards for her concert, which is to come
off on Wednesday. If Casement dies tonight, no-one in the village will go,
and it will be a great loss to her, with whom, it is a matter of necessity.
And still worse, has happened to the poor Muchalls. Tom was hired at 15
dollars per month as a marker of timber at the shanties but came home
coughing himself almost to death; but was getting better and was to have
started this morning with the team, when he fell upon the slippery river

path by the mill and dislocated his right shoulder. He suffered terribly in
having it put in, and looks as pale as a ghost. Will not be able to use it
for three weeks or a month, and they have not a copper to buy even bread.
Poor kind Mary, when are her troubles to cease? The dear little boy,
dresses and undresses the poor father, with wonderful tenderness. He is a
fine creature, is nurse and help and everything to his Mother and
though only nine years old,[6] split my wood for me, and his Grandmother's
and earned his dollar. Every copper of which, he gives to his Mother.
Mrs. Hargrave sent him five dollars about a week ago, and he gave it to
his mother to buy some warm things for his poor sick father, when he
went to the shanties. Oh, these are sore sore trials – I don't know what
they will do now. Aunt has only a few dollars in the bank. But she will
entertain, and never thinks of the [torn bottom of page] ... I feel very sorry
for the death of Mr. Burrowe's. He was such a strong looking big
headed man; he looked as if he could almost defy death. She is a lovely
little woman, and the sweetest singer I ever heard in this country. She
was very kind to me, and I felt quite an interest in the pretty little fairy-like
woman. I am glad that the dear girls are enjoying themselves this bright
winter weather. It is very cold again this morning. I had to leave off my
letter, last night, cover up the fire, and go to bed. My hands are quite
numb, though I am writing close to my stove. I shall not regret the breaking up of this cold winter.

Your letter cheered me, for I felt very low-spirited, reading of the old
letters made me sad, and conjured up, so many ghosts of the past. We
never realize how much we love the dead, until these silent voices speak
to us from their graves.

But I must banish this subject, or the old fit of gloom will return. I think
Victor, very like Mr. Vickers. Billie is like Moodie and yourself. I have
Historic Scenes[7] for him – a book hard to get now. It has Aunt's picture
for frontispiece, and dear old Reydon, and her autograph, and I now
prize it very much as it is the only book she ever gave me. If ever I should
see Toronto again, I will bring it up for him. What a graphic picture you
give of the accident to the poor gray horse. It is fortunate, that his life was
saved. I should have thought, that the porter would have poisoned him,
I always think it a vile mixture. I told you in my last, that I got the prize
money – I was a *little* disappointed, not much. Mine is a day of such
small things now, that I am used to it.

I got a nice perfume box the other day, by Express from Ottawa, the
carriage paid to Peterboro, but that old fox, who stole the wine you sent,
charged me as much for bringing it up to Lakefield. It contained a sprig of

English Holly and berries, one of Lauristinus and of Daphne laurel –
the latter perfumed the whole box, with its delicious scent. I suppose
Maime sent it, but where did she get the contents?

I think the cold weather, must have frozen all David Edward's bees for
I have seen nothing but the prospectus of the Hive.

I am reading Tennyson very carefully, and with much pleasure. He has
written a vast amount of very poor stuff, and much, that is *very beautiful*,
and is a greater poet, than I have hitherto considered him. I will not abuse
him any more. A great deal he has published, will [pass] with him, but
enough will remain, to immortalize him. I have a vile scrapy pen, and you
cannot get good ones here. I meant to buy some in Ottawa, but went
away too suddenly to get several things I wanted. I am out of card-board
too, and painting with me, is almost a necessity; for I spend at least nine
hours out of the twelve alone; and too much reading makes my eyes sore –

Give my kind love to dear John. May he live to nurse children of the
new babe on his knees – and with much love to your dear self and all
the bonnie bairns, believe me dearest Katie –

> Your affectionate old Mother
> Susanna Moodie

All here send love – I have not seen Louise since the week before last –
The snowdrifts prevent much travelling – Love to the dear Tullys.

1 In the United States shin-plaster was slang for a paper bill, first printed in 1837, worth
   various denominations of less than one dollar. In Canada, shin-plasters were only
   printed in 1870, 1900, and 1923 and were always worth twenty-five cents.
2 Her own paternal grandfather, Samuel Strickland of Finsthwaite Hall
3 Robert's place of appointment was probably Brantford, Ontario.
4 Robert Casement became the Lakefield postmaster in 1847; he was later a justice of the
   peace.
5 Adela Wigg, Tom Strickland's daughter, taught piano in Lakefield.
6 Hargreave Henry Muchall (born 1865), the Muchall's eldest child. Mrs Hargreave was his
   paternal grandmother.
7 Agnes Strickland's *Historic Scenes and Poetic Fancies* (London 1850)

---

117 To the editor of   25 July, 1874
the *Globe*, Toronto

Sir – Will you permit me to use one of your columns to correct some of the
statements which have appeared in the public papers respecting my

sister, the late Miss Agnes Strickland, the author of the well-known histories of the Queens of England? My sister was not born in the present
century, nor a native of the County of Suffolk, as they have stated, but in
the County of Kent, in the vicinity of London (which was the birth-place
of the five elder sisters) July 19th, 1796. Consequently, had she lived until
the date of this communication, she would have completed her 78th
birthday. This may seem a matter of small consequence; but as she has
become an historical character, it places her ten years beyond her real
era, and makes her the youngest of the large family that my father, Thomas Strickland, had by his second wife, of whom she was the second
daughter.

My Father had one daughter by his first wife, who died in her infancy.
His two sons, the late Col. Strickland, of Lakefield, Captain Thomas
Strickland, and myself, were born in Bungay, in Suffolk. In the year 1808
he purchased Reydon Hall and removed thither with his family, and it
remained the family residence for nearly 50 years.

I can remember very little of the very early childhood of my gifted sister.
I was but a child, when she was a beautiful, high-spirited girl, just entering upon her teens; but the family traditions abounded with stories of her
wit and genius, the record of which would fill a volume.

My Father, a man of excellent abilities, was her principal instructor.
We never had but one governess, and she left us at the end of the first
year, having joined another Lady in the management of a large school at
Chapham. From her, Agnes received her first rudiments of French, but,
having a great facility in acquiring languages, she taught herself Italian
and French. Her love of history was a passion. We had a good old-
fashioned Library, and she soon made herself acquainted with all its
historical works, while she knew the finest passages of the English
classics by heart. How we little ones used to gather round her in the fire-
light, during the long winter evenings, to hear her repeat to us the parting
of Hector and Andromache, the death of Julius Caesar, from Shakespeare; and often she would frame little Romances for us, founded
upon passages from English history, to which we listened with breathless
attention. No historical romance in after life was ever read by us with
such zest. Her conversational powers were as great as her literary ones.
Possessed of an excellent temper, great flow of natural eloquence, and
playful repartee; her descriptive powers never seemed to flag. Whether in
her grave or gay moments she knew how to charm her listeners.

When my dear father was confined to his bed with gout, she shared the
task of reading him to sleep of a night, with my eldest sister. The

newspapers were her expected task. Perched on the foot of his bed, she would read with grave interest the political events of those stirring times, and the long speeches of the Ministers in the House of Commons. Her attention was so deeply engaged that she would arrange our school-room into a House of Commons, and give us a grand speech from Mr. Canning, whom she was supposed to represent, and we thought it great fun to cheer and cry 'Hear, hear!'

Oddly enough, the Father and his child politician seldom agreed upon historical subjects. He was a Whig and a great admirer of William III, whom she detested being a devoted champion of the unfortunate House of Stuart. Yet I never remember any trouble arising out of their opposi-tion. She loved her father and was ever constant in her attachment.

I have no recollection of the poem of the 'Red Cross' but I have a very distinct one of a poem she commenced entitled 'The Spirit of Freedom,' which she never finished, and I fear that it is no longer in existence,[1] being rather of a little radical, even in those early days. The following spirited lines have remained in my memory for over sixty years.

> 'Yes, glorious Sparticus! to thee belong
> The patriot's wreath – the poet's noblest song;
> Not thine, proud chief, to wear a servile chain;
> Better to die than bear so foul a stain.
> To strike a blow for altar, hearth and home,
> And dare the conflict with Imperial Rome.
> She paused astonished at the venture brave
> And the world's mistress trembled at a Slave:
> A Slave no more! Thy chosen Champion stood,
> Free and as unconquered as the ocean flood, –
> And long recording history shall tell
> The spot where Sparticus and Freedom fell.'

She would not have exceeded fourteen years, when this generous burst of enthusiasm was written. In the same poem she eloquently held up the wrongs of Poland;[2] while I have seen her shed tears over the barbarous murder of Hoffer,[3] the hero of the Tyrol, at the command of Napoleon. The first poem she published was *Worcester Field*, which was very well received. Then followed *The Seven Ages of Woman*, *The Rival Cru-soes*, a very popular and charming tale for young people – written in con-junction with our eldest sister Elizabeth, a woman possessing talents as great as her own. At this period she contributed largely to magazines and annuals, with a daily increasing reputation. *The Patriotic Songs*, published by Mr. Green of Soho, was a joint volume of music and songs, dedicated by permission to King William IV, who had just ascended the throne. We each furnished three songs for the composer, but the music was so poor that it spoiled the popularity of the songs – and the book has long been out of print. The King through his private secretary (Sir Herbert Taylor) wrote us a very complimentary letter, in which he was pleased to say that 'He considered us an ornament to our country,' which made the two country girls very glad.

After the publication of the *Patriotic Songs*, in 1830, I was married and emigrated to this country with my husband, and my literary aspirations were quenched in the struggle to obtain bread in the backwoods. All my sister's great works were published after we left England, and with most of these the reading public are better acquainted than I am myself.

Space will not permit me to say more of this truly great woman. Her genius is too well appreciated to need it. But I cannot close this brief notice without a slight sketch of her private and domestic character, in which she bears the dearest relation to her friends and family.

An affectionate, loving daughter, a faithful sister and friend, kind and benevolent to the poor, and possessing warm sympathies for the sick and suffering; she never let the adulation of the world interfere with the blessed domestic charities. A sincere Protestant, and a firm adherent of the Church of England; nothing but illness ever prevented her from joining in the Sabbath duties, and partaking of the sacred Communion. For years she conducted the first Sabbath-school in our parish church, instituted by herself, and her literary labours were never allowed to interfere with what she considered sacred obligations.

Her long useful life is at an end, and she has descended to the grave, full of years and honours. We have lost a beloved sister, but it is a great comfort to know how wide felt is the sympathy with us in our bereavement.

> (Signed) Susanna Moodie,
> Lakefield, North Douro
> July 19th, 1874

1 The mention of 'Red Cross' here presumably comes from one of the obituaries of Agnes; that poem and 'The Spirit of Freedom' do not appear in her published volumes.
2 It is difficult to know whether Susanna is referring here to Frederick II of Prussia, who proposed a partition of Poland to Catherine II of Russia in 1772; or Koscinsko, who led an heroic revolt of independent Poland in 1794; or Napoleon I, who created a Polish buffer state in 1807.

3 Andrew Hoffer (1767–1810) led the Austrian resistance against Bavaria and the French in
  1809; he was made governor of the Tyrol, but was later betrayed to the French and
  executed.

---

118 To Sarah Gwillym   [mid-1870s][1]

The October my dear John died there appeared an advertisement [in] the
Montreal *Gazette* offering a hundred dollars prize for a poem for the
approaching All Hallow E'en Festival. We were living in the little cottage
in Belleville when John read the advertisement, and he had a great wish
to try for the prize. 'Mother' he said, 'the 100 dollars would buy you so
many useful things you want.' Well for two days he tried but in vain. He
took up his flute, and tried to play some of his favourite Scotch airs, but
the dear hand had lost its powers. 'Dear auld wife,' he said putting
down the flute with a sad smile, 'It is of no use – I shall never play or write
a Scotch song again.' 'Let me try Johnnie to write it for you!' 'You' he
said. 'Why Susie you are not Scotch. It would not have the ring of true
metal.' 'Ah' I replied 'I am Scotch in sight of my husband. Give me your
pen!' I scribbled off this enclosed song, in a few minutes and handed it over
to him. The dear creature was pleased with it but still shook his head.
This was just two days before he died, and I forgot all about the song.
Mrs. Traill happened to send it among some papers I wanted to Ottawa
and the good Colonel would send it to the society. I never imagined it
would be taken. I had twenty competitors, Scotchmen who doubtless
wished me at the bottom of the Ottawa river.

1 This letter may have been written on one of Susanna's mid-1870s visits to the Chamberlins shortly after her now-lost song won the Caledonia Society prize of twenty dollars.

---

119 To W.W. Vickers[1]   Lakefield
                                    January 16, 1876

You careless fellow! – What, lost your mitts,
Ain't you afraid I'll give you fits?
Punch your head, or slap your face,
Or send to a corner, in dire disgrace? –

Were I a lady young and fair,
You would certainly take the greatest care,
Of the smallest thing her love could proffer,
So what excuse my lad can you offer? –
But *'Some one stole them!'* – A lack a day –
Had you no pocket to stow them away?
You will lose your heart as sure as a gun
One of these days, and find it no fun
Without you can catch the thief who got it,
And transfer the stolen goods to your pocket –
Now here me Billie, while I declare
I will not knit you another pair!
I'll leave it to younger hands than mine,
To keep warm that heart and hand of thine,
When I take up the pins in your behalf
I give you leave my boy to laugh –
At old Knitty Knotty, who loves you well,
And hopes to see you a learned swell;
Lawyer or preacher, or Statesman grave,
That can keep his *own* and for others save –
Your letter is short, there is no denial
And not very sweet – make another trial –
But I give you fairly to understand,
That I prize it, though penned by a mitless hand –
That is better far, than a witless head
But that of you could never be said
So farewell W.W.V.
May heaven send a happy New Year to thee,
And so I close my first epistle
To you dearest Billie – Pray don't whistle! –
I've told the truth, and said my say,
And hope you will write some other day,
No rhyme for Moodie can I find,
But remain, your Grandmamma loving and kind

                    Susanna Moodie

---

1 Her grandson William, a student at Upper Canada College, a private boys' school
  founded in 1829 and by 1876 situated on King Street in Toronto near the site of the
  present Royal Alexandra Theatre

120 To Katharine Parr Traill   Dec[r] 2, 1877

My dear little Katie,[1]

Many thanks for your nice kind letter. If you don't forget me, I assure you that I do not forget you. A very dear and pleasant remembrance you are to me. I hope God willing to see you again and visit all the pretty nooks in your vicinity. About ten days ago, we had a visit from your Mother. Was I not surprised to see her walk in, about dusk with dear Robert and Nellie.[2] She only stayed one night and slept with me. Little Nellie walked down with her to the station. Oh such a wet dull day, but she would go, though Mrs. M. wanted her to stay for fine weather. What a shame of the thieves to steal your pretty chickens. But I don't think they were thieves on *two* legs, but *four*. That nasty small hound, was always springing at them, and then, Job looked often hungrily at them, and hawks eat such small game. They would not make a very large meal for a hungry boy.

I must tell you about our dog – Such a beauty as big as Mr. Kanes bear and much fatter. Jet black a real Newfoundlander, but taller than the table. It is a lady – Juno by name. Gives her paw in a most graceful manner and never steals though meat is quite close to her. She is only six months old and, if she grows much larger she will be too big for a plaything. She lets baby ride on her back all round the room, and put her hand into her mouth with all the white glittering teeth and never hurts her though baby pulls her about just as she pleases. The other day, a terrier, was killed upon the rail road track, which runs past the garden, and is buried in the garden. Jack having put a headstone over it, to mark the spot. Of course, I am a great favourite with Juno, who looks at me with her large loving brown eyes, and gives my hand a lick to notice her. Is poor old Tom in the land of Cats yet? and does Job ever pay you a visit. If so give them both a friendly pat for Aunt Moo.

How are all the dear little cousins – especially Hargrave. I hope you are getting along well with all your lessons and very good to dear Grandma and Aunt Kate. I must now say goodbye darling, for I am not very well and tired, and wishing you a happy Christmas and a merry new year –

remain your loving Aunt
Susanna Moodie

Nellie and Bess send love to cousin Kate who they think they should love as I love her –

1 Katharine, Susanna's great niece, lived with her Grandmother Traill and Aunt Kate Traill in Lakefield.
2 Susanna is living in Weston, near Toronto, Ontario with her son Robert.

---

121 To Catharine Parr Traill   Howell Street[1]
                                     Avenue, Toronto,
My dearest Sister,   April 2, 1878

I am ashamed of my long silence, and yours was such a sweet letter; but we have been in such a muddle with our sudden moving from Weston that I could not get an opportunity of writing. And here we are at last, and my room fit to sit down and write peaceably, and out of the dirt. We had thought to remain in Weston until June, when Robert's year's rent expired, but the man, a rough Englishman, wanted to sell the place, directly, having a good chance; and Rob thought we might as well get the bother over now as then.

We have a very nice house in the Avenue, close to the Park, and are surrounded by lovely trees, in which the birds salute the morn. My room looks directly up and down the broad avenue and is very bright and cheerful. All the fashionable idlers come here for walking and riding, and babies in their cabriolars, and pretty well dressed children. Nellie is enchanted with the place and hopes that this may be the last move. She has been working herself half to death to get things in their places, and our good Scotch girl has consented to remain with us for the next month at least.

Katie came out to Weston a few days before we left, and insisted upon my coming to her during the muss. I had not been well for some time, and, Nellie insisted upon my going, as she said, I was ill and the change would do me some good, which indeed it has, as Dr. Hall[2] gave me medicine which made me feel better in a few days. I was sorry to leave my kind little daughter-in-law when she had so much to do, but I packed up all my things, ready for the carting before I went. I really was sorry to leave Weston – It is a pretty place and must be very nice in its springtide dress, and the few people who visited us were very nice.

You cannot think my beloved how glad I was that dear Tom and Mary,

had at last settled down in a home of their own. May God bless all their
efforts to support their family. They are rich in their fine children. As to
yourself, my dear sister, I feel certain that God will extend the same
care over you, that he has ever done, and that you will find things go on
just as usual. I often picture you and dear Kate in the old familiar
places, and wish that I could step in for a pleasant chat, and see all the
dear nephews and their families, and look into the dark depths of the
beautiful river, but I begin to doubt whether I shall be able to come for a
month's board, during the summer, though I should like it much. Poor
Nell, begins to feel her burthen and is very nervous and wants petting
and cheering all the time. She is growing very fond of me, and so is the
wild, bright, shy babie. On my return last Friday from Adelaide Street, the
little creature rushed into my arms and kissed and twezzed me to my
hearts content. I was very comfortable with dear Katey and her baby
made much of me too. They have had capital letters from Georgie, who
was at Nice when she last wrote. I had no idea, that such a silent girl,
could write such capital letters. She describes every thing in such an
amusing, clear-headed manner it is as good as a book, but the dear home
and the home-faces seem always to engage her best thoughts. Her
letters give such delight to her family it is a real pleasure to see and hear
it. All the children but the baby write to Georgie. Her class in the
secondary school (boys) have rebelled; they don't mean to come to school
until Miss Vickers comes back; they love her and don't want to learn of
any one else.

However, Katie has taken her sisters class last week and they begin to
think her almost as good as Georgie. Mrs. Gwillym has written to
Georgie to come and stay with her on her return from abroad. A very kind
letter (as hers always are), but I hardly think Georgie will be able to go.
She has to visit her father's friends in Dublin, and Mr. Maguire, the
celebrated Preacher of St. Thomas' church London, her father's first
cousin and school-mate, has written expressly for her to stay sometime
with him in London. I hope she will go, for he is such a hard-working,
God-fearing man. You may have seen pictures of him in the *Illustrated
News* some years ago – Both a portrait and memoir – and his preaching to a crowded audience in London. He writes charming letters and
seems quite anxious to see his Canadian cousin.

I have not heard from dear Agnes for some time. James says that she is
better, and Donald has not written to me for many weeks, which always
lays heavily on my heart. Dunbar is getting on well and his two oldest
children are at the head of their respective schools. He seems greatly

taken with Josephus, and says that it has 'greatly shaken his infidelity.' This to me was the best news in his letter. I have not heard from Cherrie or dear Sarah since the beginning of February and I have not been able to write, nor have I seen dear Maria. I set off to walk over to call yesterday but could only accomplish half the distance. It is a very long walk from the head of the avenue and that odious hernia is tormenting me again, and making walking very tedious and painful to me. So you have heard from dear Willie – Is this a new baby or the one he was expecting when he was in Canada? Did he ever get the flowers? I have not painted anything since I left you, nor do I expect to do so. The Cromes[3] are so lovely, that anything I could do, are mere daubs. I have finished working my table for dear Nellie; and Rob took it to be made up at Jacques and Hays,[4] who greatly admired it. I wish they would order one of me. I had no idea that it would look so well; but it is hard work, to draw with a needle, so many groups out of your own head – 16 groups of flowers, it took a group to every vandyke. I must take a rest now for the gay colors have made my eyes weak. I saw from my window at Weston the funeral of poor Col. Richard Denison. The cemetry was just opposite our place at Weston. It was a pouring day, but there was a great number of gentlemen came by train and carriages to the funeral. His death was very sudden. He had some small growth of flesh cut out of the nose that impeded his breathing and went out one cold day soon after, before it was healed. Erysypelas set in and he died in a few hours. I see Dr. Lister of B.V. is gone, but have heard no particulars of his death.

I saw Malcolm at Katey's last week, but he looks very thin and pale, and consumptive. Katey was much struck with Philip Wiggs appearance. I didn't see him, but I like him much. Arthur Strickland had been there but I missed him also. I have met with a man who don't believe in a God, nor in the bible, nor in any first cause; Who thinks that death is death, and that man is perfectly irrisponsible, and in no degree superior to the animals. It was of no use arguing with him for he denied all evidence of God in the creation, in revelation or in the human soul. Poor miserable creature. He seemed to me a sort of intellectual monster. I could find no better words to suit the madness of his folly but 'the fool has said in his heart – there is no God.' The belief in a God is the central belief in the heart of man, on which his very existence depends. Oh, to hear him quote from the works of all our modern infidels, and to say that they were in advance of the rest of the world just showed what deadly nightshade is being planted in the garden of God. He writes too in Newspapers and thinks himself equal to any God. Alas, alas, ever alas!

Now darling, you must give my very hearty love to dear Robert and his beloved wife and dear girls, to Percy and Susan, Roland and his household, and to all who think old Aunt Susie worth a thought, but their love and well-being is very dear to me. I need not send love to you dear Sis, for you know I love you and dear Kate and Mary and the little ones, and believe me now and ever, your attached

Susie

Rob's eye looks very bad. He sends love to you and so does Nellie. God bless you all. I hope this may find you all well. People are planting ferns in their garden plots. I suppose this summer weather will take Kate to the woods in search of her treasures. We have a wee bit plot of grass behind the house which Jack is digging up for turf and flowers. My poor old Puss – peace to his ashes. I hope the cats gave him a decent funeral.

1 Caer Howell Place (see Letter 123), Toronto, located just south of Queen's Park, running west off Avenue Road to McCaul Street
2 Dr C.B. Hall (1816–80), assistant surgeon to the Queen's Light Infantry during the 1837 rebellion, went on to teach medicine at Victoria College
3 A 'crome' is a type of drawing done with a hook-like needle.
4 For forty years from its founding in 1843, a fine furniture manufacturing firm in Toronto

---

122 To Catharine Parr Traill   [1878]

You forgot to send me the card dear sister K.S.[1] sent me, which you said you would when you returned home. I greatly prize these souvenirs. Cherrie sent me such a lovely one – English blue white and purple violets and buttercups. I was just going to smell them they were so sweet looking. I must hasten to finish. I have been writing letters all day for Rob to post tomorrow and back and brain are both tired. Love to dear Robert, Caroline and the darling girls, to dear Susy and Percy, Mrs. Richard and R. and to dear Roland and wife, with kind regards to Mrs. Lilycrap, FitzGerald and the Grahams. If the latter have read Dr. Guthrie[2] get it home for me or I shall forget where it is.

1 Postmark gives 1878 (day and month unclear); K.S. is Katharine (Rackham) Strickland.
2 Thomas Guthrie, DD (1803–73), Presbyterian preacher, author of *Studies of Character from the Old Testament* (1868) and *Sundays Abroad* (1871)

123 To Catharine Parr Traill

2 Caer Howell Place
The Avenue, Toronto
July 29th, 1878

My Dearest Catherine,

I received your last kind letter, and was right glad to get it. But I did not see dear Charlotte until last week, she having only just returned from Brantford. The darling girl looked as sweet as usual. The light of Heaven on the dear face. I hope I shall see her again before she leaves. When Robert returned in the evening he told me that your Walter had been in his office, and would give me a call upon his return, but I suppose he has not had time, without he is still with you. Robert says that he is a fine clever fellow. How glad you will be to see him. I hope you and Kate will have a good time while he stays. I wish I were with you, but I do not think I shall be able to command funds to come down for a month, or I would just to see you all again, young and old. Perhaps when Charlotte returns I may. Mrs. H Traill may be able to pay me the four dollars she owes me which would be a help.

Your 'Forest Trees of Canada' is in this month's *Canadian* – To my mind a capital article – The best in the new issue.[1] I would send you the Mag. if they had sent it to me, but they have not been so liberal. I think if they would publish the whole series in their Mag., they might perhaps bring out the volume and give you something for it worth having. I find my not being able to walk much hinders me from going to hear about it. But you can write to the Editor who is one of the Belfords. Dear Georgie is home all safe and sound. She is much pleased with Douglas Moodie, and says Cherrie looks very well and very happy. Georgie seems to be a great favorite with dear Sarah who says in her letter to me, that she is a girl after her own heart. She cannot bear to part with her. She gave her a magnificent set of pearls, beautiful exceedingly – tiara, necklace, broach, earrings, bracelet, and hair pins. I fancy that they must have cost a lot of money, but had belonged to either Agnes or Eliza. She sent me a black shawl like my best one, and a nice p^r of gloves which was very kind. Mr. Vickers forwarded a box to you free as far as Peterborough. I have no doubt that you will find in it lots of nice things.

Nellie and the girls have just returned from their visit to Northport on the Bay of Quinté where they enjoyed themselves amazingly that very hot weather. The girls learned to row and to swim, and look all the better for their trip. You did not tell me of Richard Traill's marriage. He has a good berth in Chicago and she, the bride, is a nice girl. I hope they may be happy. Mrs. James had gone to stay with them.[2]

I should have liked to have seen those sweet children of yours – the little darlings especially – If ever there was a human angel, it is that lovely little Florence.[3]

Dear Rob is not so well as I could wish, but he has to work whether ill or well. Nellie is well and looks quite young and pretty. If I should come to Lakefield it would not be for more than a month and I could not pay more than 12 dollars, but if I could hire a couple of rooms in the village, I could keep myself, and not give much trouble. I would go to the Hotel at Stoney Lake at once, but I would rather be among the dear friends, most likely for the last time, and I could not afford to pay for the board. Robert would give me passes to Port Hope and back. I do long to see you all again. The dear Muchalls and the Stricklands. The day is the eclipse of the sun, but the clouds hide him and it is bitterly cold after yesterday's great heat, and the sudden change affects my stomach and makes me feel quite aguish. I have had great fits of toothache of late and try to bear it as well as I can, but the pains of those electrical thrills I feel in my ears and throat.

Katey and Mrs. Vickers have just come back from their trip to Fort William, Katey as much delighted with the scenery as ever.[4] Inspite of the heat, 98 in the shade, she contrived to climb up a high mountain. She is quite well and all the dear children. The little Agnes is very sweet. We live about a long mile from the Tullys, either to go by the Avenue and Queen Street, or to go by Caer Howell, or Beverly Street and St. Johns. I have not seen Louise since she returned. I thought dear Mrs. Le Fevre looked beautiful when she was last here. She and the sweet baby would have made a good picture of the Madonna and child. Her face is so sweet and pure, I don't know a lovelier woman. Her maternity is charming. I heard that Mrs. Walter was very sick last night, but of what nature her illness I do not know. She is quite beyond my reach, about five miles off and no cars from here for a mile or more. But, the situation here, though inconvenient for the city, is very lovely and I think the large Elm opposite to my window, on the other side of the Avenue, the most beautiful one I ever saw, lofty and vast, and full of birds. I saw two cat birds this morning at sunrise fighting a flock of English sparrows, that have their nest close to my window. How they tormented the big birds, it was quite amusing to watch them. We had great doings in the Avenue on the 12th of July all the processions went up our road with their flags and bands. I believe every baby car in the city was there. The poor lambs sitting in state in their Cabs, dressed in blue cloaks with orange ribbons. What business have they among the rowdy young Britains. Fortunately it went off without any serious riot. A few days before, the Physiogeys paraded through the avenue, in the most outrageous costumes you ever saw, and hideous music of tin pans and kettles. Every carriage had some dreadful looking monster on it, that wagged tails and snapped crocodile jaws at the passers by. I think that they must have borrowed Snap for the occasion. It was very droll and I laughed as much as the children. I did not go to see the performing horses and dogs in the park but Robert and the boys went and were charmed with it.

My dear Katey, I cannot write with these greasy pens and ink to my best. It is enough to make Patience tired of her monument and really I can't smile at my grief. I bought the ink only two days ago and this is the way it serves me.

I might have inflicted you with another page but I feel too cross. Give my love to all the good nephews and nieces; lots to the dear Muchalls – I am so glad that they are more comfortable. Hargrave is a good darling and God will bless him. I suppose Norman is grown beyond knowledge and little Carrie.

I hope your new parson will turn out a good one and not persecute dear Charlotte. If you see the Garb[io]ts give my kind love to them and to Mrs. Lilycrap. To dear Susan and Percy and dear Robert and Caroline, and with much for you and dear Kate and wee Kate, believe me ever your attached Sister

Susanna Moodie

Rob and Nell send love –

Direct to me here –

1 'Our Forest Trees,' *Rose Belford's Canadian Monthly and National Review* (July 1878), 90–5
2 James Traill's widow, Amelia, had moved from Belleville to Chicago to be with her son Richard and his wife.
3 Catharine's granddaughter, Florence Marion Atwood (1874–1957)
4 See 'A Letter from Catharine Moodie Vickers to Her Mother, Susanna Moodie,' *Thunder Bay and the Kaministiquia Half a Century Ago* (Thunder Bay Historical Society 1925).

124 To Catharine Parr Traill

2 Caer Howell Place
The Avenue, Toronto
13th October, 1878

My dear Sister

I wrote a long letter to you last week, but concluded not to send it. Robert has since been ill, confined to his bed with attack upon the lungs, and I was too anxious about him to think of anything else. He is about again, but thin and pale with a deep trying cough. May God spare him yet awhile to his wife and family, but I cannot repress a dread that it may not be for long. His wife fears it too, and is most attentive and kind to him, as much so, as her restless temperament will allow her to be; and he is intensely fond of her. I wish that they could both view it in a religious sense, but – there is little thought of the future here. And this indifference extends to the whole family.

I had hopes at one time, that the girls might feel an interest in sacred things, but they are so taken up with other occupations; that words fall to the ground without producing the least effect upon them. Poor things, they are eager to learn, but not in that direction. I can only hope and pray for them. They are both very clever, especially Nellie, who is a fragile delicate creature but with many excellent qualities. I am very fond of her and when I tell her of any glaring fault, she will not only own it, but try to overcome it. She has a great taste for drawing, and has painted some flowers, really wonderful for a beginner. Robert has engaged a teacher for her at the Art Union; and she is delighted with going to her lessons 3 times a week. She is so persevering and industrious she must succeed. She works beautifully in the Berlin wool and has made her mother many pretty things. I have been looking out for dear Maime for the last fortnight, but no word of her yet. If she was on the Great Lakes during the heavy gale on Tuesday, she must have had a severe tossing. I am quite impatient to see my old darling again. Not a word have I received from Cherrie since her marriage, or from dear Sarah, or old Mrs. Moodie. Agnes has heard from them lately. But not about Alice's advent in London or how she likes England and her new brother. I must say that I feel very anxious to hear from any of the parties. You may have some news of them however. Dear Nellie called with me on Mrs. Vickers on Thursday, but she had no word of them, but told me of the burning of the Hotel at St. Julians.[1] I was deeply grieved – For it must be a great loss to the dear Stricklands. It was in the *Telegram* but I did not see the paper. She said that there was no insurance upon the property. She likewise told me that Arthur Strickland's engagement with Miss Huff was broken off and Agnes' with Gerard. I did like Gerard very much, but of course, knew very little of his mind or disposition. And so poor Mrs. FitzGerald is gone – A dear good soul and a kind neighbour. I was afraid when I kissed and bade her good bye that I should never see her again. I do long to see you all, but I do not see my way clear. I am low in funds, and have no little sum laid by for extra expenses, as I generally had heretofor, and I had to buy some flannels and a few necessaries that I could not do without as the cold weather is close at hand. But should I be able to command the means, I would come down during the winter months to spend a few peaceful happy days at dear old Lakefield. I was glad to hear from Mrs. Le Fevre that you were looking so well, and that all your dear ones were well. I saw so little of the darling Charlotte while she was here, and it would have done me a world of good to have heard one of her sweet lectures and her prayers. I did not go to the exhibition but saw the grand torch-like procession for Lord Dufferin, as it passed the front of the house which commands a fine view up and down the ave-nue. Such a crowd, I have not seen out of London. It was a fine night *without* the moon, and to me a novel sight. Our house was full of company – Mr. Way of Belleville and his niece, Mrs. Morden of North-port and her sister and son, and Mr. and Mrs. Broddie, and their girls. All went off to hear the speeches and left me to watch the crowd that lined the avenue and keep guard over the house. All my folk took a bad cold for the night was cold, and the crowd was so dense, they could not get into the Park to hear the Earl's speech. All parties seem to regret his going. Malcolm is back to his studies looking well and improved every way, and quite at home with Katey, who makes quite a pet of him. Donald is still with dear Agnes and is steady as long as he has no money. Malcolm, says 'it is disease and he cannot help it.' But it cannot be hereditary in his case, as Moodie never drank, nor any of my people but poor Tom, and that, not until the death of his wife. He has taken the pledge again – Let us hope that he may stedfastly adhere to it. But in his own strength he never will; it requires the sword of the spirit to overcome one of Satan's most terrible emmissaries. He has never written to me or sent his love to me since March. It is a hard cross, but I must bear it. Thank God, I love him none the less, but the wounds we receive from those we love are always the worst to bear. I rejoice that the dear Muchalls are so much more comfortable. God will never let them want. Give my love to dear Mary and Tom and to them all – in fact, to all my dear friends in Lakefield. My heart always goes out to meet them. What lovely fall weather we have. The maple tree opposite my window in the little grove and the one at the bottom of your garden, must all be aglow now. I am not able to walk much. The old trouble hinders me but I sit at my window and admire the trees as day by day they put on their glorious robes before they decay forever. Give my fond love to dear Robert and Caroline and the dear girls, and tell them not to forget old Aunt in their prayers. I never forget them in mine. How has Walter sped in his visit to England?[2] Has he seen Aunts' Jane and Sarah? I think both would be pleased with him. You saw the death of poor old Mrs. Benson in the papers. There was a long obituary of her in the B.V. papers someone sent me, giving her all the virtues under the sun. Poor soul, such extravagant laudations would really grieve her could she be conscious of it. I hope no one will write one word about me, or place a stone over the clay that covers me. 'Vanity, vanity, all is vanity' – is the only true epitaph – and I feel the truth of the royal preachers words more every day. I have just been reading a very fine book called *That Lass of Louries*[3] – It is a mining story, one full of pathos and fine natural painting. It made a fool of me for it drew many tears from my eyes. I think I told you, that I would gladly accept the two dollars Graham offered for Dr. Guthrie, and if Lily could send me the 4 dollars she owes me, she could do so by post. It has been due a long time. She called upon me lately, but I was out. I had gone to Young Street to see after a dyer to redip my faded black dress, for I shall not be able to afford a new one this fall. I did not send anything to the show. Rob said my flowers would have taken a prize, and Katie said there was none so good there, but I am not very ambitious about these things. And now my beloved sister of old, I must close up the long dull rambling letter. I know that I have forgotten many things I wanted to say which will return to my fading memory when this is in the post. Love to the two dear Katies and much, much for your dear self. Ever Your faithful old

Susie

Give my love to the Maria if she is still with you, and to her lovely daughter. Tell her I miss her very much. Once more farewell dear Katie. Peace be with you all –

1 The Toronto *Globe*, 11 October 1878, reported a fire the day before at the Mt Julian Hotel causing $10,000 damage.
2 Having returned from the west for a visit, Walter Traill went on to England in the late summer of 1878.
3 Subtitled 'a Lancashire Story,' it was written by Frances Hodgson Burnett and published in London and New York in 1877.

125 To Catharine Parr Traill [October 1878][1]

I was sorely puzzled about the card enclosed in your letter. It was a long time before I found out who the nephew John was who had sent it. At first I thought it was some one whom I had offended who sent the word forgiven and I could not imagine who it could be. At last, I thought of dear John Taylor,[2] and the mystery disappeared. He had heard me say, that I could not positively say, that I was forgiven and was certain of salvation – and he sent the card to cheer and strengthen my faith. The dear noble loving creature, what a darling he is. Tell dear Charlotte to thank him much for Aunt Susie. When she feels very desponding, she will think of her text and feel more hope –

Love to all the other kind friends who ask after me and believe me your own loving –

Old Susie

1 Postmark appears to be this date.
2 The Rev. John Taylor was to marry Charlotte Strickland in 1879.

126 To Katie Vickers [Toronto November 1878][1]

My Dear Katie

I should have come to pay my regards to dear little Aggie in person, but I have been in bed for several days with the most atrocious cold which any poor mortal ever sneezed under. I feel somewhat better today but am melting away – No news of any moment. Heard from dear Maime – all well there. Had the queerest letter from Mrs. G. Moodie, my old correspondent, I ever read. I think the disease in her heart has attacked her mind, or that she was under the influence of alcohol when she wrote. I don't think [she was]. It is spiteful and unladylike and I can't imagine what she means by it, as her blows are dealt pretty equally to all. How I pity poor Cherrie being shut up in the same cage. She lets out that Mrs. Gwillym is delighted with Alice. Good for poor Alice. She does not mean to write again for a *very long time* and seems rather doubtful of her ill-natured letter. I was so vexed with it, that I burnt it to get rid of it. My poor trinketts seem to have stirred her bile. She compares them to an English plum pudding too heavy and rich. Well, I got over it ... she – and now I can laugh at it, but it was so unprovoked I cannot imagine how I have offended her. She all but calls Cherrie a liar for saying that Col. Chamberlain has a salary of 2000 dollars, as she hears on all sides that he is *desperately poor*. Now this is no *bubbling*, as she *calls it*, but a simple fact – only she reckons English currency instead of Canadian.

Nellie is not very well, but a kind nurse to me, and Rob has the same cold with me. Give my pretty Aggie a sweet kiss for me, and love to all the dear girls. Your loving old mother

S. Moodie

I am writing in the dark and with a very shaky hand. Don't send Dr. Hall. I shall get well without him. Give my love to dear John and my Billy and Arthur.

1 This letter was likely written at Robert's home on Caer Howell Place since Dr Hall might be sent for readily. It refers to the birthday of little Agnes Vickers (6 November) and to Geraldine (Cherrie Fitzgibbon) Moodie staying with her mother-in-law in London shortly after her marriage in 1878.

---

127 To Catharine Parr Traill   [March 1879][1]

Give my kind love to dear Hargrave and little Katie. We have a nice pup, I named Tim, who is as fond of me as old Tom was, and a pretty little Skye Terrier, who sleeps in Ted's arms every night, called Tinie. By the bye, there was an advertisement in the *Telegram* for a '*Fine Tom Cat,* a reasonable price to be paid upon delivery.' I wonder what they would consider 'reasonable.' I once read an advertisement in *Good Words* for a young cat, who had been brought up in a 'Christian Family.' This was rather carrying things too far, and looked very quizzical. Is there any talk of building up the M. Julian's Hotel again?

I had a line from dear Sarah telling of the birth of the great great Niece. What a pet it will be among them all, and a nice letter from Alice. Dear Thay was complaining of her cough – Mine is a little better. Tell dear Kate that Brown's Bronchial Troches are good.

The uncertainty of our remaining here hinders me from giving you a positive answer. If I do come, it would be for two or three months, and I would pay for my board at the rate of 15 dollars per month, which I pay to Mrs. Robert. I could not afford more, as Donald takes every copper I can spare to help clothe him. I have suffered terrible mental distress about him. Agnes has been obliged to get rid of him, and I know not where he will now go, or what will become of him. He will again be a houseless wanderer on the face of the earth. I sent 24 dollars last week to buy his passage to Chicago, whither he means to go. But his case seems a hopeless one. He never writes to me now. So that I do not know what he intends doing. You will find me very old looking, when you see me, for constant anxiety bites deeper than the teeth of time – That *dread uncertainty* –

We have terrible weather just now – Hail, rain, snow, thunder and lightning – 3 storms of the latter, on three successive days, one in the night, which reminded me of the Douro storms, and which was felt all over the country.

I am so sorry for poor dear little Jose.[2] Tell dear Susy, that I saw a girl of 15 at Belleville perfectly cured of this horrid disease, by receiving a shock of electricity, every day for 3 weeks. Reylid, the dentist, took Mr. Moodie and myself, several times to see him administer it on Carrie Pritton, the butcher's daughter. It is good for the jerking paralysis which acts just like St. Vitus Dance. The will power seems lost in both diseases. My dear daughter-in-law is sick in bed with one of her terrible headaches, and little Essie, suffering agonies of toothache, is growing thin and pale, and without the teeth can be extracted will be very ill. She is only three years old, but they talk of giving her chloroform, as nothing will prevail upon her to open her mouth to have them taken out. She bites if they try. You would pity the poor little thing, her agonizing cries when the fit is at the worst quite frighten me. She can neither eat nor sleep.

All the rest are well and dear Rob and Nellie send kind love to all. I had a very nice letter from dear Dunbar. He was nursing 7 children all down with measles, and his wife sickening for it, but he says that he thinks they will all come out right. He has renounced drink of all kinds for ever and everything is prospering with him. He is president of the Temperance society and never was so happy in his life. What he says about the effects of drink upon himself is admirable. I hope he will die a good Christian yet. I have a great lot of letters to answer so, dearest, I must conclude with love to all your dear ones, and to our dear nephews and nieces and remain with much love to your dear self, your loving

Susie

1 Letter dated by reference to the birth of Melville Mary Moodie at Lewisham, Kent, on 3
    March 1879
2 Jose (Susan Josephine), the fourteen-year-old daughter of Susan and John Percy Strickland

---

128 To Catharine Parr Traill   19th May 1879

My Dearest Sister

I have been so far from well, that I could not write to you or indeed to any
one. The cough was too cruel to let me be still two minutes at a time.
The two last warm days have much relieved me, but my nights are spent
sitting up coughing till I feel an agony of weariness. But it must be
borne and I console myself with the thought that it might be worse, and
can't last forever.
    Dear Maria Tully came for me to spend a few days with her, and meet
the bride and bridegroom. But I could only stay three days, and did not
meet them there, but Walter S. came for me in a cab on the saturday and
they came to lunch on the Monday following. They both looked very
happy, and Agnes very pretty. As to Philip, he is about the handsomest
young man I ever saw in Canada. Isabel Murney was quite right when
she said he was beautiful. His noble features and frank bright face would
make a charming picture. I hope he will turn out as good as he looks.
    Chassie was very kind to me and Walter and she[1] made all sorts of
good things to make me better but I do not believe that I shall ever get
over this attack of Bronchitis. I have dear Dr. Canniff attending me,[2] but
he does not seem very hopeful and admits that it is a very dangerous
cough, and at my age you know, dear Katey, cure can hardly be expected.
We have had such cold chilly weather, have been in all the horrors of
moving, fortunately I was away at Brocton and escaped the worst of it. I
found my room very nice. Dear Nell had made me a new carpet, and
bought a nice what-not and a book shelf of black walnut for my books
which cheered me a good deal. Rob is well and the children all very
kind. We are about half a mile further from Katey Vickers and I find the
walk too much for me. I have had to give up walking over to dinner on
Sunday. They are all well. Our street is a new one back of the avenue
planted with trees and Boulevarded with green grass and iron chairs. I
have six handsome plants in my windows and most delightful painted
blinds to keep out the sun and let in the fresh air. On the whole, we

have made a good exchange. You can direct to 30 Baldwin Street, Toronto. It seems a propitious name.

I met your clergyman Mr. Bell at Walter's. He seems a nice agreeable man, and Mr. Raikes called upon us – You remember him.

Ah, how you will miss dear Charlotte and her parents. I fear, I shall never see them in this world again, but they will always live in that world of memory the heart. I was sorry to hear that your Kate had been so sadly – I hope the opening Spring will revive her. I heard from Agnes last week. Mary and the Col. had been ill but were better. I had a long kind letter from poor Donald. He is still in Chicago and unemployed, but God has raised him up friends, as he has hitherto done, among the good of the earth, and I hope he will be given strength to overcome the horrible temptation. Where he is now he cannot indulge in it – and writes hopefully of finally overcoming it. I dare not be too sanguine, but I feel more contented in the idea that the worst is already over. His reformation would shed sunshine on my last days upon earth.

I met some pleasant people of the name of Moody at Brocton and a charming old lady, the grandmother, who was so like you that I liked her all the better for it. I did not see Mrs. Lee this time, only Hetty Dennison, who is so unlike her former self that I never should have known her. Brockton is greatly improved; it is quite a pretty suburban town now. It is hardly probable dear that I shall be able to get down to Lakefield this summer. I have given up all idea of it.

Everyone appears to have been delighted with your speech at the wedding. I wish I had been there to hear it. How are dear Mary and Tom and all the young ones. You never tell me anything about Walter and Willie – did the latter ever get the paintings I did for him? Do you ever hear anything of Minnie Bird and her husband. I seem to have lost sight of many of the Lakefield old friends. I have not heard from Aunt Sarah or Geraldine for some time, but I fear dear Thay is suffering from the same Bronchial cough that is killing me, for I feel certain that I shall never recover from mine and nature is gradually lessening my hold on life and pointing towards that better brighter shore, the glorious gift of God Eternal life. May we meet there dearest sister in peace and love.

Give my love to dear Mary and Tom and their children, to all my dear nephews and nieces and all who think me worth a thought – to Annie and her pretty bairns and to dear little Katie. My poor cat died the day I left the avenue, but Tiny has 4 innocent little Scotch terriers who are idolized by Essie and the boys. I am writing this on my knee so do not look at the bad writing. I cannot steady my hand to write legibly. Why don't

Mary try to sell her 'poetical history of England for children?'[3] I never saw but one which had a sort of ridiculous chorus;

> And saving the bother
> The one and the other
> Were all of them kings in their turn –

Mrs. Barrel used to repeat it to us. Love to dear Kate. All send theirs, and I remain ever

Your affectionate Susie

1 Charlotte and Walter Strickland
2 Dr William Canniff (1830–1910), surgeon and antiquarian whose main works are *A Manual of the Principles of Surgery* (1866), *A History of Early Settlement in Upper Canada* (1869), and *The Medical Profession in Upper Canada* (1894), all published in Toronto.
3 Although Mary Muchall had published *Step by Step: or, the Shadow of a Canadian Home* (Toronto 1876) and several pieces of poetry and prose in the *Canadian Monthly and National Review*, there is no evidence of publication of the manuscript mentioned here.

---

129 To Catharine Parr Traill 30 Baldwin Street
June 20th / 79

My Dearest Katey

The letter you forwarded to me from Geraldine only reached me on Wednesday. I send you the Photo of my first great-grandchild which was enclosed with mine, for you. It is a nice sensible looking baby for its age, but any child of only three months old bears no likeness to anyone, but to other babies of the same standing. To the parents, of course, it is the most beautiful of living creations

She says nothing of dear Aunt Sarah, only a casual remark that she had returned to Abbott's lodge and was busy in her garden. But, I was thankful for this, having felt very uneasy about her, the date of her last letter being March.

All through our cold stormy May and until two days ago, my throat complaint troubled me so that I could not stoop forward to write without bringing on a spasm of coughing. The two last days, I have felt better than I have done for the last year, for which I am grateful, even a short respite is a great relief.

We have quite got over the trouble of moving, and I am settled in a very nice room, with two large windows fronting the south, and a good view up and down our short broad street which is turfed and planted with trees. I miss the lovely trees in the Avenue, but we are only a few minutes walk from it. The tremendous storm last Sunday, washed off all the chesnut blossoms, and did a good deal of damage in the city. It began on Saturday, bombarded us all night, and culminated on Sunday evening after setting several houses on fire. I feel less timid of it than I did at Lakefield, and can shut out the lightning with the Venetian blinds which I find a great comfort. You can sleep with them down and the windows open, but the weather has been too cold for that.

I have been looking out for your Walter, but hear no tidings of him yet. I find that he is a great favorite at Katies, and will be sure to be welcome. Robert had his best great coat stolen off the rack in the hall, and when moving – a whole suit of clothes. We are so beset by tramps, that if the maid turns from the door for a minute they are apt to steal anything at hand. Nellie had a good many things stolen while moving. I was away at Brockton, but lost a few things I had left unlocked up. I have scarcely left the house since we came here, and have only been able to walk over to see Katie two or three times, and I cannot think of Cab hire. Poor Donald needs all I can spare. I have no good news of him yet. When I heard from him, he had left the Home, not having means to pay 5 dollars a week board, and I don't know how he is getting food since. This keeps me very anxious, and yet when a letter comes I feel so nervous it is some time before I can get courage to open it.

I have no news whatever. Nellie was sick abed last week but is better again. Her mother too, has been very ill and looks not long for this world. I believe she is a *saved woman* and affords a wonderful proof of the power of the gospel to convert the most obdurate heart. The change is so astonishing and the altered expression a sort of miracle, which to me is a sure proof of the reality. I feel a great interest for her, and am glad to see her so gentle and patient. Our little Jack too comes to my room every night, and begs me to read a chapter to him, and tell him what it means, and reads it himself in his own room ...

The salary is small but he is determined to stick to it and will board at the Washington home to keep out of harms way. Thank the good God for his great mercy.[1]

1 This is a cross-written note added to the top of the letter. Apparently, Susanna has just heard from Donald.

130 To Catharine Parr Traill

30 Baldwin Street
Jan 5th 1880

My dearest Sister

Many happy returns of the day and may the year upon which we have just entered, prove happy and prosperous to *you* and *yours*. You are very often in my thoughts and I wish I could fly like a bird and give you all a personal greeting – I will live in hope until the spring, if God grants me life, that I may see you and all the dear friends in Lakefield once again –

I was ill and had to call in the doctor and for several days suffered severe pain but I am better again and have just returned from a visit to Mrs. Vickers, and the quiet and good nursing set me up once more. I really enjoyed my visit the girls and boys were all so good to me, especially my dear Billie who is nearly a man now. The girls are very lovely and have everything in the way of dress to set them off. But they are very loving and kind to each other, and you never hear harsh words of any sort. A very happy household. Old Santa Claus brought me several nice presents. A black dress from dear Aunt Thay a pair of black silk and fur trimmed gloves and a breakfast shawl and better than all a very affectionate letter –

She[1] seems broken hearted about her baby and regrets the departure of the Moodies. Mrs. Moodie she tells me, was a beautiful and accomplished woman, and she was charmed with her. Dear Mrs. Moodie, I miss her clever letters very much. How much reason we have to be thankful when so many good ships foundered at sea that our travellers had such a prosperous voyage. I heard from Agnes and Cherrie on Saturday last. Moodies had moved into a nice cottage near Mrs. Chamberlin where they will remain until spring. Agnes and the Col. are delighted with old Mr. Moodie.[2] He is, A. says, a charming old gentleman so kind and courteous and quite an acquisition to the family. It seems that he very much resembles my dear husband and is about as infirm as father was. I always saw a likeness in the photographs. Douglas is coming up to Toronto on business when we shall all see him.

I saw James Fitz several times during my stay at Aunt's, and his lady love called upon me.[3] I was not much struck with her. She is like Alice, but is not so pretty and has a sharper cleverer look – she struck me as much older but I only saw her by gas light which is not a good medium. I was introduced to the family into which young Katie is to be married. Her lover is a handsome young fellow, and they are very fond of each other.[4] The old gent is a nice old man with fine blue eyes and snow white hair quite a darling of an old man, whose heart still clings to the highland hills. The old lady is very nice, with a simple kind face. Two married sons and their wives dined with us. The family is numerous four sons and as many daughters, but all married but James who is the youngest of the family. He introduced me to his Father and Mother as *his dear Grandmother* and the family all treat me as such. I don't think they will marry for some time and I don't know the young fellow's calling or profession but his father is among the wealthiest of the Toronto merchants. Kate would never let her daughter marry if the husband could not support a wife. They both seem very happy.

On New Year's Day a great many gentlemen called upwards of 50 among them Dr. Chapman, professor of geology in the College of Science in the park. A fine venerable old man, whom I met years ago at Daniel Wilson's.[5] He asked me for a copy of a little poem of mine 'The Canadian Herd Boy' as he wished to recite it at a lecture he was going to give next week. We had a very interesting chat about many things. I also met a Mr. Rowe who has been a missionary and travelled all over South America. He was a firm believer in the Jewish origin of the Anglo-Saxons and thinks that the millenium is close at hand. He thinks that all the Indians of the American continent are of Asiatic origen. He showed us many lovely photograph views of places in Chili, Peru and Mexico taken by himself. He spent two evenings with us and I should have liked much to have seen more of him. The conversation of such men is quite a refreshment after the flippancy of the men of the rising generation. I am so sorry for poor Mr. Gough. Mrs. Tully knows a certain cure for his disease. She can tell you all about it. You will be glad to hear that my poor Donald is still true to his pledge, is giving great satisfaction to his employers and has had his salary raised – dear Mr Cameron who called upon me the other day is rejoicing in his improvement. He writes beautiful letters both to Rob and me and no longer asks for pecuniary aid. He sent me some beautiful Christmas cards. I hope dear that your fears for poor Hargrave have not been realized and that his health has stood the test of cold and hard work. Give Mary and Tom my kindest love they have my prayers and heartfelt good wishes for a favourable change in their circumstances. No people deserve it more. It seems hard to deprive poor Tom of the tax-collecting, particularly as he did it faithfully, but his connection with an unpopular family, may be the real cause of it for I have been told that the S. family is no favourite in Lakefield – since the last crash –

The winter here so far has been very mild. Only one very cold night, but the thermometer never fell so low as it did in other places. I have not felt the cold at all – and work and write in my room with only a stove pipe passing through it after having traversed the hall and another room before mine. I must lay down my pen for my head aches and it is time to go to bed. Rob and dear Nelly send kind love and good wishes to you and yours in which old Susy heartily joins and with much love to your dear self and the two other Kates believe me ever your attached sister

Susanna Moodie

Horrid writing the paper is greasy ditto the ink and the pen blots. Give my love to all the dear nephews and nieces.

Maime's book on Manitoba has been accepted by Richard Bentley who succeeded his father.[6] The book must have merit to be accepted by such a publisher. I don't know on what terms.

1 Sarah Gwillym
2 George Moodie, 7th of Cocklaw, born 4 September 1799, moved to Canada with his nephew and niece-by-marriage, and died at Medicine Hat in February 1888.
3 James Gerald Fitzgibbon was married to Katy Sutherland 14 June 1880.
4 On 20 September 1882 Katey Moodie Vickers married James Playfair McMurrich, a professor of anatomy at Michigan State and Toronto universities.
5 Edward John Chapman (1821–1904) was also the author of several books of poetry, some published in Britain, some in Canada. Daniel Wilson (1818–92) came to Toronto in 1853 and eventually served as president of the University of Toronto; he also wrote poetry but is noted for several books on archeological, ethnographic, literary, and historical subjects, including *Caliban, The Missing Link* (London 1873), his contribution to the debate over Darwin's theory of evolution.
6 *A Trip to Manitoba; or Roughing It on the Line* (Toronto: Rose Belford 1880); also published by Richard Bentley, grandson of Susanna's publisher, in 1880

---

131 To Marcia _____ July 2 1880

My Dear Marcia[1]

The weather is so very dismal that I dare not venture to accept your *most kind* and *tempting* invitation. I dare not risk damp feet in the wet streets. I feel how good you are in wishing to see such a talkative old woman. But never fear – If I live to return from Lakefield, I will come and see you, or if a good day comes between this and the end of next week I will try and shake the little white hand once more. Mrs. R. Moodie has been suffering much with headache and is confined to her room. If she is no better in a few days I will not leave her. The rest are all well.

Thank your dear mother for me. I hope she and Marion and the good husband, and the sweet baby are all well. Bessie is just going a trip to Rochester on the boat, to see how they keep Independence day in the States.

All here unite in kind love and good wishes: and believe me dear Marcia,

> Yours most affectionately
> Susanna Moodie

Horrid pen, ink and paper, pray excuse it. Alex Dwight has promised to leave this as he passes the door and I write in haste.

1 An unknown Toronto friend within walking distance of Wellington Square

---

132 To Catharine Parr Traill

14 Clarence Terrace
Wellington Square
Toronto
July 4th, 1880

My dear Katey

I have deferred writing until I could say something definite about my going down to Lakefield.

Mrs. Barlee[1] is not quite certain of the day of her return but thinks it will most likely be the saturday of the coming week. If so, I have made up my mind to come with her. At any rate, you need not dear sister make any preparation for me. I shall be contented with anything you give me if only bread and cheese.

I have felt much better since the warmer weather set in, and my cough is nearly gone. I do not know whether I am to lay the improvement to the warm sun or to various remidies I have tried. The *German Syrup* did me little good and cost me a good deal. I have changed that for *Hot Bitters* which really has been an improvement but both medicines cost a dollar a bottle, rather more than I can afford to give – so I trust, that

the change of air and scene and the dear company of the loved ones, will
set me up once more. I dread the long journey and grieve, that I shall
not see dear Robert and Caroline whom I fear, I never shall see more in
this world.[2] I feel rather afraid of leaving dear Nellie who has been
suffering a great deal with her head of late, and has no servant just now
and the girls are reckoning on their holidays to pay visits at a distance
and will be sorely disappointed.

I did not go to James wedding[3] but Rob and Nellie did, and Katie and
her girls and all seemed to enjoy it very much. I called with Nell the
night before on the bride. She seems a nice kind girl. One, who will be
able to take care of her husband in sickness and health. She is just one
year older than him 28 – but looks younger. Her mother told us her age or
I should not have thought it. I supposed her to be about six and twenty.
James looks terribly delicate. Marriage will either kill or cure him but the
wife has some spinal complaint, a bad look out for children. Aunt Kate
made him a present of 50 dollars which she thought would be of more use
to him on his wedding tour. She is very fond of him. His Mother could
not come or Maime. Rob and Nell made him nice presents in plate and
cutlery and I could only add my mite, in a painting very elegantly
framed and the best thing I ever accomplished, and odd to say, it was admired by all the guests and thought the best thing there especially by
James, which was very gratifying to me.

I had a short visit from Flora McLean on friday looking rather thin and
pale I thought, but you cannot ever see anyone's face through those
spotted black veils. I was sorry I could not ask her to tea which had been
just cleared away. Yesterday I spent the evening at Katey's to meet
Mrs. Dale and her daughter Mrs. Monroe. She is a strange excentric
woman, very clever and very amusing and as full of the woman's rights
as ever.

I could not go to Mrs. Ardagh's on thursday, which I much regretted.
They are so nice but the thunder and the downpour lasted for the whole
day and I have no money to lay out in cabs.

Agnes talks of coming up when Cherrie and her baby go to Manitoba,
she expects about September. So I can stay in Lakefield for a month or
six weeks. I do long to see you all so much. Flora gave a very good account
of you. I have been reading Madam De Mesurat's [sic] memoirs of
Napoleon.[4] A most amusing book but it has destroyed all my childish
admiration of the great Emperor who is a most disagreeable, selfish
and vain man, what as children we should have called a perfect *beast*
and Josephine is a weak vain creature. Hortense the only person of

interest in this strange drama. Napoleon the III seems an angel to his uncle. Madam De Mesurat was many years hand lady of honor to Josephine and had every opportunity of seeing him as he really was. I will bring the book, it will amuse you and dear Kate.

The 'Light of Asia'[5] Rob has lent out somewhere but I think I have Jules Verne's 30,000 miles below the sea, without that is gone too. I cannot write with this horrid pen it has not affinity with the paper but scratches instead of writing. I cannot keep a decent pen. What wet weather we have had, scarcely a day without thunder and rain. The grass and the trees are gorgeously green, and we are surrounded here by noble trees and the large square carpetted with such soft grass. It is a lovely spot, we only want a fine view of the lake to make it perfect, but the line of the houses on the opposite side of the square shuts out the water. You would be amused by the English sparrows they have multiplied by thousands and are as impudent as if they knew there was a fine to be paid for shooting them. I laugh to see them in large flocks picking up crumbs in the middle of the most populous thoroughfares. Mr. Tully feeds a pet flock from the parler windows who come at his whistle. My canary is a lovely fellow, he will miss me, and I have some fears lest he die while I am away. I must say goodbye darling. I will send a postal card when I know the right day. May God bless you all and keep you in health until we meet

Your loving old Susie

Rob and Nell send kind love

1 Emma Barlee, Samuel's daughter, visiting Toronto at this time, lived in Lakefield.
2 Robert and Caroline Strickland were about to travel to England.
3 James Gerald Fitzgibbon, Susanna's grandson, married Katey Sutherland, 14 June 1880.
4 In 1879–80, Madame de Remusat's memoirs of her life at Napoleon's court were published in three volumes and became 'all the rage.'
5 Sir Edwin Arnold, *Light of Asia, or, The Great Renunciation* (London 1879)

---

133 To Catharine Parr Traill   Clarence Terrace
January 3 1881

My dearest sister

I hope that this may meet you happy and well on your birthday. I begin a few days in advance, for fear I should be prevented in writing to you on

Saturday. How I wish I could spend the day with you and dear Kate in a long friendly chat, but it is in vain to crave after pleasure placed beyond our reach. We have had a cruel cold Christmas. Not a quarter of an inch of snow but the thermometer very low for Christmas and for several days below zero. It looks very snow-like today. I was so glad to see our dear nephew Robert S. though only for a few brief minutes. He looks in better health and spirits but talks of going back to England shortly. He did not give me very encouraging accounts of dear Charlotte's health. I hope the darling will be spared to bring up her baby. One good piece of news was that you were looking well, ditto dear Kate and Mary.

Among our new year calls I had one from Mr. Dupont. He looks stout and well, and spoke of the beauty and promise of your young Katie with evident satisfaction. He thought her much handsomer than Eva Muchall. I was glad to hear that his opinion and mine coincided about the talents and amiability of Charlie,[1] but like you he fears that he is studying too fast for health.

You will be glad dear to hear that dear Robert has been promoted to a higher position, on an increase of 500 dollars per annum. It is a government appointment as General Freight agent of the Intercolonial railroad but his residence is to be here in Toronto. I don't know if we are to move again, if we do, I should not like to go any distance. I would rather come and board with you in the dear cottage by the bright waters. My cough has not been quite so bad this last week, but during the cold weather it was dreadful, I could get no rest by night or day. Nothing seems to restrain it beyond a few minutes. The receipt Donald sent me is excellent in catarrh but does little good to chronic Bronchitis and asthma. I have had very nice letters from Donald and beautiful cards. His little son has been sick nigh to death, with malarial fever. The doctor paid him 13 visits, which must be very expensive. I sent him 10 dollars which was only a drop in the bucket for they charge 2 dollars for every visit. I don't know how the poor fellow is to get along, but the Lord will provide – if I were able to work I would go to him, but my strength is a thing of the past and board even for a child is most expensive. I did not go to Vickers' since my birthday, until yesterday, and I found the walk greatly beyond comfort. Young Katie is much better, but the weakening effect of her disease (sunstroke) has made her very thin and stolen much of the charming blush pink of her cheeks. My own Katie gave me a nice cup and breakfast shawl for a birthday present. Things very useful and much wanted. My dear Nellie gave me a new ink stand and pretty cards and how lovely some of the cards are. We may give up flower painting

altogether now it will soon be a thing of the past. How did your bazaar
come off. Some of the embroidery in the shop windows is very beautiful, and has quite taken the vanity out of me but I am a thing of the past
too. I have read *Endymion* by Lord Beaconsfield.[2] I was much disappointed, it is the poorest of all his works that I have read. The hero is
Napoleon the III as Prince Floristan and Myra is Eugenie. The character
he calls the Queen is Hortense, the mother of Louis III. The book is more
curious than amusing. I think I told you that I had read Maime's book.
She has had capital reviews of it in some of the first English periodicals,
but Rose says that he can't sell it at all here – I don't wonder at that – A
prophet has no honor in his own place and among his own kith and kin,
was a sentence pronounced by Divine wisdom – and it is very true – I
think the book will stand upon its own merit yet – Donald is agreeably
disappointed in it and I know that he is very fastidious about books, he
likes it very much. How are dear Mary and Tom and all their dear ones
coming on – You must give my kind love to them all and to dear Susan
and Percy it must be a comfort to you to have her home and near you. I
hope your old friends the Garbiots are well. I often recal the pleasant
evening we spent with them give them my very kind regards. I hope the
pumpkin pies were good. I heard from Dunbar – a more agreeable
letter than he usually writes. He seems very anxious to try his luck in the
mines again, though his farm yield is very good this year 7000 bushels
of wheat being one of the items. I am happy to say no further increase of
family. Mrs. Vickers had a letter from Logan Russell with his photo.[3]
I did not see the letter but he sent kind love to me. He is rising to eminence
as a scientific man and great surgeon and has lectured before the Prince
of Wales – I like the face much, I always did like the lad. He was so
superior to his sisters. Douglas went through to Ottawa the other day,
but was too anxious to get home to his wife and babies to stop on the
journey. They will all be here soon on their way to the land of mud and
mosketoes. My dearest Sisy – I have forgotten how to spell you must
forgive me. Goodbye darling love to all and my blessing to the little
ones and hoping that we may meet in this world, believe me in all loyal
love

                              Your affectionate old Susy

   Love to the Marquis
   Have you seen the awful things expected of the new comet.[4] No less
than the destruction of all life upon this planet. I would send you the

paper but it is not mine. It /that is the comet/ has not shewn its face in our hemisphere yet but is expected daily. Tell dear Mary that I have looked in vain to find her name in *Grip*.[5] There is a new paper to come out in place of the *Truth*.[6] One that I subscribe for, that might pay for facetious stories or scraps. I forget its new name but shall see the agent for it in a few days and will get the address from him. I have not heard from England since I last wrote. Jack is waiting for this letter so I must reluctantly say goodbye

S.M.

Robert and Nellie send much love and kind wishes for health and happiness

1 Charles Henry Strickland Traill (born 1865)
2 Disraeli's *Endymion* (1880), his last novel dealing with English political life of the period 1834–41
3 Logan D.H. Russell, author of *The Affects of Inspiration as Relating to Various Diseases of the Lungs* (London 1876)
4 This may have been the comet 'Faye,' which appeared in the Toronto area in January 1881.
5 *Grip* (Toronto 1873–94), a literary and political periodical noted for the cartoons of J.W. Bengough
6 *Truth, for the People*, a Toronto periodical of which the fifth series (1883–5) is extant

---

134 To Catharine Parr Traill

17 Wilton Crescent[1]
Toronto
June 23rd 1881

My dear Sister

I have been looking and longing for a letter from you for many days, and I begin to feel afraid that you or Kate are ill. So pray let me know by postcard how you all are. I have been hoping for an opportunity to see you before the end of this month but I fear I must give it up. Mrs. M. is going visiting among her friends and so are all the children during the end of June, and of all July and I have to remain here to take charge of the house and the youngest child. My heart rebels against this for I had so longed to see you. To enjoy rational conversation and the blessing of social peace. But you know the old saying 'There is no peace for the wicked.' I have only crossed the threshold twice since we came here, and I grow despondent as we have few books to fill up the long hours.

Mrs. V. is so far away that on foot I cannot reach her and we have no street cars here, that I seldom see or hear from them. It is the same with dear Maria and I miss them very much. Bessie left for Goderich two days ago. Dear Rob went with her, and returns by Detroit and may not be here for a week as his business is now chiefly travelling for the Company to which he belongs, which belongs to the Government and is pleasant enough as all his expences are paid. He was going to Chicago but was ordered to Detroit. We are very pleasantly situated here but it is awfully dull and my eyes have grown too weak for painting or even for much reading. Thank the good God I have lost the dreadful cough for awhile and sleep better in consequence. Dr. Canniff says I am much better. He told me frankly that a cure at my age was not to be expected but much relief could be obtained. Bearing down of the womb and its interfering with the bladder makes the worst difficulty and hinders my walking without pain. I had long expected this from the miserable retention of water. But I am willing to bear my burthen as long as my intellect remains. There is little sympathy here for sickness and patience is my best nurse. Did I write to you after Geraldine's and Maime's visit? I cannot remember – After three disappointments they came at last. Fortunately they had no nurse and we got on very well without her. Cherrie looks very sweet but much older than I expected to see her and Maime looks more than her age. The babes are *perfection* such an innocent good pair of darlings. They behaved charmingly. Among their baggage they had a *Puss* and two lovely kittens. Mother Grimalkin did not approve of us, and I met her going out of the house with a fat kit in her mouth. Jack caught the female emigrant and nailed up her box but for all that she tried twice after to get out. Cats are at a premium 20 dollars, often being given for a promising Puss. By the way, talking of cats, How is the dear Lorn? I hope he has not left you forlorn but you have not mentioned him for some time past. Never since your return to the dear cottage. We are surrounded by cats but I see none to compare with the Marquis. Nellie will not suffer one in the house, but our maid *Lovina* has a big tom she keeps in the cellar on the sly to kill the rats. I had kind letters from both Sarah and Jane. Sarah's cough was better and Jane writes in good spirits a really charming letter. She seems very fond of Alice whom she thinks if not so handsome as Cherrie far more interesting. Aunt and Alice were going to spend the summer in Sutherlandshire on the moors with the Rawstones who have a hunting box there – young Rawstone a Barrister goes with them – a good chance for Alice. We have since heard of Cherrie's safe arrival in Winnipeg. They had fine weather and the babes behaved like trumps. Maime's book has been splendidly reviewed in London and

Bentley thinks it will be a success. He sent her thirty pounds as the first fruits of her share of the work and hopes to send more soon. This is all very nice and will help poor Maime and perhaps lead to better things.

I had a strange visit the other day from a very handsome lady whose name at this moment I cannot recall. She wanted to know if I was the Mrs. Moodie who was the friend of Mrs. Welstead as she had a message from the dead to deliver to me if I were. I told her that I was, that Mary had been one of the dearest friends I ever loved. Well, she said, she begged of her daughter on her death bed that if she would try and find out that you were living and give her heart felt love and blessing to you and that she had never forgotten me, though we had never been able to meet since we had parted in London'[2]

Mary has been dead four years left one son and 3 daughters, two of the latter are wives and the daughter who remained with her to the last had made enquiries for me everywhere and only by mere accident, through the lady who came to see me, heard that I was living with a son in Toronto. Poor Mary. How it recalled the past. The hours I used to sit on her bed and the sweet kind face. What a wonderful photographer memory is. Surely darling its images are not imprinted on the heart and brain in vain. Mary was among the few people, like poor Laura Harral, that loved me to the end. Caroline Black[3] is living still in N.Y. all the rest of that large family are dead. The lady who came is a lovely woman who promised to call again.

I went on the Queen's birthday to see the Horticultural gardens with Nellie, it is only a few steps from here. It was my first walk for so many weeks. It is a charming place full of lovely trees and flowers and grass green as an emerald. Numbers of ladies and their children were scattered among the trees which are greener than I ever saw them. As I get better used to walking I will try often to visit the place for it is free for everyone – body. How are all the friends at Lakefield and our dear little Katie and Mary and Tom and their bonnie bairns – Percy and dear Susan. I was sorry to hear that Josephine was threatened with a return of her old complaint, pray give my kind love to them all to George and Roland. I hear that Chassy is home and not much better. Has the beloved Robert left for England if he has not tell him I never forget him in my prayers. Is Arthur's baby a boy or girl and have you any news of dear Charlotte and her Mother and babe. How is Lily and her husband, where does she live now and what is his profession.[4] She will make a capital wife and he looks a kind man. My old friend Mr. Ricketson is married again. I am very glad for he will write no more sentimental love letters. The lady is a fair Quakeress whose ancestors came out in the

Mayflower. I must shock up for this writing is shocking. I pity you my
dearest Sis the trouble of decyphering it but there are some days when I
cannot write at all. God bless and keep you my beloved and your invaluable Kate in good health and believe me ever

Your affectionate old Susie

All here send love and good wishes
   Have you read 'Sunrise' by W. Black[5] it is a most interesting book one
of his very best – Donald is well and doing well – but I have not heard
from him for a week

1 Robert has moved again; Wilton Crescent was south of the Horticultural Gardens, between Jarvis and Sherbourne streets.
2 Mary Wolstead, probably the subject of the poem 'To Mary, Leaving England,' *La Belle
   Assemblée* (May 1827), 221
3 Daughter of Colonel James Black of Darlington (see Letter 78, note 7)
4 Lily Maclean Traill has apparently remarried.
5 (1841–98), a popular English novelist

---

135 To Catharine Parr Traill   [Toronto
fall 1881][1]

I have not seen dear Mrs. V. since Agnes left us. It is a good thing that I
did not go to Ottawa, as I should have been obliged to come home. I
had a nice visit from old Mrs. Burnham, the good Colonel's sister.[2] She is
quite a model of what an old woman ought to be. Two of the Davys
came this week to chat over the old times in BV., Mary Donaldson and
Louise Davy. How my heart warms to these old friends. They had
scarcely gone when Nellie Murney came and has been to see me since. Oh
time, how it alters people – the pretty blue-eyed child who used to sit
on my knee to hear stories, a staid woman of thirty. No longer pretty but
very nice. She was not the cleverest of the girls, but always a pet of
mine. People from BV always treat me with great respect and affection,
which is very pleasing. I am glad that dear Tom and Mary are well, and
that his gardening was successful. They deserve to be rewarded for all
their honest labor. They are often in my mind among those friends
whom one never forgets. We have been greatly bothered with moths, the
only inhabitants of the house for years. It is wonderfull what mischief
these morsels of creation can do. They ate holes in my new bunting dress

and several in the weather proof that Mrs. V. gave me. I had never worn it but twice. We are doctoring the imps with scotch snuff, and so far, have got rid of them. The Persian Insect Destroyer is a sure cure they tell me. Is dear Maria still at Lakefield? If so, give my kindest love. I am glad that you had some return from your apple trees. It is a poor year for them here. They are small with the insect at the heart. A near neighbor sent us about a bushell of grapes which grew on the roof of their house and shed. They were excellent. Most of the folks train them over the roofs of outhouses and they bear abundantly, and are very ornamental and make nice pies and preserves. My dear Katie, I always enjoy your living and think you make delicious family roasts and pies and puddings. Butter is 38 cents a pound here, but I never eat any and seldom suffer from bile now. Butter is a very serious item in our housekeeping. Give my love to the dear Percys to Roland and his household divinities, and to George and his family. I have not been able to go up to call upon Fanny. It is so far away and I have not always the money to pay for cab hire. Remember me to Lily. Where does she and her husband live? Give your dear Kate and number 3 my fondest love, and believe me ever your faithfully attached sister.

Susanna Moodie

Rob and Nell send much love –
My hand has lost the art of writing.

1 Letter dated by references to autumn produce and the fact that the closing greetings are very similar to those in the previous letter suggesting it was written in the same year; references to cab hire suggest Toronto.
2 Likely the sister-in-law of Colonel Zaccheus Burnham, a prominent founder of Cobourg, Ontario

---

136 To Catharine Parr Traill

17 Wilton Crescent
Toronto
January 3rd, 1882

My beloved sister

I will write today for I fear that I might not get a chance tomorrow to wish you all happiness on your birthday and that you may live to see many more. Your happy, cheerful, hopeful heart seems to bid fair for length of days. May God bless and keep you long on earth to make others happy.

I was indeed much disappointed in not being able to come and spend a few weeks with you, but should I live until the spring I hope to be more fortunate. I have not been very well during our warm, damp, dripping December, nor have I left the house for the last two months.

Fortunately dear Nellie is over her great trouble and has as lovely and healthy an infant as I ever saw. No baby could exceed it in beauty and the dear Mother is doing remarkably well. The dear little thing is to be called *Katie* greatly to my joy who love the name. She was confined – Nellie I mean – on the 13th of last month after nine months of great physical suffering and I felt great anxiety about her but the last anguish was sharp and short. She cannot however nurse the dear wee pet, who by the bye, weighed 12 lb. and is as big as most babies of three months. She took to the bottle directly and we have no trouble with her for she sleeps like a top. I only hope that she may hold in this humour until the cold weather is over. The snow is coming in good earnest today and I hope it may last for the sake of the many sick in the city.

Alas, while I was so glad of Nellie's safety I had a sad, sad letter from poor Dunbar. In two days God took to Heaven his two loveliest and best. A clever sweet girl of 13 years and his dear little Alice of 10 years – while his wife still is lying in a sick bed desperately ill. He has nursed his dying and dead for three weeks without once undressing or going to bed, and his heart seems breaking. I cannot think of his distress without tears. A more heart broken letter I never read it makes tears come whenever I think of it. But there is a silver lining to the dark cloud. This sad event has converted the poor father and brought him to God, for he had no God, but Nature, and in his infinite distress he has found that there is a God and a happier and better world, in which he hopes to find his lost darlings. His stern will once subdued is not very likely to change, and while I weep for the two dear children I must rejoice that their loss has brought life to the dear father. The disease of which they both died is called Peritonitis. I don't know what sort of distemper it is by that name poor Jessie the eldest girl died in great pain. Alice two days before her. I am afraid by what he says of his wife that it is more than probable that he may lose her, in her weak state, and grief for the loss of her children. Ah, me, it is a sorrowful world. It has been a very gloomy Christmas anyway. But I am so glad that dear Nellie is recovering. We had but a few callers yesterday and all young men just out of their teens, to whom our girls seem a great attraction. Mrs. Vickers was here on Saturday and wanted me to come and stay this week but I could not. I have so many infirmities that belong to the aged that it is difficult to go out at all. I saw dear Louise

Tully and Alice Bolton on Saturday both looking very sweet. She tells me
that Mrs. Lefevre is coming to stay with her Mother during the winter. I
am so glad for I think it will do dear Maria good to have her dear child
near her. I want overly to see Mrs. T. for I am very fond of her but I
have not been able to manage it. She lives so far away 2 miles at the very
least and and I cannot afford cab hire and no street cars go near John
Street. I send you a card dear which I thought very pretty. Give my love to
dear Kate and Mary and Tom and all the dear nephews and nieces. I
heard from Maime last week. All our emigrants are well and delighted
with the country although they are 25 below zero. Mr. Leacock[1] bought
his cottage 2 miles from Winnipeg for 1200 dollars and is offered 20,000 in
cash for it. The gambling for land is in full blast just now. Goodbye
darling God bless you all is the sincere wish of your old loving

Susie

1 The uncle of Stephen Leacock, and the subject of his 'My Remarkable Uncle.' Georgina
  (née Vickers) and her husband went to Winnipeg soon after their wedding and their
  three children were all born in Manitoba.

---

137 To Katie Vickers

My dear daughter Katie,

Wilton Crescent
Toronto
Sep. 5th 1882

I was just putting on my dress to come and see you all, when I got your
kind invitation to our dear young Katie's wedding.

Now don't be angry darling with the old mother when I say that I
cannot come. I wish the dear young people all the happiness that they
can possibly wish themselves and that God's blessing may rest upon them
for time and Eternity but I do not feel myself fit for a wedding guest, and
as I did not see dear Georgie married it would seem unkindness to her.
Katie will forgive me for she knows that I love her much and though
absent in person I shall be present in spirit.

Nellie and I, have both been prevented from coming to see you by the
illness of the baby who has been cutting more teeth and suffering much
pain from the process and has kept her dear Mother awake for several
anxious nights. To day she has quite a rash out on her body and seems
a little easier. Robert had to leave for Barrie yesterday night, and as he
was suffering from summer cholera we feel very anxious about him. I

hope to be able to see dear Katie before she changes her name. There is no news in our part of the world. Vennor[1] seems right at last about the weather which is just now as bright and beautiful as any bridal party could wish.

Give my love to dear John and all the dear girls and boys. I have not heard from aunt Traill or from Ottawa. No news from England and not a word about dear Maria Tully or any of the Lakefield boys. Does Agnes Chamberlin and Alice, come up to the Exhibition, or will Georgie and her baby come to the wedding? I have not been out since I saw you last. I seem to grow more helpless every day and almost forget my own name. I *feel quite a doited auld wife now,* but it is no use finding fault with the inevitable. I had no idea that age was such a ruthless destroyer of the senses and so perfectly obliterate[s] the past, by mingling it up with the present. To many it must be an act of mercy. It has its laughable sides too if it were only the blunders one makes of the names of people and places. Do you want a beautiful young black cat – without a pale hair – a lovely thing. I could send her by Jack for I don't like to hurt her, or for dearest Arthur – I call her Topaz – and wish I could keep her, but cats are too plenty in our neighbourhood.

I quite long to see you all, it seems an age since I was in Adelaide Street, but you must be awfully busy just now. I was glad to see Billy looking so well after his trip to Manitoba. God bless you my dear child, may Wednesday prove a happy day for all parties, though absent I shall feel all your joy and ever remain you loving old Mother

Susanna Moodie

1 In 1877, Henry George Vennor (1841–84), an ornithologist, geologist, and meteorologist, began producing almanacs that were surprisingly successful at weather forecasting.

---

138 To Catharine Parr Traill   December 25th 1882

My dearest Sister – I wrote *myself* by postal early last week to tell you that I was a little better. My lungs have been tested by an able Physician. Right *lung sound* – left much affected also Bronchial tubes. There's some hope, but not much, owing to my feeble state – System very low – I am quite resigned to God's will – Your letters very precious to me. Many thanks for pretty Cards. I *am well taken care of* will let you know if able to write on the 7th

A happy Christmas to all the dear ones at Lakefield –

1884~1885

Afterword

B Y LATE 1884 IT WAS EVIDENT that Susanna required constant super-vision. Her eyes were weak, her body frail, and her mind distorted the world around her into echoes of the past. Robert's Wilton Cres-cent house was not large enough to accommodate the nurse Katie felt her mother should have; thus she was moved to the Vickers' house on Adelaide Street for the last three months of her life. Catharine came down from Lake-field to be with her; on 28 March 1885, she wrote her friend Ellen Dunlop:

... I have a charming room with a fire and Mrs. V. sits a great deal with me and the nurse brings my poor sister in to sit with me till she gets restless and then she leads her back again to her own comfortable room where she has every comfort and every attention paid to her. She looks the picture of neatness and is dressed so nicely with a lovely cap of mauve ribbons and warm delicate shawl and elegant lace collar and handsome dark dress and warm slippers. She looks a perfect picture as far as hands can make her, but she is much bent and requires support, yet though so weak looking, she can put forth muscular strength that makes me feel like a baby myself.

Saturday morning – My dear Ellen, I have lost a mail and lost a day and now I find my letter will not reach you this week. The case is when I go into my sister's room and when she comes into me she keeps talking and rambles so that I lose thought of any thing and every one else. What a strange change – what a wreck. Do you know, dear, that my sister who used to rail against dolls and call them hideous idols and find fault with mothers for giving little children dolls to play with has a great wax doll dressed like a baby and this she nurses and caresses and believes it is her own living babe, and cannot bear it out of her sight – puts it to sleep, talks to it and has it placed in a chair that she may look at it or has it fed and laid to sleep. This is to me the saddest sight for it shows the entire change that has come over her fine intellect – she is a child again in very truth. Poor dear old sister. Well thank God she is unconscious of it herself. She gets very much confused between her daughter and me. She thinks I am Mrs. Vicker's mother, and she – Mrs. V. – my Kate Traill, only she says – she has grown a great deal bigger than she was. Sometimes she gets strange fits of terror about robbers, and is difficult to pacify. It is wonderful to see the patience and care that her dear daughter treats her with and the good clever way the nurse has in humouring her vagaries. She seems today to recognize me as 'her own Kate' – and pats my cheek and says it is very pretty. She has just gone back to her room. But she does not listen to the Bible as she did. She gets tired and does not attend. She eats and drinks well and sleeps in the day but is often very troubled at night. This is the state she is in. At times it is a great trial, when she is *wilful* and obstinate – but, dear Ellen, she is not responsible for the powers of the mind are shaken. God be gracious and merciful to my dear sister. Her speech is very difficult to understand but her own hearing is good ...

On 8 April 1885, death claimed her. Catharine sent word the next morning to her daughters Kate and Mary in Lakefield:

The end has at last come, and the wearied spirit is now at rest – Your dear aunt Moodie was released from the body yesterday between the hours of four and five p.m. ... She now lies peacefully sleeping in her death robes among the lilies and sweet flowers that she dearly loved in life.

Let us thank God that she is at rest from all the trials that wore and wearied her too active brain. I believe softening of the brain had been long at work – I cannot now dwell on the sad details of the last weeks – but she was most kindly attended in every way, and this is a comfort to all about her.

On 11 April, Catharine, still in Toronto, wrote to her daughter Annie Atwood near Rice Lake:

My Own Beloved Annie

You will most likely have heard ere this reaches you of the death of your dear Aunt Moodie. I had left the Vickers house on Saturday as she showed no symptoms that any particular change was likely to ensue for some time though she was restless and uneasy but not more than usual. On Sunday Easter Day – there had been a new church bell put up close to Adelaide St. and the first tolling of it for church had greatly disturbed her poor brain. She exhibited great signs of uneasiness and fancied it was tolling for the execution of some murderer who was to be hanged for cutting off her – your poor Aunt's – head. For you must know, my dear Annie, that the poor Aunt's head was all in a deranged state lately, she was the victim of all sorts of terrible delusions. The nurse who never leaves her only for a few minutes found her charge out of bed kneeling by a chair praying that this man might not be hung for killing her – for she lost her own identity at times. Well, dear, she got worse after that night. On Monday she fell into a state of unconsciousness; from daybreak she never opened her eyes. Mrs. Vickers sent a message to me and I went at once – but my beloved sister was never conscious to the last moment. We watched beside her – her mother Isabel [Mrs Vickers, Sr], myself and the good nurse – till rest and peace came and it was all over. The total loss of your dear Aunt's faculties had indeed reconciled us to the final close of her life on earth consoled by the hope that it was the entrance by death of the frail body to a higher state of life where death had no power – for the Lord in whom she believed had overcome the sharpness of death having purchased by His life and sufferings on the Cross eternal life for all believers. When Christ who is our life shall appear then shall we also appear with Him for that is His promise – God grant it be ours to realize these words, my dearly beloved

The Moodie grave in Belleville

child. The restful peace of God seems to have taken the place of all the sad harassed pained expression that was for so long sad to witness. As she lay among the lilies and lovely flowers that in life were so dear to her – I felt indeed that it was well that the toil and mental strife were over – so like in death to my own dear mother as if I saw her loved face once more calmly sleeping as I so often had done some fifty years ago. The remains were taken to Belleville as she wished and her husband and two children will be buried in the new cemetery above the bay east of the city …

358

GENEALOGIES

THOMAS STRICKLAND   m.   (1) Susanna Butt (d.c. 1790; no issue)
(1758–1818)   (2) Elizabeth Homer (1772–1864)

| Elizabeth (Eliza) (1794–1875) | Agnes (1796–1874) | Sarah (Thay) (1798–1890) | Jane Margaret (1800–88) | Catharine Parr (1802–99) | Susanna (1803–85) | SAMUEL (1805–67) | Thomas (1807–74) |

Sarah (Thay) (1798–1890)
m.
(1) Robert *Childs* (d. 1837)
(2) Richard *Gwillym* (d. 1868)

Catharine Parr (1802–99)
m.
THOMAS TRAILL (1793–1859)

Susanna (1803–85)
m.
J.W.D. MOODIE (1797–1869)

SAMUEL (1805–67)
m.
(1) Emma Black (d. 1826)
(2) Mary Reid (d. 1850)
(3) Katharine Rackham (d. 1890)

Thomas (1807–74)
m.
(1) Anne Thompson
(2) Margaretta

- Walter
- Julia Lily
- Mary
- Diana
- Adela Margaretta
- Elizabeth Marina

THOMAS TRAILL m. Catharine Parr Strickland
(1793–1859) (1802–1899)

James George (1833–67)

Katharine Agnes Strickland (Kate) (1836–1922)
m.
Amelia Keye Muchall
- Richard Henry (b. 1858)
- Thomas Edward Strickland (b. 1859)
- Agnes Strickland (b. 1863)
- Earnest George (b. 1866)
- Herbert

Thomas Henry Strickland (Harry) (1837–70)
m.
Lilias Grant Maclean
- Charles Henry Strickland (b. 1865)
- Katharine Parr (Katie) (b. 1867)
- James George McManus (b. 1869)

Anne Traill Fotheringhame (Annie) (1838–1931)
m.
James Parr Clinton Atwood
- Henry Arthur Strickland (1860–4)
- Emily Grace (b. 1863)
- Clinton Arthur Strickland (b. 1865)
- Katharine Stewart (b. 1868)
- George Evan (b. 1869)
- Anne Traill Fotheringhame (b. 1871)
- Florence Marion (b. 1874)

Mary Ellen Bridges (1840–1)

Mary Elizabeth Jane (1841–92)
m.
Thomas Muchall
- Hargreave Henry (b. 1865)
- Evelyne Mary (b. 1867)
- Caroline Gwillym (b. 1870)
- Norman Stewart (b. 1873)

Eleanor Stewart (d. infant 1842)

William Edward (1844–1917)
m.
Harriette McKay
- Walter (b. 1870)
- Katharine Parr (1871–8)
- Mary (1873–4)
- William McKay (b. 1875)
- Henry (1877–9)
- Ethel (b. 1878)
- Jessie (b. 1881)
- Mary (b. 1884)
- Harriet (b. 1888)
- Catharine Barbara (b. 1892)
- Maria
- Anna

Walter John Strickland (1847–1932)
m.
Mary Gilbert

JOHN WEDDERBURN DUNBAR MOODIE
(1 Oct. 1797–22 Oct. 1869)

Catherine Mary
Josephine
(14 Feb. 1832–24 Dec. 1904)
m. 1 Aug. 1855
John Joseph *Vickers*
(b. 1818)

Georgina Eliza
(b. 28 May 1856)

John Alexander Dunbar (Jack)
(b. 22 May 1858)

Katie Moodie
(b. 28 June 1860)

William Wallbridge
(b. 6 Aug. 1862)

Isabel Josephine
(b. 7 Aug. 1864)

Victor Gilmore Ridgeway
(b. 1 June 1866)

Ethel Rosina
(b. 4 March 1868)

Henrietta Moodie
(b. 2 March 1870)

Arthur Algoma
(b. 26 March 1872)

Agnes Strickland
(b. 6 Nov. 1874)

Agnes Dunbar
(9 June 1833–1 May 1913)
(1) m. 23 Aug. 1850
Charles Thomas *Fitzgibbon*
(d. 22 Feb. 1865)

Mary Agnes (Maime)
(b. 18 June 1851)

James Gerald
(b. 2 Feb. 1853)

Geraldine (Cherrie)
(b. 31 Oct. 1854)

Eliza Dunbar
(24 Feb. 1856–14 July 1856)

Charlotte Alice
(b. 8 Aug. 1857)

Katie
(10 Feb. 1859–8 Aug. 1859)

John Wedderburn Dunbar
(18 June 1860–16 March 1865)

William Winder
(12 April 1862–18 Oct. 1866)

(2) m. 14 June 1870
Brown *Chamberlin*
(22 March 1827–13 July 1897)

Agnes Gertrude Mary
(b. 7 April 1871)

John Alexander Dunbar
(20 Aug. 1834–14 May 1927)
m. 20 March 1862
Elizabeth Roberta Russell
(1834–2 March 1882)

Agnes Strickland Dunbar
(b. 11 Feb. 1863)

Robert Russell
(b. 28 Nov. 1864)

Elizabeth Dunbar
(b. 24 Aug. 1866)

Janet Ethel
(28 Aug. 1868–20 Dec. 1881)

Alice Dunbar
(4 Aug. 1870–16 Dec. 1881)

Clutha Roberta
(b. 28 Nov. 1873)

Elsie Helen
(b. 6 Aug. 1877)

m.   Susanna Strickland
4 April (7 Dec. 1803–8 April 1885)
1831

Donald	John	George	Robert Baldwin
(21 May 1836–27 Dec. 1893)	Strickland	Arthur	(8 July 1843–3 Feb. 1889)
m. 16 Feb. 1866	(16 Oct. 1838–	(19 July 1840–	m. 27 June 1863
Julia Ann Russell	18 June 1844)	8 Aug. 1840)	Sarah Elizabeth (Nellie)
			Russell
			(17 Nov. 1847–8 Feb. 1930)

Donald's children:
- Daniel Edward Prodhead
  (b. 1 Jan. 1867)
- Walter Brewster
  (Nov. 1868–14 June 1870)
- Charlotte Peachy
  (b. 1 Jan. 1872)
- Julia Edith Strickland
  (b. 14 Oct. 1875)

Robert Baldwin's children:
- Bessie Perry
  (b. 12 April 1864)
- Nellie
  (b. 17 Sept. 1865)
- John Wedderburn Dunbar
  (b. 4 March 1868)
- Thomas Edward Strickland
  (b. 8 May 1871)
- Esther Edith
  (b. 23 July 1875)
- Susanna
  (b. 15 May 1878–1878)
- Catherine Agnes
  (b. 13 Dec. 1881)

362

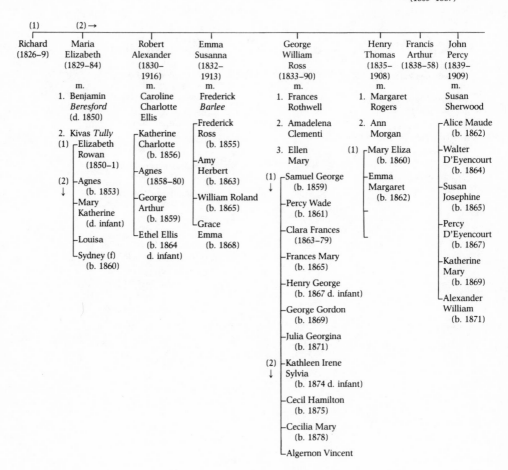

(1)	(2) →						
Richard (1826–9)	Maria Elizabeth (1829–84)	Robert Alexander (1830–1916)	Emma Susanna (1832–1913)	George William Ross (1833–90)	Henry Thomas (1835–1908)	Francis Arthur (1838–58)	John Percy (1839–1909)
	m.	m.	m.	m.	m.		m.
	1. Benjamin *Beresford* (d. 1850)	Caroline Charlotte Ellis	Frederick *Barlee*	1. Frances Rothwell	1. Margaret Rogers		Susan Sherwood
	2. Kivas *Tully*			2. Amadelena Clementi	2. Ann Morgan		

(1) Elizabeth Rowan (1850–1)
(2) Agnes (b. 1853)
↓ Mary Katherine (d. infant)
Louisa
Sydney (f) (b. 1860)

Katherine Charlotte (b. 1856)
Agnes (1858–80)
George Arthur (b. 1859)
Ethel Ellis (b. 1864 d. infant)

Frederick Ross (b. 1855)
Amy Herbert (b. 1863)
William Roland (b. 1865)
Grace Emma (b. 1868)

3. Ellen Mary

(1) Samuel George (b. 1859)
↓ Percy Wade (b. 1861)
Clara Frances (1863–79)
Frances Mary (b. 1865)
Henry George (b. 1867 d. infant)
George Gordon (b. 1869)
Julia Georgina (b. 1871)
(2) Kathleen Irene Sylvia (b. 1874 d. infant)
↓ Cecil Hamilton (b. 1875)
Cecilia Mary (b. 1878)
Algernon Vincent

(1) Mary Eliza (b. 1860)
Emma Margaret (b. 1862)

Alice Maude (b. 1862)
Walter D'Eyencourt (b. 1864)
Susan Josephine (b. 1865)
Percy D'Eyencourt (b. 1867)
Katherine Mary (b. 1869)
Alexander William (b. 1871)

m. 1. Emma Black (d. 1826)
    2. Mary Reid (d. 1850)
    3. Katherine Rackham (d. 1890)

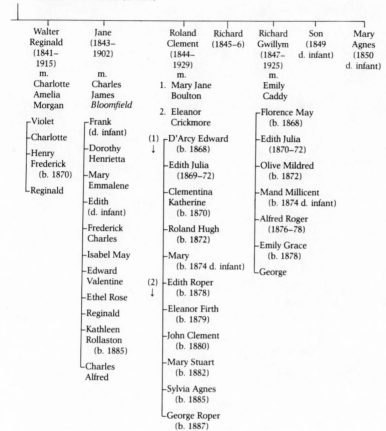

Walter Reginald (1841–1915) m. Charlotte Amelia Morgan
- Violet
- Charlotte
- Henry Frederick (b. 1870)
- Reginald

Jane (1843–1902) m. Charles James *Bloomfield*
- Frank (d. infant)
- Dorothy Henrietta
- Mary Emmalene
- Edith (d. infant)
- Frederick Charles
- Isabel May
- Edward Valentine
- Ethel Rose
- Reginald
- Kathleen Rollaston (b. 1885)
- Charles Alfred

Roland Clement (1844–1929) m.
1. Mary Jane Boulton
2. Eleanor Crickmore

(1)
- D'Arcy Edward (b. 1868)
- Edith Julia (1869–72)
- Clementina Katherine (b. 1870)
- Roland Hugh (b. 1872)
- Mary (b. 1874 d. infant)

(2)
- Edith Roper (b. 1878)
- Eleanor Firth (b. 1879)
- John Clement (b. 1880)
- Mary Stuart (b. 1882)
- Sylvia Agnes (b. 1885)
- George Roper (b. 1887)

Richard (1845–6)

Richard Gwillym (1847–1925) m. Emily Caddy
- Florence May (b. 1868)
- Edith Julia (1870–72)
- Olive Mildred (b. 1872)
- Mand Millicent (b. 1874 d. infant)
- Alfred Roger (1876–78)
- Emily Grace (b. 1878)
- George

Son (1849 d. infant)

Mary Agnes (1850 d. infant)

Sources of Letters and Illustrations

Rev. A.G. L'Estrange, *The Friendships of Mary Russell Mitford* (New York 1882). Ellipses within the letters taken from this source indicate L'Estrange's deletions. Letters 15, 19, 21, 24 to Mary Russell Mitford

Suffolk County Public Records Office, Ipswich
The John Glyde Papers, originally located here, are now available on microfilm, Reel A-1182, in the Susanna Moodie Collection, Public Archives of Canada. Ellipses within the letters taken from this source indicate Glyde's deletions. Letters 1–10, 12, 14, 17–18, 20, 22–3, 25–7, 29, 31–4 to James and/or Emma Bird; letters 89, 93, 99–100, 103, 106, 111 to Allen Ransome

British Library, London
The Richard Bentley Papers, Manuscript Room, are now available on microfilm, Reel A-1411, Susanna Moodie Collection, Public Archives of Canada. Letters 44, 47–9, 55, 60, 77, 82, 84 to Richard Bentley

Public Archives of Canada, Ottawa
Susanna Moodie Collection, MG29 D100
The letters loaned to the editors by Mrs Hope Vickers and Miss Kathleen McMurrich are now housed in this collection. Letters 94, 112 to John Vickers; letters 95, 97, 98, 108–10, 116, 137 to Katie Vickers; letter 118 to Sarah Gwillym; letter 119 to W.W. Vickers
Traill Family Collection, MG29 D81
Letters 51, 57, 63, 66, 69, 71, 73, 75–6, 80, 85, 96, 101–2, 104, 113, 121–5, 127–30, 132–6, 138 to Catharine Parr Traill; letter 83 to Mary Muchall; letter 120 to Katharine Parr Traill
Henry Morgan Papers: letter 72 to Henry Morgan

Archives of Ontario, Toronto: letters 114–15 to Maggie Rous

National Library of Canada, Ottawa: letter 90 to Mrs Kersterman

Boys and Girls House, Toronto Public Library
The Osborne Collection of Early Children's Books: letters 11, 16, 28 to
Frederic Shoberl

Canadiana Room, Corby Library, Belleville: letter 92 to the County Council of Hastings

The Historical Society of Pennsylvania, Philadelphia: letter 36 to Sumner
Lincoln Fairfield

UNIVERSITY COLLECTIONS

Rare Books and Library Manuscripts of the University of California at Los
Angeles (microfilm of all American Bentley holdings available at Mills
Memorial Library, McMaster University, Hamilton): letters 13, 30 to
Frederic Shoberl; letter 81 to Richard Bentley

Rare Books and Manuscripts, Houghton Library, Harvard University,
Cambridge: letter 91 to Anna Ricketson

The Bentley Papers, Special Collections, University of Illinois, Chicago:
letters 45–6, 50, 52, 54, 56, 58–9, 61, 64–5, 67–8, 70, 78–9, 81, 87–8,
107 to Richard Bentley; letter 86 to George Bentley. Substantial excerpts
from letters 59, 61, and 68 appeared in 'A Glorious Madness: Susanna
Moodie and the Spiritualist Movement,' *Journal of Canadian Studies*, VII
(winter 1982–3), 88–100.

Special Collections, Douglas Library, Queen's University, Kingston:
letter 40 to John Lovell; letter 62 to Charles Sangster; letter 131 to
Marcia ———

Thomas Fisher Rare Book Library, University of Toronto: letter 105 to
Richard Bentley

Special Collections, Bata Library, Trent University, Peterborough: letter
53 to Dr Lister; letter 126 to Katie Vickers

Special Collections, Scott Library, York University, North York: letter 42
to Louisa May Murray

NEWSPAPERS

Albion, New York: letters 35, 43 to the editor, Dr John Sherren Bartlett
British American Magazine, Toronto: letter 74 to the publishers
Examiner, Peterborough: letter 37 to Sumner Lincoln Fairfield
Globe, Toronto: letter 117 to the editor
Literary Garland, Montreal: letters 39, 41 to the editor, John Gibson
Palladium, Toronto: letter 38 to the editor, Charles Fothergill

---

ILLUSTRATIONS

ii Susanna Strickland Moodie, photographed by G. Stanton of Toronto, c.1850.
Courtesy of Miss Kathleen McMurrich
3 Reydon Hall, photographed by Elizabeth Hopkins, 1980
7 Susanna Strickland. Courtesy of Miss Kathleen McMurrich
8 Catharine Parr Strickland. Courtesy of Miss Kathleen McMurrich
10 James Bird, from an engraving by M. Harvey, published in *Aldine Magazine
of Biography, Bibliography, Criticism and the Arts* (June 1839), 297. Courtesy
of the British Library Photographic Services
78 John Lovell, photographed by William Notman of Montreal, c.1860. Courtesy
of the Notman Photographic Archives, McCord Museum, McGill University,
Montreal
84 The Moodie Cottage, photographed by Michael Peterman, 1981
86 J.W.D. Moodie, photographed by William Notman, 1866. Frontispiece from
Scenes and Adventures of a Soldier and Settler during Half a Century (Montreal: Lovell 1866)
106 Richard Bentley, an engraving by Joseph Brown from a photograph by Lock
and Whitfield of London, c. 1860. Courtesy of the British Library Photographic
Services
113 Cross-written letter to Catharine Parr Traill, from Traill Family Collection,
MG29 D81. Courtesy of the Manuscript Division, Public Archives of Canada,
Ottawa
200 J. Allen Ransome, photographed in Ipswich, c.1860, from the Ford Collection. Courtesy of the St. Edmondsbury Borough Council and the Bury St.
Edmunds branch of the Suffolk County Public Records Office
203 Susanna and J.W.D. Moodie, photographed in Belleville, c.1860. Courtesy
of the Archives of Ontario, Toronto
258 Susanna Moodie, photographed in 1866. Courtesy of the Notman Photographic Archives, McCord Museum, McGill University, Montreal
263 'Blue Iris' watercolour, 1869. Courtesy of the Canadiana Department, Royal
Ontario Museum, Toronto
356 Moodie grave, photographed by Roy Ingram, 1981. Courtesy of the Hastings
County Historical Society, Belleville

Index

For references to correspondents, see Sources of letters.